D0707763

HOW SC
TRUMPED TEACHERS

Change Without Reform in
University Curriculum, Teaching,
and Research, 1890–1990

HOW SCHOLARS TRUMPED TEACHERS

Change Without Reform in University Curriculum, Teaching, and Research, 1890–1990

Larry Cuban

Teachers College, Columbia University
New York and London

For David Tyack

*Outstanding scholar, gifted teacher,
and dear friend*

Published by Teachers College Press, 1234 Amsterdam Avenue, New York, NY 10027

Library of Congress Cataloging-in-Publication Data
    Cuban, Larry.
    How scholars trumped teachers : constancy and change in
university curriculum, teaching, and research, 1890-1990 / Larry
Cuban.
        p. cm.
    Includes bibliographical references (p.   ) and index.
    ISBN 0-8077-3865-4 (cloth : alk. paper)
    ISBN 0-8077-3864-6 (paper : alk. paper)
        1. Stanford University—Curricula—History. 2. Universities and
colleges—United States—Curricula—History—Case studies. 3.
Curriculum change—United States—History—Case studies. 4. College
teaching—United States—History—Case studies. I. Title.
    LD3013 .C83 1999
    378.1'99'0979473—dc21   98-56523

ISBN 0-8077-3864-6   (paper)
ISBN 0-8077-3865-4   (cloth)

Printed on acid-free paper

Manufactured in the United States of America

06 05 04 03 02 01 00 99   8 7 6 5 4 3 2 1

CONTENTS

Acknowledgments vii

Introduction 1

Chapter 1

How the Invention of the University-College Led to a Century
of Dilemmas and a Tradition of Reform at Stanford 13

Chapter 2

How Universities Tame Reform to Preserve the Research
Imperative: Or Why There Is Change Without Reform 61

Chapter 3

Scholar-Teachers in the Stanford History Department,
1891–1990 91

Chapter 4

A Sturdy Way of Preparing Physicians: The School of
Medicine, 1908–1990 133

Chapter 5

How Research Trumped Teaching in History and Medicine 165

Chapter 6

Scholars or Teachers: How Much Change Is Possible? 191

Notes 207

References 251

Index 265

About the Author 280

ACKNOWLEDGMENTS

FOR WELL OVER A QUARTER-CENTURY, my experiences in public schools as a teacher and administrator served as the wellspring for my writing. Invariably, I became intrigued—as I lived the experiences—by questions that eluded easy answers and institutional tensions that seldom eased. What I have written for practitioners, policymakers, scholars, and the general public, then and now, has tried to answer these questions and simultaneously reframe institutional conflicts. My writing has drawn upon my daily experiences in schools and offices and been enriched by the work of other educational researchers. So it is now for universities.

I became a university professor in 1981 and entered a very different world than I experienced as a superintendent or high school teacher. *How Scholars Trumped Teachers* has grown directly from almost 2 decades of experiences as a professor through teaching, advising students, researching, and writing. As with my public school experience, over the last decade troubling questions began to form in my mind about why faculty and administrators did what they did and the institutional conflicts that I saw. I began to read deeply and widely about the history of American universities and their growth over the last century. I created a course on curricular and instructional reforms in higher education and examined with students the history of efforts to make major changes. As before, I have tried to merge my experience-produced knowledge with that of research-produced knowledge to offer a university practitioner's perspective on unasked questions and enduring dilemmas.

During my intellectual journey to understand both the wonder and the tensions within universities, I have become deeply indebted to many colleagues, students, and friends who have taken time out of their complicated lives to read drafts and offer suggestions.

I am deeply appreciative to the students in Education 271 over the years for their patience and high interest in working through early versions of my thinking on higher education and for the questions they so thoughtfully raised.

For those hardy readers of early drafts, I am indebted to them for their comments, disagreements, and suggestions. In particular, I want to thank Elisabeth Hansot, Donald Kennedy, Gary Lichtenstein, Richard Lyman, and David Tyack.

Because I had to learn a great deal about medical education, I want to especially thank those whose patience, good will, and deep program knowledge helped me grasp much that had eluded me about the complexities of preparing students to become physicians. In particular, I appreciated very much the librarians and archivists at the Lane Library of the Stanford University School of Medicine who so graciously helped me during 1992 and 1993. Professor Mark Nelson, M.D., and Professor Charlotte Jacobs, M.D., brought me into the medical education journal club at the School of Medicine where, for 5 years, I joined in spirited discussions. Their prodding and suggestions in those biweekly meetings and their willingness to read drafts of the medical school chapter were unusually helpful to me in avoiding major factual errors and quirky interpretations of the evidence. Also, I want to thank David Stern, M.D., Kelly Skeff, M.D., and my dear friend Joel Merenstein, M.D., for reading and commenting on drafts of that chapter.

None of the people mentioned above, of course, bear any responsibility for what appears in *How Scholars Trumped Teachers*. That responsibility, as always, remains both my personal delight and individual obligation to readers.

Larry Cuban

INTRODUCTION

SINCE THE EMERGENCE of research-driven universities over a century ago, the question of whether these institutions are reform-resistant or reform-prone has been debated often. To Irving Kristol, for example, "the university has been—with the possible exception of the post office—the least inventive (or even adaptive) of our social institutions since the end of World War II." Yet to Jacques Barzun, writing at the same time, "since 1945 the universities have been doing nothing but innovate." As Derek Bok, then president of Harvard University, concluded, "both of these critics cannot be right."[1]

What deepens this apparent paradox is the century-long history of university reform, which even challenges how these scholars frame the issue of change. Wars, economic depressions, and rising public expectations for higher education have unrelentingly swept over universities, creating problems that prompted strong criticism of, and pressures for change in, these institutions. Not a decade has passed without academic reformers promising major changes in university governance, funding, organization, curriculum, and instruction. Universities competed with one another in generating reforms in the decades bracketing the turn of the 20th century, the post–World War I and II decades, the 1960s, and since the early 1980s. Reforming universities, if anything, had been, and remains, steady work.[2]

Yet, as scholars and critics of higher education have noted repeatedly, amid this century of reforms—many of which aimed at reconstructing curriculum and elevating the status of teaching—the research imperative has so dominated academic work as to become a truism. The contradiction of professors being hired to teach yet rewarded with tenure and promotion for publishing research has become an academic cliche. Hence, those who agree with Kristol's observation about a lack of change can point to the durability of research eclipsing teaching within the university. Others who would agree with Barzun can point to the frequent reform efforts aimed at improved courses and recognition of excellence in teaching.

While many studies have reaffirmed that research is the core mission of universities—the equivalent of scholars rediscovering that mice like cheese—few researchers have investigated exactly why and how the imperative to inquire and publish has subordinated teaching to its demands. Few historical studies have inquired into the tangled connections between frequent reforms aimed at university structures and academic norms and their linkages to scholars doing research. This lack of systematic inquiry into how university structures and processes might be linked to the primacy of research prompts the questions that drive this study.[3] The two key questions are

1. Over the last century, how have university structures and processes, including curricular reform, influenced the academic work of research and teaching?
2. Why has scholarship trumped teaching in universities?

To answer these questions, I need to first make clear to readers why I chose universities. Although the 125 major public and private research universities included in the Carnegie Foundation's classification of Research I and II universities in the early 1990s were less than 4% of the nation's higher education institutions, they enrolled almost 20% of all college students. These few institutions (over 3,600 are considered in the pool of higher education) nonetheless set implicit standards for other universities, 4- and 2-year colleges, and even secondary schools since the early 20th century.[4]

Moreover, this small group of research-driven universities has had a disproportionate influence historically on curricular and instructional practices in higher education both in the United States and abroad. The establishment of Johns Hopkins, Clark, and the University of Chicago in the last decades of the 19th century, for example, spurred reforms in existing colleges. Curricular reforms at Columbia during World War I, at the University of Chicago in the 1930s, and at Harvard in the 1950s attracted the attention of hundreds of other less-prestigious institutions' administrators and faculties. Since then, U.S. research-centered universities have been imitated by many nations.[5]

Over a century ago, university presidents set the gold standard for their institutions when they framed their mission as that of advancing knowledge through publishable research, especially in the physical and natural sciences. As faculties published their scholarship, the upward path to national (and international) prestige for other institutions narrowed into one model of a research-driven university to copy. And mimic they did. Reduced teaching load, sabbaticals, and large graduate schools spread among less-prestigious and status-seeking institutions to reproduce an academic culture congenial to research-minded faculty. Other evidence of the major universities' trickle-down influence on upwardly mobile institutions can be seen in each generation of the professoriate receiving its graduate training in top research universities and serving on faculties elsewhere. Hence, an inquiry into the historical relationship between research and teaching, curricular reforms at major universities, and commonplace structures and processes is an inquiry into stability and change in academic work.[6]

Finally, an in-depth case study of one representative research university may provide insights into the connections between curricular reforms, university structures and processes, and how scholarship eventually subordinated teaching. There is, however, another, more personal, reason for answering these questions.

When I came to Stanford as an associate professor in 1981 after a quarter-century of being a public school teacher and administrator, I eagerly looked forward to being a teacher, scholar, and adviser to graduate students. The thought that I would be paid to read, think, write, and teach (four courses an academic year) utterly astounded me. After all, I compared a university work schedule over which I could control my time to the frenetic, action-driven life that I led for decades as a superintendent and high school teacher, in which my time belonged to others. I was told (and I believed) that the academic tasks of teaching and inquiry could exist in harmony and indeed even reinforce one another. Yet within this precious freedom that I had to manage my time and determine what I could teach and investigate, I encountered some puzzling questions that nudged me toward doing this study.

At Stanford, I observed the faculty's repeated attempts to improve the undergraduate curriculum by adding and deleting electives and required courses. These attempts culminated in the late 1980s with the Faculty Senate voting, after an extended and heated debate, to revise the Western Culture course. A few years later, Gerhard Casper, a new president, convened the Commission on Undergraduate Education (CUE), the first such review since 1968. The Faculty Senate debated CUE's modest recommendations to add and revise a few academic requirements, leaving the elective system largely in place. After a decade of faculty-driven curriculum reforms, it was unclear to me exactly how much in the undergraduate curriculum had actually changed.

Similarly, I observed efforts of a Stanford president to heighten the importance of teaching. In the early 1990s, then-President Donald

Kennedy launched an initiative to recognize the importance of teaching and improve its quality. New awards were established, and there was much talk about the compatibility of teaching and research and the need for cross-departmental cooperation. There was also much talk about redefining the tenure criterion of excellence in research to incorporate what effective teachers do in their classes. A few years later, the Faculty Senate received a report from one of its committees charged to evaluate teaching in the university, urging that teaching be reframed as a scholarly activity and that peer review be considered as another way of improving the quality of teaching. Faculty concerns over autonomy and obligations to do research arose. Since then, little has been done by the faculty or administration to implement the committee's major recommendations.[7]

What surprised me in all of these moves and countermoves involving new electives and required courses, teaching, and research were published reports of faculty surveys revealing that most professors relied upon lecture for undergraduate courses. Nontraditional forms of teaching, including the rich technologies available to each professor, were used sparingly. This baffled me. I had gone to undergraduate school in the 1950s and attended graduate school in the 1960s and 1970s, and here, in the 1980s, colleagues reported that they taught in strikingly similar ways to the professors I had decades earlier. This perplexing continuity in teaching, moreover, had persisted despite major changes in university enrollments, curriculum, facilities, governance, organization, new instructional technologies, and, of great importance, reduced teaching loads. Constancy in teaching patterns was not what I had expected in a selective, well-endowed, high-prestige university.

What gave me further pause was the strong similarity between what I observed in higher education and the research I had conducted years earlier on curriculum, pedagogy, and attempted reforms in public schools. What I was seeing at Stanford was that professors and public school teachers taught in much the same manner, despite the divergent settings for instruction and the vastly different institutional forces for change. Thus, coming to Stanford from a quarter-century of public school work and having completed historical research on efforts to reform public school teaching, I was bothered by these puzzling issues.[8]

These events and connections left me uneasy about their meaning. In what ways had the array of electives really changed for Stanford undergraduates? Why did faculty modes of teaching seem so stable over decades? What links, if any, were there between departmental authority, professorial freedom, the quality of teaching, and the duty to publish scholarship? Would mainstream definitions of research shift in making tenure decisions, as proponents urged? On this latter question, highly publicized dismissals of assistant professors seeking tenure during the 1980s and 1990s spoke more loudly to both tenured and untenured faculty than any presidential initiative or faculty resolution.

What I observed over almost 2 decades of change was a sturdy stability and apparent linkage between the mundane structures and norms of academic life, such as the elective system, departmental organization, faculty autonomy, and frequent curricular reform—all of which seemed to be connected to the supremacy of research. In my previous historical research into the reform of teaching and curriculum in public schools over the last century, I had noted how organizational and political factors interacted to shape how teachers taught. Likewise, my Stanford experiences prompted me to turn to the literature in higher education.

What I found in the literature was no surprise: The primacy of doing research and publishing scholarly work over teaching has been an enduring pattern in universities since the turn of the century. Amid repeated presidential and faculty claims for the signal importance of teaching and affirmations that harmony, not conflict, characterizes teaching and research, critics and scholars have noted the research imperative as dominating academic work again and again. No news here.[9]

What remained puzzling, however, was *why* the patterns arose and *how* they persisted. Many explanations have been offered that use theories drawn from economic, political, organizational, and institutional models to explain the enduring superiority of research over teaching. Few scholars, however, have inquired into how the subordination of teaching was accomplished organizationally and sustained politically throughout the century. Even fewer scholars have investigated how the tensions between teaching and research have played a role in repeated curricular reforms. Examining such disparate but commonplace entities as the structure of the undergraduate college embedded in the research-driven university, the elective system, departmental influence, and professorial autonomy to make sense of the enduring superiority of publishing scholarship over teaching students emerged as a central task for the study. To do this within one elite university might reveal how very different factors interact and, perhaps, explain the connections between so much talk about curricular reform and the importance of teaching yet so little relief of the grinding tensions among faculty over balancing the demands of both crucial academic tasks.

But why Stanford? The university has been considered a research-oriented institution since it joined the Association of American Universities in 1900, and its place in national rankings of "best" universities began in that same decade. Subsequent growth made it a strong regional institution on the West Coast until the early 1950s. By the mid-1960s, Stanford had moved into the first tier of universities reputed to be of national stature in quality of faculty, students, size of endowment, and available research funds. By the 1990s, reputational rankings of departments and undergraduate and graduate programs by both popular news magazines and scholarly studies had continually placed Stanford in the top five institutions in the country. As a selective Research I university, Stanford is representative of similar upwardly mobile, elite institutions, both public and private, in the United States.[10]

Stanford also possesses many structural and cultural features common to other high-status institutions. These features include dispersed governance split between administration and faculty, decentralized organization of departments, faculty autonomy to inquire and the freedom to teach what is deemed important to the individual professor, professorial entrepreneurship to secure research grants, structure of the university-college, elective principle in curricular organization, and, finally, commitment to the ideals of creating and disseminating knowledge.

What also makes Stanford typical among its sister institutions is that it has had to face dilemmas that have arisen from these academic ideals, structures, and processes. Tensions over how much faculty time should be spent teaching undergraduates while working on research projects created conflicts for professors, especially when university decisions on tenure were clearly linked to the volume and quality of scholarly publication, not teaching awards. Being hired to teach but rewarded to do research emerged early in the 20th century as an uneasy paradox confronting professors in all of the elite institutions. Conflicts among departments arose frequently over how much time and which courses faculty should build into the curriculum to ensure that undergraduates were exposed to essential knowledge in the humanities and sciences and still leave sufficient time for professors to specialize in a discipline. The tough question of how much breadth and depth of knowledge should students possess has faced university faculties throughout this century.

It does not come as a surprise that in the early 1990s Stanford was the first university to be investigated by a congressional committee for its budgeting practices in allocating federal research funds. The investigation testifies less to Stanford's uniqueness—since the university's budgeting rules were similar to other research institutions—and more to the broad view that Stanford was typical of major universities.

Finally, Stanford and other private and public universities sought to strike a balance in this century between maintaining stability and encouraging innovation as they negotiated their path through turbulent, unpredictable times. This was difficult in a constantly changing society in which students expected good teaching, corporate leaders called for more applied research, public officials sought advice from university experts, and parents wanted diplomas to open doors to high-paying jobs for their sons and daughters.

Yet to argue for Stanford's representativeness is not to ignore how this century-old university is unique by its history, privateness, and rise to prominence. Stanford's locale and roots differ considerably from Ivy League institutions. Wealth derived from mid–19th-century Western railroads, not religious impulses to train clerics, underwrote Stanford's origins. Its rise to national prestige came swiftly after World War II, not slowly as with Harvard and Yale. As a private institution, Stanford has had more flexibility in policymaking, hiring faculty, and selecting students than its sister public institutions.

Stanford, then, is both distinctive and typical of the highly influential group of institutions. Yet most studies of selective universities have concentrated on East Coast, Midwestern, and occasional West Coast institutions, usually Berkeley. While archival sources are rich at Stanford, and while the university has been included in many other studies of elite institutions (further testifying to its typicality), there is yet no single volume of scholarly history of Stanford over the last century. While I make no claim for this study filling that niche, a sharply focused historical description and analysis of one selective institution offers rich comparisons and contrasts with other research-driven universities. What such a study further offers, that few have done thus far, is to probe deeply into why there are tensions between teaching and research and how those tensions might be linked to departmental authority, the elective system, professorial autonomy, and frequent curricular reform.[11]

Using Stanford as a case study, however, might obscure the inevitable variations that occur in institutions that are bottom-heavy. At the turn of the century, most universities were top-heavy, that is, largely governed by their presidents. Since World War I, research university governance and organization have been shared between central administration, department chairs, and faculty. As with every research-driven institution, Stanford has been (and is) organized into disciplinary-based departments. Such departments are Stanford's basic unit for appointing and promoting faculty, allocating resources, organizing curriculum and instruction, and developing strong to weak cultures in support of research and teaching. As a bottom-heavy institution, market competition among departments has led to inescapable differences among the scores of quasi-independent units.

To capture the variation and commonalties among departments, I examine two between 1891 and 1990. Not only do such internal sub-case studies provide the detail necessary to see curricular and teaching practice up close, but they also avoid researchers' common practice of generalizing about the character of an institution as if it were the same across schools and departments.

Since views of knowledge and teaching vary by discipline, I include departments in both the humanities and sciences. Investigating the Department of History offers insight into a discipline straddling both the humanities and social sciences. In the School of Medicine (originally the Department of Medicine), I examine overall changes in curriculum and instruction while concentrating on the teaching of anatomy in the preclinical years of study. Again, I will compare and contrast Stanford's experiences in these two settings with both private and public research universities and national patterns of reform for the same period.

This rationale for investigating the connections between repeated curricular reform and common elements of university structures, professorial freedom, teaching, and research at one selective research-oriented university omits the ultimate reason for using Stanford. The point of studying Stanford is less to impress readers with the details of the case but more to cast a sharp light on important questions raised by the example of Stanford. In doing so, reframing familiar perspectives and offering new ones to illuminate those abiding questions becomes the obligation of any scholar using a case study. What follows is a condensed version of the argument and themes that I will elaborate in the next six chapters for which Stanford becomes both the foreground and background.

THE BASIC ARGUMENT

In the face of substantial economic, social, political, and demographic changes in the larger society, Stanford's presidents and faculties, like their counterparts in similar institutions, adjusted to those larger social changes in order to preserve the core ideal of creating new knowledge—the research imperative—while continuously seeking to carve out a high-status niche among competing universities.

This ideal of creating knowledge was embedded in a larger ideology of scientific inquiry that had been embraced as the secular mission of the university in the closing decades of the 19th century. In admitting undergraduates, however, the emerging research-driven universities had to contend with the religiously based moral mission within the antebellum college of professors who were charged with building student character and cultivating citizenship—the teaching imperative. Facing the dilemma of reconciling conflicting ideals, presidents of these turn-of-the-century universities pursued different compromises. Some sought to split off the early undergraduate years from advanced instruction; others considered hiring some professors just to teach undergraduates and others just to conduct research. None of these compromises survived for long.

The uneasy compromise that university presidents eventually worked out in the early 20th century at Stanford and its sister institutions was the hybrid invention of the *university-college*. Within this organizational structure, the mission of teaching and minding the moral life of its undergraduates became embedded within departments, the elective system, and, later, required liberal arts courses called "general education." Amid these innovations, faculty continued their core duties of conducting research, publishing their findings, and guiding doctoral students. This restless détente of institutional ideals now embedded in university structures permitted presidents and professors to strike a balance between conflicting values while striving for higher institutional prestige.

Yet the balance between the teaching imperative buried within the college and the research imperative buried within the graduate school went awry as decades passed. The unrelenting spread of the research-based graduate school culture to educating undergraduates produced far more emphasis on creating mini-academics than on molding citizens. In constructing this early 20th-century compromise of the university-college, then, the hybrid structure generated new tensions that have accompanied it ever since.

In curriculum, the perennial question became how much breadth and depth of liberal arts should undergraduates attain within 4 years? Committed to the elective principle of students choosing which courses to take and professors choosing what they will teach meant that answering the question became more difficult as expert knowledge grew and pressures for vocational preparation increased. Moreover, occasional surges of interest in general education, often mirroring deep societal changes stirred by wars and economic turbulence, moved faculties to reconsider the steady drift toward academic specialization and question the principle of student choice of courses. At different times, faculty-driven curricular reforms mandated new courses for all undergraduates. These surges of general education reform, however, ebbed, returning to fewer requirements in the initial undergraduate years and a renewed embrace of the elective principle.

Yet another paradox buried within the hybrid structure faced research-oriented professors responsible for teaching both general education courses and their specialties to both undergraduates and doctoral students: They were hired to do research but paid to teach; then they were retained or fired on the basis of published scholarship.

Universities required a Ph.D. degree to become a professor, established a ladder of academic rank, and awarded tenure and promotion to those who excelled in getting their research published. These structures and norms were anchored in a traditional core belief that teaching and research were inherently compatible within the university-college. For those presidents and professors who believed that the two tasks were intertwined, there was no contradiction. However, in this century each time an assistant professor renowned for teaching excellence was denied tenure for inadequate scholarship, the incompatibility of the two academic duties became clear with the unambiguous message that what counted was research, not teaching. The deep tensions that faculty experience at Stanford and elsewhere in allocating their time to teaching and research strengthened the view that the struggle continues in the university-college as the 21st century begins.

As major reforms swept over higher education after World Wars I and II and during the 1960s and 1980s, these intractable institutional paradoxes within the university-college provided an enduring framework for Stanford faculty, including historians and medical scientists, to make symbolic changes in curricula and pedagogy. Symbolic reforms within the university framework of enduring beliefs, structures, and academic culture are not, however, straitjackets of either constancy or uniformity. Among research-driven institutions, increased ideological, organizational, and cultural homogeneity in this century has not eliminated the diversity embedded in private and public, religiously affiliated and secular, and large and small institutions. Moreover, within these institutions there has been sufficient slack due to professorial freedom and departmental organization to permit variability in how much administrators and faculty honor teaching. In short, within particular departments individual professors at Stanford and other institutions have experimented with nontraditional forms of teaching and have been recognized by students as first-rate teachers. But they have remained a tiny fraction of faculty who have entered and exited university classrooms. This, then, is the argument that threads through the next six chapters.

In Chapter 1, I describe and analyze the tradition of curricular and pedagogical reform that evolved at Stanford since its founding. The chapter documents the invention and subsequent career of the university-college. I describe key moments when presidents and faculty groups launched curricular reforms and analyze how those reforms affected teaching, advising, and research. In Chapter 2, I offer a framework for analyzing change in universities and apply it to the century-long experience of Stanford with the university-college. Chapters 3 and 4 return to Stanford and trace both the curricular and instructional changes that occurred in the Department of History and the School of Medicine, respectively. In each of these chapters I take the earlier analysis of change and apply the concepts to what happened in each setting. In Chapter 5, I compare and contrast the experiences of these two units within the university. In making these comparisons, I concentrate on the distinct commonalties that emerged at Stanford and in other universities. In Chapter 6, I return explicitly to the two questions that I set out to answer and explain: How has the academic work of research and teaching influenced university structures and processes, including curricular reform, over the last century? Why has scholarship trumped teaching in universities? I end the chapter by asking whether the dilemma of scholars versus teachers can ever be fully reconciled.

I undertook this study to better understand an institution that had entranced and confounded me for almost 20 years. Coming from a quarter-century career as a teacher and administrator in the public schools, I was exhilarated by the precious freedom that I had to think, read, write, teach, and—most important for me—to learn. Yet, in stumbling over surprising commonalties between reforming university curriculum and teaching with my earlier work on public schools, I found even more jarring paradoxes in how university faculties managed their curricular and pedagogical affairs that both startled and puzzled me. This study documents my journey to understand better the persistent tensions within the teaching and research in which I (and many colleagues) have been fruitfully if not frustratingly engaged.

═ 1 ═

HOW THE INVENTION OF THE UNIVERSITY-COLLEGE LED TO A CENTURY OF DILEMMAS AND A TRADITION OF REFORM AT STANFORD

IN THE 1990s, at Stanford University, as elsewhere in the nation, there was much talk about teaching and its relationship to published research. Stories of gifted teachers being denied tenure became common news items in campus newspapers. Proposals to reduce the conflict between research and teaching ranged from cash awards given to university professors for excellence in teaching to altering criteria for awarding tenure.

In the previous decade, there was tumult over changing the curriculum, especially the "Western Culture" courses. The question of exactly what knowledge and values university graduates must possess had been seriously debated by faculties across the country. Reformers had made many curricular changes. Yet few reformers or researchers had examined the sources of the persistent tensions between teaching and research and conflicts over what knowledge is essential to see if such tensions were connected. I claim that they are linked.[1]

Within the birth of the American university were planted the seeds of conflicts that sprouted enduring dilemmas over research and teaching and curricular breadth and depth. In creating the modern university at the end of the 19th century, strong-willed presidents and founders borrowed from German and British higher education to invent a hybrid institution adapted to American soil: the university-college.

The ideal of unfettered faculty freedom of inquiry was embedded in the 19th century German university. The ideal of teaching youth in order

13

to furnish their minds with essential knowledge and values while strengthening their character was embedded in the medieval British college and transplanted to 17th century America. In the last quarter of the 19th century, at new institutions such as Cornell, Chicago, and Stanford, and at established ones such as Harvard and Yale, presidents and professors grafted together the two ideals of research and teaching into an innovative structure called the university-college.

But the imaginative invention of the university-college contained within it much tension. The ideal of a professor seeking truth through disciplined inquiry competed with obligations that the very same professor would teach advanced students aspiring to be researchers as well as students who had just completed high school. For graduate students, the professor could design tailored elective courses; for undergraduates, the professor would teach a required introductory course that would provide entry-level knowledge of a discipline. Hired to do research and publish findings yet paid to teach courses to undergraduates created a bind for professors.

These ideals conflicted because of constraints of money and time facing administrators and faculty. University presidents might have lessened tensions if they had sufficient funds to pay professors to do either research or teaching. They did not, so faculty had to do both. Eliminating the undergraduate college might have eliminated conflict. After all, Johns Hopkins and Clark began as solely research-driven institutions in the late 19th century, accepting only graduate students; within a few years, however, both amended their mission to become university-colleges. Presidents at Stanford, Chicago, and Harvard had tried to lop off the first 2 years of college and let junior colleges absorb undergraduates. All efforts failed. So, individual professors experienced the conflicting ideals in their daily lives. They had insufficient time to complete all that was demanded of them: investigate unsolved problems in their field, publish their research findings, teach courses to undergraduates and graduates, advise students, serve on university committees, stay abreast with their disciplinary colleagues, and, perhaps, have a life outside of the campus. Because of these constraints, administrators and faculty had to make daily choices among the competing ideals. Tensions surfaced and persisted.

The invention of the university-college fundamentally changed American higher education, but, in doing so, it created in its wake conflicting ideals and obligations that have prompted continual reforms to eliminate these tensions without signal success. The dilemmas of conflicting ideals, buried within the structural innovation of the university-college, have endured for a century. And so it was at Stanford.

I begin with the founding of the university-college at Stanford over a century ago where, as one pioneer faculty member put it, "one could almost feel the hot breath of the desert."[2]

Leland Stanford, the wealthy senator, ex-governor, and former head of the Central Pacific Railroad, and his wife, Jane, sought to create a living memorial for their 15-year-old son who had died of typhoid fever on a visit to Italy in 1884. Within a year, a grant of endowment established the framework for a new institution that would "qualify students for personal success and direct usefulness in life." Their fervor inspired the many tasks that face founders of a university: securing a state charter to open a university, hiring a president, appointing architects to design classrooms and buildings to house students of both sexes, and providing enough money to keep the new university solvent through its early years. Their determination was unflagging.[3]

In 1891, Leland Stanford Junior Memorial University welcomed its first class of over 550 young men and women (who paid no tuition), 17 youthful faculty (most under the age of 40), and the new president, David Starr Jordan, formerly the head of Indiana University and himself just 40 years of age. On a small section of the 8,000 acre Stanford estate ("The Farm" as it was called), near the newly created tiny village of Palo Alto, 12 classrooms, an engineering laboratory, separate male and female dormitories, and cottages for the faculty, with paint still drying, were ready.

Leland Stanford died in 1893. His death led to years of financial uncertainty since the U.S. government had sued to recover federal loans made to the Central Pacific, and the estate was frozen. Jane Stanford, as the remaining founder, worked closely with President Jordan to keep the infant institution alive. She used personal funds to pay faculty, maintain existing buildings, and construct new ones until 1896, when the U.S. Supreme Court finally rejected the federal claims.

For the next decade, although she traveled extensively, Jane Stanford kept in close touch with university affairs to the point of demanding that Jordan fire economics professor Edward A. Ross in 1900 for his outspoken views on the silver and Chinese immigration issues and his support for presidential candidate William Jennings Bryan. The subsequent national and local furor over Jordan's firing of Ross (and loss of a few key professors who resigned in protest) damaged the university's reputation, but did not deter the surviving founder from being involved in key decisions. At her death in 1905, the terms of the grant of endowment (1885) formally transferred all decision-making powers to the president and the board of trustees, although Mrs. Stanford had turned authority over to them earlier.[4]

David Starr Jordan served as president for 22 years before retiring in 1913 to become chancellor, an honorific post especially created for him. Jordan, a man of enormous energy who delighted in the play of ideas, was a member of the pioneer class of Cornell (1869–1872) and knew its president, Andrew White, well. White had even recommended Jordan, then head of Indiana University, to the Stanfords after turning down their offer to head the new university. Under White, Cornell's newly installed elective system gave the first generation of students the freedom to choose courses, a freedom that left a strong impression upon the young Jordan. He majored in botany, minored in geology and zoology, and sampled courses in history and five languages, including Chinese.[5]

After graduation, Jordan taught elementary and secondary school. He also went to medical college and received an M.D., although he never practiced medicine. He eventually became a college professor of zoology and ichthyology, and he continued to do research on fish and publish articles in scientific journals even after coming to Stanford. In this zigzag career path, Jordan recalled the singular learning experiences he had had at Louis Agassiz's "Summer School of Science" on Penikese Island off the coast of Cape Cod. Working daily with other young scientists in collecting and examining animals under the close scrutiny of Harvard University's premier scientist, Jordan believed that he learned there to think for himself. Between White and Agassiz, the young Jordan saw the power of an administrator and teacher to inspire and mold a student's mind and character. Both the creation of knowledge and a youth's moral development were one in his mind. He applied the lessons of Cornell and Penikese, brief as they were, to Indiana and, later, Stanford, particularly in organizing a curriculum, teaching, and conducting research.[6]

THE MAJOR-SUBJECT SYSTEM

From Stanford's founding until 1920, Jordan's views of curricular structures and his expectations for professors as teachers, advisers, and researchers were institutionalized into the major-subject system, a blend of student choice and professorial prerogative.

Organizing a Curriculum, 1891–1920

Bringing from Indiana University, and even earlier from Cornell, the concept of a "major" and the principle of electivity, Jordan and the faculty agreed that the only required subject that all students had to take at Stanford was English composition. The notion of 1st-year students choosing a major and subsequent courses, save one, implicitly made all subjects offered by each department equal in worth and permitted a student to specialize as his or her professor had done.[7]

Basically, the major-subject plan organized the official curriculum around the disciplinary-based (and specialized) interests of professors and departments. Each 1st-year student would pick a professor with whom he or she would like to work and the two of them would then plan an individualized 4-year course of study in the major and any minors that the professor thought necessary. The student would take the courses that the department required for the major (no more than one-third of the units required for graduation) and then choose among other departmental offerings. The professor would be the academic adviser and his or her recommendation (of the original faculty, two were women) would be necessary for graduation.[8]

For example, in 1894, 3 years after the university opened, professors in 24 departments enrolled 1,100 students. A student who wanted to major in history might choose Professor George E. Howard as adviser and the two would work out annually a schedule of which courses to take in history (only two were required—the "Historical Training" course and a seminar for 4th-year students) and courses elsewhere to complete minors in which the student was interested. Other departments were more prescriptive. A professor in mining engineering would inform his advisee that 17 hours a week of certain courses were required by the department for 5 years; in addition, the adviser would explain that Spanish was required and summer fieldwork also had to be completed in order to graduate.[9]

Teaching, Advising, and Research, 1891–1920

Jordan's curricular organization located the professor-student relationship as central to forming the student's moral character, inspiring a love of learning, and finding a practical use for what had been learned. Jordan, who viewed his experiences with Louis Agassiz and Andrew White as crucial to his intellectual and moral development, saw the major-subject system as essential in making the university-college hybrid work. The system would produce the unity of morality and knowledge in a faculty-student bond where friendliness, respect, and cooperation could be cultivated.

Within this curricular structure, the professors' primary tasks were to teach, advise their students, investigate in their fields, and publish their research. Other tasks that occupied professors were departmental meetings, work on various university committees, and attendance at meetings of the entire faculty in the Academic Council. Given these diverse obligations, the president still expected scholarly excellence from his faculty, first-rate teaching and advising, and the growth of an intellectual community among students and faculty. Even before Jordan became president, in a letter to Leland Stanford summarizing the main points upon which they had agreed, he wrote: "each professor be supplied as soon as may be with the books, apparatus, or machinery which he needs for instruction or for research. . . . That provision be made for the publication of the results of any important research on the part of professors or advanced students." That these goals, constrained by limited resources and competing obligations, may have been in conflict, Jordan, like fellow presidents, disregarded.[10]

Of all that professors were expected to do, teaching absorbed most of their time. And Stanford's president prized this morally charged task. In the early years of his tenure, he enjoyed lecturing to students. "The great teacher," he wrote in 1899, "never fails to leave a . . . mark on every young man and young woman with whom he comes in contact."[11]

How did professors teach in these years? Since later chapters will examine teaching in specific subjects, I briefly mention here the generic approaches used at Stanford and common to other American universities. Lectures, recitations,[12] weekly quizzes, and major exams were familiar fare for students in these decades, and the introduction of laboratories in the sciences and seminars in history and other disciplines broadened the teaching repertoires that professors used in their courses. The most common teaching practices were lectures, recitations, the use of laboratories in the sciences, and exams throughout the 1890s and early 1900s.

In the student-written newspaper, the *Daily Palo Alto,* the editors asked professors in 1895 to be more aware of the style of teaching large classes.

> In some of the larger classes where the students are not called upon daily to recite, there springs up a strange hesitancy to speak when a class question does arise. The professor, although he prefers to spend most of his time in lecturing, finds it discouraging, when he does ask something to be met with an appalling silence savoring of stupidity. . . . The students . . . often know perfectly the answer, but are not used to speaking in a lecture class, [and] hesitate about breaking the silence and drawing all the attention to themselves.[13]

Students were also concerned over the length of professors' assignments for recitations and the recommended time of 2 hours preparation for each daily recitation when they had to read hundreds of pages for their different courses.[14]

By World War I, formal, scheduled recitations had largely disappeared from Stanford's catalogs although many professors would continue to use different versions of it in smaller classes; by the 1920s, the recitation section had been transformed into weekly discussion sessions largely taught by graduate students. Seminars for undergraduates also appeared.[15]

As much as Jordan extolled teaching, he expected his faculty to do original research. While Jordan was presiding over Indiana University, he said bluntly that "a professor to whom original investigation is unknown should have no place in a university." In his first speech to new Stanford students, faculty, and guests in 1891, he sounded the same theme and predicted,

> Some day our universities will recognize that their most important professors may be men who teach no classes, devoting their time and strength wholly to advanced research. . . . They set high standards of thought. They help to create the university spirit, without which any college is but a grammar school of little higher pretensions.

A decade later, he echoed similar sentiments. "The real university," he wrote in *Popular Science* in 1902, "is a school of research. . . . It is an institution from which in every direction blazes the light of original research." Jordan required annual departmental reports to include publications of each professor. If research inspired teaching, according to Jordan, publications were also instrumental in achieving tenure and promotion. When Edwin Slosson visited the campus and spoke with faculty, students, and administrators, he found much evidence for Jordan's views and actions. He concluded that "skill as a teacher, helpful personality, executive ability, or long service, though taken into consideration, are not held to justify promotion above the grade of assistant professor without thorough and therefore productive scholarship."[16]

With Jordan openly expressing competing expectations, the conflicts among these ideals deepened as the university grew in size and led to the gradual erosion of the major-subject system. Stanford expanded from the original 30-odd faculty and 550 students in the pioneer class of 1891 to over 1,300 students taught by 75 faculty in 1900. A decade later, there were almost 1,800 students and 112 faculty. By the time Jordan retired, Stanford was no longer a small community of faculty and students whose face-to-face contact softened official policies and procedures.[17]

As the university grew, administrators bureaucratized admission requirements, the curriculum, and departmental regulations. Expectations for faculty duties, however, remained the same. They lectured and heard recitations 8 to 12 hours a week depending upon the department, pursued research, wrote articles and books, advised students, and attended committee meetings. Jordan was loath to reduce teaching hours. He would "grant freedom from cheap and sterile activity—from reading papers, sharpening knives, and copying letters"—but not from teaching students. Jordan had also seen the moral and academic mission of the university distilled in the professor-as-adviser role: "The college must furnish its lower classmen with advisers ... men who come near the students, men whom the students can trust and who at the same time are in touch with the highest ideals the university teachers represent." As a consequence, for many professors facing these conflicting obligations, the personal relationship with students mandated by the major-subject system, especially around advising, frayed.[18]

As early as 1894, complaints over faculty inattention to advising students led to the introduction of the *study card,* a way of holding both students and professors accountable by listing courses that the student would take each semester; it was counter-signed by the "major" professor. Within a few years, however, the idea of each professor doing all of the advising gave way to the department being responsible for specifying which courses each student should take. Still, complaints about advising persisted.

Faculty opinion about the flaws in advising focused entirely upon the students. A questionnaire returned in 1905 by two-thirds of the faculty found most faculty agreeing that many 1st-year students were too immature to choose wisely either their major or other courses. Such students, professors said, often took easy courses or ones calculated to leave much time for extracurricular activities.[19]

What to do? Framing the problem as faculty inattention to advisees led to the invention of the study card. Yet the pattern of many faculty disregarding students' academic needs persisted. To define the problem as, for example, faculty wanting to spend more time on their research and other duties than on listening to students would have probably offended busy faculty. I found no such example in recorded discussions and published reports.

Another way of framing the problem was that 4 years of college was unnecessary. College studies could be compressed into 2 or 3 years. University of Chicago's president William Rainey Harper coined the phrase, "four year fetish." Charles Eliot proposed to the Harvard faculty in 1901 a 3-year bachelor's degree. Unprepared and immature students who in their initial 2 years displayed an unreadiness for advanced work with research-minded faculty specialists could attend the newly emerging junior colleges. The Harvard faculty turned down Eliot's proposal. For those who framed the issue in this manner, as David Starr Jordan did, the solution was to abandon the innovation of the university-college and send undergraduates to enroll in junior colleges, or to add additional years to their stay in public high schools.[20]

Jordan, like other presidents, began to argue that no single institution could be a college, graduate research institute, and professional school simultaneously. Students vary, institutional purposes differ, and the manner of instruction must be tailored to fit student and institutional differences. Jordan sought a university committed to research and teaching, not a college solely committed to high-quality teaching, and this could be best done, he felt, by dropping the first 2 years. So between 1907 and 1910 he recommended three times to the board of trustees his "bisection" plan of retaining only the last 2 years of the undergraduate curriculum. Each time, the board rejected the plan on the grounds that the loss of entering students would seriously restrict growth of Stanford as a university, since few sources for graduate students existed other than undergraduate enrollment. The major-subject system that permitted a topsy-like growth of departmental curricula for majors and minors with the habitual problem of faculty inattention to student advising also remained in place.[21]

Not until the end of World War I did faculty sentiment coalesce around an energetic new president, Ray Lyman Wilbur, to end the major-subject system, to finally shift from the continuously criticized semester system to a four-quarter academic year, and to attack the nagging issue of professors signing without more than a passing glance the lists of courses that students chose. Similarly, within universities nationally, the 1920s and 1930s were years of both consolidation and modification of earlier reforms after the founders and high-profile presidents had passed away.[22]

A REORGANIZED CURRICULUM, 1916–1956

In 1916, the board of trustees appointed Dr. Ray Lyman Wilbur as president. Wilbur had graduated from Stanford in 1896, completed Cooper Medical College in San Francisco in 1899, and become an assistant professor of physiology in 1900. He left the university in 1903 to enter private medical practice. Six years later, after Stanford University and Cooper merged, he returned as a professor of medicine and eventually dean of the School of Medicine in 1910.[23]

After Jordan's successor as president, John Branner, retired in 1915, alumnus Herbert Hoover, by then a wealthy engineer who was deeply involved in World War I relief, became a trustee and led a campaign to make Wilbur, his longtime friend, the next president of Stanford. Within a year, the board of trustees appointed Wilbur as president of the university. His intimate knowledge of the university and appreciation of corporate efficiency permitted him to make organizational and curricular changes that had been discussed for many years among faculty, trustees, and administrators but had gone unaddressed.[24]

Within 5 years, Wilbur had reorganized curricular structures by moving from the semester plan to the quarter system, ending the major-subject system for 1st- and 2nd-year students (while still requiring them to take certain courses) and splitting the undergraduate curriculum into lower and upper division courses. Within a decade, he had also restructured 26 departments into five schools, or super-departments (Biological Sciences, Social Sciences, Engineering, Physical Sciences, and Letters), and added more professional schools (Nursing, Law, and Business).

This surge of organizational changes occurred during a period of rapid university growth—from 2,200 students (and 118 faculty) in 1916 to nearly 4,000 in 1925 and over 5,000 (and almost 300 faculty) by 1940—including the lean years of the Great Depression. In seeking efficiencies and consolidating these organizational changes, he gave the university a remarkable stability, sufficient to earn Stanford a strong regional reputation and the beginnings of a national one. He also tried (and failed like Jordan) to eliminate the dilemma embedded in the university-college by abolishing the first 2 undergraduate years. Stanford, like its sister institutions of Harvard, Berkeley, Johns Hopkins, Chicago, Michigan, and Yale, has remained ever since an uneasy hybrid of college and university.[25]

Reorganizing the Official Curriculum, 1919–1920

Wilbur wasted little time in addressing the curriculum, as it had grown like kudzu through interdepartmental negotiating over the major-subject system. Wartime opened many opportunities for change. Many universities, driven by a strong patriotic impulse, accepted federal funds to train cadres of soldiers. Faculties jerrybuilt a basic curriculum in order to instill in recruits what it meant to be an American. As a result, at Columbia and elsewhere, faculties and administrators began to rethink what a university should offer as a common intellectual experience to all undergraduates about to become voters.[26] Wilbur was no exception:

> It seemed to me that no student in the so-called classical or humanities curricula should graduate from a university without some laboratory experience in gathering information firsthand. . . . Nor should any science or engineering or medical student graduate without a good working knowledge of the cultural, social, and economic forces upon which the demand for his professional services and his quality as a citizen depend. We were training more than mechanics and technicians.[27]

In 1919, Wilbur appointed a five-man faculty subcommittee, and it presented to the Academic Council in 1920 a reorganization of the entire curriculum. The faculty swiftly adopted the recommendations.[28]

The curricular reorganization maintained departmental specialization for 3rd- and 4th-year students, thus retaining the major-subject system for what became known as the upper division while introducing required "liberal education" courses for lower division students in their first 2 years. In reorganizing the curriculum in this manner, the faculty sought to ease the persistent tension between the values of student choice and specialization embedded in the major-subject system and the faculty's concern, ripened during World War I, about all students having a common intellectual experience.[29]

The new plan called for 1st- and 2nd-year students in the lower division to fulfill "distribution requirements" in English, foreign languages, natural sciences, and history. High school graduates admitted to Stanford who had already taken required courses in languages, science, and history would receive credit. However, even these students would still have to take four mandated university courses: English composition and three new survey courses that had yet to be created. These included a natural science course, a history course, and a newly developed "Problems of Citizenship" course. For those undergraduates entering the university who were less-favored in their high school preparation, their course load would be heavy with requirements, but would still leave room for one-third of their lower division courses to be electives.[30]

Apart from renewed university interest in "liberal education," there were pressing social reasons for particular survey courses. Citing similar courses at Columbia, the University of Chicago, Williams, and Dartmouth, the faculty committee argued forcefully for the mandated "Problems of Citizenship" course.

> Generally speaking, all freshmen are either now or soon to be voters. Does not the University owe them a duty as such? If our tritest sayings

are true, these freshmen are destined to become leaders in their respective communities. They are forming the political, economic, and social ideas that will characterize that leadership. And they are forming them now while the air is full of strange doctrines and without waiting for a critical and scholarly insight. Can the University not render a substantial social service by providing a sound basis of elementary scientific facts and principles by which the validity of these doctrines may be tested?[31]

The committee reasserted the ideal of private universities performing a public service by educating the young to be good citizens. The familiar quasi-religious moral mission of the undergraduate college had now been secularized.

Between 1920 and 1956, many changes in course content occurred within departmental offerings, but there were few modifications in the structure of required and elective courses. The only concerted effort to review the reorganized curriculum was a faculty committee that met for 2 years (1936–1938) during the debate over whether the 4 years of undergraduate work should be reduced. Within that heated debate, which involved alumni, the faculty concluded that nothing should be done to change distribution requirements or the organization of lower and upper division courses. There was a faculty faction that wanted to stretch the 2 years of distribution requirements for "liberal education" into 4 years, but this group failed to convince enough colleagues; the group issued an innocuous statement of support for the existing curriculum in 1938.[32]

Teaching, Advising, and Research, 1920–1954

Having taught at both Cooper Medical College and Stanford, President Wilbur knew the demands of the job and had strong beliefs about what distinguished a fine teacher from a "hack professor."

> The professor has to perform from one to four times daily, often on as many different subjects, to as many audiences. . . . He must also organize his own material, as well as present it in a way that will arouse enough inquiring interest to make it stick in the minds of his students. . . . Outside of his classes, student conferences, student papers, and other work of review or organization claim his time. . . . And crowning all, the drive of some original research project of the professor's own nags him day and night, keeps his mind taut, and leads to more nervous tension than is generally realized.[33]

Wilbur also summed up popular opinion on teaching undergraduates and graduates. "Teaching ability," he said in 1930, "is rarer than research ability. . . . Good teachers are born, not made, just as geniuses are born, and . . . they are hard to capture."[34] If he believed in the genetic basis of effective teaching—a position that leaves little ground for self-improve-ment—his opinions on research were more grounded in hard work and productivity, regardless of their sources.

To Wilbur, as important as teaching was, published research made the university shine. At a dinner in his honor, he said, "the thing that gave me the most satisfaction . . . was to see the name of a Stanford man after a scholarly or creditable piece of work, be it in the *Journal of Philology,* the *New York Times,* or in a medical journal." He acknowledged the ten-sion between teaching and research but nonetheless argued that a pro-fessor investigating a problem and publishing the results spelled the difference between merely teaching and being a full-fledged faculty member.[35]

To highlight the importance of research, Wilbur's administration designed criteria to use in making faculty appointments, reappointments, and promotions. In order of importance, they were scholarship, teach-ing ability, ability in research, personality, and future promise. Although national associations of college officials and faculties had begun to raise questions in the 1920s about the inferior quality of teaching and its voca-tional importance—those receiving a Ph.D. essentially became profes-sors and taught—at no time in these years was the supremacy of schol-arship seriously questioned by Stanford's president, faculty, or students.[36]

With the reorganization of the official curriculum, the array of famil-iar teaching practices continued: lectures and labs in the lower division, and lectures, seminars, and independent work in labs in the upper divi-sion. Lectures continued to dominate teaching practices in most uni-versities, including Stanford. *The Quad,* a student-written yearbook, jested about this common method of instruction:

> The greatest tragedy that can happen to a professor is to enter his class-
> room and find all the chalk gone. The next greatest tragedy is to have a
> dog fall asleep during one of his lectures. The third greatest is to have
> a student fall asleep.[37]

In the 1920s, the faculty and administration approved merging lectures with "discussion" sections (replacing the older and familiar "recitation" sections). In large lecture courses, groups of 30 or so students were taught by graduate assistants, as in the lower division survey course "Problems of Citizenship." These interdepartmentally designed survey courses were intended to reduce the autonomy of key departments. The "Problems of Citizenship" course, for example, sought full professors in the economics and political science departments who would not only collaborate in integrating subject matter from different social sciences but also devote a few years to teaching the course. No volunteers from either department, however, stepped forward to organize or teach such a course. Instead, both departments scheduled lecturers to appear on given days.[38]

History Professor Edgar E. Robinson volunteered to coordinate the "Citizenship" course. In a confidential memo written in 1925, he described the reduction of lectures from 90 in 1924 (or 3 a week for each quarter) to 60 a year later. He recruited 15 professors from economics, political science, and law to lecture weekly and 6 instructors (mostly graduate students) to lead discussion sections of about 30 students each twice a week.[39]

Criticism, however, mounted each year. Students complained about uncoordinated lectures and discussions divorced from lectures. Instructors complained about infrequent meetings with lecturers. Faculty complained about lecturing to uninformed 1st-year students. Running through the criticism was the debate over just exactly what should 1st-year students know about the world and their civic obligations. Temporary agreements among faculty on core concepts stilled criticism, but consensus faded quickly as new charges arose. In 1935, the faculty dropped the "Citizenship" course and replaced it with "History of Western Civilization." This course, sponsored by the history department, contained lectures and discussion sections, and it became a lower division requirement.[40]

For the survey courses on biology and physical sciences, there was some collaboration between departments because particular professors chose to work together. After a few years, however, the collaboration atrophied, and the pattern of lower division required courses becoming a sequence of cameo appearances from different professors without much effort to coordinate lectures became routine.[41]

What about that form of teaching called advising? Strong criticism of the major-subject system for decades concentrated upon faculty neglect in advising students. The 1920 reorganization placed responsibility for advising advanced students with the departments. For 1st- and 2nd-year students, however, advising was located in a new administrative organization called the Committee on the Lower Division. The committee referred lower division students who already knew what major they wanted to the department, whereupon a faculty adviser was assigned. For most students who had not yet declared a major, the published requirements were expected to guide the completion of the study card.[42]

By 1954, it was clear that the quality and frequency of advising again varied considerably among faculty. In that year, under President J. E. Wallace Sterling, administrators and faculty raised serious questions about both advising and teaching, and the earlier reorganization.[43]

TINKERING WITH THE OFFICIAL CURRICULUM, 1954–1968

During World War II, Stanford professors served in the armed forces, taught servicemen sent to the campus, and conducted government-funded research. "When I came to Stanford in 1945," Wallace Stegner, novelist and longtime director of the university's creative writing program, recalled, "there were only a few men on campus. It seemed like a girls' college. . . . And then came September and the GIs and the place just exploded."[44]

After the war, the campus overflowed with returning veterans seeking degrees financed by the Servicemen's Readjustment Act (the G.I. Bill). Professors in the natural and life sciences and medical schools settled into working on federal research contracts. Sizable increases in university enrollment, faculty, and budgets were common throughout the 1950s across the nation, and Stanford was no exception.[45]

With the retirement of Ray Lyman Wilbur in 1943, after 27 years as Stanford's top official (with time out to serve in the cabinet of President Herbert Hoover), the board of trustees turned to one of their own, businessman Donald Tresidder. An admirer of Herbert Hoover and deeply committed to making the university managerially efficient, Tresidder also sought closer ties to industry. He created the Stanford Research Institute and appointed Frederick Terman dean of the School of Engineering to forge those linkages. After only 4 years in office, shepherding the university through the war and its immediate aftermath, Tresidder suddenly died.[46]

In searching for a successor, the board of trustees turned again to an alumnus and appointed J. E. Wallace Sterling as the university's fifth president. He served for 19 years, leaving office in 1968. Thus, three men, the founding president and two alumni—Jordan (1891–1913), Wilbur (1916–1943), and Sterling (1949–1968)—headed Stanford for 68 of its initial 77 years, providing a climate for both innovation and stability to thrive, which many sister institutions could only envy.

Like Jordan and Wilbur, Sterling came to the office a relatively young man at the age of 42. Born and raised in Canada, he graduated from the University of Toronto with a Bachelor of Arts degree in history. He taught history (and coached football and basketball) at the University of Alberta while securing his Master's degree. What brought him to Stanford in 1930 was the Hoover Institute and Library where he pursued a doctorate in history. After 7 years of being a graduate assistant and teaching in the history department, he received his Ph.D. He began teaching at the California Institute of Technology as an assistant professor. In 1942, Sterling was promoted to full professor. He also served as a news analyst for CBS radio network between 1942 and 1948, covering national conventions and the founding conference of the United Nations. With the death of Tresider and after Herbert Hoover and other trustees determined that Sterling's political views were correct (the candidate said that he had never voted for Franklin Delano Roosevelt and would support Republican Thomas Dewey in the next election), the board appointed Sterling as Stanford's fifth president. At Sterling's inauguration, Herbert Hoover said: "Character, understanding, scholarship, administrative ability, and love of youth are all combined in him. Stanford will march ahead under his leadership."[47]

Amid the sharp growth in enrollments, the faculty's demands for higher salaries, and the decay of the physical plant, Sterling had his own blueprint for raising Stanford into the first echelon of major American universities, a purpose that he brought to the post and made clear to the student body. Stanford senior Derek Bok (class of 1951 and later president of Harvard) recalled a speech in which Sterling announced his ambition for Stanford: "We will become the Harvard of the West." Bok thought that was overreaching and wrote a letter to President Sterling saying that "Stanford would never be like Harvard because it lacked an . . . unrelenting commitment to intellectual excellence" because it chases too many goals at once. "The result of all this," Bok concluded, "is that Stanford manages to be pretty good in everything but outstanding in nothing." The next day, Sterling called Bok to his office and the senior remembered that the president spoke "eloquently, even passionately, of his vision for a future Stanford. I replied politely . . . [and] [w]e parted, neither one persuaded by the other's view.[48]

Reaching for national prestige meant copying Ivy League institutions. Sterling sought to raise private and public monies to underwrite higher faculty salaries, expand the pool of first-rate professors, renovate physical facilities, and undertake major improvements in the university program. He convinced the board of trustees to merge the two campuses of the medical school into one university-based facility (needing almost $20 million—in 1954 dollars—for construction). He also helped the board of trustees begin planning for developing thousands of acres deeded to the university, by leasing parcels of land to industrial corporations—initially in 1951 to Varian, and later to Hewlett-Packard—to create what later became Stanford Research Park. He appointed Dean Frederick Terman as provost in 1955 to upgrade the faculty and make the sciences the envy of sister institutions. And he charged the faculty to undertake two comprehensive reviews of undergraduate education, the first in 1954 and the second in 1968, the year he decided to leave the post. That this determined drive for higher status occurred at a time when the federal government began its policy of investing in university research—particularly in the physical and life sciences—can be noted as brilliant strategy, luck, or, more likely, a bit of each.[49]

Pursuing national distinction was tied to a strategy of securing federal and industrial-strength research dollars and bringing star-quality faculty to Stanford. In the mid-1930s, when he was being interviewed for the presidency of Harvard, James B. Conant stated clearly his belief in what made a university great: "A university [is] a collection of eminent scholars. If the permanent professors [are] the most distinguished in the world, then the university [will be] the best university." Provost Terman, sharing Conant's belief, laid out clearly his view (and that of Sterling's) for securing a national reputation.

> Academic prestige depends upon high but narrow steeples of academic excellence rather than upon coverage of more modest height extending solidly over a broad discipline. Each steeple is formed by a small faculty group of experts in a narrow area of knowledge, and what counts is that the steeples be high for all to see and that they relate to something important. The number of steeples and the breadth of knowledge that each covers are quite secondary. The strategy thus indicated is to build up very great faculty strength in a few important but very narrow areas at the expense of broad coverage.

By the time Sterling left the president's office, there was little doubt in most informed observers' opinions that Stanford had entered that small circle of universities known nationally as the best.[50]

Changing the Official Undergraduate Curriculum, 1954–1956

Enough criticism of the existing curriculum, largely unchanged since it was implemented in the 1920s, had made it clear to President Sterling that organizational changes in the undergraduate program were necessary. Harvard had already undertaken a review—the *Redbook* had appeared in 1945—and its faculty had adopted a new policy of prescribed courses and distribution requirements in 1949. In the fall of 1954, after securing a grant from the Fund for the Advancement of Education, Sterling wanted a full-scale study of undergraduate education that would eventually improve university programs to "warrant favorable comparison with any . . . in the nation."[51]

The Executive Committee of the Stanford Study of Undergraduate Education established faculty groups to examine the quarter system, student advising, lower division course offerings (especially for general education), instructional methods, and how student performance was judged. They compiled the results of student questionnaires, faculty interviews, and written statements from both students and faculty.[52]

After 2 years of study and faculty deliberation, the Academic Council approved the committee's curricular recommendations. The faculty extended general education (Stanford's version of a "liberal education") for an undergraduate's career rather than restricting it to the initial 2 years as it had been since 1920. Moreover, all students had to take particular English, history, and language (or mathematics) courses and then choose subjects within two nonmajor "area requirements" in humanities, social sciences, and natural sciences. Less a major change than a structural enhancement of an already existing commitment to general education, the revised official curriculum largely reaffirmed the 1920 compromise between electives and required courses by extending the commitment to 4 years.[53]

When it came to teaching and research, however, this major evaluation of undergraduate education openly acknowledged for the first time linkages between different disciplines, how content was taught, the imperative to conduct research, and the many demands upon faculty responsible for both undergraduates and graduates.

Teaching, Advising, and Research

The competing demands of teaching and research had initially surfaced in an entirely different investigation made a few years earlier by visiting scholars from other universities. Their final report recommended:

> We would like to see good teaching rewarded as a prime value in the life of the university. We do not wish to imply that good teaching should be rewarded to the neglect of scholarly and scientific research. We are, however, perturbed by a fairly general impression, and particularly among younger faculty members, that advancement is achieved almost exclusively through research and publication.[54]

When the Study's executive committee surveyed faculty views in 1955 on the relative weight given to research and teaching, they found that it was not only the importance of the teaching imperative in a research-driven institution that was at stake, it was also the quality of teaching. As before, lecturing-cum-discussion groups, seminars, bench work in laboratories, and independent study within certain departments filled out the teaching repertoire of most professors. While lecturing remained the dominant mode of teaching, with graduate students handling discussion sections—"History of Western Civilization" easily serves as an example—professors in the sciences and humanities varied in their teaching practices but more importantly in the attention they gave to lecturing, leading seminars, and conducting laboratory instruction.

Determining the quality of teaching is difficult for researchers, much less professors, administrators, and students. I need to interrupt the flow of the narrative for a brief mention about assessing "good" teaching. Evidence about the quality of teaching at Stanford or, for that matter, at most universities is scanty, anecdotal, and contested. University presidents and faculty have periodically (and fervently) sought ways of determining teacher effectiveness over the last century. I will report what faculty, presidents, commissions, and students have concluded about the quality of teaching at Stanford, including anecdotes, but I will avoid making summary judgments about whether teaching was "good," "poor," or "effective" for three reasons.

First, to determine what is "effective" teaching within a university (or elsewhere), there needs to be at least explicit consensus over the goals of teaching within a university to determine whether the pedagogy is consistent with what is desired. Such a consensus over aims is rare within higher education save for the few colleges that have clearly specified what they expect from teachers and students. It was absent from Stanford and most universities in these years.

Second, there are competing views of what constitutes "good" or "effective" teaching that are anchored in centuries-old differences about the purposes of teaching (usually bundled into words like *traditional* and *progressive* or *subject-centered* and *student-centered*). One example should suffice. A few decades ago, two professors won the award for outstanding teacher at the University of Chicago. Joseph Schwab in the biological sciences cross-examined students until they retreated into chagrin and silence; Norman Maclean in English conducted his classes with such a gentle, caring version of the Socratic exchange that students returned his kind probing with boundless affection.[55]

There is no clear preponderance of evidence to demonstrate that one form of teaching (lectures, seminars, or labs) is superior to another. Researchers have said repeatedly: The effectiveness of the method of teaching depends upon what the overall goals are. This lack of explicit consensus over goals for teaching and strong preferences for different ways of teaching have continually frustrated those who have sought reforms in university pedagogy, including Stanford administrators and faculty. Some researchers have reasoned that characteristics of teaching that students rate highly, such as clarity of presentation, organization of subject matter, knowledge of the field, receptivity to questions, and so on, can be used to define effectiveness. Instruments to evaluate teaching have been constructed around the subject-centered view of teaching. Few instruments, however, have been constructed that are anchored in a student-centered view of effective teaching.

Finally, there is no agreement on the means to determine "good" teaching even were consensus on goals to be reached. Student ratings, peer evaluation, administrator judgment, and self-reports are the common ways to assess teaching performance. There are strengths and weaknesses to each and no agreement among researchers as to which one or ones are best.[56]

For these reasons, I have concentrated on reporting what contemporaries have said about the quality of teaching and on describing how professors have taught over time. Return now to the evidence offered in the mid-1950s.

During the Stanford study, many professors wrote to the executive committee about what this letter writer explicitly labeled "poor teaching":

> An undue amount of poor and incompetent teaching is done by... members of the faculty who are recognized, and perhaps distinguished, in other areas of professional interest.... Some, perhaps a majority, of these able men are not really college teachers at all, however, competent they may be in conducting research and in guiding graduate students.[57]

Anecdotal evidence was often garnered from student accounts of their professors, since few, if any, faculty had direct knowledge of how their colleagues taught. Stories lacked the heft, however, to persuade most faculty that a problem in the quality of teaching existed. Other data were needed. Hence, the executive committee displayed its concern for teaching by citing a study that pointed out which of the nation's top 50 colleges had undergraduates who had gained distinction in scholarship and science (Swarthmore, Princeton, Reed, etc.). Stanford was absent from the list. This was construed as indirect evidence of Stanford's professorial neglect of undergraduate teaching.[58]

The executive committee also stressed—the first such group at Stanford to do so—the importance of evaluating professors. They suggested that the absence of any criteria to judge teaching and no mechanisms for its appraisal might well explain why scholarship had more salience in appointments and promotion than teaching. The executive committee, however, pleaded in its final report that with an already full agenda of recommendations the task of developing such criteria be taken up by a new committee to be appointed by the president. That recommendation was ignored by both administration and faculty for a decade.[59]

What makes this surrender of the executive committee and subsequent avoidance of both faculty and administration striking is the unusual concern for the quality of teaching in this mid-1950s study. The amount of space set aside to deal with teaching quality (two entire chapters of seven in the book or 37 pages of text out of 118) made it unique compared to previous university reports.

What may account, in part, for the attention given to teaching were the jarring comments of visiting scholars, cited earlier, and the availability of alumni and senior students' questionnaire results between 1950 and 1953. Both men (60%) and women (71%) wanted smaller classes. Between 55 and 62% of the replies asked for fewer lecture courses and more discussion groups. As for contact with faculty, 89% of the women and 80% of the men wanted more "personal direction in studies and course selecting" than they had thus far. "Hence," the executive committee wrote, "the conclusion is inescapable that . . . seniors and the alumni regard class size, the need for more discussion groups, and the need for closer contact with the faculty, both in the class and in advising, as the most pressing items in need of attention." Because the faculty had the discretion and authority to reduce lecturing, the committee made no recommendations on these points.[60]

Then there was the durable issue of faculty advising, identified as far back as the 1890s as a problem and now viewed in numerous surveys of seniors and alumni as being held in "low esteem." Faculty inattention to advising still persisted, but too many other pressing issues pushed it off the executive committee's agenda; it was referred to the newly created Committee on General Studies and, subsequently, ignored.[61]

As a result of this major, 2-year study of undergraduate education at Stanford, modest changes were made in how the official curriculum was organized by extending general education to the entire 4 undergraduate years. Still it was both the collective faculty and separate departments that determined which issues and suggestions made by the executive committee were addressed in this decade. When a dean asked the chair of the biology department in 1961, for example, whether more faculty could teach the introductory course, the chair rejected the request. Increasing the faculty's undergraduate teaching load would reduce time for biologists to do their research. "The awkward but inescapable fact," the chair concluded, was that "at Stanford, as well as in all American universities, we are attempting to accomplish two quite different and almost incompatible things"—undergraduate teaching and research.[62]

Thus, while President Sterling and Provost Terman nudged the university toward a national reputation, the freedom of departments and faculty to set their agendas for majors, what courses to teach, and what methods to use still remained, as it did under Jordan and Wilbur, securely within the grasp of the faculty. In this way, the earlier compromises made in 1920 to reconcile the conflicting values embedded in the hybrid university-college, that of unfettered inquiry for the faculty and concern for the moral character of undergraduates, were strengthened and extended to the mid-1960s as Stanford administrators reached for national recognition.

And the university's prestige did grow. Stanford's rank among the nation's graduate programs had moved from 13th in 1959 to 5th in 1966. If that didn't convince skeptics of Stanford's stature as a research institution, perhaps *Time* magazine, with its signature zinger judgments, would:

> Along with dollars came scholars: Stanford is raiding blue- chip faculties all over the East. . . . For academic larceny, Stanford is fast matching the University of California at Berkeley—the only other Western U.S. campus that cares or dares to compare itself with Harvard.[63]

National distinction or not, it is fair to ask: What happened in subsequent years to those student and alumni concerns over excessive lecturing, expanding teaching repertoires of professors, and increasing faculty attention to student advising? To answer the question, I turn to the *Study of Education at Stanford* that President Sterling initiated in 1968, more than a decade after the executive committee issued its final report.

ELECTIVITY REDUX, 1968–1980

For some former students and faculty, the 1960s and early 1970s were exhilarating; for others, this was a time of trouble. There seems to be little middle ground on judging the tumult that jolted Stanford and other universities across the nation. Beginning in the early 1960s, the civil rights movement touched Stanford when contingents of students and faculty went to the South in 1964 to register voters and teach black children. Student and faculty pressures to admit minority students grew from this involvement, and hundreds of minority students enrolled at Stanford, irreversibly changing its complexion. By 1966, the growing resistance to U.S. involvement in Vietnam triggered protests, again from activist students and faculty, leading to major disruptions of classes and violence on the campus. In 1968 alone, 60 black students disrupted a colloquium on the assassination of Martin Luther King Jr. and demanded increased admissions of minority students; 250 students staged a sit-in at a university building to protest the suspension of 7 students for demonstrating against CIA job recruiters on campus; and arsonists destroyed President Sterling's office.[64]

After Kenneth Pitzer (former Berkeley professor and head of Rice University) was appointed Stanford's president in 1969, demonstrations against both the war and the university's involvement in U.S. Defense Department research escalated. In 1970, President Richard Nixon's announcement of the invasion of Cambodia triggered class cancellations, building take-overs, police intervention, and arson. Shortly thereafter, Kenneth Pitzer announced his resignation and Provost Richard Lyman was appointed as the seventh president of Stanford. In 1971, at a noontime rally to protest the U.S. invasion of Laos, Professor H. Bruce Franklin allegedly urged a crowd to close down the university by taking over the Computation Center. Within a few hours, 80 men from the sheriff's office arrived and arrested the 150 demonstrators. President Lyman suspended Professor Franklin. A formal hearing a year later determined that Franklin had incited the crowd, and the president fired the tenured professor. Lyman, quoting a phrase from a book's chapter title about these years, called these turbulent times "Years of Hope, Days of Rage."[65]

While the "Days of Rage" may be self-evident in the events, "Years of Hope" can be summoned up by the spurt of remarkable growth in the university between the 1940s and early 1970s (see Table 1.1). Not only was there an increase in students and faculty, but the dollars to fund new programs and build world-class facilities—the brand-new medical school to cite one example—poured into university coffers. When Sterling arrived in 1949, the endowment was $35 million; when he retired in 1968, it was $268 million. It is within this sheer expansion of the student body (especially at the graduate level), faculty, and university funds amid growing national and local turbulence in the 1960s that led President Sterling and many faculty to believe that the character of the university had changed sufficiently to examine education again.[66]

By early 1967, Sterling had appointed a steering committee of six faculty and three students, with Herbert Packer, professor of law, as chair of the Study of Education at Stanford. "We were free to discuss a curriculum we thought was best," a former member of that committee recalled a quarter-century later. He added, "there was . . . certitude among faculty about what was best for students." Certitude there may have been, but a durable consensus over which values within the university-college should be stressed was missing.[67]

TABLE 1.1 — *Enrollments and Faculty, 1940–1970*

Year	Undergraduates	Graduates	Faculty
1940	3,218	1,146	309
1950	4,794	2,841	372
1960	5,603	3,636	619
1970	6,303	5,159	1,029

The steering committee produced 10 volumes of over 900 pages and hundreds of recommendations for the Stanford community to digest. They urged overhauling the earlier compromise between competing values in breadth and depth of distribution requirements and elective courses that had marked the undergraduate curriculum between 1920 and 1968. Their recommended compromise resembled strongly in spirit David Starr Jordan's views of curriculum and the relationship between the teaching and research imperatives.[68]

Reorganizing the Official Curriculum, 1968–1980

The steering committee's analysis of the existing General Studies Program was scathing. They concluded that the requirements were "rigid, . . . superficial, . . . and excessive."[69] They then said:

> It is time for us to face the fact that this compromise leaves the teacher and student with the worst elements of two attractive but conflicting ideals: From the ideal of general education it leaves prescription in form but not prescription in substance; from the ideal of freedom to teach and to learn it leaves incoherence of purpose. The underlying problem is both intellectual and institutional. There are no easy solutions, but we are persuaded that the current General Studies Program will no longer suffice.[70]

The steering committee found that the 1920 reconciliation of the tensions within the university-college to be "totally impracticable as a dominant curricular pattern in the modern university." It recommended that no specific courses (e.g., "Western Civilization") be required but that undergraduates must take introductory courses geared to writing and history from the many offered by different departments. Moreover, to increase intellectual contact between senior faculty and 1st-year students while still avoiding large lecture classes, a freshman seminar program was strongly recommended. Beyond that, students would still have to meet distribution requirements in humanities, social sciences, natural

TABLE 1.2 — *Survey of Seniors' Experiences with Modes of Instruction, 1968*

| | Percentage of seniors | | | |
	Engineering	Science	Social Science	Humanities
Independent work	11*	24	18	18
Seminars	17	9	18	33
Medium-sized lectures/ discussion	80	67	75	68
Large lectures	28	63	64	50

*This figure means that 11% of all respondents in Engineering had "independent work" in their classes.

sciences, and technology, but they would have far more choice than before.[71]

Loosening the structural components of the official curriculum considerably, compared to what it had been, the faculty accepted these recommendations and further agreed to let students concentrate (i.e., major) at any point in their career at Stanford. In accepting these recommendations, the faculty reasserted the elective principle with which Harvard's Charles Eliot and Cornell's Andrew White in the 1870s and Stanford's own David Starr Jordan in the 1890s would have blessed: "Let the objective of curricular planning be to encourage the faculty member to teach what he likes to teach and the student to learn what seems vital to him."[72]

Teaching, Advising, and Research, 1968–1980

The professorial teaching load both across the nation and at Stanford had shrunk from an average of 8–12 hours a week at the turn of the century to an average of 4–6 hours a week by the early 1980s (depending upon the department and professional school). Yet, overall teaching practices largely remained the same. In a 1968 survey, Stanford seniors reported the kinds of teaching they experienced (see Table 1.2).[73] Commonly in selective universities, large-group lectures and discussion sections early in an undergraduate's career gave way to seminars, colloquia, research projects with faculty, and independent laboratory work. As the Stanford seniors reported, however, the dominant pattern of large-group lectures and discussions persisted with clear variation among departments in the natural sciences, social sciences, humanities, and engineering.

The range in teaching practices across departments in these years can also be caught in an unusual collection of faculty-written essays in one volume of *The Study of Education at Stanford* and in Hugh Skillings's seminar on teaching in the School of Engineering. There were also some technological innovations—such as computer-assisted instruction, desktop personal computers, and televised lectures—introduced in the 1970s.[74]

In the volume on teaching, the chair of the study, Herbert Packer, pointed out how the essays "emphasize the integral relationship of a man's teaching to his research." He returned repeatedly to the theme that marked the entire study by quoting Gerald Meier (Graduate School of Business): "Although the best teacher is a catalyst for the student's discovery, he teaches in such a way that the student can learn to do without him." Packer stressed that what these professors have written supports the study's central position that "teachers have the freedom to teach what they want to teach and to work on the problems that interest them." For three-quarters of a century, this belief in research and teaching strengthening one another had become secular doctrine, albeit one without compelling evidence to support it. Such words would have gladdened the hearts of American academics returning from German universities a century earlier who had pursued *lehrfreiheit* and *lernfreiheit* (freedom of teaching and learning).[75]

Fully aware of the constraints that faced professors who tried to meet multiple obligations of teaching, research, and service to the university and to the discipline in which they labored, the steering committee straddled the uneasy conflict by setting forth a hybrid model of the "teacher-scholar." The professor would be committed to research and "at the same time initiate students into the world of self-motivated learning."

Yet it was the dominant imperative of research and publishing, not the teaching imperative, that kept turning up in faculty responses to surveys. The Subcommittee on Teaching and Research had commissioned various faculty surveys and conducted interviews about teaching load, research, advising, and perceived obstacles to integrating teaching and research. The results: Most faculty felt that research was more highly regarded by the university than teaching, although many felt that university incentives and rewards should help correct the imbalance. When asked if the demands of research interfered with their teaching, three out of four professors said that it did not. But when the subcommittee examined the few research studies on the linkage between research productivity and teaching effectiveness, they found no clear answers.[76]

The steering committee obviously recognized the strong institutional bias toward research. As one subcommittee reported,

> There is little likelihood that Stanford's great emphasis on research will be reduced for the sake of improving teaching. No one has yet argued seriously that this approach to the improvement of teaching at Stanford should be taken. Rather, the problem should be viewed as one of finding ways to improve teaching without any reduction in the amount and quality of the effort that Stanford's faculty devotes to research.

"We do see a need," the steering committee concluded, "for a reorientation of the system of expectations and rewards so that imbalance is discouraged."[77]

The steering committee's response to the abiding tension between the imperatives of teaching undergraduates to be upstanding men and women and creating new knowledge was a 2-fold recommendation of student assessments of faculty teaching—a recommendation made 12 years earlier—and helping faculty to improve their teaching and advising.[78]

Advising, that informal face-to-face teaching outside of the lecture hall, laboratory, and seminar room, was also on the steering committee's agenda. The Committee on Advising and Counseling interviewed students and faculty about this form of teaching and their report was unsparing:

> A single word would fairly accurately sum up the situation of advising . . . at Stanford and the principal problems to which we addressed ourselves. That word is "indifferent." The faculty are, on the whole, indifferent to advising; the advising they give is generally indifferent in quality; students are indifferent to it. . . . As a result of this indifference, students progress haphazardly in many ways.[79]

The committee urged the entire faculty to adopt the policy that "advising is a central function of the faculty, comparable in educational significance to teaching and research, and considered along with them in decisions regarding appointment and promotion." The Faculty Senate failed to adopt this recommendation.[80]

The steering committee did seek improvement in teaching. The importance and quality of teaching has been made explicitly central to the major studies of Stanford's undergraduate education in 1954–1956 and 1968. Concern for teaching also had been present in David Starr Jordan's decision to fire one professor of the four he terminated during the 2 decades that he served the university.[81]

The steering committee recommended that all faculty must teach; that appointments and promotions "require a commitment to teaching and a reasonable degree of proficiency in it"; that the university provide funds for innovative classroom projects and prizes for teaching excellence; that the university establish a center to help faculty interested in improving their teaching; and that, finally, there be student- and university-developed instruments for appraising the quality of instruction.[82]

Many of the 1968 study's recommendations concerning teaching were implemented. In 1971, the Walter J. Gores Award was established to recognize teaching excellence for a senior professor, a junior faculty member, and a teaching assistant. In 1973, the Faculty Senate approved the idea that for tenure and promotion decisions "some formal procedure of teacher evaluation" be used. After much experimentation with different evaluation instruments, the senate adopted in 1979 the faculty-designed "University Student Evaluation Rating Form" that had to be used by schools where no rating form existed. The Danforth Foundation Grant established a campus Center for Teaching and Learning (CTL) in 1975 that was eventually underwritten by the university. Since then, CTL has offered interested faculty, graduate teaching assistants, and undergraduates aid in preparing courses, lecturing, teaching with small groups, self-evaluation through videotaping, and other services.[83]

The tension over the balance between teaching and research persisted after the 1968 report. In 1974, the Committee on the Professoriate, in a report to the Faculty Senate, again reaffirmed the traditional hierarchical relationship of research over teaching. For appointments to the tenure-line, faculty must consider "excellence in scholarship (research) and an active commitment to the university's goal of combining scholarship with teaching."[84]

Having reinstated the Stanford tradition in making appointments, the Committee on the Professoriate then tried to reconcile the durable conflict between research and teaching imperatives. In language echoing the 1968 study (and one articulated in the 1954–1956 study), the committee concluded,

> *Students come, or should come, to a major university more to learn than to be taught.* And the unique element in the offering of a university (compared to a college) derives from the student's *association* with independently creative scholars: From them, above all, students can *learn* what the mind can do and how creative work is done. We must state this position strongly at the outset because it is open to serious misunderstanding. We do not advocate and cannot justify neglect of the university's [teaching] function, nor do we say that the [teaching] function should be secondary to the research function. However, the unique, and

> therefore indispensable, element in a university education as such is a
> faculty of first-rank scholar-researchers who teach as much by their atti-
> tudes and approaches to human knowledge as by evident pedagogic
> skills. They provide the intellectual environment in which the students
> *can learn.* [Italicized words were emphasized in original text.]

They concluded that for appointments "the normal expectation ought
to be that scholarship is indispensable and teaching is important to
advancement." The ideal of the scholar-teacher that motivated earlier
generations of presidents and faculties was again recertified.[85]

In 1979, a group of anthropologists interviewed and shadowed 46
professors across different departments and found that almost half of
the professors "most admired" a colleague who had demonstrated competence as a scholar. Teaching ability was "most admired" by only 9%.
No surprise, then, that among the criteria 82% of these Stanford professors ranked highest in hiring new faculty was ability as a researcher. Nor
was there any surprise that 73% of the Stanford professors saw scholarly achievement weighing most strongly in university tenure and promotion decisions; only 28% said that a professor's teaching effectiveness
mattered greatly in making these decisions. So a robust consensus over
the importance of research emerged from this study of academic culture
and it was largely consistent with the university's history of highly prizing research.[86]

This durable tension between teaching and research lasted throughout the 1970s in the turbulent aftermath of changes that called for more
student choice in the curriculum. That tension, of course, mirrored the
much longer three-quarter century effort to negotiate a balance between
breadth and depth in the curriculum.

Concerns over the balance between requiring students to take prescribed courses and letting them choose among electives reemerged in
the early 1970s. In those years, professors who championed the restora-
tion of general education courses slowly won supporters among colleagues who had begun to lose confidence in virtual electivity. The Faculty Senate (a legislative institution invented in 1968 to represent the
entire faculty on the Academic Council) resolved in 1976 that a required
course in "Western Culture" be redesigned for 1st-year students. The
redesigned, yearlong "Western Culture" course, first offered in 1980,
became mandatory. By the early 1990s, students had to take one course
in each of eight specific areas. They also had to meet the new gender
studies requirement and demonstrate proficiency in a foreign language.
Academic bookkeeping, the bane of an earlier generation of reformers,
had returned.[87]

THE FITFUL RETURN OF GENERAL EDUCATION, 1980–1995

With the reintroduction of the required yearlong "Western Culture" course, which had been abandoned in 1968, the tension between depth and breadth of knowledge with which each generation of Stanford faculty had contended reappeared, but with a twist this time. Major demographic changes in Stanford's student body produced diverse opinions that reopened debate in 1986 over the reinvented "Western Culture" course. That debate led to both local and national furor over curricular changes and redirected attention to the relationship between teaching and research, and to the unhappy condition of advising.

Reorganizing the Official Curriculum

Stanford's student body had changed dramatically since the 1950s when it was largely white, male, and prosperous. Not only had the university grown in size (from 7,600 students in 1950 to over 13,000 in 1990), but also its complexion and gender had shifted. In 1970, of the entering class of undergraduates, just under 17% were minority (black, Hispanic, Native American, Asian American); a quarter-century later, the entering class was 41% minority. While only one out of three 1st-year students were female in 1965, 3 decades later, half were women.[88]

A new generation of white and minority, male and female students in the 1980s brought to the campus different perspectives, shaped by their experiences. By the mid-1980s, concerned students and faculty began questioning the yearlong "Western Culture" course as being too narrowly conceived for a world that is composed of many cultures and whose history was shaped by not only the Western tradition.[89]

By 1986, the three-quarter "Western Culture" course, with weekly lectures and discussion sections, had eight tracks from which students could choose: Great Works; Humanities; History; Literature and the Arts; Conflict and Change; Philosophy; Values, Technology, Science, and Society; and Structured Liberal Education. For all tracks, a "core list" of readings became the official curriculum; the list included Genesis in the Bible, Plato's *Republic,* St. Augustine's *Confessions,* Doctor Johnson's *Rasselas,* Voltaire's *Candide,* and Freud's and Darwin's writings. While each track could, and did, assign other texts, it was the core list that became labeled as the "canon."[90]

Beginning in 1986, student groups and faculty members began pressing the Faculty Senate to make changes in the "Western Culture" course. The senate asked Provost James Rosse to form a faculty and student committee to review the course and recommend changes. After strong reactions to an earlier draft, the task force proposed to rename the course "Cultures, Ideas, and Values" (CIV), require study of non-European cultures in all tracks, and permit instructors to make flexible use of the core list (even ignoring the readings if they chose). Opponents of this proposal swiftly submitted an alternative that retained the existing "Western Culture" course but amended the core list to include texts by women and persons of color and expanded the curriculum to include issues of race, gender, class, and ethnicity.[91]

Protests escalated as charges were exchanged over what it meant to alter the "Western Culture" course and its core list. A rally in 1987 to support the demands for more minority students and faculty at which the Reverend Jesse Jackson spoke soon turned into a 500-strong student and faculty demonstration against the "Western Culture" course. In January 1988, both proposals came before the Faculty Senate. For 3 months, the faculty debated the issue as student supporters of the CIV proposal demonstrated across campus. Journalists picked up the struggle over curriculum and it became a made-for-media event in which the Stanford president even debated the U.S. Secretary of Education. Televised interviews, articles in *Time* and *Newsweek,* and editorials in the *Los Angeles Times* made Stanford's curricular debates national gossip. Faculty members worked out a compromise between the two proposals, and, on March 31, 1988, the senate approved a new Area One Requirement called "Cultures, Ideas, and Values" (CIV).[92]

Since 1988, the only changes to the distribution requirements have been modest ones, in effect, strengthening Stanford's return to a 1950s version of general education adapted to a demographically different university in the 1990s. President Gerhard Casper, soon after he assumed the presidency from Donald Kennedy in 1992 and facing budget cuts due to the withdrawal of federal funds, called for another reexamination of undergraduate education. Citing the historic struggle between breadth and depth in the curriculum, between electivity and prescription, Casper quoted David Starr Jordan and cited earlier examinations of the undergraduate curriculum to justify his call for yet another study.[93]

In 1993, Casper appointed 14 professors, two students, two alumni, and one top administrator to the Commission on Undergraduate Education (CUE). He asked History Professor James Sheehan to serve as chair. "Reform in a university," Sheehan said, "is a matter of lots of small victories. There is no single great triumph that is going to alter our lives." What concerned the commission most was what also concerned previous faculty task forces and commissions: "Our worst fear is not that the commission's recommendations will be rejected, but that they will be ignored." The CUE's report was issued in 1994.[94]

The commission's recommendations fell into two categories. First, there were those that aimed to increase "the rigor, coherence, and clarity of the undergraduate program." Suggestions included creating a new requirement for teaching science, mathematics, and technology to nonscientists; strengthening the foreign language requirement; and further clarifying the CIV requirement. In line with previous attempts to return the academic calendar from quarters to semesters (1932, 1954, 1968), the commission reaffirmed its commitment to the quarter system. Second, CUE proposed "processes" that would lead to "better use of technology in teaching and learning" and improving evaluation of teaching and advising by more "recognition of these activities in faculty appointments, promotions, and compensation." By 1997, President Casper had concluded that the recommendations had "sparked significant reform . . . of how undergraduates are taught and learn at Stanford."[95]

Teaching, Advising, and Research, 1980–1995

The teaching load for the average Stanford professor remained about the same as it had been in the mid-1970s: that is, 4–6 hours a week of teaching, with much departmental variation in attending to teaching and monitoring its quality. Thus, a few departments had strong teaching cultures while most had weak ones.[96]

In settings characterized as strong teaching cultures, such as has existed for many years in mechanical engineering at Stanford, one would expect faculty-supervised orientation for teaching assistants, departmental practices of peer visiting of lectures and seminars (as the Law School and English departments have established), and scheduled discussions of pedagogy in formal meetings. Further indicators of a strong teaching culture would be a chair's making sure that introductory courses were taught by senior faculty rather than by part-time faculty or instructors; such a chair would be reluctant to reduce teaching loads or permit professors with amply funded research projects to "buy off" courses. A chair in such a department would review student evaluations to see if patterns of low ratings emerge from particular courses and, if they did, discuss these ratings with the professor. Such a department would also have guidelines for faculty appointments and promotions stipulating that "outstanding" teaching or research (with "acceptable" in the other area) can secure an appointment, tenure, and promotion (as does the Graduate School of Business).[97]

Departments with weak teaching cultures would have such strong norms for research that professorial autonomy is unrestricted when it comes to buying out of teaching commitments. There would be few explicit collective discussions of teaching. Systematic preparation of teaching assistants for their primary duties would be left to chance or to a junior staff member. One professor, to offer an example of a social science department at Stanford with a weak teaching culture, described his department's attitude toward teaching succinctly:

> I don't think this is a department that cares much about whether teaching is effective or not.... They have let teachers continue to teach who have gotten abusively bad ratings.... There are many cases where people just refuse to do teaching that needs to be done.[98]

This particular department has no requirement for undergraduates to have an adviser. In 1995, there were 427 majors and 80% had no faculty adviser, another clue to the malign neglect of both teaching and advising.[99]

That departments vary in strength of their norms about teaching would surprise few at Stanford and similarly situated institutions. After all, departments are disciplinary-based homes for specialization. And disciplines vary in the amount of collaboration built into each one's mode of inquiry. It is the discipline, then, housed within the department and married to the university norm of professorial autonomy that drives the acquisition of knowledge.

For a university department to create a strong teaching culture, it would take uncommon joint administrative leadership, at the minimum, of the chair, a dean, and a central administrator. Such leadership would have to cultivate and sustain shared beliefs among faculty about the importance of teaching and advising and incorporate those beliefs into departmental recruitment and socialization of new faculty. In 1995, some evidence of that leadership was noted in a memo to all department chairs urging them to apply for grants that would elevate the practice of teaching through a variety of ways. "Since at least the spring of 1991 Stanford has been professing more vocally, and trying to implement more systematically, the idea that teaching is as important in the faculty's responsibility as is research. No one expects teaching to eclipse research at an institution like ours. Nevertheless, teaching and research can become more mutually reinforcing." Although such cooperation has occurred at Stanford and stands out precisely because it has been the exception, swimming upstream against a strong current is seldom sought by tenure-seeking or tenure-secure faculty.[100]

If Stanford was well within the national mainstream on departmental cultures dominated by the research imperative, so was its faculty's use of familiar teaching practices, including the recently emerging professorial and administrator interest in adapting new technologies for instruction. Nationally, random samples of professors were questioned on what methods they used in their classrooms. The responses yielded familiar results: Lecturing to large groups of undergraduates dominated practice across disciplines. Wagner Thielens Jr.'s study found that in physical sciences, mathematics, life sciences, social sciences, and humanities 80% of the randomly selected 829 professors (representing a 79% return of questionnaires) lectured for the entire period, while an additional 9% said that they lectured from 15 to 25 minutes. The remainder of the sample said that they used other teaching approaches.[101]

At Stanford, the evidence documenting teaching practices is fragmented but nonetheless suggests that lecturing to large undergraduate classes has remained solidly entrenched, if not dominant, in the 1990s. In a 1995 survey of 113 Stanford professors from across the university (representing a 20% return), Nira Hativa found that 78% lectured and answered students' questions "frequently" or "almost always," and 66% of the professors said that they lectured and then had separate discussion sections that they or teaching assistants led. She found some variation in lecturing and time allotted for student questions in engineering, math, natural sciences, and social science courses. Humanities departments combined lectures with discussions. When asked what tools they frequently used to enhance their teaching, 54% checked the chalkboard, 32% the overhead projector, and 27% reported that they used short films, videotape clips, computer presentations, and physical models. These figures suggest that the vast majority of professors lecture, with over half relying on the chalkboard and one-quarter to a third using other tools.[102]

An earlier faculty survey done in 1994 under the auspices of CUE found even less variation in classroom practices. The survey went out to 750 professors who taught undergraduates. There was a 35% return of the questionnaires. Six of every ten professors said that they never used a computer in their classroom; 19% said that they used computers occasionally, while 8% said they used them often (the remaining responses were unusable). Similar levels of limited use were reported for videotapes and laserdiscs.[103]

Other evidence, however, suggests a growing use of small-group discussions in colloquia, seminars, and group-work. Periodic surveys of graduating seniors in the 1980s and 1990s asked if students had had "sustained small-group contact with Stanford faculty." On five surveys between 1986 and 1994, over 60% answered "yes." When asked if they had opportunities to work directly with faculty on projects—implying that students knew professors well enough from classroom contact—over one-third of the seniors consistently marked "very good" to "excellent" (one-third also judged those opportunities as "fair" to "poor"). Also, in 1988, a question was asked about how much classroom contact seniors had with faculty. Almost 30% said "a lot," while 65% said "some," and the remainder said "none." In subsequent chapters of this book, when particular departments and schools are examined, a finer-grained analysis of the teaching methods will be made to determine if, indeed, changes had occurred in teaching practices.[104]

Even with this contrary piece of evidence, what does appear in the 1980s through the 1990s, albeit fragmentary, is the familiar phenomenon of lecturing to assembled undergraduates as the prevalent pedagogy, even in the face of curricular changes and increased access to classroom technologies. One of the few explicit admissions of this practice from a top Stanford official came with the announcement in 1996 of a $25 million initiative from President Casper to ensure that 1st- and 2nd-year undergraduates have the opportunity to take seminars with senior faculty. "We know," Casper said, "that courses taken predominantly by freshmen and sophomores are larger and less frequently taught by regular faculty members than are courses aimed at upper-level students."[105]

When students and faculty reported on advising, that highly personal form of teaching, the same dismay with the faculty's poor performance (now a century old) reappeared. In its 1994 report, as earlier reports had done, CUE identified advising as the source of the most dissatisfaction among students. The Stanford model of advising combined the use of professionals in the Undergraduate Advising Center (a recommendation from an earlier study), faculty, and staff. But faculty participation was low: Of the over 1,300 professors on the Academic Council, less than 10% "take the time to help students begin their academic careers."[106]

The "indifference of faculty" to advising led CUE to investigate other models in use at Yale University, where advising is an obligation for each professor, and the University of Chicago, where the task is given completely to professionals and faculty play no role as formal advisers. CUE members found a problem with each of the models and therefore concluded that no "single dramatic remedy for the ills in our advising system" is available. Recognizing the linkage between size of class and growth of personal relationships with faculty, CUE recommended the institutionalization of seminar experiments that had begun in the early 1990s. Finally, the commission pledged to seek integration of the faculty role of adviser into the formal university salary and reward system.[107]

This common (and, by now, traditional) pattern of teaching and advising practices across campus, including much variation by department, echoed earlier generations of Stanford faculty behavior. What about the linkage between teaching and research?

Linkage Between Teaching and Research

In earlier decades, the tensions between the two were obvious, but even Presidents Jordan, Wilbur, and Sterling urged that the two complemented one another. Presidents Kennedy and Casper in the 1980s and 1990s also believed in the compatibility of research and teaching. The ideal of synergy between the two remained alive and well.[108]

But when other professors and critics spoke and wrote of teaching and research, they pointed to the inherent conflict that arose from the constraints upon professors' time and energy in performing competing tasks and the contradictory messages in university presidents' speeches and tenure decisions. Historians Alan Brinkley at Harvard and Stephen Ferrulo at Stanford in 1985, for example, received university-wide teaching and service awards but were denied tenure. President Donald Kennedy recalled that when he was hired by the biology department in 1960 "it was becoming clear that my research record would be important in my promotion—perhaps more important than how I did with my large captive audience in Memorial Auditorium." Such stories became part of the folk beliefs of the professoriate: Producing high-quality scholarship, not high-quality teaching, is the way to win the game.[109]

There is more than folk beliefs and anecdotal evidence about the conflicting tasks, however. From faculty studies done nationally and at Stanford, the tension between research and teaching was evident in the 1980s and 1990s. In a 1984 national faculty survey, about two-thirds of university professors reported that they were either very heavily oriented toward research or did both research and teaching but tilted toward research. In another survey of 35,000 faculty at almost 400 institutions conducted in 1989–1990, 80% of university professors said that conducting research was the highest priority, even exceeding their response to another question, that the highest priority was students' intellectual development (70%). Where the internal conflict emerges is in the 98% of the respondents who said being an exemplary teacher was an essential goal yet only 10% of the professors believed their institutions rewarded such teaching.[110]

At Stanford, the figures for the decade are comparable. A mid-1980s survey (with over half of the professors responding) found that 77% of the faculty gave the highest rating to their research as opposed to teaching role (49%). Still professors were enthusiastic about teaching and felt that it was important (73% rated it as very high or high). Almost half of the faculty (46%) also believed that the university placed a low value on rewarding teaching.[111]

What, then, would motivate professors to invest time and energy into their teaching? In the 1995 survey of 113 faculty, over 95% of the professors said intangible rewards spurred them to teach well: satisfaction from teaching and students' personal comments about their performance. Ranking lower were the tangible awards: 80% said if evaluation ratings of their performance were seriously considered in tenure and promotion decisions they would be motivated to teach better; 57% said the same for published recognition through excellent teaching awards; 43% said cash awards. Written comments on these surveys further revealed faculty angst over combining high-quality teaching and research.

> They say teaching is important, but if you want tenure, you'd better publish, and publish a lot.

> My main frustration is the sense that teaching has to suffer or be compromised in order for research to happen. There doesn't seem to be enough hours in a day.[112]

One effort to cope with the persistent tension locked into this conflict-ridden linkage between teaching and research was the ambitious report of the Faculty Senate's Committee on the Evaluation and Improvement of Teaching (1995). This committee continued Stanford's traditional loyalty to the belief in compatibility between the prized values of research and teaching but reframed the issue by redefining research to include the act of teaching.[113]

The committee asserted that the teaching function is "central to a scholar's role in a research university." Moreover, "to teach is to engage in an act of scholarship" because the act of teaching creates and transforms knowledge as it is communicated to students. Since teaching is central to scholarship, excellence in teaching "deserves to be supported and evaluated in ways that are comparable to other scholarly activities." To do so, the university "must require that substantial evidence of teaching quality and scholarship be integral parts of any argument for appointment, promotion, and tenure in the university." The committee's report recommended that student evaluation of teaching and peer review be used to provide systematic evidence of teaching performance for appointments and promotions.[114]

This report represents another halting step in a 40-year effort to compel professorial attention to the quality of teaching. That effort began with the 1954 Stanford Study of Undergraduate Education, in which student evaluation of teaching was recommended for the first time but was ignored by faculty and administration for 15 years.[115]

In 1968, another campus-wide study addressed the importance of teaching and its quality and called for student ratings of faculty teaching and university support for helping professors improve their instruction. Student evaluations of faculty would create a "countervailing force" to the research imperative. "Such a force will raise teaching, in the eyes of the faculty, to the level of research as an avenue to the rewards that the university has to offer." Such a recommendation frames university teaching and research in conflict with one another; resolving the tension depends upon the metaphor of the stubborn donkey: introducing carrots (awards and help for faculty) and sticks (student ratings) to elevate the importance of teaching. In the 1970s and 1980s, instruments for students assessing their professors' teaching were approved, awards recognizing excellence in teaching multiplied, and the Center for Teaching and Learning (CTL) was established.[116]

By the late 1980s, however, faculty dissatisfaction with the official student rating form had become widespread. Such dismissal of formal student evaluation and limited use of CTL by senior faculty amid a growing national concern over faculty research crowding out undergraduate teaching fueled the efforts of President Donald Kennedy and other prominent university leaders to again address the quality of teaching and its priority on campuses.[117]

President Kennedy's initiative in 1990–1991 sought to reconcile the competing ideals by asserting that teaching is central to scholarship and that traditional definitions of research had to change to incorporate the centrality of teaching—a creative spin to the familiar argument that teaching and research reinforce one another. The 1995 report to the Faculty Senate argued that to improve teaching two forms of evaluation were necessary: student and peer. This is the "countervailing force" of the 1968 study, that is, faculty need incentives and hints of sanctions in order for them to address the quality of their teaching.[118]

That such a restatement of an historic fundamental dilemma anchored in the university-college hybrid would ensure the sought-for accommodation, given previous faculty reluctance to reconcile this dilemma, is doubtful. Presidential words and committee recommendations were symbolically important for both internal and external consumption but ultimately weak in changing significantly the age-hardened asymmetry between research and teaching.

What makes such change unlikely for the immediate future are the factors that probably account for 40 years of neglected recommendations. One need look no further than the institutionalized beliefs, structures, and cultural norms that have developed over a century and that clearly favor research over teaching, electives over prescribed courses, departmental and faculty autonomy over collaboration, and the core value of advancing knowledge over developing character and citizenship in undergraduates. For it is in consciously constructed governance mechanisms that faculty have exerted increasing influence over curriculum, teaching, and research. The faculty, working through departments and the senate, determine what the intellectual and moral property of students should be after undergraduate and graduate work. They decide how that student-accumulated knowledge should be distributed and counted. Moreover, individual professors design personal research agendas that guide their decisions of how much time they should spend advising students, what courses they will teach, and how the subject matter should be taught.[119]

William James predicted in 1906 what would happen at Stanford. In a speech celebrating the founding of the university, the distinguished psychologist looked into the future and said,

> Let her call great investigators from whatever lands they live in ... for the advantages of this place for steady mental work are so unparalleled.... [Stanford can become] less a place for teaching youths and maidens than for training scholars; devoted to truth; radiating influence; setting standards; shedding abroad the fruits of learning.[120]

CONCLUSIONS ABOUT CURRICULAR CHANGE, TEACHING, ADVISING, AND RESEARCH AT STANFORD UNIVERSITY SINCE 1891

Curriculum

While the official curriculum has grown enormously in course offerings and changed dramatically in the content offered, the durable internal see-saw struggle over choice and prescription in balancing breadth and depth in knowledge offered to students has dominated faculty discourse over the last century. At Stanford, the tug-of-war invariably pulled toward specialization through its original embrace of the principle of electivity.

The elective principle, introduced by David Starr Jordan and carried on by his successors, was moored to the structure of the major-subject system (1891–1920). Apart from one writing course that was mandated, students could choose what they wished from the very first year, including their majors. It was the departmental faculty, under the elective principle, who determined which courses were required for a major, and it was individual professors within a department who decided which of their specialties they would teach to both graduate and undergraduate students.

Student choice of courses was modified slightly during and after World War I by the shift to the quarter system and the strong impulse toward a general education that swept across campuses. In switching from two semesters to a four-quarter academic year in 1917, more courses could be offered that would reflect professorial specialties, especially for advanced students. On four different occasions, opponents of the quarter system sought a return to semesters, and each time faculty majorities or commission reports endorsed the four-quarter academic year. The curricular mechanism of the quarter (eleven weeks of courses per quarter) quietly and indirectly reinforced student choice, faculty specialization, and research.

Faculty also introduced distribution requirements and four prescribed courses (Stanford's version of a liberal education) for the first 2 years. In the 1950s when another wave of concern over liberal education swept across higher education, Stanford faculty tacked on more courses and distribution requirements.

A revival of virtual rather than abridged electivity occurred in 1968 during the widespread social tumult that spilled over the nation's universities. This lasted at Stanford for just over a decade. Since the early 1980s, there has been a decided return to the pre-1968 balance of a few prescribed courses, multiple distribution requirements, and much student choice in negotiating undergraduate curricula. At the graduate level, apart from flexible departmental requirements, choice reigned. The structural compromises in the official curriculum constructed by Stanford faculties and administrators between the prized values of breadth and depth of knowledge over the last century—anchored as it was in the elective principle, or in Donald Kennedy's words, "entrepreneurial consumerism"—have tilted toward specialization in the undergraduate curriculum and clearly dominated graduate studies.[121]

Teaching

The dominant teaching practices of the post–Civil War colleges (lectures and recitations) and innovations introduced in the late 19th century universities (lecture-cum-discussion sections, seminars, and laboratory work) have, with some modifications, remained largely constant over the last century at Stanford. This remarkable continuity of teaching practices in the university at large in the face of major demographic, bureaucratic, political, curricular, and technological changes suggests both institutional and personal compromises that administrators and professors struck between conflicting teaching and research obligations contained within the university-college.

Not until the 1950s did these compromises that subordinated teaching to research become a matter of openly expressed concern. Since then, teaching has been intensely, if sporadically, examined by Stanford faculty and students. Collectively, the faculty's strategies to improve its teaching since the 1950s have been to advocate student ratings of teachers, recognize teaching excellence, help individual faculty voluntarily improve their teaching, and, most recently, call for a redefining of research to incorporate teaching activities.

The emergence of quality teaching as an issue has sharpened considerably the perceived conflict between the available time to advance knowledge and publish scholarship traded-off against the time necessary to prepare lectures, set up labs, advise students, and teach classes. Although presidents and faculty at Stanford historically have been loyal to the belief in research and teaching strengthening one another, the inevitable constraints of limited time and energy have pitted one against the other with the research imperative gaining preference over teaching time and again—according to faculty surveys and reports.

What has complicated the assessment of teaching quality is the deeply revered university norm of faculty autonomy. Such unhampered individual discretion—the professor as researcher and solo teacher—has created a fierce loyalty to classroom independence and an abiding reluctance to force solutions aimed at improving teaching, such as team teaching, cross-departmental collaboration in planning courses, and using instructional technologies. Faculty resistance to reducing their autonomy also emerged in the frequent difficulties to gain agreement over what constituted proper measures to evaluate teaching (e.g., student and peer ratings, administrator judgment). The norm of the professor as commander of the classroom remained a cherished value that few administrators or faculty committees sought to either seriously challenge or abridge since the turn of the century.

These unyielding dilemmas have faced Stanford professors, like their colleagues across the country, for over a century. What has been striking in this enduring clash of ideals has been the divorce of pedagogy from subject-matter specialties. Intermittently and briefly, since the mid-1950s, teaching has been part of the faculty conversation at Stanford. Yet even when university-wide discussions occurred, teaching was treated as separate from what was taught except in a few departments where a strong teaching culture had emerged and had been linked to content. The disconnect between pedagogy and content in most departments evolved clearly, as did the divorce of teaching from advising.[122]

Advising

Advising is a form of teaching, and over the last century there has been one constant: faculty inattention to advising students about their academic programs and future plans. Student complaints about faculty advising, particularly prior to declaring a major, have been legion and documented repeatedly over the last century. Faculty concern over the widespread neglect of this important task has arisen again and again, beginning in the 1890s (with requiring professors to sign students' study cards) and continuing through the 1990s (with repeated reports from faculty committees on the "problem" of advising).

The model of every professor being an adviser—the aim of the major-subject system for the first 30 years of the university's history—and the ideal of a research university also functioning as an undergraduate college mindful of students' intellectual and moral lives gave way slowly to a different model of mixing professorial advising with special staff hired to help students. Neither model has been satisfactory to either faculty or students. For a faculty composed of researchers who are torn by competing obligations to teaching and pursuing scholarship, trying to advise 1st- and 2nd-year students on possible majors and on what courses in general studies they should take (knowledge that many of these specialists lacked) has led inexorably to student disappointment and faculty frustration, if not indifference.

Research

Even though there have been heroic words about the importance of teaching and even occasional action, there has been little doubt about the centrality of inquiry to a Stanford university professor's work.

Beyond modeling the behavior of an investigator, Stanford presidents, like their peers elsewhere, instituted policies for faculty appointments that clearly sought promising scholars and offered rewards of rank and prestige for those on campus who published their scholarship and gained national distinction. The formal institutional compromises worked out to reconcile the teaching and research imperatives in the university-college were established under Jordan and have been refined, even enhanced, but they remain largely unchanged insofar as the primacy of scholarship is used to determine the worth of a professor to the university. The scholar-teacher, not the teacher-scholar, has been, and continues to be, the desired model for a Stanford professor.

The dominance of the research imperative emerged at Stanford as a consequence of an institutional compromise to reconcile conflicting ideals anchored within the university-college hybrid. For the research imperative to become dominant, however, institutional beliefs had to be translated into formal structures and cultural norms that, over time, became commonplace. These routine organizational mechanisms and norms then evolved to shape professorial duties of teaching, advising, and the pursuit of scholarship.

HOW AN INSTITUTIONAL FRAMEWORK FOR THE RESEARCH IMPERATIVE EMERGED

I turn to the taken-for-granted features of the university: the elective curriculum, faculty autonomy, the structures of the Ph.D., hierarchical academic rank, and departmental powers.

The Ideology of the Elective System

The elective principle in curricular organization was the structural linchpin to the university-college hybrid at Stanford and other universities. The principle eased the conflict inherent in having undergraduate and graduate students working in the same institution under inquiry-minded professors. Electives expanded the curriculum to include sciences, modern languages, and other subjects that had been alien to the classical curriculum of the antebellum college. Electives meant that no one body of knowledge was intrinsically more important than another. Electives, especially for those who actively promoted choice, meant that the curriculum expanded to include advanced study in a subject specialty.[123]

The principle of students choosing courses to meet their current and future needs, which unabashedly guided Charles Eliot at Harvard University (1869–1909), Andrew White at Cornell (1868–1885), and David Starr Jordan at Stanford (1891–1913), also meant that professors could choose which courses, particularly which advanced courses, to offer in their specialty. Professorial choice in the courses to offer melded easily with their freedom to teach as they wished once the door closed or lab began. Thus, electives were wedded to the prevailing university norm of faculty autonomy.[124]

Amid these freedoms, which accrued to both students and professors under the elective principle, complications arose. The matter of blending an undergraduate college with a graduate program of specialization persistently sharpened the dilemma of how much breadth versus depth of knowledge an undergraduate should have and what constituted an appropriate mix of large lectures and small-group instruction. Ideological proponents of breadth often couched their arguments in the vocabulary of a "liberal education" (later "general education") and argued for certain prescribed courses—often crossing disciplinary boundaries. Opponents who argued for depth called for specialization in a field with no special merit attached to one subject over another. Compromises to this enduring, if not intractable, dilemma and the debates that it spawned were hammered out, implemented, and remade (after more debate) throughout the century—as this abbreviated history of curricular changes at Stanford illustrates—leading to the introduction of required courses and distribution requirements.[125]

Does the elective system also create a predisposition toward particular kinds of pedagogy? Probably not for lecturing. Both the ideology of a prescribed "liberal education" and the elective system incorporated the traditional practice of lecturing in 20th century universities. Professors in most disciplines teaching introductory courses, whether prescribed or elected, often lectured. That lectures to assemblies of undergraduates in their initial years subsidized seminars and colloquia for juniors and seniors suggest that organizational and economic factors beyond the elective principle or habit also accounted for frequent lecturing.

For small-group work with students, the answer to whether an elective system favored a particular pedagogy is probably "yes." Seminars and laboratory teaching were born in the American desire to adopt pedagogies associated with scientific discoveries and the pursuit of scholarly inquiry in German universities. For both professors and advanced students, small-group work and individual research meant duplicating the doctoral student's apprenticeship to the scholar. Seminars, colloquia, directed research, and reading courses and similar small-group or individually tailored courses played to faculty's specialization in subject matter while neatly intersecting with the belief that students could become inquirers through the elective system.[126]

Although the impulse to evaluate teaching is not ideologically driven by the elective system, a practical concern for the quality of teaching accompanied a commitment to student choice. After all, many students would seek out professors believed to be strong teachers and avoid courses where the teaching was reputed to be notoriously poor.

With the growing proliferation of specialized courses consistent with professors' research interests, it would be only a matter of time before the question of wide variation in the quality of teaching would inevitably arise, as it did when enrollments expanded dramatically in the 1950s and 1960s.

For decades, the question was ignored in deference to professorial autonomy until it became reframed as a problem, that is, when research interests of professors—enhanced by the elective system—were perceived to have crowded out undergraduate teaching responsibilities. The potential conflict involved in abridging professorial discretion by mandating student review of teaching, while still seeking ways of getting faculty to voluntarily improve their classroom practices, has remained a conundrum.

If concern for the quality of teaching accompanied the elective system, so did faculty indifference to student advising. As much as small-group work and students researching at the bench or in the library under the watchful eye of the professor were enhanced by the elective system, the task of advising students on their academic program—a crucial factor in a system geared to student choice—has been largely disregarded. Faculty time devoted to research, writing, teaching, service on university committees and national disciplinary associations left little time for individual help to students.

Since the turn of the century, then, the ideology of the elective principle has been the centerpiece for much ebb and flow in curricular structures especially in the last 2 years of undergraduate work and in securing graduate degrees. The pervasive grip of the elective principle alone, however, could not account for the institutionalization of the research imperative. Other familiar structures provided a solid scaffolding for research-driven values.

The Structures of the Doctoral Degree and Academic Rank

The Ph.D., an import from Germany, was Americanized in the late 19th century but retained its distinct gatekeeping mission of certifying that freshly minted professors had discovered new knowledge through investigation. It is, to state the obvious, a research degree, not a teaching credential. "Will anyone pretend for a moment," William James asked in 1903, "that the doctor's degree is a guarantee that its possessor will be successful as a teacher?" Depending upon the discipline, the route to the Ph.D.—over half of those who begin doctoral work fail to complete the dissertation—is structured to train the candidate in the intricacies of inquiry. Teaching experience is only gained as a necessity to subsidize the time spent in libraries, laboratories, or the field. Time spent teaching is time away from the more important work of doing research.[127]

Newly degreed doctors in their first academic job generally face climbing the ladder of rank to full professor by first meeting teaching responsibilities and, second, by publishing the findings of their research. University administrators institutionalized the mechanism of academic rank (i.e., assistant professor, associate professor, and full professor) in the late 19th century to distinguish college tutors, docents, instructors, and other titles that were clearly aimed at teaching from professors dedicated to inquiry. Rank helped to "clarify relationships between teaching and research."[128]

In the mid-1950s, for example, when Stanford's Professor H. Stuart Hughes proposed to the history department that senior professors teach sections of the "Western Civilization" course, his colleague Thomas A. Bailey replied,

> We have tried this, and it doesn't work. Senior professors do this kind of thing grudgingly; their hearts are not in it. . . . The younger men have a good deal of zest. Our promotional system is such that great weight is placed on scholarly production, and as a consequence a senior professor dragooned into section work is militating against his chances for advancement.

Hence, a rough division of labor emerged as newly appointed assistant professors in the humanities and social sciences (but not in the life and natural sciences) taught introductory courses, while advanced courses were taught by senior faculty. All were expected to publish their research.[129]

Departments

The institutional setting for Ph.D.-certified scholars to pursue independently their specialties as they climbed the professorial ladder was the disciplinary-based department. Departments were egalitarian insofar as each professor's specialized body of knowledge was viewed as equal to a colleague's. With their often autocratic chairs in the first and second generation of universities, departments became the vehicles for professors to pursue and display scholarship through teaching and writing while offering programmatic coherence—that is, a sequence of courses that constituted a "major" for students to elect. University presidents also needed departments to establish standards for appointments of junior faculty and promotions to senior rank within the particular discipline. This curricular, pedagogical, and personnel gate-keeping became the basis for departmental authority and autonomy within the university.[130]

The beliefs and norms surrounding the commonplace structures of the Ph.D., academic rank, and departments formed the university's institutional scaffolding within which research became routinized. What strengthened research and publishing scholarship even further was curtailing teaching responsibilities. Over the decades, departments across the university reduced faculty course loads and teaching hours per week; these reductions became silent university subsidies for research as surely as awarding tenured faculty grants or sabbaticals.

These familiar university structures, then, of the elective system, the doctoral degree as a credential for an entry-level academic job, hierarchical academic rank, and departmental powers wedded to strong cultural norms of professorial autonomy in research and in classroom teaching, have been institutionalized into a model of scholar-teacher.[131]

QUESTIONS TO CONSIDER

This chapter describing a century-long focus on the innovation of the university-college as a means of reconciling competing ideals inevitably raises questions about change. Stanford presidents and faculties have repeatedly called for reforms in curriculum and the relationship between teaching and research. New policies were adopted. New programs were launched. New curricula were put into place. When professors and administrators have looked back, however, few changes seemed to have remained. If anything, the problems seemed to have recycled, reappearing in different guises a decade or more later. Yet, it remains unclear exactly what I mean by *change* and *reform,* words that I have used frequently in this chapter. Is all change the same? Is there a difference between change and reform? Can change occur without reform? Can reforms occur and produce little change? It is to these questions that I turn in the next chapter.

= 2 =

HOW UNIVERSITIES TAME REFORM TO PRESERVE THE RESEARCH IMPERATIVE

Or Why There Is Change Without Reform

In the Introduction, I noted how scholars Irving Kristol and Jacques Barzun contradicted one another in stating unequivocally their assessment of the capacity and willingness of universities to change. Kristol claimed that the university was change-resistant, the least inventive institution—save the U.S. Postal Service—that he had known; Barzun indicted the very same institution for being change-prone, of not letting any innovation pass unnoticed. The previous chapter on Stanford displayed in great detail both an energetic stability and a resilient adaptiveness in changing curriculum. Can both scholars be correct?

Yes. Kristol and Barzun were referring to different dimensions of change in depth, breadth, level, and time. It is in making such crucial distinctions about deliberate changes in universities that I can claim, with ample evidence, that there have been many curricular and pedagogical changes. Yet at the same time, certain deep, far-reaching, enduring attempts at reforms have again and again fallen far short of their designers' intentions. By offering an analytic framework that distinguishes between different types of change and explaining how and why Stanford and other universities adapted to their ever-shifting environment, I can reconcile the enduring popular cliches and scholarly claims that changing universities was akin to moving cemeteries or that professors stoutly resisted change.[1]

61

As universities have endlessly adapted to larger social, political, economic, and cultural changes while also strengthening institutional goals and structures—two-thirds of the colleges and universities that exist now are over a century old—so have faculties and administrators adapted to both planned and unplanned changes as they have preserved their powers and autonomy. In this chapter, I will examine how faculties and administrators have used the elective system, professorial autonomy, departmental powers, teaching, and advising to strengthen the research imperative at Stanford.

First, I will analyze the proposed, adopted, and implemented changes to illustrate how universities tame reforms. Then, I will explain why in adapting to turbulent, keenly competitive environments universities have found mechanisms to sustain their priorities and how those structures and processes have insured stability. In using these tools, I will offer political, institutional, and organizational explanations for why change without reform is the norm in universities.[2]

SCOPE OF DELIBERATE CHANGE: A TYPOLOGY

The typology I offer examines the differences between proposed changes, ones that are adopted, and changes that are ultimately modified as they are put into practice. I will explore these distinctions between proposed, adopted, and implemented changes by examining the depth, breadth, context, and elapsed time of the changes.

I begin with two dimensions that capture the reach of proposed and adopted changes: depth and breadth. I will analyze each and offer examples, ending with a figure that represents in graphic form the complexity of designing change. Then I will analyze how proposed and adopted changes get modified as they get implemented. Where a change is put into practice—the context—and the time involved to implement the change also shape the outcome of the change. After considering these four dimensions, the notion of "change without reform" should be apparent to the reader.[3]

Depth

Depth of change indicates the degree to which the designers of a particular innovation seek to make minor, modest, or major changes, even transformations, of the key structures, cultures, and processes that constitute the essential features of a university.[4]

By structures, I mean the basic organizational features that make a university a university: multiple goals (research, teaching, service); public and private funding to support multiple institutional functions, including nonacademic activities such as athletics; admissions policies; decentralized departmental organization for allocation of university functions and professorial resources; policies for determining hiring, tenure, and promotion; curricular and instructional policies based upon the elective principle, including large undergraduate lecture classes and small-group experiences for advanced undergraduate and graduate students; division of labor between administrators and faculty in governing nonacademic and academic matters. All of the foregoing are what I call structures.

By cultures, I refer to overall stories, beliefs, language, rituals, and practices that have come to give meaning to those in the university. In addition, there are the professorial beliefs in, and norms of, academic freedom and autonomy in research and teaching, as well as shared faculty beliefs about what portions of the university's mission are more important than others. Because there are many departments and schools within a university, each with their subculture anchored in a discipline and their history within the institution, the pulse of the university-wide culture will vary in strength across a campus.

By processes, I mean formal and informal conduits of communication and of allocating resources, legislative and judicial procedures, intra- and interdepartmental bargaining, and actual teaching and advising practices.

These structures, cultures, and processes, then, are the basic building blocks, the core organizational features, that constitute a university and become targets for reformers.

The poles that anchor this depth continuum, I call "incremental" and "fundamental." The depth continuum does not consist of either/or, or absolutes; it is a matter of degree. Enough incremental changes in one domain over time, for example, can accumulate into a fundamental change.[5]

Incremental Change

Designers of incremental changes aim to improve the efficiency and effectiveness of existing structures, cultures, and processes, including classroom teaching. They adhere explicitly to rational theories of organizations. The premise behind incremental change is that the basic structures are sound but need improving to remove defects that hinder effectiveness and efficiency. Synonyms for *incremental* to signal the depth of the planned change would be *additions, enhancements, modifications,* and *alterations.* To offer an obvious analogy, a car maybe old, but it still

has a lot of miles left in it. Its chassis and motor can be in decent condition, but it may need new tires, brakes, a battery, and a tune-up.

Illustrations of proposed incremental changes within Stanford University would be extending the 2 years of general education mandated
in 1920 to 4 years in 1956, adding the "Western Culture" course in 1980
as another distribution requirement for graduation, and adding a student
to the university board of trustees. Applied to the classroom, incremental changes would include decreasing the number of hours students
spend in labs, adding in-service workshops to have professors use computers to present multimedia lectures, and reducing professors' teaching load from five classes a year to four.[6]

Fundamental Change

Proposed changes are those that aim to alter drastically the core
beliefs, behaviors, and structures of the university. The original notion
of reform was to transform, to form anew, or revive existing institutions
to reach some moral vision—past or future—of a better life, even a
utopia. Examples of such reforms are the Protestant Reformation, the
mid-19th century evangelical impulse in the United States, Reform
Judaism, and 19th century reformatories for youth. Notions of both individual and social reform were embedded in the Western idea of progress
and were at the center of such movements for the establishment of common schools in the mid-19th century, the governmental and social
reforms of the Progressives at the turn of the century, and the civil rights
movement of the post–*Brown vs. Board of Education* decade.

Advocates for this kind of change assume that basic university
structures, cultures, and processes are flawed at their core and need a
complete overhaul, not simple renovations. In other words, the old car
is beyond repair. What is needed is a completely new car or a very different form of transportation. Synonyms for *fundamental* would be *revolutionary, radical, major, substantial, structural, significant,* and *transfor-
mative.* In this study of universities, I equate *fundamental change* with
the word *reform.*[7]

The late 19th century emergence of American universities is an
instance of fundamental change or reform of the previously college-dom-
inated system of higher education. Other examples would be when
Robert Hutchins, president of the University of Chicago (1929–1951),
took a research-driven institution totally committed to the elective principle and professorial autonomy and, with the help of key deans and faculty, transformed a moribund undergraduate program into a college with
a required curriculum using external examinations. Gerald Grant and
David Riesman write about "telic reforms" of the 1960s in which admin-

istrators and faculty created new institutions (e.g., Kresge College at the University of California, Santa Cruz; and the College of Old Westbury in the State University of New York system) to counter the dominant multiversities with their impersonal bureaucracies, errant teaching faculties, and vast impenetrable curricula.[8]

Applied to the classroom, fundamental changes had occurred almost a century ago with innovative forms of teaching accompanying the rise of American universities, such as seminars, laboratory work, and clinical work in hospitals for advanced medical students. Advocates of fundamental change in teaching practices would, for example, transform the perennial role of lecturer and occasional discussion leader into one where the professor actively engages students and advises undergraduates; they would convert the familiar professor who is the central authority on subject-matter to that of a coach-like figure who guides students to find meaning in what they learn from one another. Teaching would become less telling and more listening, questioning, and probing.

Examples of such reforms that have substantially altered how professors teach would be problem-based learning that has been incorporated into a handful of medical schools (e.g., University of New Mexico, and Harvard University). Such changes in the basic faculty teaching repertoires would represent fundamental alterations in the ways professors think about what is knowledge, teaching, and learning, as well as their actions in the classroom.[9]

Depth of change, then, means distinguishing between incremental and fundamental changes intended to improve or transform the basic structures, cultures, and processes of the university. Breadth of change adds another dimension.

Breadth

The poles that anchor the breadth continuum are "narrow" and "broad." Again, the breadth continuum, like the depth continuum, is not a dichotomy of mutually exclusive absolutes; it is a matter of degree. Narrow breadth means that the designers of innovations aim at one or two structures and processes for change. Broad breadth, of course, means that the reach of the change goes beyond a few systemic features; the intent is to modify several elements or the entire system.[10]

Moreover, the two continua of depth and breadth interact. An example of a narrow, incremental change would be the reduction in faculty teaching load of five to six courses to four in the 1960s. Broad, incremental changes would be when the Stanford faculties altered the curricular organization by establishing new courses and creating distribution requirements in this century. A narrow, fundamental change would be when the City University of New York went to open admissions in 1970 and dramatically changed the composition of the student body without corresponding changes in curricular and instructional practices until years later. A broad, fundamental change would be a design intended to reform multiple elements of the existing system, such as transforming the conventional University of Buffalo (part of the State University of New York) into the "Berkeley of the East."[11]

Breadth of change, then, means distinguishing between the narrowness and broadness of the intended change to alter a few or many of the university's structures and processes. Breadth interacts with depth to form a four-celled matrix of change into which instances of innovations and adaptations can be inserted in distinct quadrants (see Figure 2.1). But a university is a large, complex, multilevel operation. Does the matrix only apply to university-wide change? To answer the question and underscore that the figure is a useful tool to make sense of change and stability in a university, I turn to the dimension of level.

Level

The matrix I offered in Figure 2.1 is useful in categorizing changes that are *proposed* and *adopted*. Not until the matter of level and, later, time are introduced can analysis occur of what happened after adoption and whether *implementation* led to the incorporation of the change in routines. Because the university is a decentralized organization of nested, quasi-hierarchical layers of authority and decision making interspersed with many semiautonomous units, the level at which the intended change (incremental/fundamental, narrow/broad) is targeted becomes ever so important for implementation. The university, in Burton Clark's vivid phrase, is a "bottom-heavy" organization.[12]

Since this study concentrates on curriculum content and organization, departmental and faculty autonomy, and pedagogy as they interact with the research imperative, the "bottom" is the lecture hall, laboratory, faculty office, and seminar room where professors decide what to investigate and what to teach. The next level of authority or target for change would be the department or school that in universities receives funds and grants, allocates office space, schedules teaching load, and recruits faculty for posts and current professors for tenure and promotion. It is the disciplinary and cultural home for faculty. The aggregate faculty becomes the next level. At Stanford, it would be the Academic Council and its representative body (since 1968), the Faculty Senate, which is authorized to decide on academic policies. Finally, there is the institutional level with

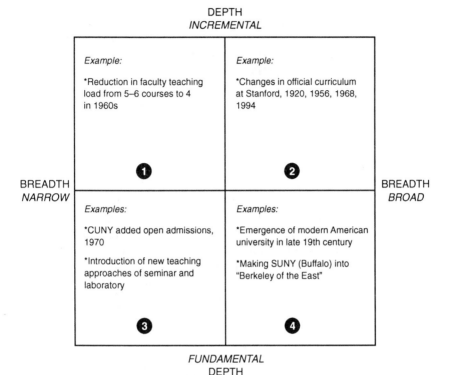

FIGURE 2.1 — Proposed changes.

the board of trustees, president, and administrators, all of whom are expected to give direction to the entire enterprise. Thus, the level at which a change is directed within a university moves the analysis beyond simply the design of an innovation or its formal adoption.

Two important points need to be made about levels within the university where authority is broadly dispersed and the organization is decentralized into schools and departments. First, in "bottom-heavy" institutions, individual professors and departments are relatively independent in their actions as compared to top-heavy, hierarchically organized institutions, such as General Motors and the Postal Service. Second, as a consequence of fragmented authority and decentralized organization, powerful departmental cultures, and strong norms of individual autonomy, the linkages between university levels is relatively loose, meaning that directives from a higher level to a lower one may be explicitly noted, partially or wholly heeded, or even ignored. In this study, university-wide, faculty-sponsored school and departmental efforts to alter the balance between teaching and research, then, are subject to the broad, individual autonomy that professors have in determining what they investigate and teach. There is, then, little certainty, and even less conviction, that decisions made outside of the professors' offices will affect what they do.[13]

To return to the above matrix, the breadth and depth of change can now be applied to each level of authority and decision making in a university, including the classroom. Each application of the matrix, say, to the professor's classroom and then to a department or school, would need to consider the interacting linkages to other levels in an institution where governance is so dispersed and the organization so bottom-heavy.

What's missing from this matrix and discussion of level in applying depth and breadth is what occurs as time passes. The matrix is a snapshot of what change looks like *before* implementation; it is not a photo album documenting changes that occurred to the innovation a decade or even a century *after* adoption. Furthermore, I have used the words *intended* or *designs* for change to distinguish reformers' plans for change from what was implemented and what evolved, often unanticipated, years later.

Time

The implementation of new policies and programs aimed at modestly improving or transforming stable features of the university depends a great deal upon the organizational level and the passing of time. What begins as a broad, fundamental change may end up, a decade later, as a narrow, incremental change. What was introduced as a narrow, incremental change may slowly spread into a broad, fundamental change. Or what was initiated as either of the above kinds of change simply may have disappeared within 5 years.

Putting a planned change into practice, then, is a chancy operation that reveals itself as the years unfold. So, to capture the differences between intentions of reformers and the anticipated and unanticipated outcomes of the designs, there needs to be many matrices. The first is a matrix for adopted changes or the designers' hopes; it is the snapshot before implementation (refer to Figure 2.1). The second and subsequent matrices record what happened to innovations after full or partial implementation as years passed; it is the album documenting the zigzag journey in the life span of a planned change (see Figure 2.2).

There are several ways that organizations modify adopted changes as they get implemented and subsequently become routine features,

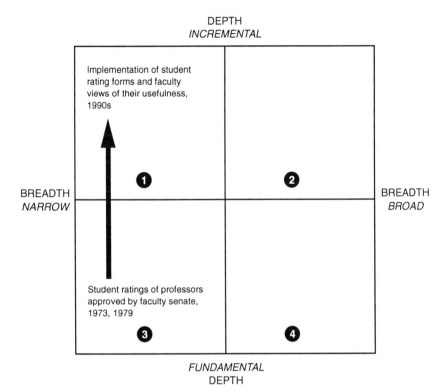

FIGURE 2.2 — Incrementalizing a fundamental change.

become marginalized, or even disappear. A common pattern is when intended fundamental changes (broad or narrow) shrink into incremental ones—or, to refer to the change matrix, move from quadrant 3 or 4 to 1 or 2. An example illustrates this process.

Fundamental Into Incremental: Evaluating Teaching

Two major reports on education at Stanford, one in the mid-1950s and the other in the late 1960s, recommended that faculty teaching should be evaluated. Their recommendations derived from deep concerns over the university's commitment to teaching expressed by external visiting committees, in faculty and student interviews, and by growing public recognition that faculty responses to the research imperative had impacted the quality of teaching undergraduates. Both reports recommended that students evaluate their professors' teaching.

Not until 1973, however, did the Faculty Senate decide that all professors must submit to some form of student evaluation. Not until 1979—a quarter century after the first recommendation for evaluation of teaching—did the Faculty Senate require any form ("The University Student Evaluation Rating Form") to be used. There is, of course, variation across the campus in evaluating classroom performance. For example, the School of Law, in addition to the university forms, uses a peer-review process that has senior faculty periodically visiting nontenured junior colleagues.[14]

Here, then, was a narrow, fundamental reform in its concentration on a core task in academic work: the conduct of teaching. It was fundamental in three respects. First, the intent was to correct the sheer imbalance between teaching and research that faculty and administration had come to see as deleterious to the university's mission. Second, it finally broke through the privacy of classroom teaching, opening it to quasi-public inspection. Although a student-published guide to undergraduate courses with judgments about professors—the *Course Review*—had circulated for many years, the Faculty Senate now put its stamp of approval on opening the officially closed door to the professor's classroom. Third, these student ratings and other ways of assessing teaching were given official weight in making formal judgments on hiring, granting tenure, and promoting professors, thus modifying a core structure in the university.

By the mid-1990s, however, it had become clear to both faculty and students that the standard evaluation form had incurred much dissatisfaction. Comments from four focus groups of faculty and students to determine what the primary issues were on teaching evaluation found "frustration, cynicism, or apathy." The focus group report said that "many seemed to feel that no real change would come; therefore no effort was currently justified in re-orienting their personal priorities or actions." The dream of an earlier generation of reformers to make student ratings of professors' teaching a "countervailing force" to the research imperative had turned into an end-of-quarter bureaucratic procedure where clerks would run forms through machines and produce a summary for the professor 4 months later. Student ratings of teaching had become both incrementalized and marginalized.[15]

Fundamental Into Incremental: Enclaving

Enclaving can be seen in the Kresge College at the University of California, Santa Cruz, in the early 1970s. Clark Kerr, appointed president of the University of California system in 1958, envisioned the Santa Cruz campus to be a cluster of colleges that could combine the small academic community that he had experienced as an undergraduate at Swarthmore with the intellectual feistiness of Berkeley, where he had served as chancellor. "Make it seem small," he urged the first chancellor of Santa Cruz, "as it grows large."[16]

The first residential college opened in 1965 and the eighth in 1972, each having a particular focus: science, the third-world, social science, humanistic psychology, environmental planning, and so on. Colleges generated courses for their students, an easy enough task since each of the first generation of provosts and faculties were established scholars from first-rank universities inside and outside the University of California system. Committed to cultivating faculty-student bonds beyond the occasional contacts that usually characterize professor–undergraduate student relations, the original design and subsequent adaptations created different curricular, governance, and faculty structures, such as the residential college, pass/fail grading, written evaluations, and faculty that had to be jointly hired by departments (called Boards of Study) and colleges. Teaching was strongly emphasized in each of the residential colleges, although criteria for tenure and promotion continued to be research-driven.

Within this attempt to create an undergraduate cluster of colleges committed to experimentation and innovation in creating teaching and learning communities, Kresge College was established in 1970. It opened a year later with 275 students and 18 faculty living together. From its very beginning, the ideas of Carl Rogers about teaching and learning—concepts drawn from humanistic psychology and organizational development circa the late 1960s, including heavy emphasis upon small-group encounters exploring feelings, and interpersonal conflict—infused the first generation of faculty and students. Student living space—clusters for eight students (octets)—was partition-less, more so to create a sense of community. Core courses were jointly shaped by faculty and students who met countless times for extended periods to figure out what should be taught and how.[17]

Governance decisions about core courses, allocation of space and funds, and other college-wide issues were initially made in "families" (subsequently renamed "kin groups") and in periodic "Advance" sessions of the entire community. Questions of authority and full participation proved to be inescapable as the years passed. Demands for constant meetings led to many faculty and students reducing their involvement in the frequent "sensitivity-training" sessions that marked both kin groups and Advance gatherings. As the original founders tired, expressing disappointment with divergences from the original design, and as the initial class, imbued with the ideology of Kresge, graduated— changes occurred in the core courses, organization, governance, and tenor of the college.

Student surveys in 1974 confirmed the designers' intentions: Sixty percent of students said that contact with the faculty was one of the most important factors in their years at Santa Cruz; in an earlier survey, almost the same percentage of faculty reported that they interacted frequently with students outside of class (as compared to 20% for Berkeley faculty). In a 1972 University of California survey, faculty and students at Santa Cruz gave the highest ratings of any campus in the system to individual personal development, humanism, aesthetic awareness, and innovation. Faculty ranked Santa Cruz the highest in the University of California system for innovation and experimentation.[18]

By the 4th year, however, enrollment had reached almost 600 students with less than half in residence. Only about half of the students had marked Kresge as their first choice; the rest had only a superficial knowledge of what the college represented. By the end of 1974, faculty had decided to create a special program within Kresge called "Corner of the College" to continue the original dream of the designers. Only residents of Kresge could be members of this school-within-a-school. Faculty advisors to kin groups were replaced by students who had been trained in encounter-group methods. In the apartments, walls began to go up to ensure more privacy than had existed earlier. Rather than the required core courses of earlier years, faculty began offering electives, many of which were interdisciplinary. In 1975, a new provost was appointed who moved to establish interdisciplinary academic clusters that resembled majors.[19]

Kresge, a subunit within the university with very different goals, was designed to be a deep and broad change in undergraduate education; it became an enclave. After 5 years, Kresge had begun to adapt to changes in its student body and university demands for convergence. The enclave has had, at best, marginal influence on the rest of the university. It remained sufficiently different, however, to be kept at arm's length (see Figure 2.3).[20]

Thus far in this implementation analysis, I have detailed how deliberate reforms get incrementalized within organizations. These unforeseen adaptations and unintended results usually disappoint reformers. What about the reverse? Can incremental changes accumulate slowly over time to create unintended fundamental changes? Such a change would be less of a deliberate reform designed by faculty than an unexpected outcome that just happened as decades passed.

Incremental Changes Unintentionally Accumulating Into Fundamental Changes

One example of this process is how the research imperative, so thoroughly embedded in the graduate school, slowly penetrated the

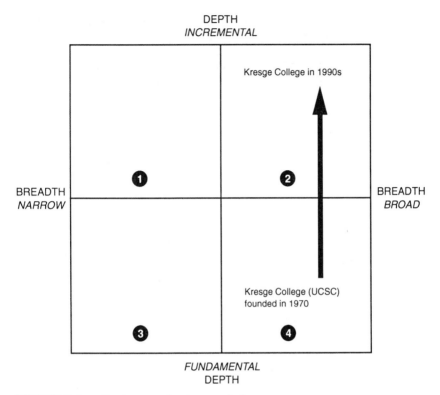

FIGURE 2.3 — Enclaving a fundamental change.

undergraduate colleges in many universities during this century. Without a deliberate plan, through an addition here and an improvement there, specialized colloquia and seminars, honors programs, reading periods, comprehensive exams, and research projects steadily captured the junior and senior years of most colleges housed within universities. Surely, in the decades after World War II, the growing number of undergraduates planning to continue in graduate and professional schools accelerated the quiet changes; but these changes were seldom planned by university faculties and administrators with the intent of converting the last 2 years of college into mini-graduate schools. For example, at Yale, in the 1930s, with the generous gift of Edward Harkness, who also gave money to Harvard for its Houses, residential colleges were built on the Oxford-Cambridge model that aimed at creating moral and intellectual communities of undergraduates. Yet, in the previous decade, the faculty had adopted a series of changes that introduced graduate school practices into the undergraduate college, including compulsory comprehensive exams and independently written essays.[21]

At Stanford, this process began in its very first decade with the introduction of seminars for both graduate and undergraduate students. With so few advanced students enrolled in the initial decades and so few undergraduates continuing into professional and graduate schools, little movement in that direction occurred until post–World War I curricular changes had created the upper division. In the economics, political science, and history departments during the 1920s, for example, undergraduate majors took research-based seminars, entered honors programs, and sought out faculty for independent research projects. Faculty offered more specialized courses for majors and, because enrollments were small, combined undergraduates and graduates into the same class. Changes in the official curricula and pedagogy in these departments reflected the research-cum-specialization ethos of the graduate school far more than the teaching-cum-general-education aim of the liberal arts college.

This slow, uncalculated, ad hoc incrementalism created an unplanned, fundamental change that, in turn, spurred university presidents and faculties to launch reforms in undergraduate education (see Figure 2.4). At Stanford and its sister institutions, strong reactions to the transforming of undergraduate work into preparation for graduate school occurred in the mid-1950s and, again, in the late 1970s, spilling over into the 1980s with the renewed debate and subsequent curricular changes in general education courses (as it did elsewhere in the country).[22]

The typology of change I have offered includes four dimensions (depth, breadth, level, and time) arrayed in matrices to show the range of differences, especially differences between intentions of the designers and the outcomes—both expected and unexpected—that occurred during and after implementation. These matrices reconcile the contradiction that Kristol and Barzun posed. Kristol's charge that universities are change-resistant translates into his disappointment over few fundamental changes; Barzun's indictment of universities chasing every fad refers to his view of faculties and administrators mindlessly adopting many incremental changes. If the subtitle of this chapter becomes clearer, the obvious questions arise: How does change without reform occur and why?

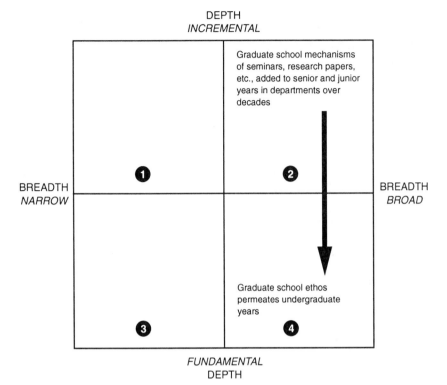

DEPTH
INCREMENTAL

Graduate school mechanisms
of seminars, research papers,
etc., added to senior and junior
years in departments over
decades

BREADTH
NARROW

BREADTH
BROAD

Graduate school ethos
permeates undergraduate
years

FUNDAMENTAL
DEPTH

FIGURE 2.4 — Incremental changes accumulating into a fundamental change.

HOW DOES CHANGE WITHOUT REFORM OCCUR?

Stanford adapted continually to its students and surroundings as decades passed. These adaptations, for the most part, were ad hoc, incremental changes that sustained the beliefs of its founders, as interpreted and institutionalized by subsequent presidents and faculties, and meshed with a larger web of social beliefs and practices in other universities.

One obvious example of makeshift incrementalism is what has happened to the enduring research and teaching imperatives. Both impulses were present at the very birth of Stanford University and were institutionalized into the uneasy hybrid structure of the university-college by a string of long-tenured presidents (Jordan, Wilbur, Sterling, Lyman, and Kennedy cover 91 years of the century—none serving less than a decade and two serving more than 2 decades). Rhetorically, each president made clear that both imperatives were entwined and essential to the national reputation of the university. They claimed that professors could be both first-rate teachers and researchers. And while some professors fulfilled that institutional belief with great elan, university structures, processes, and cultures made it unmistakably evident for most faculty during the entire century that of the two imperatives, what available time there was had to be spent on research first, then teaching.

Establishing awards for excellent teaching, the Center for Teaching and Learning, student ratings of teaching performance, and using the quality of teaching as a criterion for hiring professors, granting tenure, or promoting associate professors to senior rank were encased in richly symbolic language. Still the far-reaching vocabulary of reform used by administrators and faculty leaders could hardly mask what were plainly incremental changes charged to heighten the importance of teaching.

Yet in implementing these modest changes, paradoxically, the recognition and awards for teaching strengthened rather than weakened the asymmetrical relationship between the two competing imperatives. Heightened recognition and new awards increased the symbolic importance attached to teaching by external and internal constituencies without challenging the basic beliefs, structures, and cultures that favored research over teaching. Leaving untouched the systemic building blocks that kept in place the asymmetric relationship unintentionally strengthened the research imperative. By increasing recognition for teaching and doing little to restructure existing policies governing the hiring of new professors, granting or denying tenure to junior faculty, or promoting associates to full professors, a protective shield was erected around the research imperative.

Few professors surveying the panoply of teaching awards available in the early 1990s were swayed to say—as the results from faculty questionnaires prior to and after the increase in recognition for teaching clearly show—that teaching was now equal to or even more important than research at Stanford. Perhaps, the steady accumulation of these symbolic changes aimed at bolstering teaching at Stanford may eventually tip the balance and make it equal to research. Most likely, it will not. These incremental changes aimed at bolstering the importance of teaching have become routine parts of the organization but have yet to fundamentally alter the unbalanced relationship between the two imperatives. Hence, change without reform.

Change Without Reform in Stanford Curriculum

Stanford's major-subject system with jerrybuilt adaptations lasted for almost 30 years, from its founding through World War I. The first reform intended to overhaul this virtually elective system was proposed in 1919. Joining a national movement among universities to generate common curricular content that would offer undergraduates the essentials of the Western tradition, Stanford's presidents and faculties, using the vocabulary of reform, reorganized the curriculum into lower and upper division courses, created distribution requirements, and mandated core courses for all 1st- and 2nd-year students.

These arrangements lasted for over 3 decades, until another national movement in the early 1950s drove universities to revise again both course content and curricular mechanisms to embrace a general education encompassing all 4 years of college. In 1968, the faculty's decision to reinstitute a virtual elective curriculum abandoned prescribed general education courses and retained only a few distribution requirements, thereby charting a course that returned the university to a familiar, albeit earlier, direction. By the late 1970s, however, and throughout the 1980s and 1990s, the faculty decided to reinstate mandated general education courses while steadily increasing distribution requirements.

These improvised shifts in content and curricular structures, as described earlier, were Stanford's faculty responses to both the explosion of specialized knowledge in various disciplines and the enduring tensions embedded within the university-college at similar institutions. These episodic adaptations in breadth, depth, and fixity of courses, each accompanied by the rhetoric of reform and extensive departmental logrolling, sought to strike a balance between the faculty's search for value-free knowledge and the value-laden teaching imperative unique to the undergraduate college. A reform tradition, particularly in the use of language that promised major changes, arose from faculty coping with the recalcitrant dilemma of the university-college, mushrooming specialization of knowledge, and events occurring at other prestigious universities.

To cope with these dilemmas, a rhetorical tradition of reforming curricula had emerged. The language of reforming undergraduate curricular organization and teaching practices pledged deep, even radical changes. Yet once implemented, reforms dissolved into modest changes.

Change Without Reform in Other Universities

Were the tradition of reform a Stanford-only phenomenon, then an explanation for recurring efforts to reform curriculum and pedagogy would need to be located within the unique details of the university's history. But the phenomenon of similar curricular reforms appeared at other research-driven universities during the last century. Presidents and faculties at Columbia, Harvard, and Chicago, to cite three similar settings, have repeatedly wrestled with the issues of breadth, depth, and fixity of curricular content and structures.

Columbia University's venture into general education, like Stanford's, began during World War I with the creation of the "Contemporary Civilization" yearlong course in Columbia College. From one such course, it expanded to a second yearlong course in 1929. All undergraduates shared a common intellectual experience in these courses. There were no majors. There were no student-filled auditoriums to listen to lectures. Classes of 25 students engaged in discussions about the required readings under the tutelage of a professor or instructor.

Columbia College's pioneering approach to general education in developing yearlong courses married to a pedagogy of small-group discussions lasted from 1919 until 1954. In 1954, the faculty established the major for 3rd and 4th-year Columbia College undergraduates and the option to substitute other courses for the "Contemporary Civilization" ones. In 1959, the faculty dropped the 2nd-year course that had begun 3 decades earlier. Again in the mid-1960s and mid-1970s, university-wide studies and debates pivoted on structural questions of required general education courses, distribution requirements, and to what degree electivity should be abridged.[23]

Harvard University's history of curricular debates over breadth, depth, and prescription of courses date from the presidency of Charles Eliot and his introduction of the elective principle in the 1870s, which, in ending the fixed classical curriculum, broadened and specialized the curriculum as it strengthened graduate and professional education. Seeing the individual choice embedded within the elective system as serving American democracy and industrial development, his successor, A. Lawrence Lowell, was far more concerned about how the very same premium placed upon choosing courses had exacted harsh costs from Harvard undergraduates' education. In his inaugural address in 1909, Lowell pointed out that it is in the college "that character ought to be shaped, that aspirations ought to be formed, that citizens ought to be trained, and scholarly tastes implanted." To such words Eliot might have nodded his head in agreement. Yet the former president would see Lowell taking his Harvard in a different direction than he had for the previous 40 years. Under Lowell, Harvard college students were expected to live in freshman dorms (and later upperclassmen houses), take tutorials followed by oral exams, and concentrate in one area of study while taking courses in other departments. It was a general education, Harvard-style, that tried to reverse the freedom to sample courses and specialize that Eliot had so enthusiastically unleashed decades earlier. With the gift of

Yale alumnus Edward Harkness, Lowell could introduce the House system to bring all undergraduates together, the rich private school scion along with the Cambridge schoolboy, which would become "seminars in living" where students' diverse ideas could clash around the dinner table in the Common Room. The pedagogy of this version of general education was anchored in large lectures, discussion sections, tutorials, and informal exchanges between residential masters and professors and their students.[24]

Not until World War II did the issue of the quality of undergraduate education arise publicly again at Harvard. President James Bryce Conant's charge to faculty to lay out the purposes of a college education led to the publication of *General Education in a Free Society* (or, the *Redbook*). The *Redbook* sought a balance between specialization and education for a common citizenship and balance between the creation of knowledge and the value-loaded task of teaching undergraduates. The report proposed required courses in the humanities, social sciences, and natural sciences similar in thrust to Columbia's "Contemporary Civilization" courses.[25]

Although the faculty approved the recommendations in 1945, not until 1949 was general education made compulsory. Yet in those 4 years the aim of providing a common experience had been revised by giving undergraduates numerous alternative courses in the required fields. These courses, taught by senior faculty, were basically large lecture courses that brought star professors to speak to 1st- and 2nd-year students. From the 1950s until the mid-1970s, these "great men" lecture courses were taught in Harvard College.[26]

In 1973, Harvard President Derek Bok appointed Henry Rosovsky as Dean of Arts and Sciences, and within 2 years Rosovsky had launched a comprehensive review of the college's offerings. The faculty study produced the core curriculum, a broad series of new courses in six prescribed areas (literature and the arts, science, historical study, social analysis, foreign cultures, and moral reasoning). Students had choices within each area but had to complete all six. The faculty voted in 1978 to adopt the core curriculum and replace the general education survey courses that had begun in the late 1940s.[27]

If Harvard's post–World War II version of general education was driven by "great men" and Columbia's program between 1919 and 1954 was distilled into "great courses," then Chicago's model between the 1930s and 1950s was forged in "great ideas."[28]

The experience of the University of Chicago prior to and after the presidency of Robert Hutchins, "the genie of the university" in Daniel Bell's apt phrase, underscores the tensions that have inexorably trailed the university-college in its efforts to balance breadth and depth in organizing the curriculum. Moreover, that history displays the "radical" and "revolutionary" changes (words used by commentators decades later) that a president, a succession of deans, and a hard-working faculty created—in an institution devoted to graduate research—to achieve a single coherent program of general education for all of their undergraduates (some of whom were admitted after completing their 2nd year of high school). For over 2 decades, Chicago's general education program was a distinct alternative to the research-oriented, graduate school-dominated university.[29]

To Clark Kerr, Hutchins was "the last of the university presidents who really tried to change his institution and higher education in any fundamental way." In Hutchins's determination to combine the last 2 years of high school with the first 2 years of college into a 4-year program leading to the bachelor of arts degree, he was retooling the old bisection notion that Gilman of Johns Hopkins, Jordan of Stanford, and Chicago's own Harper had advocated at the turn of the century. Hutchins, of course, did this to create an alternative to graduate school because he believed that most Americans who attended college would end their formal education with a bachelor's not an advanced degree.

Faculty committees and deans had created four yearlong courses (social sciences, humanities, physical sciences, and biological sciences), with syllabi listing the required books that all students had to read. Senior faculty delivered introductory lectures and junior staff led discussion groups, the teaching practice of choice. Students, on occasion, formed extracurricular evening groups and invited eminent professors to speak. To receive course credit, students were no longer judged on their attendance, responses to a professor's questions, or performance on quizzes and tests. Instead, they took comprehensive examinations (a total of 15 by 1937 to complete the 4-year program). These exams, designed by faculty committees, determined whether the student had satisfactorily grasped the central ideas in the yearlong courses. They could take the exams without even attending classes. What counted was student initiative, self-motivation, and academic competence in completing the requirements. An intellectual community no longer was restricted to graduate school, and 17- to 20-year-olds could be engaged in the play of ideas.[30]

Not only was the college a curricular experiment in general education, but it was also an experiment in faculty collaboration in designing courses and preparing examinations across disciplines. College faculty was organized by courses rather than departments, so cross-disciplinary planning and teaching were endorsed. Teaching (including lecturing, leading seminars, and guiding discussions) was considered the primary task of college professors. In 1932, cash awards for excellence in teaching were established. In 1943, an alumnus gave $100,000 to be used for college faculty development in teaching.

With the departure of President Hutchins in 1951, his successors approved changes in the program that undid general education, slowly returning it to the tradition of a research-driven university that its founding president, William Rainey Harper, had so ardently sought. In 1953, only high school graduates could enter the college, not 15- and 16-year-olds. In 1957, the university reorganized the college into a lower division with 2 years of prescribed core courses, a few of which students could avoid, and an upper division with 2 years of electives geared toward a major. By the mid-1960s, Provost Edward Levi, who later became president of the university, had divided the college into area colleges, each offering a specialty. In moving clearly toward the mainstream university-college model of distribution requirements, specialization, and few prescribed courses, the university had, in Daniel Bell's words, "finally reversed the original intention of a common 4-year education."[31]

WHY IS THERE CHANGE WITHOUT REFORM?

Stanford's experience in reforming its curricular content and structures over the last century was matched in different degrees by what occurred at similar universities. Both public and private universities across the nation during this century have had their faculties engaged in calm to acrimonious debates over the breadth and depth of the curriculum and what, if any, courses should be required. These strategies of improvised incrementalism, over time, tamed reforms to preserve the web of institutional beliefs, structures, and cultures. Why?[32]

No one crisp explanation can suffice to fully answer the question. Any answer, however, must begin with the constantly changing environment in which American universities are nested and to which they must respond if they are to survive—as most have for over a century. Unceasing social, political, economic, and cultural changes have impacted universities through direct intervention (e.g., federally subsidized scientific research and the G.I. Bill following World War II, shrinking or expanding market for occupations requiring advanced degrees) and indirectly through each generation of increasing numbers of students who enter as undergraduates. The intellectual and vocational aspirations students bring to campus, clothed in the garb of ever-shifting cultural attitudes, have direct effects on the courses students take, the causes they promote, and the activities they pursue.[33]

Universities, then, adapt to fit these constantly changing surroundings. While resilient adaptation is a plausible response to the ample evidence of societal changes impinging upon universities, it fails to explain *why* universities are impelled to adjust to their surroundings, the recurring popularity of content and structural changes in the official curriculum, or the subordination of teaching to research.

Researchers have pointed out the obvious to college presidents and deans: To survive as institutions, universities must not only compete for students and faculty, but also for public esteem, financial support, political power, and legitimacy from a variety of elite political, economic, and social constituencies. Constituents' views on what purposes universities serve and their roles in society differ, yet have become, over time, shared social beliefs of what universities ought to be and do. These shared beliefs, often embracing contrary expectations, become insistent demands upon universities to conform.[34]

In responding to these uncoordinated demands from varied constituencies, universities have become, since their origins in the United States over a century ago, places where knowledge is created and stored in libraries, archives, and laboratories. Universities harbor research facilities that seek cures for lethal diseases, innovative ways of powering vehicles, and laborsaving devices. Universities also disseminate the oldest and newest of knowledge and skills to students who seek the life of the mind, to a public that can apply what is learned to their communities, and to corporations eager for marketable inventions.

These familiar beliefs about what universities are expected to do have been supplemented, as decades passed, by equally vigorous notions of what else they should be doing. Universities are expected to be agencies that certify undergraduates as having a liberal and technical education sufficient to join the labor market or to gain advanced credentials to enter law, medicine, business, education, engineering, or other professions. They are expected to solve social problems. They are expected to provide a social escalator for upwardly mobile working-class and middle-class youth. Furthermore, they are expected to offer an arena for the display of athletic and cultural activities.

Clark Kerr's coining of "multiversity" as a word describing the university in the late 1950s had its beginnings in the early years of Stanford, Chicago, Johns Hopkins, Berkeley, and other late-19th-century institutions. Thus, the purposes of universities so easily summed up in the oft-repeated trinity of creating knowledge, disseminating it, and serving the public get far more complicated by additional public expectations. The mix of explicit and implicit goals reveals the deep ambiguity of purposes and their underlying conflicts within universities as they compete for students, faculty, funds, and public esteem.[35]

Over the decades, then, a notion of what a "real university" is has emerged that embraces all of these contrary expectations: A "real university" has eminent faculty who do research in libraries and modern laboratories as they gladly teach students and offer expert advice to public officials and corporations. A "real university" offers a variety of courses both prescribed and elective, schedules 50-minute lectures in large halls for undergraduates and seminars for advanced students, selects the best and the brightest to admit, offers at least 4 years of schooling for undergraduates, awards bachelor's and advanced degrees every spring, and has extensive facilities that include stadiums, theaters, professional schools, and hospitals.[36]

To meet these varied but shared social beliefs about what a "real university" is, these institutions, particularly the ones that have become highly selective in choosing students and faculties, have often imitated one another. The Ivy League and select Midwest and West Coast universities, both public and private, have constituted what sociologists call an "organizational field" for almost a century. They look to one another to maintain standards, secure a degree of uniformity and predictability, and adopt innovations from sister institutions that appear to be successful in order to maintain their competitive edge. Stanford's "organizational field" can be traced to the founding of the Association of American Universities (AAU) in 1900 (Stanford was a charter member). The group listed three objectives: Establish uniformity in Ph.D. requirements, achieve foreign recognition of the American doctorate, and strengthen standards of the weaker American universities. Currently, the Carnegie classification of institutions clearly demarcated a first tier of universities mundanely captured in the term *Research I*. The spread of reform-tinged curricular mechanisms and new disciplinary subject matter within this organizational field of AAU and Research I universities offers one example of this mimicry.[37]

Following World Wars I and II and between the mid-1970s and mid-1980s, waves of interest in the balance between prescribed general education courses and specialization swept across university campuses, touching Stanford in each case. Examining Stanford's structural changes in the 1950s compared to those at Harvard, Columbia, and Chicago (after Hutchins departed) reveal strikingly common features. So reforms are contagious; they return again and again because universities competing with other highly ranked institutions adapt to social changes in the larger environment to maintain the support of important constituencies.

In adapting to these social beliefs and conflicting, ever-increasing demands to maintain social and political prestige and legitimacy, universities, inexorably since their emergence in the last quarter of the 19th century, have developed a sponge-like capacity to absorb and respond to their turbulent surroundings. That capacity for resilience is located in the dispersed governance, decentralized organizational structures, sub-cultures, and processes that have arisen in universities to cope with diverse constituencies and powerful beliefs within the larger society about what universities are expected to do. This answer may also explain how universities convert proposed fundamental changes into modest alterations by using the language of reform while practicing ad hoc incrementalism, creating traditions of change, and enclaving. Thus, university presidents and faculties tame reforms.

But how does this happen? Simply claiming that ad hoc incrementalism explains these occurrences is inadequate. What is missing from this analysis is how political, organizational, and institutional processes within the university accounted for reforms being modified. The example of reforms aimed at improving teaching and advising may illustrate the process.[38]

Major reports by Stanford faculty in 1968 and 1994 had publicly reaffirmed the critical importance of improving teaching and advising. In the mid-1970s, the Center for Teaching and Learning was established and the Faculty Senate approved formal student evaluation of teaching. In the late 1980s and early 1990s, President Donald Kennedy initiated his plan for improving teaching through cash awards and recognition. A Faculty Senate committee reported in 1995 on how teaching could be reframed as a form of scholarship in making appointments and that peer review could improve the quality of teaching. For over 40 years, then, university presidents and faculty have sporadically attended to teaching and advising by making major pronouncements, undertaking massive studies, and launching new programs.

Within this Stanford context, however, there is, as I have already noted, the basic dilemma of teaching and research within the university-college and the professional school. While both teaching and research are prized, constraints of time and energy mean that professors and departments must make choices about how they use their limited resources. Yet university incentives, structures, and norms clearly have favored research over teaching and advising insofar as recruiting of faculty, securing tenure, and getting promoted are concerned. With the freedom that individual professors and departments have had at Stanford, their responses to exhortations about teaching, massive studies, and new programs have been largely benign, and, in the case of advising, indifferent. Allowing for the variation that exists among individual faculty in their passion for improving teaching, and even granting as accurate the shared belief that some star researchers are also star teachers, professorial and departmental interests in research have not been, by and large, advanced by devoting more time to teaching and advising. In effect, the interests of faculty, as a corporate body, are best served by those policies and programs that strengthen their research agendas. But what about the changes instituted to heighten the importance and quality of teaching mentioned above?

What helps to explain the scaling downward of an intended fundamental shift in the historical imbalance between research and teaching into a few incremental changes is that they are essentially compromises negotiated among practical-minded faculty, department heads, and administrators. Over the century at Stanford, negotiations over changes occurred often among individual tenured faculty within and across departments as they sought to maximize their autonomy to inquire, teach, set their own schedules, and write. Departmental logrolling occurred often as chairs jostled for larger undergraduate enrollments to justify the university allotting more faculty billets and graduate student financial aid to the department, allocating more time for research and reducing teaching hours. Some departments won and acquired more resources and status, others lost.

Administrators and department heads compromise also. They know that individual faculty will largely welcome public recognition of teaching prowess to improve teaching but not coercion, even when instruction may be seriously flawed. Thus, few tenured professors who are viewed by administrators, colleagues, and students as ineffective have had to go to the Center for Teaching and Learning to improve. Faculty committees, over the years, have negotiated the items on the official evaluation forms to be so generic as to confound everyone as to exactly what the tallies mean or how the responses can be used to revise courses. Yet the rhetoric about the importance of new programs and rewards for teaching have great symbolic value to alumni, faculty, administrators, and parents of applicants. University officials can point with evident pride to the speeches, programs, and dollars aimed at teaching.

Hence, the last 40 years of episodic interest in improving teaching and the few incremental changes that have been made (noting that hardly a ripple of attention to the subject occurred in the first half-century) are largely due to the considerable power that faculty and departments have in determining which academic items receive attention from students and administration and the pace of change that occurs once attention is given. As tenured faculty's interests in their freedom to inquire, publish, and teach have, over the decades, converged with their power to govern academic issues involving curriculum and instruction, preserving those interests has become a political priority. Faculty self-interests do matter.

This elaborated answer may explain why universities adapt and how they tame reforms. What the answer omits, however, is why, of all the targets for reform, curriculum turns up again and again.

WHY CURRICULUM CONTENT AND STRUCTURES?

At different times in the history of universities, particular aspects of university mission, funding, organization, governance, student admissions, curriculum, and instruction have come under faculty scrutiny. Of all of these, none has attracted the most public attention consistently over time, certainly in the last half-century, as the content and structures of the official curricula.

Clear examples of intense public attention are seen in the Columbia experiment with general education following World War I, in Hutchins's designs for Chicago in the 1930s, and in the Harvard *Redbook* following World War II. During the 1960s, academics and journalists published accounts, engaged in fiery debates, and rendered analyses of colleges and universities creating entirely new curricula. In the mid-1980s, the hullabaloo over changes in Stanford's "Western Culture" course produced a televised debate between President Donald Kennedy and the U.S. Secretary of Education, William Bennett; articles in the national press; and books devoted to the change in one course that all 1st-year students were required to take. Writing at about the same time, President Derek Bok of Harvard University summed up this history:

> Anyone who studies the history of curricular reform since 1900 will emerge stripped of the notion that this subject holds the key to many insights about the course of American civilization. Over this period, all of the fundamental issues have remained the same. Almost every important proposal has already been tried. No permanent victories are ever won, nor are serious arguments ever conclusively defeated.[39]

What is there about changing the content and organization of the official curriculum that generates such intensity with so little gain?

First, debates over subject matter or prescribed courses offer a forum for faculty to elaborate ideological conflicts over prized values. Is the mission of the university to prepare students for the job market or to be active, informed citizens? Should medical schools prepare students to be medical researchers or doctors who practice first-rate medicine? Such tough questions arise from erratic but persistent concerns over the conflicting imperatives of teaching and research within a university-college. Concentration upon research and specialization within the university may fit well with graduate students in professional school seeking a license to practice, but it distorts the academic experiences of undergraduates who are expected to receive a "liberal education." Thus, curricular debates become volatile proxies for the endemic tensions over competing values within the university-college. Such fiery exchanges are not to be dismissed as mere words of sound and fury amounting to little.

To the degree that ideas matter and to the degree that consciousness about values can be changed, such debates incubate proposed changes that become eventual compromises hammered out of contending interests among faculty, administrators, and students. The forum for curricular debates permits advancing compromises to satisfy conflicting parties without creating permanent fractures in the organization. Much yelling and shouting reported by the media is then followed by new proposals drafted by peacemakers on the faculty who seek to reduce conflict and gain consensus for reconciliation. So the content and structures of the official curriculum are where the many competing values of a university nest. Proposed changes invoke different values, and such changes matter to the faculty, even if they cannot permanently resolve conflicting ideals.[40]

Second, there is an important symbolic function served by changing subject matter and how the official curriculum is organized. It reduces internal conflict by offering a stage for displaying verbal positions; it also reduces external criticism of the university. Adding new courses and special interdisciplinary programs, for example, may signal critics that something important has happened without necessarily modifying the asymmetry of the research and teaching imperatives. Few of those hopes have materialized in a half-century. Such changes, then, function initially as a forum for hammering out compromises, then as a distracter, and ultimately as a way of downsizing reform expectations. New courses and programs become visible trophies of change that still critics' charges of inattention to problems—for awhile.[41]

Third, altering curricular content and structures avoids talk about how the curriculum is taught. Consider the organizational conflict that would arise from mandating that professors use more technology in their instruction or from elevating teaching to equal status as a criterion for gaining tenure. Such open conflict threatens organizational stability.

Hence, faculties search for ways of avoiding destructive intramural bat-tles. One way to do that is to divorce content from pedagogy. The dom-inant belief is that *what* is taught is far more important than *how* it is taught. Curricular reform, then, signals critics that some changes are underway while the fundamental structures, cultures, and processes—especially the balance between research and teaching—continue largely undisturbed.

None of this, of course, is meant to suggest that faculties act con-spiratorially or even intentionally to divert external criticism, avoid tack-ling tougher organizational issues, or create the illusion of reform. These outcomes, often unanticipated, are the consequences of shared beliefs in the elective system, departmental authority, faculty freedom, and the compatibility of research and teaching. As the previous chapter on Stan-ford and examples of other universities have shown, such beliefs and fac-ulty decisions about the official curriculum seldom revise pedagogy or reconcile underlying dilemmas of purpose and action in universities.

What I have argued, thus far, is that continual efforts to revise the official curriculum, regardless of faculty intentions, have created an insti-tutional tradition of reform complete with symbols and the common practice of improvised incrementalism. Both symbols and practice are means of coping with the enduring dilemmas of purpose in the univer-sity-college. These stubborn tensions inherent to the teaching and research imperatives within the university-college hybrid have made reform initiatives a routine faculty behavior. This tradition of reform per-mits each generation of professors to debate conflicting values in the curriculum, consider proposals for change, and then act modestly on questions. In taming reforms, faculties preserve their prerogatives and maintain continuity in practice. Institutionally, however, this tradition and practice depends on organizational forgetfulness.[42]

Perennial dilemmas arising from the history of the university-college generated tensions that needed to be reconciled by each generation of faculty. Faculty turnover and reluctance to consult the past strengthened organizational forgetfulness, thus preserving the institutional habit of reform and ad hoc incrementalism. Such habitual behavior provided comfort to faculty, students, alumni, and administrators since proposed reforms seized temporarily the attention of significant constituencies inside and outside the university, signaling that important issues were being considered and addressed without calling attention to the imbal-ance between research and teaching.

The reform tradition and improvised incrementalism also helped the larger public see that universities change, yet hew closely to what is expected of these resilient organizations. In universities adapting to the constant turmoil of a changing larger society while seeking high-status among rivals, this tradition of curricular reform, modest changes, divorce of teaching from subject matter, and organizational forgetfulness provides stability for presidents and professors to cope with enduring, irreconcilable dilemmas.

Here, then, is the argument and evidence to answer the question of how universities shrink reforms into modest changes. The typology of change and organizational, institutional, and political explanations for university adaptability make the point that ad hoc incrementalism, enclaving, and rhetorical traditions of reform reduce proposed fundamental changes to manageable proportions while sustaining institutional stability in core beliefs, structures, processes, and cultures.

A skeptic, however, could claim that the argument and evidence is pitched at the university level and the oft-cited pattern of internal variation may give the lie to the tidy generalizations that I have made about how the elective system, professorial autonomy, departmental powers, teaching, and advising all work toward strengthening the research imperative at Stanford. Many organizational and institutional theorists have pointed out that large, multifaceted universities such as Stanford are hardly tightly coupled in curriculum, teaching, advising, and research. Presidents and deans are limited in their reach into professors' labs and classrooms. Professorial and departmental autonomy linked to the elective system suggest much looseness in the institution that no amount of bureaucratic rules or plans for realignment could tighten. Entrepreneurial values and political logrolling among departments within bureaucratic organizations occasion incremental changes, even major reforms, elsewhere in these bottom-heavy, loosely connected organizations.[43]

For the statements that I make in this chapter to have rigor, they need to be tested against what goes on in specific settings within the university. What follows, then, are chapters on the Stanford history department (which bridges both the humanities and social sciences) and the medical school (embracing the life sciences) over the last century. By choosing two different large-university settings with contrasting subject matter and purposes—the history department is committed to both undergraduate and graduate education, while the School of Medicine, once a department but now a professional school, focuses on graduate education—I can find strengths and weaknesses to the claims that I have made about how the web of beliefs, traditions, structures, and processes work to preserve institutional stability at Stanford.

3

SCHOLAR-TEACHERS IN THE STANFORD HISTORY DEPARTMENT, 1891–1990

EPHRAIM DOUGLASS ADAMS climbed the academic ladder of assistant, associate, and full professor of European history at the University of Kansas between 1891 and 1902. In 1903, he accepted President David Starr Jordan's offer to become an associate professor of history at Stanford. Why would a full professor travel almost 2,000 miles for a lesser post at an institution barely over a decade old? At least one clue comes in a letter that Adams wrote 2 decades after he arrived at Stanford.

> When I came to Stanford University... from Kansas University, where under a populist regime I could be compelled to teach as much as 20 hours a week, I made it a point with... the [chair] and with President Jordan that I should never be called upon to teach more than 7 hours per week unless I voluntarily chose to do so. This was agreed to. ... I should be thus free to pursue my own work and writings and not give all my time merely to teaching.[1]

Adams, knowing well the inner conflict he faced over trying to do his research while negotiating a heavy teaching load at Kansas, found far more time at Stanford for archival work and writing. In his first 5 years at Stanford, he "merely" taught six courses a year (five lecture, one seminar), averaging 6 to 8 hours weekly. By then, Adams, who knew that writing a book was necessary for promotion, had published a monograph (1904) on late-18th-century British foreign policy. He was promoted to full professor in 1906 and appointed to the chair (then called *executive head*) of the history department in 1908. In 1909, he gave the "Albert Shaw Lectures in Diplomatic History" at Johns Hopkins University, which appeared the next year as *British Interests and Activities in Texas, 1838–1846*. His major archival work was completed in 1925 with the publication of the two-volume *Great Britain and the American Civil War*.[2]

As a teacher, according to one of his former students who recalled a lecture course that he had taken with Adams in the early 1920s, he did well.

> He stands out in my mind as a very engaging gentleman, rather small in stature, who lectured with machine-gun rapidity. His lectures were beautifully organized and delivered with extreme clarity. . . . He did, however, have a curious mannerism: He would remove his pince-nez glasses about 50 times in the course of the lecture while looking at his notes.[3]

Adams's first 7 years at Stanford were spent teaching European political history and British diplomatic relations. Not until 1909 did he switch to teaching U.S. history and American diplomatic history to sustain his deep interest in foreign relations between Britain and the United States during the Civil War. Until 1930, when he died, he taught introductory lecture courses on 19th century America and advanced lecture courses and seminars on U.S. diplomatic history.

For the two introductory U.S. history lecture courses ("1789–1848" and "1848 to Present"), enrollments before World War I were between 90 and 100 students. By the mid-1920s, Adams faced between 200 and 300 students in each of these courses. He had students sit in alphabetical order and took attendance (or graduate assistants did, if they were available). Exams and quizzes were given periodically, with a final exam administered at the end of the term. Students purchased an outline for each course, which included reading assignments, collateral readings, and brief notes on each lecture.[4]

Lecture titles for these introductory courses reveal a decided preference for politics, foreign affairs, and wars, although there were also lectures on immigration, slavery as an institution, the westward movement, American literature, industrialization, and other topics that a later generation of historians would call social and cultural history. For the 2 decades that Adams taught these survey courses to undergraduates, anywhere from two-thirds to three-quarters of the lecture titles remained largely the same each year between 1914 and 1928.[5]

As a scholar and teacher, Adams established the field of diplomatic history at Stanford. He worked closely during World War I with Herbert Hoover (who had become a member of the university's Board of Trustees) in gathering European documents that became the core archives for a subsequent Stanford library. He knew well the scholarly lineage within which he worked. Adams and his departmental colleagues, as he wrote, "adhere to the historical traditions regulated by the Ranke School, to seek to avoid personal bias in their courses." Such sought-for objectivity plunged Stanford history majors into painstaking analyses of primary sources to determine their accuracy.[6]

Yet Adams, as a scholar and teacher, like many of his contemporaries in university-college hybrids, pursued competing goals. He sought the Rankean ideal of objectivity—creating value-free knowledge—in his written scholarship. Each year, however, he taught hundreds of undergraduates largely innocent of "scientific history" to be active citizens— a clearly stated objective in the Stanford annual catalogue for the history department since 1917—and this was, if anything, a value-laden task.[7]

Why are these competing goals? The scholarly audience for history and one composed of beginning students differ dramatically. The latter audience is filled with future and current citizens who may profit from the historian's knowledge about the past—the moral "lessons" that Americans should heed when voting for the best candidates and making public policy. Teaching this audience demands clarity, moral commitment, and the students' engagement for the knowledge to be used well in the future. Writing for fellow scholars who believed at that time in value-free historical analysis calls for very different knowledge and skills in constructing and communicating accounts of the past. Two audiences, two duties. Is it the historian's moral duty through writing, teaching, and personal action to make better citizens? For Stanford undergraduates, the answer was yes. Yet historians were expected also to be faithful to their professional obligation as scholars who trained graduate students to be impartial and analytic. Within a university-college structure, historians were expected to do both seamlessly.

Those expectations aside, there was another conflict, one that Adams tried to reconcile early in his career by leaving the University of Kansas. As Carl Becker put it with characteristic clarity, "No doubt the truth shall make you free . . . but free to do what? To sit and contemplate the truth?" In short, obligations to civic advocacy and scholarly detachment were (and are) highly prized values that conflicted, for example, when historians wrote books for school children—Adams was working on a high school text before he died—or when historians decided what role they should perform during wartime insofar as their scholarly duties and displaying their patriotism were concerned. Adams's son served in France in World War I, and the Stanford professor supported wholeheartedly those patriotic historians who wrote and spoke for the allied war effort. These competing goals seldom surfaced in Adams's letters or public utterances, but the tensions existed within the department, especially at times of national crisis.[8]

Ephraim D. Adams, then, for almost 3 decades, was the star performer of the department. As a scholar-teacher, he had published books and articles and was admired for his thoroughness in the lecture hall by peers and students. He chaired the department for almost a decade and was active in the American Historical Association (AHA). In the first quarter of this century, he and his fellow historians also established departmental norms that continued for another half-century of publishing scholarship in national journals, attending to teaching duties, and changing departmental offerings to keep pace with new knowledge in the field.

Were Adams to have returned in the 1990s to the refurbished History Corner (originally built in 1903 and completely restored in 1980) that so nicely anchors the south side of the academic "Quad," he would surely have felt at home touching the marks left by the stonecutters' tools on the sandstone columns and seeing the richly appointed interior wooden trim and escalloped railings along the stairs. Were he to have also entered the 12 classrooms and 7 seminar rooms, he might swallow hard at the obvious differences in student (and faculty) dress and informal demeanor but would easily recognize familiar teaching practices. He might have expressed surprise over professors' lighter workload of lectures and seminars. But such changes would have probably pleased him.

Were he to have attended a departmental meeting, the mix of agenda items and issues, including the digressive conversation so common among academics, might have triggered fond memories of earlier gatherings. And were he to have listened carefully to the discussions of tenure and promotion linked to the all-important production of books and articles, he might have mused to himself how little things had changed since David Starr Jordan applied the same criteria.

Where Adams might have been startled (even if pleased) however, might well have been in the growth of the department, its strong national reputation, and its radically altered demographics and new specialties represented in the curriculum. It is to these changes over the last century in the history department that I now turn.[9]

THE HISTORY DEPARTMENT'S CURRICULUM AND TEACHING, 1891–1991

In organizing the official curriculum, Adams and his successors built strong departmental norms of professional autonomy to teach what they specialized in and design personal research agendas while providing service to the rest of the university by teaching hundreds of under-graduates. These departmental norms interacted with and were rein-forced by university norms that clearly prized scholarship in hiring, tenuring, and promoting faculty. Such expectations overshadowed those of individual historians' who tried to raise questions about the direction of the department and related issues of teaching quality and advising. In short, by the time Adams died, 4 decades after the university's found-ing, a departmental curriculum and culture favored doing research and publishing scholarship, paying much less collective attention to teach-ing and advising.

The Organization of the Official Curriculum

Four factors largely shaped the official history curriculum over the last century: university-wide course requirements that the history department adhered to (e.g., "Problems of Citizenship," "Western Civi-lization" courses); research specialties that historians brought to Stan-ford when they were appointed (e.g., diplomatic history, Latin-American history); fields of study common in other research-driven universities to which Stanford compared itself (e.g., Harvard, Johns Hopkins, Yale); and Stanford's location on the West Coast.[10]

History was one of the original 15 departments that Jordan staffed when Leland and Jane Stanford greeted students, parents, and faculty on that sunlit October afternoon in 1891. Professor George B. Howard (who resigned in 1900 protesting Jordan's firing of another professor) offered seven courses covering ancient Greece and Rome, U.S. history from the colonial period to the present, and the French Revolution, and a seminar (or "seminary" as it was then called) investigating special top-ics about American institutions.[11]

When Adams arrived in 1902, the department had grown to five fac-ulty (two professors, two associate professors—of whom Adams was one—and one instructor). They offered 36 courses, which were catego-rized by the complexity of the content (introductory and advanced) and the customary organization of historical study at the turn of century: ancient history, Europe in the middle ages, English history, modern Euro-pean history, U.S. history, and graduate-level courses in the nature of his-torical study. Also, professors offered seminars in their specialties. Because of Stanford's location on the West Coast, Assistant Professor Mary Sheldon Barnes, who taught from 1892 to 1897, had also intro-duced courses on the westward movement and Pacific Slope history, which were still taught when Adams arrived.[12]

In 1929–1930, the last year that Adams served, there were nine history faculty (six professors, one associate professor, and two assistant professors) and additional visiting professors who offered 61 courses reorganized into introductory and advanced lecture courses, and introductory and advanced seminars. Professors no longer offered ancient history—it had been taken over by the classics department—but the customary divisions of medieval, renaissance, modern European, English, French Revolution, and U.S. history remained intact. The specialized subject matter that professors brought with them was converted into advanced lecture courses and almost 20 seminars.[13]

The steady growth in departmental enrollments, history faculty, course offerings, and specialties, though interrupted and slowed by wars and depressions, continued into the 1990s (see Figures 3.1 and 3.2). As faculty joined the department, specialization in course offerings increased. Americanists and Europeanists dominated the department, although, by the 1920s, Stanford historians also taught courses on the Far East and Near East (as both areas were then labeled) and Latin America and Canada. In the 1940s, Stanford history courses covered seven areas of the world. In the 1960s, the Middle East was added and the Far East was renamed East Asia. The first course on Africa was offered in the mid-1960s. Like other universities, Stanford's history department expanded its official offerings as national and international events impacted curricula in higher education.[14]

The growth of specialties became particularly evident in the mid-1940s, when the department formally offered for the first time doctoral work in 5 areas of history: European, British, United States, Latin American, and the Far East. By the mid-1960s, the faculty had grown sufficiently to offer specialized doctorates in 9 major fields (now expanded to Africa, Russia and Central Europe, and the Near and Middle East). A decade later, major fields for doctoral work had increased to 11 (Central Europe had become a separate field called Eastern Europe; East Asia was subdivided into two fields of study before and after 1600); in 1994, there were 12 (Jewish history had been added).[15]

As with other universities, growth in student enrollments, course offerings, and specialties added more professors to the department. The faculty had grown but changed little from its initial composition of a largely white Protestant male department.[16]

The first female faculty member (I have excluded instructors or lecturers) was Assistant Professor Mary Sheldon Barnes (1892–1897). Not until the mid-1970s did four female assistant professors join the faculty—one female associate professor had been appointed in 1956 but she stayed for only one year. The 1960s and 1970s also were years that

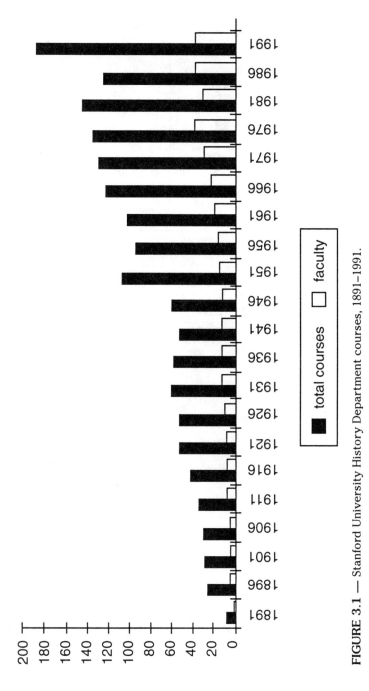

FIGURE 3.1 — Stanford University History Department courses, 1891–1991.

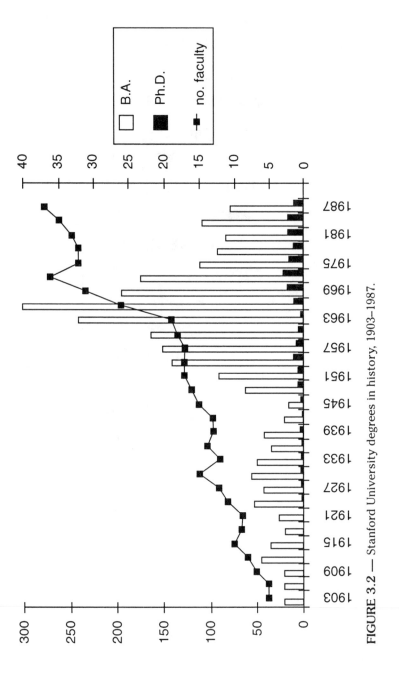

FIGURE 3.2 — Stanford University degrees in history, 1903–1987.

Jewish (in 1966), black (1970), and Hispanic (1974) junior faculty joined the department. By 1991, of 34 faculty members in the department, 6 were female, about 12 were Jewish, 2 were black, and 1 was Hispanic. Compared to the stark uniformity in background among Stanford historians for the first 70 years of the department, its composition had changed substantially in the last 3 decades.[17]

Teaching

Over the decades, the faculty teaching load fell from a norm of six courses to five, and then to the present four, usually split evenly between lecture courses and seminars. Figure 3.3 of Americanist historians' workload over the last century suggests the decline in numbers of courses and weekly hours in class.[18]

Lecturing to large groups of undergraduate students continued as the dominant teaching practice for introductory courses until the mid-1960s. Although small-group instruction through seminars had been introduced in Stanford's inaugural year for a few graduate students, not until 1917 did seminars become institutionalized for undergraduates. In that year, a significant move signaled the increased influence of those professors who sought to inject specialized historical inquiry into undergraduate work: The department required history majors to take seminars. Juniors took the Introductory Seminar, focusing on the research methods that historians use, analyzing primary and secondary sources, taking notes, and annotating sources while writing articles and monographs. Seniors were required to take a seminar geared to producing a research paper. As one former student recalled,

> We learned to take notes, not in notebooks, but on four-by-six note cards or slips that could be filed under proper headings. ... We learned how to provide footnoted support for information that might be challenged, complete with the "garland of ibids."

What was most important, he said, was that "we learned to detect propaganda, forgeries, hoaxes, exaggeration, misstatements, and other pitfalls that await the amateur historian." In his Senior Seminar, he wrote a 65-page paper on "Republican Presidential Campaign Expenditures, 1920."[19]

One retired professor recalled how he taught these seminars:

> For the junior seminar, every week they had a problem to work on. The idea was to get them acquainted with ... standard works. Individuals had topics to report on each week. For the senior seminar, I would make up a list of projects. ... Students would choose a topic. The idea was to

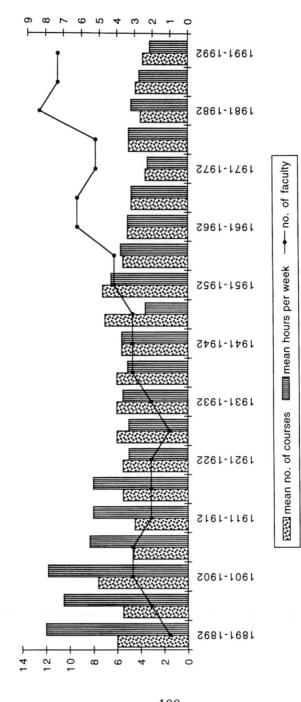

FIGURE 3.3 — Americanists' workload in the Stanford University History Department, 1891–1992

mean no. of courses   mean hours per week   no. of faculty

have students make use of what they learned in the Introductory Seminar. They were expected to prepare a publishable paper.[20]

In the mid-1950s, the department abolished the Introductory and Senior Seminars. Replacing them were the Basic Seminar that all majors had to take and the Advanced Seminar open only to majors with a *B* average who wanted to enter the newly created Honors Program in history. The aim of the Basic Seminar was, in the words of Gordon Wright in 1961, "to give to a dozen majors who won't be professional historians the kind of introduction to problems and methods of research and writing that will enable them to understand better how history is written and to read history books more intelligently." As Executive Head Thomas A. Bailey put it to his dean, "We felt that it is better to give our professional training to exceptional students rather than to the run-of-the-mill students."[21]

Colloquia, or small-group courses aimed at analysis and discussion of secondary sources, replaced the Basic Seminar in the mid-1960s and were introduced for doctoral students also. These small-group courses, according to Richard Lyman, were different than seminars in that they focused entirely upon specialized readings. Students wrote short papers and met at the professor's home to discuss the articles and books. For doctoral colloquia, he instituted mini-orals in the last weeks of the quarter to prepare students for oral examinations, since he felt that it was unfair and counterproductive to have students' first exposure to an oral exam (Ph.D. orals) carry such high stakes.[22]

In 1984, the Introductory Seminar required of all majors was reestablished, again reasserting the insistent impulse within the department to prepare juniors and seniors for graduate work. The purpose of this required course was to

> introduce undergraduate majors...into the historian's workshop and provide first-hand experience in interpreting documents, in constructing a coherent story from them, in interpreting their larger implications, and in discovering why it is possible to agree on the facts but to disagree on what they mean.[23]

For seminars and lecture courses over the century, few technological aids entered the historian's lecture hall or seminar room. While departmental reports note that maps, opaque projectors, spectroscopes (for slides), movie projectors, and other teaching tools were available to the faculty in the early decades of this century, only occasionally did professors integrate these machines (including film projectors, television, and the computer) into their lectures and seminar discussions.

Campus publications highlighted a few members of the department for their efforts to integrate information technologies into their teaching. In the mid-1990s, the department did appoint a technology aide to help faculty use computers for instruction. What little evidence is available, however, seems to support the conclusion of one member of the department when he said, "the slowness that [technology] penetrates this environment is really quite remarkable."[24]

Even if technological tools were infrequently used by historians in teaching their courses, the faculty was thoroughly committed to small-group instruction through elective seminars and colloquia. Since the late 1950s, the steady growth in these courses, reflecting professorial research interests, rose to even exceed the lecture courses offered to undergraduates (see Figure 3.4).[25]

The pattern of increased offerings of seminars—strengthened considerably by the proliferation of historical specialties and subspecialties, or, to put it more bluntly, the penetration of graduate school norms into the undergraduate curriculum—also encompassed other universities. That the surge in seminars occurred at different times in public universities than at Stanford and that lectures (which are less costly to offer) still dominated course catalogs suggest possible differences in institutional histories and public and private resources; these differences, however, cannot mask the steady increase in seminars at other universities in the 1960s and 1970s (see Figures 3.5–3.7).[26]

The sharp increase in small-group courses at Stanford in the 1950s and 1960s can be attributed to various factors. Some members of the department saw increased small-group work as a faculty initiative: "Such individualized methods," a 1953 report asserts, "constitute our effort to break the lock step in education, to achieve the advantages of a tutorial system." Other explanations point to possible trickle-down effects of university commissions (1954–1956 and 1968). These faculty-dominated groups, including members of the history department, recommended reductions in lecture courses and increases in small-group seminars, especially for undergraduates. Such recommendations were both noted and, probably to some degree, heeded. The history department increased colloquia and seminars during and after these reports were issued at the times when the university reduced the number of courses professors were required to teach. David Kennedy recalled that in his first year on the faculty, he heard at a meeting like a "bolt out of the blue that the dean said we should teach five courses a year [rather than six], and we did."[27]

Of notable influence was the growing linkage between a university's national reputation and graduate research, published scholarship, and

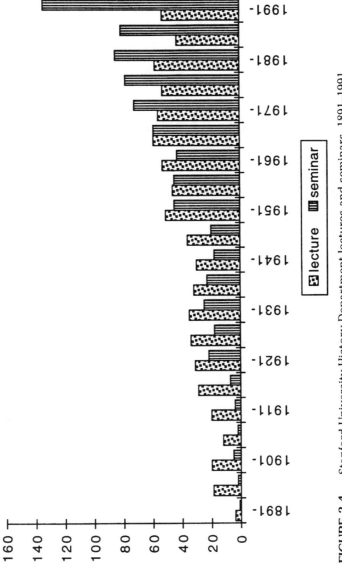

FIGURE 3.4 — Stanford University History Department lectures and seminars, 1891–1991.

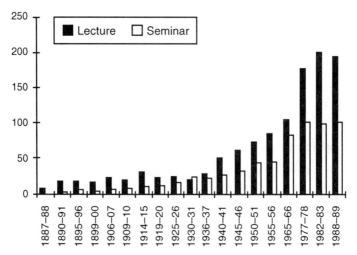

FIGURE 3.5 — University of Michigan lectures and seminars, 1887–1989.

the training of doctoral students. Once that linkage was forged in the minds of university boards of trustees and their presidents (and it occurred at Stanford in the 1950s under President Sterling and Provost Terman), the university's commitment to the elective principle wedded to the specialization naturally occurring within the research enterprise led professors to offer courses that were closely related to their inves-

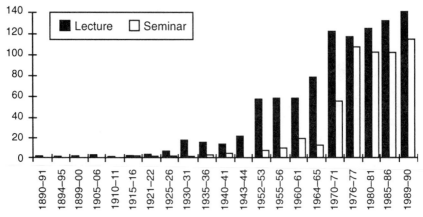

FIGURE 3.6 — University of Virginia lectures and seminars, 1890–1990.

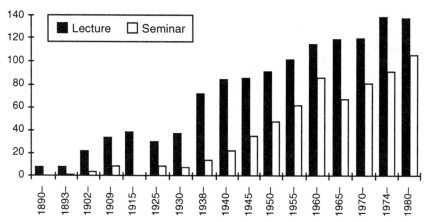

FIGURE 3.7 — University of California at Berkeley lectures and seminars, 1890–1980.

tigative work. Consider further the feverish acquisition of star-quality professors (e.g., attracting Europeanist Gordon Craig from Princeton in 1960 and Americanist David Potter from Yale in 1961) who came to Stanford with promises of "light" teaching loads and the chance to offer advanced seminars in their fields. These factors, more than a unilateral effort by the history department to break the "lock step" of instruction, may help to explain the dramatic increases in seminar offerings after 1950, as historians' teaching loads shrunk.[28]

Yet increases in small-group offerings failed to curb criticism about another form of teaching: advising. Beginning in the late 1950s and continuing since has been student concern (among both history majors and graduate students) over faculty availability.

Advising

With the university review of the entire undergraduate program in the mid-1950s, the history department examined how it compared with other departments in preparing majors. A three-man faculty committee investigated the requirements for the history major, the academic standing of its majors and faculty advising load compared to other departments, and, for the first time that I could find, a formal inquiry into student opinion of advising and access to faculty.[29]

History faculty had the largest number of majors among the 23 departments in the School of Humanities and Sciences; the ratio of professors to advisees was 1:18; the next closest were political science with 1:15 and biological science with 1:10. The lowest ratios were in classics, anthropology, music, and mathematics, where each professor was assigned 1–3 students each.[30]

Hence, it comes as little surprise that when juniors and seniors returned questionnaires about advising, instruction, and accessibility to the faculty (21 were returned; no mention was made of what percentage response this represented), replies about advising were largely negative. Of the 19 students who responded to this question, 12 complained about infrequent and perfunctory contact with the adviser and "resentment at being only one of a fairly large number of advisees." They wanted more frequent contact. Although student responses were highly favorable to seminars and small advanced lecture courses, majors pointed out the difficulty of getting to faculty. One student said: "The greatest weakness is the generally cold, far away attitude of the professor to his students." In light of these strong statements, it may be a surprise that the three-man committee recommended eight minor improvements with the only mention of advising being that faculty should have more secretarial assistance.[31]

A decade later, another survey was sent out from the department and the History Undergraduate Student Association to 107 majors (and 5 nonmajors). On the matter of advising, almost one-third responded that they "never" spoke with their adviser and well over half marked that they "seldom" met with their adviser. Just over 10% checked "often." When asked if they "find it easy to speak with professors," 52% answered "no." When offered reasons for the "no," 53% chose either faculty "attitudes" or "inaccessibility" (47% also responded that it was their [i.e., students'] lack of time and attitude that accounted for avoiding their professors). When asked if students knew a professor in the department "well enough to get a letter of recommendation," only 43% said "yes."[32]

In 1990, to prepare for a major review of the history curriculum, the department sent out over 1,000 questionnaires to undergraduate alumni who had graduated in 1970, 1978, and every year since 1981. The return rate was 40%. Particular questions concentrated on faculty-student relationships. On a 10-point scale, faculty regarded students marking an 8, 9, or 10 as satisfactory. Just under half (49%) marked that they were satisfied with their advisers (23% had given it a 1 or 2, which indicated a "poor" relationship). Regarding their general relationship with faculty, 52% said that they were satisfied.[33]

The data are fragmentary, yet isolated bits converge on the same point: A substantial number of history majors and alumni had strong reservations about the quality of advising and accessibility of faculty, similar to their counterparts in many other departments across campus as described in Chapter 1.

Intersection: Curricular Expansion, Teaching, Advising, and the Research Imperative

The steady growth in elective courses, faculty, specialities, and seminars at Stanford and similar institutions reflect, of course, the history faculty's reconciliation of the tensions within the university-college hybrid that they faced daily. They fashioned an intuitive compromise from conflicting values by primarily pursuing their research agendas and preparing doctoral students while secondarily teaching and advising undergraduates. Such intertwined commitments were so deeply embedded in the basic structures and belief systems within American university life that such commonplaces as the Ph.D. degree, faculty rank, and departments masked the steady institutionalization of the research imperative and the marginalizing of undergraduate teaching. Over the decades, as in other departments and other universities, the history department professionalized undergraduate curricula with seminars, reduced faculty course loads, and mandated fewer teaching hours per week.

Other obvious indicators of the institutionalization of the research imperative over the teaching imperative are the sheer growth, beginning in the 1950s, in graduate students seeking doctorates and university support for doctoral work through fellowships and teaching assistantships. Decades earlier, hiring graduate assistants to help professors in large lecture courses for grading exams and reading papers had become accepted practice. For example, in a letter to a former student in 1932, Thomas Bailey wrote that he is "not burdened with classroom duties, for I have only a 4-hour teaching load this quarter, with plenty of assistants to handle the papers." Such markers explicitly signal the emerging priority given to research over teaching within Stanford's history department.[34]

Less obvious markers of the primacy of investigation over teaching was the common practice, beginning in the 1950s, of using a job offer from another university as a bargaining chip to secure a higher salary and less teaching time. Such tactics also signaled to junior faculty that successful teaching was secondary.

In 1948, Thomas A. Bailey sent a telegram to Edgar E. Robinson (his executive head) of an offer that he received from the president of the University of Maryland offering him a position to head their department of history for $9,000 a year. In the margin of the telegram, Bailey noted that he was not interested, but that Berkeley, in another offer he had received, would go to $10,000. If Berkeley does, "I shall have to give it very earnest consideration." An undated note in Bailey's files summarized his subsequent conversation with a Stanford vice-president that he would receive $12,000 to exceed Berkeley's offer. Moreover, Bailey would get another office in the library to do research, be in line for an endowed chair after Robinson retired, and be relieved of university and department administrative work, and, finally, there would be no increase in his teaching load.[35]

Another clue to the departmental preference for advanced work and individual research agendas over teaching comes from the shared, but seldom expressed, institutional attitudes and beliefs that often shaped professors' classroom practices. The autonomy of the researcher, for example, to investigate whatever he or she chose was easily transformed into professorial freedom to teach what and how he or she pleased. If the laboratory was the place that bench science could be practiced without intellectual constraint, then the lecture hall and seminar—especially after the principle of academic freedom became accepted by universities— were settings for the professor to display knowledge and teach in ways that he or she deemed proper.[36]

In 1903, to cite one example of this freedom, Max Farrand— then executive head of the department—wrote to Henry Cannon, who had been just appointed as an assistant professor, about what to expect at Stanford. "In the first place," Farrand said, "you will be absolutely free to conduct your courses as you see fit." Farrand did say that he would visit Cannon's classes and even offer suggestions but that Cannon had the choice of accepting them or not. "Results are what we want," he told Cannon, "and I believe the best results can be obtained by allowing each man to work in accordance with his own ideas." Over a half-century later, Professor Thomas A. Bailey wrote a colleague at the University of Pennsylvania that "here at Stanford, the instructor is king in his own classroom."[37]

Yet departmental norms about teaching emerged also from the crucible of faculty's past experiences as history majors and doctoral students listening to lectures, taking notes in archives, and drafting articles for publication. As apprentice historians, they learned that the central task of teaching was to convey acquired knowledge to the uninformed through lecturing.

Certainly, historians also led seminars for advanced students. In these settings, the skills of questioning, listening, and guiding discussions were acknowledged as important and quite different from lecturing. Among the faculty, many professors recognized that some colleagues were better with small groups than with 500 or more students in the Memorial Auditorium. But it was lecturing to hundreds of undergraduates that was a public performance and one that required much time to prepare. Such performances were viewed as an ineffable combination of personal presence, organization, and grasp of content intertwined with a pleasing voice and a capacity to nicely turn a phrase. This braid of qualities was closer, many faculty believed, to a genetic gift than a set of skills that could be learned easily.

Embedded in such views was the belief that teaching was not a science like biology—it was a task anyone of modest intelligence could do as long as they had a grip on the knowledge that they were supposed to convey to others. That teaching was also the primary work of those who labored in public schools, people with far less formal education than professors possessed, and, furthermore, that it had become an occupation dominated by females (by 1900) may well have added a social odor to the work from which professors sought to distance themselves.

Such views that teaching is basically knowing one's subject, personal traits, and trial-and-error were rarely expressed publicly, but they can be rescued from private letters. For example, in 1917, in a letter to President Ray Lyman Wilbur, Adams recommended reappointment of Henry Cannon on the grounds of his scholarship—he had just completed a book—and on teaching. "Professor Cannon is not exceptional," Adams wrote, "yet he is distinctly good. He does not appeal to all students. This, I think, is the result of a personality which is appreciated by some, but not by others." Stanford historian E. M. Hulme wrote to Thomas Bailey recommending one of his graduate students for a post at the University of Hawaii where Bailey was then teaching: "He has never taught but he is a fine looking, self-possessed young fellow. He has a good deal of common sense. I feel sure he will get along very well in the classroom." Such expression of societal and institutional attitudes linked to the freedom of professors to do as they saw fit in their classrooms left the department in these decades decidedly ambivalent about teaching.[38]

The private letters of these historians and the public pronouncements of President Jordan extolled the importance of teaching (i.e., lecturing in an organized, enthusiastic, and clear fashion sufficient to attract students to class and get them to listen, take notes, and do well on exams). Yet tenure and promotion went to those, as Jordan so often repeated, who had books and articles published. The history department was no exception to the rule. Max Farrand wrote to Ephraim Adams in 1908 that he could not recommend a colleague for promotion to full professor because he "could not endorse his request on the basis of scholarship." E. E. Slosson, visiting Stanford at about the time Adams began serving as executive head, interviewed students and faculty and said, "Skill as a teacher, helpful personality, executive ability, or long service, though taken into consideration, are not held to justify promotion above the grade of assistant professor without thorough and therefore productive scholarship." In an imperfect world where both teaching and research were prized but limited time was available to do both well, Stanford, like its sister institutions, invariably chose scholarship first.[39]

MANAGING THE CONFLICTING PURPOSES
WITHIN THE HISTORY DEPARTMENT

Clearly, the department had grown in students, faculty, course offerings, and specialties since Ephraim Adams taught at Stanford in the decades before and after World War I. But toward what ends was the history department moving? Most undergraduates who took history courses then and since were uninterested in becoming academic historians. Most history majors pursued diverse careers in business, law, and medicine when they graduated. So the department offered courses that served the university's larger aim of providing a liberal education to undergraduates. Billets-for-service courses was a *quid pro quo* that seemingly satisfied both the department and the university administration. But for those students who wished to major in the discipline or secure an advanced degree in history, what did the department seek?[40]

Preparing Generalists and Specialists

By 1918, Adams and his colleagues had begun to standardize the history major by specifying in the catalogue a required course in "Historical Training," the number of units for the major (45 of 180 needed for graduation), which seminars had to be taken, and additional requirements for minors in other departments. Still acknowledging the service function of teaching undergraduates and the preparation of those seeking to become secondary school history teachers, Adams concisely laid out two purposes for students taking history courses. For the nonhistory major, "the underlying principle of these courses is that they shall be useful, not in the utilitarian sense, but in the sense that they... equip the student for his duties as a citizen." For the history major, the purpose was to become a specialist: "The curriculum... is designed to familiarize the student with the fundamentals and methods of the chief branches of knowledge, and with the methods of historical science."[41]

These competing generalist and specialist purposes of presenting history to undergraduates—surrogates for the conflicting values within the university-college structure—have continued as Stanford launched and completed major curricular changes in 1954–1956, 1968, and 1994. Thus, the citizen-building purpose of taking history in *Courses, Degrees, and Information, 1994–1995* is the same for nonmajors as it was in 1918, except for minor word changes. For majors, the language in 1994–1995 had changed but the apprentice-historian purpose remained the same: "Majors are required to complete an introductory seminar exposing students to the practices of the historian and an undergraduate research seminar in which the student conducts research." The history major has become increasingly oriented to training undergraduates to do research.[42]

As the requirements for undergraduate history majors became increasingly geared toward preparing students for a professional career, the tensions between generalist and specialist values also became apparent for professors. First, there was the strain over time spent doing research and teaching introductory and advanced courses, and, second, there was growing departmental nervousness over preparing doctoral students to teach.

Teaching Introductory and Advanced Courses

Historians discover new facts in archives. They reinterpret existing facts and construct new meanings through explanatory frameworks or narratives (or both) for fellow scholars. They do this through the primary medium of doing research for books and articles. Through publishing their scholarship, historians speak to one another in their field; they are a professional community dedicated to discovering and interpreting the past.

Scholarly writing often collides with their duties of teaching introductory courses to undergraduates. Presenting the central issues, concepts, and interpretations of scholars to large groups of students is a complex pedagogical task that requires historians to determine what can be squeezed into 11 or 18 weeks of teaching and how the content should be presented engagingly to a largely uninformed audience, and to have some degree of awareness about who their students are.

Formidable as the task is, academic historians traditionally have approached such an introductory course through weekly lectures, discussion sections led by graduate assistants, textbooks supplemented by readings in primary and secondary sources chosen by the professor, and periodic examinations. This familiar organization of large-group lecture courses, however, reduces historical knowledge to the barest minimum, softened considerably by those personable and well-organized professors who thoroughly engage their audiences. Teaching introductory courses as ventures in communicating basic concepts in a field becomes synonymous with lecturing.[43]

It is uncommon for historians to recognize publicly these differences between teaching introductory history courses and the essential academic duty of writing for other scholars. David Kennedy, for example, noted that lectures are closer to a "cartoon than [to] a full-length portrait." Department head Edgar E. Robinson openly acknowledged the split between teaching undergraduates history and performing scholarly duties. "The professional historian," he wrote in 1947, "is a research specialist rather than a teacher." Moreover, "the historian 'teaches' history as the physician 'practices' medicine, yet in most instances the historian has not *thought* of teaching as the physician has . . . [of] practice." Robinson's recognition that the act of teaching needs to be examined carefully was unusual for his department and, I might add, for faculty across the university.[44]

Elsewhere, historian Forrest McDonald brought this cleavage down to specific terms in spelling out these differences in teaching and writing history:

> In the first place, most of us realize that what we teach in the classroom is not and cannot be an account of "history as it actually happened." As for myself, in a semester, after holidays, quizzes, and other such things are allowed for, I have the opportunity to deliver about 38 lectures in a given course, and I can expect my students to read roughly 15 books or the equivalent [for courses covering decades or almost a century]. . . . Under such circumstances, it is absurd to deceive ourselves into believing that we can convey any real knowledge of what has happened in the human past. . . .

> [W]e find it valid, useful, and necessary to resort to various devices in the classroom which would not be tolerable in our writings. We oversimplify; we exaggerate; we depend upon secondary sources of questionable reliability; we attempt to stimulate our students by stating as fact theories we have not verified and have no intention of even investigating; . . . we even challenge them occasionally by advancing as fact statements which we know to be false. In the classroom, I repeat, these are perfectly legitimate devices.

> But when the class is over such devices must be left behind, and that is not always easy; indeed, the teacher-historian's most dangerous and insidious occupational peril is the tendency to confuse and intermix the functions and methods of the teacher with those of the historian.

In short, the pedagogy for introductory courses differs considerably from what historians do as scholars.[45]

Teaching advanced seminars, however, comes closest to preparing apprentice historians for the scholarly work that they will be expected to do once they become professors. For the most part, professors organized seminars in their specialties to help students become thoroughly familiar with the historiography of the topic by doing research in libraries and archives on the question that they have posed, and by presenting their work for scrutiny from fellow-students and the professor. Advanced seminars began the process of scholarly work that doctoral students would do once they graduated and became professors. Teaching a small-group course in the intricacies of historical research, analysis, interpretation, writing, and presentation created a very different set of pedagogical tasks than teaching an introductory course or doing one's own scholarly work. These fundamental differences between doing research, writing, and teaching—the central academic work of historians—and the complex pedagogical decisions that have to be made when teaching introductory and advanced courses have remained largely unexamined issues within the department.[46]

Preparing Doctoral Students to Teach

For most graduate students, the point of securing the doctorate in history is to become a professor. Professors have to teach. Is part of the graduate training of a historian then to include formal preparation for teaching in colleges and universities? Despite increasing numbers of doctoral students since the 1950s, the history department has remained ambivalent about its answer.[47]

In 1948, Edgar E. Robinson offered a new elective for graduate students called "Historical Writing," a course on the study of materials used in teaching American history. The elective disappeared after he retired in 1952. In 1967–1968, when the department overhauled its requirements, the course "Methods of Teaching History" was required of doctoral students. It could be given by the student's adviser or someone else designated by the adviser. For students who had served as teaching assistants (TAs), their experience could be offered in place of the requirement. In 1970, the department required each candidate for the degree to teach undergraduates for one quarter, stipulating that such a course must consist of leading two weekly discussion sections. Five years later, the requirement was raised to two quarters of teaching; in 1984, faculty increased it to three and then, in 1993, to four quarters of teaching. Finally, in 1993, the department, assisted by a private foundation grant, offered a voluntary workshop for Ph.D. students on the philosophical and methodological issues in university teaching. The workshop would deal with "recent trends and innovations in historical pedagogy" but also with "practical matters."[48]

Such a bald recounting makes clear departmental ambivalence about the importance of preparing its Ph.D.'s for the craft of teaching. The need to provide help to embryonic professors was strengthened considerably by university pressure for more small-group courses and undergraduates' desire for more contact with faculty.

Yet there were strong counterforces within the department opposed to satisfying student concerns, university pressures, and professors who were passionate about teaching. First, interviews with past and present Stanford historians suggest weak norms for discussing the quality and performance of teaching duties at departmental meetings. What discussions occurred did so informally between colleagues and among professors and their TAs. Visiting other colleagues as they taught and even team-teaching were isolated events. Second, allocating more professorial time to helping Ph.D.'s to learn how to teach would have subtracted from time spent on their research agendas and other teaching responsibilities. Moreover, the widely shared institutional belief that teaching can be learned by teaching itself undercut formal efforts to introduce doctoral students to teaching. What help the doctoral students did receive occurred accidentally as a result of an adviser or friendly professor who was deeply interested in the art of teaching, from trial-and-error in teaching sections and lecturing, and from peers. Such university norms and widespread beliefs interacted with the disciplinary ethos of history (individual scholars work alone to produce monographs) to produce a weak teaching culture in the department.[49]

Not until the early 1990s was there a formal departmental effort to prepare doctoral candidates for their teaching responsibilities. Professor Richard Roberts wrote that before 1990, "there was little attempt to structure the way students learned how to teach in the discipline." Since then, the department has introduced a voluntary three-quarter sequence in which doctoral students in their 1st year can take the workshop described above; in their 2nd year, they prepare for their teaching by taking part in an all-day workshop run by veteran TAs on such matters as delivering effective lectures, preparing exams, and leading discussions. In the 3rd year, there is a seminar to help history TAs prepare a syllabus for the Introductory Seminar that they will be teaching.[50]

None of the foregoing facts about departmental ambivalence toward graduate students being prepared for their future teaching responsibilities should obscure the individual professors' passion for teaching or efforts to improve lectures and seminars. Nor should the collective pride that faculty have taken in colleagues who have received awards for teaching over the years go unnoted. For example, department head David Kennedy wrote to current students and alumni in 1993 that "in the last 2 decades, fully 13 members of our faculty have been recognized with the Dean's Award for Distinguished Teaching," and he went on to note those colleagues who had received other university-wide honors for their teaching and research.[51]

The gap between rhetoric over the importance of teaching and the preparation of Ph.D.'s to teach had begun to close by the early 1990s, but a weak teaching culture merged with unvarnished university and departmental policies and norms that openly favored the practice of scholarship.

These cross-cutting purposes of doing historical research and producing scholarly work while teaching undergraduate courses in a university committed to both undergraduate and graduate education were deeply embedded value-conflicts that the department and each generation of Stanford historians endured, yet seldom explicitly faced, during the century. Tensions arising from these conflicts rose and fell within a department dependent upon the university for allocation of faculty billets to teach undergraduates; so, too, did conflicts reside in each professor seeking tenure and promotion, who had to juggle the multiple responsibilities of publishing, teaching, and providing service both to the university and the discipline.

What became increasingly clear over time, however, was how the university's institutionalization of the research imperative wedded to the department's disciplinary ethos of individually crafted scholarship, faculty autonomy, and weak teaching culture tilted the history department toward specialization and graduate education. The evidence is unmistakable: reductions in the number of courses to be taught and hours spent teaching and advising, the providing of sabbaticals, the expansion of graduate norms for research downward into departmental mandates for undergraduate majors, and the incentives for tenure and promotion in publishing books and articles. All of these institutional beliefs, structures, and norms made for a strong, individualistic research culture that retarded efforts of those historians interested in improving teaching across the department for both professors and doctoral students.

From this persistent conflict in the department's purposes, there also derived the core professional dilemma: How can teaching and writing history be juggled sufficiently to do both well? Each generation of historians at Stanford and its sister institutions wrestled with these questions openly or covertly in arriving at their answers. What the earliest generations did at Stanford, however, was to construct durable answers to the questions that have been refashioned to fit subsequent decades, but have largely kept its essential features undisturbed.[52]

SETTING THE MOLD: SCHOLAR-TEACHERS OR TEACHER-SCHOLARS

The first generation of Stanford historians believed in history as a science and in a pedagogy consistent with this notion. The phrase "historical science" that appears in the department's description of itself in the 1918 *Register* is an outward sign of that inner commitment to a value-free history. The idea of a "scientific historian"—the phrase remained in the annual catalogue until 1945— was commonly used among peers across the country in the waning years of the 19th century and continued through World War I at Stanford, although it was to be challenged by the generation that followed Ephraim Adams.

The first historians to hold positions in universities across the country saw history largely as an enterprise of uncovering facts through exhaustive archival research, publishing their scholarship, and teaching civic lessons to undergraduates, public school students, and the larger public. As scientific historians, they saw narratives written by amateur historians about kings and their courts as merely vivid stories filled with romantic flights of language. Scientific historians sought a systematic inquiry into the past and compiled monographs drawn from primary sources. From these many, often tiny, microsplinters of the past, which university-based scholars systematically mined from archives, historians would then construct a macroedifice of truth that could be used by academic peers and students.[53]

These university-based historians also believed that a scientific pedagogy must accompany the new scientific history. While later generations of historians largely divorced the act of teaching from their research and writing, seldom discussing the connections, many of these professors were passionate about pedagogy.[54]

According to contemporaries and subsequent scholars who have written about this generation of historians, interpretive lectures, use of multiple sources, essay exams, and the seminar slowly replaced the pedagogy dominant in post–Civil War colleges, such as informational lectures, the use of a single textbook, formal recitations, and tests calling for displays of historical facts. While there was much contention over which methods could be used best with graduate students rather than undergraduates, to these historians content and instruction were inseparable.[55]

With history viewed as a science, novices could now learn how historical investigation was done by listening to experts lecture. Students used a research library containing detailed maps, photos, and original sources to examine evidence and reach measured conclusions in essay exams and research papers.

Beginning in 1900, every Stanford history major had to register with a professor to take 1 hour each week of work in methods of historical investigation. In 1906, majors had to take the "Historical Training" course, which included document analysis, taking notes from archival sources, and becoming familiar with standard bibliographies in the field. With the establishment of Introductory Seminars in 1917 majors took a course called "Historical Method," which concentrated on the reading, studying, and writing of history.[56]

One common teaching task was determining how much their students had learned from lectures, recitations, and library reading. Usually, examinations asked students to accurately render the facts that had been covered by professors in lectures and assigned texts. For example, Stanford's Arley Show, an advocate of scientific history who was deeply interested in the craft of teaching, asked students in 1897 to answer these questions on medieval history:

1. (a) At what point in the period covered by the year's work would you say the distinctively *medieval* [original emphasis] type of civilization begin to show itself? (b) By what criteria do you judge in making your answers? . . .

3. Did European society make any distinct progress during the first 8 centuries of the Christian era? Discuss.

The remainder of the exam asked students to list the five most important dates in Frankish history and to give reasons for their answers.[57]

As lectures and exams slowly changed, so did the German import of the research seminar,[58] a keystone to graduate history training for this first generation of professional historians and for subsequent ones. The seminar became the laboratory—analogous to physical and life scientists working at the bench—for plumbing the past's mysteries; the required seminar monograph was to produce new knowledge of the past.

Yet among these professors who lectured and led seminars were important distinctions in their attitudes toward teaching and scholarship. Most historians emphasized the production of accurate accounts of the past and believed that teaching, while important, was at best a handmaiden to research and at worst a set of practices learned early without much technical expertise and connection to scholarship. Their teaching was driven by scholarly ends. Others stressed the pedagogical complexity of teaching history and inquired into how students learned the subject. The latter group of professors stressed methodological skills in doing historical research that had to be learned *while* the content was being taught.

At Stanford, Ephraim Douglass Adams typified the scholar-teacher model of the scientific historian oriented toward academic peers and graduate students as a primary audience for teaching and publishing. Mary Sheldon Barnes and Edgar E. Robinson illustrated the model of teacher-scholar, professors who prized pedagogy and were oriented to a primary audience of undergraduates who learned about history and thinking as citizens by working with original documents. Although strain over satisfying competing values occasionally surfaced, the vocabulary of dilemmas and conflicting choices were absent from archival sources. Where appropriate, I will offer indicators and clues to infer that tensions over being a teacher-scholar or scholar-teacher were evident. The careers of Mary Sheldon Barnes and Edgar E. Robinson offer hints of these deeper, masked strains.[59]

Barnes came to Stanford in 1892 and taught and published until she left in 1897. Daughter of the educational reformer Edward A. Sheldon, who was founder and principal of the Oswego Normal School in New York, Barnes graduated from the University of Michigan in 1874, where she had taken courses with historian Charles Kendall Adams. She accepted an appointment to teach at Wellesley in 1876 and for the next 4 years developed her approach to the teaching of history.

> From the beginning no set textbook was employed. During the first three years every week a number of pages of material, prepared from original sources, were copied by the electric pen, and a copy was placed in the hands of every student. Accompanying this material, a dozen or more problems were set requiring independent and original thought on the part of the individual, and as much additional reading was suggested and encouraged as possible. . . . During these first three years the classroom hour was largely devoted to conversation and discussion. Every student was encouraged to express fully and freely the results reached by the other members of the class. Before the topic in hand was left the results were all summarized and placed on the blackboard in tabular form. Each student kept a notebook, into which she entered these tabulated summaries, for the contents of which each student was responsible on examination.[60]

After leaving Wellesley, she taught at the Oswego Normal School, studied, traveled, and wrote books on the teaching of history. In 1885, she published *Studies in General History,* which was one of the earliest texts that included primary sources. In 1891, Mary Sheldon and Earl Barnes, now married, wrote *Studies in American History,* a text that stressed the use of primary sources by both college and secondary school students. When Jordan came to Stanford, he brought Earl Barnes, who was at the University of Indiana to begin a Department of Education, and the next year appointed Mary Sheldon assistant professor in history.[61]

Teaching by using original sources was consistent with the notion of history as a science. In her first book, she said, "these [sources] ...deal with historic records at first hand, as the geologist deals with fossils, the botanist with plants." Moreover, to study history required much from the student. "Like mathematics," she wrote, "it involves logic; like language, it demands analysis and fine discrimination of terms; like science, it calls for exact observation; like law, it needs the cool, well-balanced judgment."[62]

In her first year at Stanford, Barnes introduced two new courses: one was a lecture course on "The Pacific Slope," and the other was a seminar on the same subject. In doing so, she established, at least for the time she was in the department, the study of local history through original sources. In one class, she had a surviving member of the infamous Donner Party speak about what had happened to the ill-fated group during that winter of 1846.[63]

In 1896, her *Studies in Historical Method* appeared. Addressed to secondary school teachers, she included classroom research studies about how children from different backgrounds developed a sense of history. In the same year, Barnes and her husband left Stanford. While traveling in Europe, she took ill and died in 1898.[64]

Mary Sheldon Barnes was a teacher-scholar deeply interested in how to help students grasp the methodology of doing history as they came to master the content. She wrote for college professors and high school teachers, offering theories of teaching history, complete with sources for teachers to use in their classrooms. Her ultimate audience was students learning history.

Another teacher-scholar cut from similar cloth as Barnes, but who was also intrigued by how university administration could foster better teaching, was Edgar E. Robinson, who came to Stanford in 1911 and retired in 1952. On the basis of a strong recommendation from historian Frederick Jackson Turner, with whom Robinson studied at the University of Wisconsin, Adams recommended that Robinson be hired to teach U.S. history courses. Although he never completed a Ph.D., Robinson stayed at Stanford for over 4 decades, establishing himself as a superb lecturer, a founder of programs that sought to turn undergraduates into thoughtful citizens, and a veteran administrator.

An executive head of the department for almost a quarter-century and serving as an adviser to President Wilbur, Robinson also displayed deep affection for the art of teaching and the university's purpose of turning undergraduates into thoughtful, loyal Americans. He took the lead in organizing and implementing the "Problems of Citizenship" course in the early 1920s. When "Problems of Citizenship" was dropped in the early 1930s, Robinson helped establish the "Western Civilization" course and gave it guidance in its early years. In 1925, he organized the Independent Study program that permitted Stanford's brightest students to work closely with individual professors, a program that became the honors program during the 1950s.[65]

For all of his teaching prowess and administrative finesse in the 1920s, due to his lack of scholarly publications he moved very slowly to associate and then full professor. Robinson recalled a conversation with Ephraim Adams, then executive head, in 1921: "[He told me] that until there was positive evidence of my ability to produce scholarly work—he meant by that a book—a promotion would not be in order." Robinson did finally complete a book on political parties. Over the course of his career, he wrote for and spoke to many audiences, including scholars but especially to students and fellow citizens. He served enthusiastically as president and governing board member of San Francisco's Commonwealth Club, a sponsor of talks on public affairs.[66]

It was lecturing, however, that gave colleagues and former students reason to celebrate Robinson's gifts on the podium. Ephraim Adams, not a gentleman to indulge in hyperbole, thought so highly of Robinson's skills that in 1915, just 4 years after the assistant professor's arrival, Adams wrote a fellow historian at the University of Chicago that Robinson "has proved himself... one of the very best lecturers for large classes that we have ever had here at Stanford." Robinson taught his Westward Movement course for over 40 years—a tribute to Turner's influence upon him at Wisconsin—and, by one estimate, lectured to 20,000 students. Students recalled more than the words. "I remembered the day you lectured on frontier characters," one wrote, "and came to class dressed as a cowboy, wearing a 10-gallon hat and a bandanna around your neck." A former student and later professor of history wrote, "I watched your every gesture, every movement of your eyebrows, your pauses, your smile. I took 'westward movement' just to study your lecture methods." George Knoles, another former student and later colleague of Robinson in the department, said that he had planned to specialize in European history, "but after my first quarter with Robinson, I switched to American history."[67]

Celebrating Robinson as a lecturer could easily overlook his concern for the entire range of university teaching. He was deeply involved in the administration of two programs that employed history graduate students as teaching assistants: "Problems of Citizenship" and "Western Civilization." Meetings with these graduate students covered what happened in section discussions, how papers should be graded, and other pedagogical issues. For the Commonwealth Fund, he completed a study of how American history was taught in colleges and universities before and during World War II. While he argued in this study for historians to reaffirm their faith in the American experiment in self-government—it was written as the war was ending—Robinson spotted, like few other historians, the gap between scholarship and teaching: "The professional historian is a research specialist rather than a teacher."[68]

As a department head, Robinson did more than identify the separation of scholarship from teaching. He helped secure funds to underwrite a series of conferences on American history that brought together high school, college, and university teachers to jointly discuss issues of common concern. After World War II, he initiated an elective course for graduate students in the "Writing and Teaching of History." When he retired in 1952, the elective vanished, not to reappear as a departmental offering to doctoral students until the early 1970s.

Here, then, was a teacher-scholar who found much personal reward in lecturing to thousands of students and fellow citizens, administering the department, and writing for general audiences. It was not easy to juggle these very different interests within an institution that regarded scholarship as its primary responsibility, especially for someone like Robinson who wanted to leave an imprint on an institution that he loved. He managed, after much inner turmoil, to construct a career that combined "a desire to create something with a desire to present it and a desire also to live a life of the mind." Robinson's signature to the model of a teacher-scholar was enhanced by an administrative career thus revealing indirectly the persistent internal dilemmas that faced professors who sought to move beyond the accepted model of scholar-teacher.[69]

While Adams, Robinson, and Barnes worked within the tradition of scientific historians at the turn of century, it was the exemplar of Adams as a producer of scholarship for peers that the scholar-teacher triumphed in the decades to come. The model historian for the Stanford history department was neither Edgar E. Robinson nor Mary Sheldon Barnes, teacher-scholars whose gyroscopes centered on helping undergraduates (and larger audiences beyond the confines of the campus) grasp the purposes and essence of historical investigation through

ces that prized both content and skills. Few Stanford his-
ıllowed their lead in so acutely attending to the complex-
ıg history.

f teaching, of course, was honored verbally—with few
evidence—in making appointments, granting tenure, and
gaining promotions. Genuine respect for professors who could lecture
well to hundreds of students was evident, but it was scholarly productivity that counted most. The academic career of Thomas A. Bailey
stretching from 1930 to 1968 illustrates well the success of the scholar-
teacher as the department's dominant model of the historian.

Thomas Bailey was a man who spent 38 years teaching at Stanford,
whose passion about teaching, especially lecturing to large classes, was
especially strong, at least until the early 1960s. He worked hard at being
an engaging teacher who would motivate listeners to think critically
about history. He saw himself as both scholar and teacher, yet acknowledged: "It is true that the man who is known locally as a great teacher,
and nothing else, writes his name in water." He saw research as giving
heft to teaching. "The excitement of treading paths never before trod;
the satisfaction that springs from sharing one's findings with others—
all this helps the teacher to be fresh and vibrant," Bailey wrote. In the
Adams tradition, Bailey wanted more than a name written in water; he
wanted to be both scholar and teacher. Yet, Bailey knew it was a struggle: "One of the many battles that the [historian] has to fight with his
conscience is where to establish a nice balance between the time
devoted to teaching and that devoted to research."[70]

In his aggressive pursuit of scholarship, Bailey still found a balance
by making a name for himself as a platform performer, diplomatic historian, and author of popular textbooks. Bailey's single-minded and systematic regime of self-improvement led him through an academic career
that gained him national recognition and local admiration. His
unadorned impulse to succeed established Bailey as a star courted by
other universities. In the 1950s, Bailey represented the kind of scholar-
teacher that President Sterling sought elsewhere in his quest for Stanford to move into the first tier of national universities.

Bailey was born and raised in San Jose, California. His mother, a
schoolteacher, dreamed of her son attending Stanford. In 1920, he took
the electric trolley up to Palo Alto and began an academic career that
ended at the same institution in 1968. As an undergraduate, he had
thought of becoming a Baptist minister (he had preached as a teenager)
and he majored in Greek and history. He earned a Bachelor's degree
before continuing for a Master's in history (1924). During those years,
he turned away from the ministry and decided to become an academic

by securing the Ph.D. (1927). He had taken classes with Ephraim Adams and worked closely with Edgar Robinson, his dissertation adviser and mentor. After Bailey spent a few years at the University of Hawaii as a fledgling professor, Robinson negotiated his return to Stanford after Adams died in 1930.[71]

For each of his lectures in his early years at Stanford, he supplied students with a one-page outline (there was no textbook). A former Stanford debater, Bailey relished the drama inherent to lecturing by presenting an argument chock full of stories and rhetorical flourishes. Each year he worked earnestly at polishing his content and delivery.

> My practice was to type or write inserts or paste on paper strips containing new information . . . such as pointed quotations, illustrative anecdotes, slogans, or even bits of contemporary doggerel. My quotations were invariably short, for I soon learned that unless the quoted material is particularly pungent, students are apt to tune out while it is being read.
>
> After each lecture, I would return to my typewriter . . . and write a brief commentary on how well the lecture was received, and include such turns of phrase, analogies, and other flashes of wisdom as occurred to me in the heat of the moment. If not captured at the time, these gems might never come to me again.[72]

Bailey saw his strengths to be in lecturing rather than in small-group seminars. "The qualities that make for success in teaching in a small class," he wrote to a former student, "frequently do not insure success with a larger group." He counted as his "most important achievement" his "success with the large elementary course consisting of around 300 students."[73]

Yet he did enjoy teaching junior history majors the Introductory Seminar on historical methodology in the 1930s and 1940s. In that seminar, he wanted students to determine the truth or falsity of a document. In one assignment, he directed the 10 juniors in the seminar to go to *Appleton's Cyclopedia of American Biography* to find 20 men that he had identified. At the next meeting, he asked students if they had found the men; all had done so. "And you are all able to report in detail," he asked, "on the careers of each of these individuals?" Heads nodded. Then Bailey delivered the punch line: "Well, not a single one of these 20 men ever existed!" Bailey described the students' reactions: "Ten jaws dropped as one. Amazement and incredulity were written on every face." Bailey explained that a scholar had discovered that 47 sketches in the *Cyclopedia* had been invented by contributors eager to make money by writing about imaginary men.[74]

To Bailey, analyzing the veracity of sources was far more satisfying than having students in their Senior Seminar "extracting history passively from a printed secondary... account written by someone who perhaps had not consulted the necessary primary... sources or had not interpreted them correctly." To teach these seminars in which seniors produced scholarly papers, Bailey would assign a large general topic that was on his research agenda (e.g., Russian-American relations). He then divided up the topic into pieces with each student working separately on a subtopic. "If the students are working on the same general theme," he advised a former student, "they not only share a common interest but they can often exchange bibliographical information." Students then prepared two short papers (with accompanying oral reports) rather than one long one of 50-plus pages, because Bailey had discovered that students were "overwhelmed before the quarter came to an end." Finally, he avoided having students read their seminar papers. "Reading aloud," Bailey said, "tends to put other students to sleep." Students presented their major findings with the understanding that Bailey and fellow students would interrupt to ask questions and comment.[75]

For seminars and lectures, Bailey was judged successful by both peers and students. What "contributed most to my success in teaching," he wrote in 1934 after 7 years as a university professor, was "an ability to see the point of view of the student, and not try to talk over his head, and considerable training in the field of public speaking.... After all, one who lectures to a large class successfully must be a good speaker and have a forceful personality." Yet, in the same letter," he concludes that "successful teachers are born and not made."[76]

Whether the implied contradiction in Bailey's beliefs about success as a teacher and its genetic basis ever became explicit I do not know. What is evident, however, is that he loved doing what historians do: lecture, read, take notes, and write. Self-improvement stands out as a cardinal feature of Bailey's unceasing effort to find just the right turn of phrase—colonial New Englanders were more concerned with "cod than God" and with "fish and ships"—in his lectures, articles, and books.[77]

Stanford historian David Kennedy recalls his first years in the department and as Bailey's collaborator in preparing another edition of the college textbook *The American Pageant*.

> He had no other hobbies or pursuits; he counted it fitting and normal to be at his typewriter six days a week, including the Fourth of July, when I once discovered him hard at work in his office. "What more appropriate date to be writing American history?" he asked.[78]

Such hard work also garnered praise from Bailey's students for the finely wrought, engaging lectures. From the *Stanford Daily* in 1936, under the section "Valentines," the student editors wrote: "To Thomas Bailey for continuing to lead the list of profs who can keep us awake in lectures."[79]

Attention to lecturing also paid off handsomely for Bailey in rising course enrollments. Between 1930 and 1937, he taught 18 introductory courses in U.S. history. Only once did enrollments fall under 200 students. His advanced lecture course in diplomatic history, which he began teaching in 1932, went from 80 students to over 130 in a few years. Course enrollments declined to under 70 when World War II began, only to explode after 1945 with enrollments of over 200 students throughout the rest of that decade.[80]

The diplomatic history course is an example of how both the scholar and teacher in Bailey merged. For the first 5 years, he organized the course around a set of topics, and each year he would try out new subjects, amend old ones, and delete others so that the syllabus was constantly undergoing small changes. By 1940, he had written a text on U.S. diplomatic history for college students that had as its core the 30 lectures that he had refined over the decade. Bailey combined teaching and scholarship in this manner.[81]

But it was the published scholarship, not teaching, that both Bailey and university colleagues counted as coin of the realm. The articles and books that he so diligently produced year in and out throughout the 1930s and 1940s moved him through the ranks to associate professor in 1940, full professor in 1945, and holder of an endowed chair (and executive head of the department) in 1956. Three years later, he was elected president of the Pacific Coast branch of the American Historical Association, and, in 1968, he was elected president of the Organization of American Historians.[82]

He knew well, however, from the career of his mentor, Edgar E. Robinson, whose teaching was praised but research productivity was thin, and from Ephraim Adams, whose scholarly reputation was built upon diplomatic history, that advancement came through published writing. And write he did. Using the same work methods (and materials) that he used for preparing lectures, Bailey prepared monographs, interpretive works, and textbooks. By 1935, only 8 years after completing the doctorate, Bailey already had completed one published monograph and 19 articles, all of which were in refereed academic journals. In 1940, his scholarly textbook survey *A Diplomatic History of the American People* appeared, soon followed by two monographs on Woodrow Wilson published in 1944 and 1945. Three years later, his *The Man in the Street: The Impact of American Public Opinion on Foreign Policy* appeared. He then turned to Soviet-U.S. relations, and *America Faces Russia* was published in 1950.

Just as Bailey had based his diplomatic history text on years of teaching, he then decided to write a text aimed at 1st-year college students taking U.S. history. *The American Pageant* appeared in 1956 and was a hit with both students and professors for its sprightly tone, vivid anecdotes, and irreverent spirit toward common beliefs about the past. By 1980, *Diplomatic History* had gone through 10 editions and the *Pageant* had been revised and was in its 6th edition—in which David Kennedy first appeared as a coauthor. After retiring in 1968, Bailey continued to write, bringing out monographs and texts aimed at high school and college students.[83]

True to an earlier generation's ideal of history as a science with a content emphasizing political, military, and diplomatic affairs and an unflagging loyalty to the ideal of value-free objectivity, his former Stanford colleagues Ephraim Adams and Edgar E. Robinson would have nodded in approval at what Bailey had accomplished as a scholar and teacher. Bailey had continued Adams's scholarly work in diplomatic history and Robinson's work as a longtime teacher deeply interested in educating the young for their civic duties. What his colleagues may have missed, however, were the tensions between his teaching and scholarly obligations, which Thomas Bailey had to negotiate in a more competitive academic arena than they had faced.

Finessing the matter of different audiences produced anxiety in Bailey over the decades. "At some time, probably in the mid-1930s," Bailey recalled, "I . . . felt that I had a new mission in life to replace the 'call' I had once received to preach the gospel for the salvation of sinners." The "call" was for Thomas A. Bailey to "educate the people to their responsibilities as citizens by teaching them the so-called lessons of history." He did this through his students who would become future leaders, ones who, he proudly noted, had become "U.S. Senators, to say nothing of congressmen, federal judges, Foreign Service officers, generals, and admirals." Writing college textbooks over the decades while teaching generations of Stanford students fulfilled that "call" to make better informed citizens.[84]

Where the conflict emerges was also in meeting the professional obligation to produce articles and monographs for a scholarly audience. In some instances, there was a convergence that, at least in Bailey's mind, eliminated conflict. His two monographs on Woodrow Wilson, for example, were written during World War II: "Early in the war I decided that I could best serve my country by trying to educate the American public, from soldier to statesman, to its responsibilities for making an enduring peace ... [so it] would not repeat the same disastrous mistakes" that Wilson had made after World War I. The title of this chapter in his autobiography is "Penman for Peace."[85]

Such a fortuitous intersection of audiences was absent, however, when Bailey wrote textbooks. Beyond the substantial differences in writing for scholars and writing for uninformed students was the fact that authoring textbooks took much time—5 years for each of his texts—and they were often dismissed by historians as nonscholarly publications. In writing texts, Bailey said, "I had a feeling that I was committing some kind of academic sin." When he decided to write *The American Pageant* in the early 1950s, he was already a full professor and author of a half-dozen monographs and scores of journal articles. He felt that he "could survive the stigma of having fallen so low as to write a basic textbook." David Kennedy, his collaborator in *The American Pageant* and a respected Americanist, recalled how Bailey had warned him that collaborating on a text would earn Kennedy no kudos from fellow scholars.[86]

Why, then, did Bailey write textbooks? Certainly, it was not to seek higher standing among his colleagues. Perhaps it was the lure of royalties. Perhaps it was, as David Kennedy claims, that Bailey was so passionate about knowing American history that he sought to overcome the general ignorance of the past held by so many Americans. Or, perhaps writing texts after gaining tenure and promotion was a compromise that Bailey had fashioned for himself over time between the conflicting obligations of being a scholar and a teacher trying to reach very different audiences. In climbing the academic ladder by publishing scholarly work in the 1930s and 1940s, he had created the security of tenure to fulfill that heartfelt missionary impulse to teach history's lessons to undergraduates and the public. He could continue as a scholar and still be a teacher and "penman" for citizenship.[87]

Bailey's nearly 40-year career and his decisions about conflicting obligations in being a scholar-teacher represent what both the department and university have sought in its professors since Jordan brought Adams from Kansas in 1902. Subsequent historians in the department have diligently pursued the scholar-teacher, some more or less aware of the conflicts embedded in combining research and teaching. Those historians who sought to be teacher-scholars in the tradition of Mary Sheldon Barnes or Edgar E. Robinson would find the history departments at Stanford and other elite universities largely inhospitable. The dominant scholar-teacher model embodied in Bailey's career makes tangible the research imperative that permeated Stanford's history department over the last century and the pattern of incremental changes in content and curricular organization that strengthened electives, expanded graduate education, and sustained professorial autonomy to inquire and teach. Norms and practices that would elevate teaching to equivalent status as research, save for those occasional historians openly passionate about what they did in their classrooms, remained in the shadows.

SUMMARY

Organizational and Subject-Matter Changes in the Official Curriculum

Similar to what occurred across the university, traditions of reform in the official history curriculum emerged over the century. As the field of history expanded, specialists brought expertise to Stanford that yielded different elective courses defined by place and time. These advanced courses provided further evidence of institutionalizing faculty research interests. While Americanists and Europeanists have dominated the content of the official curriculum over the century, there is little doubt that courses changed as subspecialties of social, economic, and cultural history became intertwined with the familiar political, constitutional, and military subject matter of the discipline.

What the "continuous . . . re-engineering and tinkering" with the structures of the official curriculum and reshaping of the details of majors and graduate work signaled was a divorce between curriculum and pedagogy. Enormous amounts of departmental time and attention have been devoted to organizational changes in the official curriculum, with little collective attention from the department upon how subject matter was taught. Departmental support for the norm of faculty autonomy bolstered by institutional beliefs and structures that clearly favored scholarship over teaching for getting hired, tenured, and promoted made the gap between an elective or prescribed course's subject matter and how it was to be taught a common occurrence.[88]

Tinkering with the content and organization of the official curriculum over the last century also reveals how incremental adaptations accumulated into a fundamental change: Graduate school norms eventually came to dominate the undergraduate history major. There was much faculty support for the notion that the department's strength was precisely in becoming specialized. Consensus was implicit: Professors and doctoral students were going to be university scholar-teachers who would teach and publish in their specialties. If the record of changes in content and curricular structures in the history department reveals anything, it is the steady trend toward professionalization of doctoral work, especially after the 1950s, to prepare future academics to be scholar-teachers in their discipline. But for undergraduates, tinkering added up to transformation of the history major.

A balance was struck within the department between service courses, such as introductory surveys of Europe, Western civilization and U.S. history, for 1st- and 2nd-year undergraduates and required courses for history majors. Beginning in 1917 and accelerating after the late 1950s, doctoral work slowly became professionalized, with the ethos of graduate work spreading to the last 2 undergraduate years for majors. By examining the entire century of the department's making changes in requirements for majors, the resulting transformation of the junior and senior years into a mini-graduate school becomes obvious.

What was discussed intensely at times were ways of organizing courses and requiring more teaching from doctoral students, especially since the 1960s, and more writing from history majors, especially since the 1980s. These collective deliberations to renovate were meant to align the overall departmental goals with organizational procedures for creating majors in history who were thoroughly familiar with the historian's craft and for preparing doctoral students to smoothly move into assistant professor vacancies in university history departments elsewhere in the nation. The latter was seemingly prompted less by a genuine concern for the craft of teaching than by severe decline in the job market for academic historians and the need to have instructors for the broad array of courses offered in the department as the teaching load for professors decreased.

Teaching and Advising

Through the entire century, there was a stable instructional organization of lecture/section and seminar/colloquium for both undergraduates and graduates. As one professor in the department noted in the 1990s, "The way we deliver the product looks in actual practice the way it did 50 years ago: stand-up lectures, around-the-table seminars, papers, [and] taking exams." Amplifying the professor's judgment is evidence of little use of machine technology over the century in historians' teaching.[89]

One change in the mix of teaching approaches that occurred as faculty teaching loads shrunk from six courses an academic year to five and now to the present four, was a steady increase in small-group courses. Declining lecture-based offerings continued through the middle decades of the century with small-group courses exceeding traditional lecture courses after the 1960s. Both the decrease in teaching load and mix of large lecture courses and seminar/colloquia provide further evidence of the university-wide institutionalization of the research imperative mirrored in the department's creating a strong culture for research-oriented courses and a weak culture for teaching.

The same powerful institutional norms favoring research over teaching may also explain why advising was hardly perceived as a problem. Advising is informal teaching, and to the degree that teaching was not dealt with openly, and to the degree that faculty viewed teaching as competing in time and energy with research duties, so, too, was advising largely ignored as an issue until the 1960s. Since then, only erratic attention has been given to it by both the university and the Department of History. Such tensions between competing values, of course, suggest that the department faced intractable dilemmas.

Dilemmas of Role and Purpose for Academic Historians

Dealing with two prized values (producing scholarship and teaching well) under the constraint of limited time and aid is the familiar institutional conflict of the university-college reduced to the departmental level and individual professor. Reconciling these contending demands, both of which are highly prized rhetorically but differentially rewarded within the university, has been managed by constructing departmental and individual compromises to ease the tensions.

One departmental compromise is stating publicly the institutional belief that teaching and research reinforce one another while unobtrusively incorporating the research imperative into those departmental structures and norms that influence faculty behavior: Who teaches which courses; how many lecture and how many small-group courses should each person teach; what is discussed and not discussed at faculty meetings; what criteria for tenure and promotion will be used; and what will be subsidies for research (sabbaticals, graduate assistants). This compromise of much rhetoric about the importance of teaching (with increasing recognition in university awards and use of student ratings since the 1970s) and organizational policies, norms, and behavior that institutionalize research as the primary value suppress the strain between the two imperatives while making it acceptable to the department, individual professors, students, and the public. Reducing the tension usually works, except on those occasions when the discrepancy between the rhetoric and actions become painfully clear for all to see, as when promising assistant professors in the department were denied tenure in the 1980s and 1990s.

The second dilemma is over the audience (writing for peers vs. teaching, writing, and speaking to students and citizens) and has been worked out differently by a succession of individual historians at Stanford, beginning with Ephraim Adams, Mary Sheldon Barnes, and Edgar Robinson, and extending through Thomas Bailey, David Kennedy, and current members of the department. Compartmentalization of different purposes has been one compromise. Being a scholar first and teacher second has been the model of choice in the Department of History, clearly mirroring the university's priorities. Staging one's career has been another compromise. Thomas Bailey, for example, while prizing lecturing and achieving local fame in his early and mid career, also made sure that his scholarly credentials were impeccable (and he had tenure) before turning to writing college and high school texts and reaching out to larger audiences. Mary Sheldon Barnes published works that were scholarly but that were focused upon pedagogy of history and created a brief career that was closer to a teacher-scholar than that of her colleagues. Edgar Robinson handled the strain between competing ideals by acquiring tenure and spending more time on teaching, administration, and reaching out to general audiences, while seldom writing for fellow scholars.

Thus, two models of historians—essentially compromises reconciling competing ideals within the university-college—emerged in the department. Both eased friction by finessing the demands of both research and teaching and balancing the competing purposes of being an academic historian: either as the teacher-scholar (Barnes and Robinson) or the scholar-teacher (Adams and Bailey), with the latter model being dominant since it so clearly institutionalized the university ideal of conducting research.

These patterns of both constancy and change in the official curricula, in how professors of history taught, and in the making of compromises to enduring dilemmas suggest that while many changes have occurred within the Department of History since 1891, they have been incremental to the official and taught curricula. The fundamental changes that occurred were less intentional reforms than consequences of uncoordinated, ad hoc faculty decisions that tilted departmental culture toward the scholar-teacher and converted the junior and senior years for history majors into an approximation of graduate school. Figure 3.8 illustrates the kinds of changes that occurred in the department.

Yet the Department of History is only one unit within the university. The discipline of history, which bridges both the humanities and social sciences, and the department's bifocal attention on both undergraduate and graduate students mark it as quite different from a professional

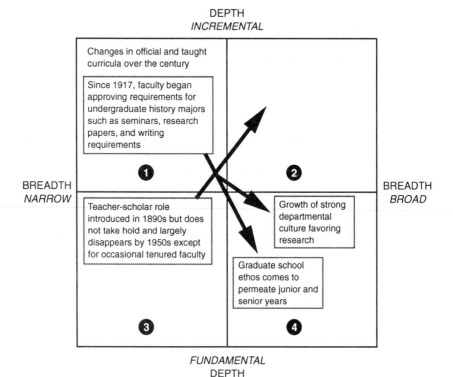

DEPTH
INCREMENTAL

Changes in official and taught
curricula over the century

Since 1917, faculty began
approving requirements for
undergraduate history majors
such as seminars, research
papers, and writing
requirements

BREADTH
NARROW

BREADTH
BROAD

Teacher-scholar role
introduced in 1890s but does
not take hold and largely
disappears by 1950s except
for occasional tenured faculty

Growth of strong
departmental
culture favoring
research

Graduate school
ethos comes to
permeate junior and
senior years

❶   ❷   ❸   ❹

FUNDAMENTAL
DEPTH

FIGURE 3.8 — Changes in the History Department, 1891–1991.

school largely devoted to the life sciences that prepares college graduates to become physicians. In the next chapter, I examine the traditions
of reform in the medical school curriculum and pedagogy to determine
the degree to which research trumped teaching, as I have described for
the Department of History.

$\equiv 4 \equiv$

A STURDY WAY OF PREPARING PHYSICIANS

The School of Medicine, 1908–1990

In 1922, Ray Lyman Wilbur, former dean of Stanford University School of Medicine (SUSM) and president of Stanford, spoke to the California State Medical Society about his deep concern over the direction that medical schools in the state and the nation (including Stanford's) were taking. What troubled him most about the "new" medical curriculum introduced at the turn of the century—a reform that he had then endorsed—was the decided trend toward specialization. "We must return," he said to the assembled doctors, "to the basic idea that the granting of the degree of Doctor of Medicine means that the student is capable of handling the ordinary problems of general practice." Wilbur saw that the unrelenting passion for laboratory sciences in research-driven universities tilted students away from the expected role of a doctor as a general practitioner who cared for the whole patient rather than a specific illness. The president minced no words: "We must frankly recognize the fact that, as a profession, we are thought of too much in terms of drugs and the knife and that we have become . . . isolated from the sick patient because of the machinery that we have built up."[1]

The conflicting purposes of a professional medical school that Wilbur identified in 1922 echoed the competing purposes buried within the university-college hybrid that Stanford had developed decades earlier. While there were obvious differences between the School of Medicine and the Department of History, managing dilemmas of purpose were common to both. Similarly, Wilbur's criticism of the medical school curriculum spoke to excessive specialization and professorial autonomy that he saw dominating medical education in the 1920s. These conflicts along with their curricular and pedagogical implications persisted throughout his tenure and since for Stanford presidents and medical school faculties (as they have in other universities) who have sought a workable consensus over what kind of physicians should receive degrees from medical school.

President Wilbur was calling into question a major reform at the turn of the century that had fundamentally altered the direction of medical education throughout the country, including Stanford. The history of SUSM between 1908 and the 1990s describes how a professional school episodically modified this reform, even introducing major changes in it at mid-century. Those late 1950s reforms of the earlier reform were dismantled less than a decade later and replaced by a totally elective program in 1968. Within a few years, the elective system gave way to a program of required courses that resembled strongly the structures of the official curriculum and its pedagogy that Wilbur would have found familiar.

Incremental changes were made to the official curriculum and instruction, but, overall, the fundamental reforms undertaken at the end of the 19th century that so thoroughly overhauled the content and pedagogy of medical education at Stanford and across the country—ones that Wilbur questioned in 1922—have largely remained in place. So have the conflicts over purposes. Thus, a puzzle emerges: Why has the basic model of preparing physicians remained remarkably durable amid enormous societal changes; sheer growth in administration, faculty, and students; and the huge influx of federal and private research funds? This question drives the chapter.[2]

CENTRAL ISSUES FOR MEDICAL EDUCATION IN THE LATE 19TH CENTURY

Contained within the content and structures of every medical school curriculum is a vision of a good doctor. To every generation of medical school reformers, the central questions have been (and continue to be): What do those preparing to become physicians have to believe, know, and do, in order to practice first-rate medicine? Technical proficiency, humaneness, serving the public, staying abreast of new knowledge, and scientific inquiry are some of the prized ingredients that go into most visions of excellent practice. Securing a faculty consensus over the proper mix of these ingredients has been the unrelenting challenge in reshaping medical education.

A second central question is: How can medical school faculty best communicate those beliefs, values, knowledge, and skills? Through formal teaching, advising, and research, medical educators have sought different ways of communicating essential content, skills, and values. Faculties often faced difficulties in confidently answering these questions because of the rapid expansion of medical knowledge in this century and the conflict over which values to stress. By the late 19th century, however, medical school reformers had agreed upon a curricular and instructional model of education that sought to keep pace with new medical knowledge while maintaining competing values. That model has lasted over a century.

Before the Reform Movement

After the Civil War, becoming a doctor commonly meant attending a privately owned medical college (there were 47 such schools in 1860) a few months a year for a few years. There were no entrance requirements, except the ability to pay fees to the doctors who owned the school. Courses were practical: anatomy, physiology, pathology, chemistry, surgery, therapeutics used for the sick, medical jurisprudence, chemistry, obstetrics, and diseases of women and children.[3]

Typically, the medical school was housed in a two-story building with two lecture halls. The first-floor lecture hall was used for presentations in chemistry and for the theory and practice of medicine. The second-floor hall, which usually contained a skylight, was used for lectures on anatomy, physiology, and surgery. Dissection facilities were either in the same building or in an adjacent one, which housed a chemistry laboratory, faculty offices, and a museum of anatomical exhibits. Most medical colleges had no library except for the private ones held by the school's proprietors.

Instruction each term from the half-dozen or so professors (who had their own practices and taught part-time) was primarily through 5 to 6 hours of daily lectures in amphitheaters, with practitioners often demonstrating procedures to the assembled students. Exceptions to the constant lectures were the times spent in special rooms where students learned their anatomy from dissecting cadavers. Also, some colleges sent students to nearby hospitals to watch and listen to attending doctors discuss their patients.

To graduate and receive the M.D. degree, students had to pass most of the oral exams given by their professors and be at least 21 years of age. Alternatives to attending degree-granting, proprietary colleges existed in apprenticeships to practicing doctors, serving as a "house pupil" or "intern" at a hospital, or, for those few who could afford the cost, going to Europe to receive training. Overall, medical education was brief, practice-driven, and for-profit.[4]

The Reform Movement

Between the 1870s and early 1900s, medical education reformers in universities and professional associations reconstructed the Harvard medical school and founded Johns Hopkins medical college and scores of other newly created university-based medical schools. To this generation of doctors, many of whom were trained in Europe, the for-profit, short-term, and unscientific approach of existing medical schools meant low standards in health care for the public and an over-populated, unprofessional occupation. They offered crisp but very different answers to the basic questions about how to produce better doctors to serve the public: merge medical colleges with universities where research and the practice of science were honored; train fewer and better doctors by raising entrance requirements for students; lengthen the time spent in medical school; make the curriculum sequential, with biological and chemical sciences in the initial years followed by time spent in hospitals learning clinical procedures; create full-time faculty posts, so that research and teaching can be combined and professors would discontinue private practice to increase their income; supplement lectures by using laboratories and hospital wards as places for scientific inquiry and clinical practice.

In short, the vision that drove these reformers was to produce scientifically trained professionals who were both skilled practitioners and medical researchers. Reformers in professional associations and universities succeeded in reducing the number of proprietary medical colleges from 160 in 1900 to 131 in 1910.[5]

In 1910, the Carnegie-funded Flexner report appeared, further accelerating the national movement to upgrade medical education that had begun decades earlier. The implicit model for a "good" medical school in Flexner's report was largely based on the curriculum and pedagogy established at Johns Hopkins University in 1893 and on what had been advocated by reformers in the waning decades of that century.

The report recommended a 4-year (2×2) graded curriculum; for 2 years students would study basic medical sciences to understand how the human body worked, then spend another 2 years working in clinical settings with the ill. The report claimed that using laboratories, hospital wards, and clinics as sites for small-group and individual teaching and research would entail learning through doing, a far more effective pedagogy than listening to lectures. Thus, reformed medical schools would graduate fewer and better-trained doctors who would think like scientists, do research, and practice first-rate medicine.

The American Medical Association's Council on Medical Education endorsed Flexner's report and became a de facto accrediting agency through its rating system of each medical school. Through these rankings and the widespread publicity garnered by the 1910 report, for-profit medical schools continued to close. By 1915, there were 95, down from 131 in 1910. The combined ideals of university-based medical school faculties engaging in research while also producing scientifically trained, humane practitioners were deeply embedded in the curriculum and pedagogy of this early-20th-century 2×2 model, especially at Stanford.[6]

MEDICAL EDUCATION AT STANFORD UNIVERSITY, 1908–1990

In examining the history of the Stanford University School of Medicine (SUSM), where frequent curricular and instructional changes occurred over almost a century, clues may emerge to answer the question: Why has this century-old model of medical schooling been so sturdy?

In answering this question, the matter of how much can be generalized from the SUSM experience arises. Stanford University's medical school is unique in its history and the particular details of the local and regional setting. It is, after all, a private university unlike, say, Michigan State University's College of Human Medicine in its mission, student composition, and history.[7]

Two facts, however, make generalizing beyond SUSM possible. First, SUSM has belonged for many years to a consortium of medical schools (in the 1980s, member medical schools of the consortium were University of Chicago, Columbia, Cornell, Harvard, Johns Hopkins, University of Pittsburgh, Pennsylvania, Rochester, University of Washington, Yale, Case-Western Reserve, Duke, and Stanford). They share the goal of preparing medical students to be university researchers working within the tradition of academic medicine. There are, then, similarly situated public and private university medical schools.[8] Second, all medical schools (there were 126 in 1994), public and private, large and small, are affected by the continuing explosion of medical knowledge, the changing federal role in financing health care and medical education that has forced universities to seek revenues in commercial ventures, physicians working more in groups rather than as solo practitioners, and, of course, numerous innovations aimed at aligning medical education with these larger unplanned changes. Finally, differences notwithstanding, medical schools seeking reforms have had to begin, as Stanford has done, by modifying the familiar 2×2 model of scientific medicine that has been in place since the turn of the century.[9]

The First Half-Century of the Official Curriculum

Well before the 1908 merger between the Cooper Medical College in San Francisco and Stanford University (or the subsequent Flexner report), Levi Cooper Lane and his successors had moved Cooper toward a 4-year sequential curriculum. Medicine became another department in the university, something that both President David Starr Jordan (who had an M.D. degree but had never practiced) and the trustees of Cooper dearly wanted; it was also what turn-of-the-century medical school reformers sought.[10]

Between 1912 and 1959, students spent 2 years on the Palo Alto campus studying anatomy, histology (cell structure), biochemistry, physiology, and other subjects that examined normal and abnormal structures and functions of the human body. These preclinical years were followed by 2 years of intensive work 35 miles away in hospital wards and clinics of the former Cooper Medical College in San Francisco. Here students cared for sick patients under the guidance of university-appointed full- and part-time clinicians.

Even within a split campus, the research imperative held sway within a professional school dedicated to producing practitioners. It appeared in student-faculty research projects and in the requirement, established in 1912, that to receive a medical degree each graduate had to complete a research-based thesis.[11]

While the official curricular structures remained largely the same for a half-century, the faculty still made additions and substitutions in content and organization. As new knowledge was carved into specialties (e.g., pediatrics, psychiatry, oncology, cardiovascular surgery), departments that were responsible for offering courses, determining teaching practices, and conducting research divided like cells. In 1913, when the Department of Medicine was reorganized into the School of Medicine, there were 10 departments. A half-century later, there were 17, and in 1990, the number of departments had grown to 22. The clear trend toward specialization in medical practice and research is mirrored in this growth.[12]

New subjects and departments complicated the teaching of an already packed official curriculum, where the goals of training medical students to become first-rate general practitioners and able researchers competed. Faculty struggled with adding and deleting courses, juggling the number of hours allocated to each subject, and managing scheduling conflicts. For example, in 1923, the medical school faculty decided that "all required work . . . be reduced by 8%," thereby dropping the number of hours of instruction below the 4,000 required by the state for licensing physicians. The faculty then mandated that students make up the difference by doing elective work in departments of their choice, prodding students to specialize and engage in research projects with their professors. "The new schedule," Dean William Ophuls reported to President Wilbur, "is a great improvement over the old one in that it has done away with a great part of the overcrowding and has made it possible to give the students in some quarters an additional free afternoon a week." Such organizational changes in the official curriculum reflected interdepartmental compromises to existing tensions over the rapid accumulation of new medical knowledge, competing goals for what kinds of doctors SUMS should produce, and the time available for faculty to teach and do research.[13]

Teaching, 1908–1959: The Case of Anatomy

Examining the preclinical courses that entering medical students had to take, such as anatomy (which included neurology, histology, and gross anatomy), offers a glimpse of how much time was allocated to the subject, the prevailing teaching practices, and the intersection between official curriculum and what professors taught. With the establishment of the medical school in the 1st decade of this century and for the next 5 decades, lectures and small-group work in labs dominated the teaching of preclinical subjects (see Figure 4.1).[14]

I chose anatomy (gross anatomy—structures and functions of systems, organs, and tissue in the human body; histology; and neuroanatomy) because it is (and has been) taught in the first 2 years of virtually every American medical school as part of the basic medical sciences. Gross anatomy, for example, has been taught through dissection of cadavers. Teaching has combined lectures, laboratory work in small groups, and informal conferences with faculty and teaching assistants. The tensions over how to teach anatomy in the initial year of medical school reflected the warring ideals of training students to be both researchers and practitioners.

During the years just prior to the merger of Cooper Medical College and Stanford University, practicing surgeons mostly lectured, stressing the practical applications of learning about the human body. A former

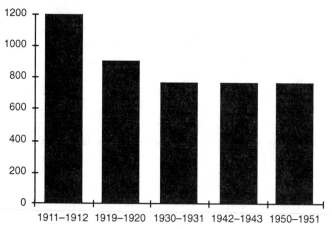

FIGURE 4.1 — Allocation of hours to anatomy subjects, 1911–1951.

student at the Cooper Medical College in the waning years of the 19th century remembered one particular professor:

> Apart from dissecting, anatomy was a didactic course taught by R. H. Plummer, primarily a surgeon; a tall, large, impressive looking man with a full apostolic beard. I suspect that he knew Gray's *Anatomy* by heart, as his lectures did not contain anything that could not be found in that well-known work.... [T]he lectures in anatomy took place soon after lunch, and, partly on that account and partly as a result of the dryness of the presentation, students were apt to drop to sleep. When ... Dr. Plummer discovered a culprit, he would stop his lecture, point an accusing finger at the slumberer, and begin to recite a poem of which all I can remember are the opening words "Oh! Sleep."[15]

After Cooper Medical College merged with Stanford in 1908, a gradual shift occurred toward teaching anatomy as an investigative science with more emphasis on animal research and less on its clinical application to future physicians. Nationally, anatomists struggled to convert their subject into a research-based field where experimentation in animal embryology and development replaced drilling information about human anatomy into students. This struggle over the purposes for students studying anatomy, of course, had consequences for deciding who teaches medical students (researchers or clinicians) and how the content is taught.[16]

In 1909, President David Starr Jordan brought Arthur W. Meyer from Northwestern University to teach anatomy. Meyer had been a student and later a colleague of Franklin Mall at Johns Hopkins, who was a leader in the movement to make the study of anatomy research-based. While Mall avoided lectures and directing students in their laboratory work—he was said to have appeared on the 1st day in the lab, announcing that there would be no lectures, and was seldom seen again by the students—Meyer spent much time with students in the dissecting rooms and laboratories. A colleague remembered his manner of teaching:

> With long forceps which had an uncanny affinity for poorly displayed parts, he moved from table to table, like a clinician on ward rounds, bringing out the essential points through searching, often disconcerting questions. . . . He had scant patience with careless work or fuzzy thinking. If, for example, in demonstrating his dissection a flustered student happened to say, " . . . and this is your femoral nerve," Dr. Meyer would retort, "Not mine!" in a tone that seemed to imply that an unpardonable sin had been committed. His visit to successive groups was always awaited with an element of apprehension; one currently well-known physician actually fainted when he looked up and saw the Professor at his elbow.[17]

In a 1926 report to the president of the university, Meyer, then the department chair, described the courses taught and research agendas of the four full-time members of the department. His brief report concluded with a list of the research papers written by members of the department that had been published or were in press. For example, he cited Professor E. T. Engle's article, "Notes on the Sexual Cycle of the Pacific Cetacea of the Genera *Megaptera* and *Balaenoptera*," in the *Journal of Mammalogy*. Meyer's own work at this time was on anatomical lesions that occurred as a result of scurvy.[18]

By the mid-1930s, research scientists, not clinicians, dominated the teaching of gross and microscopic anatomy. As members of the anatomy department in the School of Biological Sciences, professors also were appointed as faculty in the medical school. Although dual citizens, their laboratory research occupied most of their time. The university catalogue's display noted this shift in a mild expansion of elective courses mirroring faculty research agendas. Even though occasional efforts were made to link the study of required subjects to clinical practice, a heavy departmental emphasis on investigative work on mice, guinea pigs, dogs, and other animals prevailed. Anatomy professors, similar to some colleagues in the history department who taught mostly undergraduates, generally viewed teaching medical students as a necessary duty to the university.[19]

Detailed knowledge of the body, nonetheless, was required of students. Professor Arthur Meyer expected medical students to identify, by the end of their first quarter of study, each part of the human skeleton. He had students follow a general procedure for dissection. With two students assigned to each cadaver, one student initially made shallow incisions in the arm, neck, and face, and the other in the back, chest, abdomen, and lower limbs. Students would turn back the skin but not remove it. After this dissection, they turned to deeper incisions in the abdomen and chest, the deep muscles of the back, and the head and neck. They removed the brain and spinal cord and, finally, made deep dissections of the legs, feet, and hands.[20]

Lectures, of course, continued. Over the last 2 centuries, professors have used varied approaches to engage listeners in actively thinking about the content and to secure student responses to subject matter. Making lectures an active-learning experience, however, takes an enormous amount of the professor's time in planning the lectures, having outlines available for students, and determining what questions to ask and how to get responses in an orderly manner. Available evidence on lecturing does suggest that only a small fraction of university professors, including those at medical schools, invested in such planning; most presentations were done conventionally, including for anatomy. There were two types. There was the straight presentation of information drawn from texts, recent research findings of other scientists, and the lecturer's own investigations; often these would be illustrated by some visual device (in the early 20th century with stereopticon slides, preserved specimens, and models; in later decades, overhead projectors, photos of slides, and X-rays). Another popular form of lecturing was the demonstration, in which the presenter would conduct an actual experiment or do a particularly difficult dissection (called a prosection) in front of the students.[21]

Lecturing in any form puts a premium on the professor organizing the information and concepts and presenting them in such a way as to inspire and provoke students to learn and think. How much was learned directly from these lectures is unknown except in those instances when recitations and quizzes were scheduled. By the 1920s, however, both of these practices had disappeared from the printed schedule.

What occupied Meyer and his successor William Greulich more than lecturing and dissecting was their obvious pride in how much research on animals and humans their department had conducted. In a 1952 report summarizing the department's achievements, Greulich pointed out that over the last quarter-century members in the department had published four books and 350 articles in scientific journals. Moreover, at least one member of the department had served since 1928 on the editorial board of the premier journal in the field, the *Anatomical Record*.[22]

The tension between time to teach medical students gross anatomy and time to spend on animal research projects increasingly became an issue because university rewards since the 1908 merger—as Meyer and Greulich knew—went to those faculty who published their research. As anatomists specialized, they lost interest in pointing out clinical applications to 1st-year medical students, which led (in Stanford's case) to criticism years later when more assertive students objected to the quality of teaching.[23]

In summary, then, the dominant teaching methods for anatomy, until the late 1950s, were in laboratories and dissection rooms (over 80% of the time) with the remainder of students' time spent listening to professors lecture. The conflict over the purposes for studying anatomy—that is, as an experimental science or to help medical students prepare for clinical work later in their student career—persisted through the end of World War II. In these years at Stanford, the research imperative prevailed until the 1950s when another generation of faculty saw the enormous time students spent in labs as wasted in following routine procedures.

The half-century since the founding of the SUMS, then, included many incremental changes in the subject matter and the structures and organization of the official curriculum, and a clear commitment to a laboratory-centered pedagogy. Persistent tensions, however, between new and old departments over finding room to teach their specialties in a teeming curriculum were constant, suggesting that the issue of how to organize a curriculum and teach it as medical knowledge remained a struggle. Conflicts also arose between research-oriented and clinically oriented approaches in doing dissections and examining slides, and in student laboratory work. Finally, a growing unease over what kinds of doctors Stanford should graduate had begun to emerge. Expressed in the opening paragraphs of this chapter by President Wilbur in 1922 and echoed occasionally by individual professors and students, the unease was transformed into a redesign of the entire medical school curriculum in the 1950s, when a new president and board of trustees sought to move Stanford into the first rank of American universities.

REFORMING CONTENT AND TEACHING: THE FIVE-YEAR PLAN

The first major overhaul of the official curriculum occurred when the board of trustees approved President Wallace Sterling's recommendation in 1953 to merge the two campuses and build a new medical school and hospital in Palo Alto, California. Planning for a consolidated medical facility spurred rethinking of what kind of doctors Stanford should graduate, what material medical students should study, and how faculty should teach. In rethinking their mission and program, the faculty borrowed from other medical schools that had been redesigning their curricula and teaching in the 1950s. As the first (and only) challenge to the dominant 2×2 model of medical education already in place for a half-century, the *Five-Year Plan,* as it came to be called, still sought the twin ideals of preparing humane practitioners and research scientists. Where the challenge to the prevailing approach to medical education appeared was in an alternative curricular organization and pedagogy.[24]

Reshaping the Content and Structures of the Official Curriculum

The Five-Year Plan sought to deal with information overload in the preclinical curriculum and the persistent tension over the prized values of simultaneously preparing scholarly investigators and humane, competent practitioners. Because every official curriculum is anchored in a set of faculty assumptions about knowledge, teaching, learning, and a vision of good medical practice, examining the premises intended to steer the Five-Year Plan becomes important. Faculty planners set out three assumptions:

1. There should be as little separation as possible between the preclinical and clinical work and there should be "integrated teaching" that can connect to the "previous educational experience for the student."
2. "At the heart of the study of medicine lies a core of medical knowledge, which should be presented to all students, irrespective of their eventual choice of medical career." This core knowledge should be organized by subject rather than by departments. Each student will be able to go beyond the core essentials through independent study and the taking of electives.
3. "The student of medicine has passed beyond that stage of his education where the mere acquisition of facts can be defended. They are graduate students who should be encouraged to learn in terms of ... *problems of medicine* [original emphasis] rather than in terms of the acquisition of techniques or the accumulation of data."[25]

These explicit beliefs offered an alternative view to the historic and unquestioned assumptions that had been embedded deeply in the turn-of-the-century university-based curriculum, in which knowledge was partitioned between preclinical and clinical, separate departments delivered the curriculum and instruction, and neophyte doctors had to learn both scientific factual knowledge and clinical procedures to become both practitioners and researchers. Transforming the decades-old content and structures of the official curriculum meant installing another set of institutional beliefs about the mission and organization of the school: how teachers should teach, what the students should learn, and the role of departments. To a faculty who had themselves experienced a 2×2 curriculum, gaining agreement about such fundamental changes was no easy task.

Even before the steel girders for the new buildings were in place, conflict erupted in committee meetings over allocation of laboratory and lecture time to different departments. Advocates for the Five-Year Plan in the basic medical sciences, such as pharmacology Professor Avram Goldstein, believed that most laboratory time was wasted in following routine procedures in manuals and it robbed students of the creativity and curiosity that scientific experiments should offer. He called such lab work "cookbookery." In November 1957, at a meeting of the faculty's newly established Curriculum Study Committee, which was charged to implement an interdepartmentally taught laboratory course that would reduce laboratory time for certain subjects, some professors (including the head of the anatomy department) objected strongly to a proposed longer school year to accommodate new courses. They argued that adding 3 weeks for other courses would further diminish their time for laboratory work and individual research.[26]

At the same meeting, some professors, believing that the Five-Year Plan was being carried out by "a small minority," moved that the entire faculty vote immediately on the basic principle of the reform because "at least three departments . . . were utterly and vehemently opposed to extension to 36-week years." Other members of the committee quickly pointed out to their angry colleagues "that no department or group of faculty has a right to veto anything which is a decision of the School." Even the bland language of recorded minutes could not mask the threat of one faculty advocate of the Five-Year Plan who said, "It is the privilege of a faculty member to leave the school if he disagrees with such a decision but not his privilege to veto it." The motion was eventually tabled and the proposal for a longer school year was eventually approved. But the interdepartmental tensions persisted.[27]

In 1959, students entering the new SUSM buildings found that the faculty had put their beliefs about curricular and pedagogical reform into practice. First, to create a climate of graduate education and choice, the faculty had lengthened the study of medicine from 4 to 5 years (encouraging but not mandating students to spend 3 rather than 2 years to complete the basic medical sciences). The longer program gave students options to take electives elsewhere on the campus, pursue research opportunities with faculty, and specialize in a medical field. While electives and research opportunities had been available in the pre-1959 curriculum, tightly orchestrated preclinical courses had left little time for students to take them. Now the faculty wanted students to have "more time for reflection, for unhurried contemplative reading, for assimilating the best of the original literature in each field." They wanted students to learn that "real study is more rewarding than 'cramming,'" and that "all our present knowledge serves mainly as a springboard into the fascinating unknown."[28]

Second, preclinical courses were reorganized. From all departments having taught separate subjects, faculty in key departments now jointly designed laboratory-based core courses in the basic medical sciences for each of the first 2 years. New buildings contained multiple laboratories each, with bench-stations for 16 students and equipment from various disciplines, where students, working closely with faculty, could conduct research. Connecting rooms were used for demonstrations and interdepartmental experiments.

Furthermore, faculty-developed multidisciplinary courses on the "Basic Medical Sciences," "Cell Structure and Function," and "Introduction to Clinical Medicine" brought together professors who had usually taught alone. In addition, teams taught required courses organized around organ systems (e.g., cardiovascular, central nervous system), rather than separate courses on, say, the heart or stomach. Also the faculty reduced laboratory time and increased time spent on student-designed research projects. Finally, believing that medical students were mature adults in graduate school, the faculty abolished grade point averages and class ranking and replaced the former with a simpler grading system. Here were major changes in the content and structures that organized the official curriculum.[29]

Teaching Practices During the Five-Year Plan

After the introduction of the reform in 1959, faculty moved ahead with the new laboratory-based pedagogy. Once implemented, there was an overall reduction in hours of laboratory instruction in eight preclin-

TABLE 4.1 — *Laboratory Hours in Eight Preclinical Subjects*

Year	Total hours
1960–1961	1,117
1963–1964	880
1966–1967	825

ical subjects (excluding anatomy but including biochemistry, hematology, histology, neuroanatomy, etc.) (see Table 4.1).[30]

What happened to the teaching of anatomy under the Five-Year Plan? As laboratory time in other subjects fell, hours spent in anatomy labs and dissecting rooms declined also. From a high of over 90% of time spent in anatomy labs (including dissection) between the founding of the school and World War II, assigned hours fell to 80% after the introduction of the Five-Year Plan. Lectures increased. Students also became restless with the pedagogy.

By 1965, students for the first time collectively voiced their concerns over the required interdisciplinary "Cell Structure and Function" course and other preclinical subjects that, they claimed, had few linkages to subsequent clinical work. In that year, small groups of students met with professors of the required courses and complained about the lack of syllabi, unprepared lecturers, insufficient numbers of clinical applications, and visuals that had to be copied from boards rather than being given in handouts. For "Cell Structure and Function," 1st-year students gave resoundingly low marks: Between 67 and 90% rated the lectures fair to poor on preparation, clarity of presentation, enthusiasm, and communication of material—the lowest ratings of any of the preclinical courses.[31]

When students perceived little change in the teaching pattern the following year, protest escalated with formal petitions to the dean's office. According to the minutes of the faculty's executive committee, "a certain amount of student reaction and unrest is inevitable with any curriculum, and to be sure a certain amount of the present situation represents frustration with a curriculum that still has a fair amount of rigidity." The faculty acknowledged student discontent over required courses and inflexible teaching practices and concluded those students' "concerns were legitimate." Moreover, the students "have a right to expect an education of high quality."[32]

In a remarkable decision, the faculty executive committee then decided that for the remaining two quarters of academic year 1966–1967, students would not be required to attend lectures. Students who took this option could read selected course materials and take exams as an alternative to attending lectures. With the instructor's permission, they could also be excused from further attending laboratory courses. "These new provisions in the academic policy of the School of Medicine," the executive committee concluded, "are intended to be a first step toward providing students with a curriculum more in keeping with the graduate school philosophy" of the Five-Year Plan. Coming a half-dozen years after the innovation was introduced, the faculty statement rang hollow. As a way of bargaining their way out of a crisis, professors—some of whom agreed with student critics—gave a positive spin to a treaty negotiated with angry students.[33]

Such actions, however, failed to halt student criticism of teaching in the required core courses or growing faculty restiveness over the reform. Continuing dissent over the quality of the teaching and intrafaculty and departmental tensions over the research and clinical purposes for teaching the medical sciences help explain the slow demise of the Five-Year Plan. Faculty proposals for changing the Five-Year Plan, crafted in the heat of student and professorial protests, sought a new consensus for change.

REFORMING THE REFORM:
AN ALL-ELECTIVE CURRICULUM, 1968

Student dissent over the Five-Year Plan paralleled open faculty conflict. As early as 1962, interdepartmental tensions over reductions in laboratory time historically allocated to particular departments resurrected earlier divisions among faculty over scheduling courses. Departmental competition for more hours of teaching time (for which university funds were allocated) shrunk even further the prospects for faculty collaboration in those courses designed to be exemplars of team teaching. In January 1962, a frustrated Professor Frederick Fuhrman (who directed the integrated "Cell Structure and Function" course) proposed disbanding the committee appointed to oversee curricular integration and thus end the fiction of interdepartmental collaboration.

> It is clear that the development has been away from our original goal of integrated laboratory teaching toward complete departmental autonomy in planning and presentation.
>
> I believe that it is now time to recognize our failure . . . because of the lack of any real desire for this type of teaching by either the members of the Committee or their departmental executives.

What bothered Fuhrman was that incoming students were receiving false advertising about the program in the catalogue. "We are deceiving our students," he wrote, "by continuing to state that the 'medical work is presented largely in interdepartmental courses.'"[34]

To Professor Avram Goldstein, enthusiastic promoter of the Five-Year Plan, untiring advocate of research-based medicine, and the driving force behind the new interdepartmentally taught laboratory courses, Fuhrman's proposal to disband the committee was misguided. Goldstein cited the impact of Fuhrman's own integrated course, how four faculty in the two departments of Physiology and Pharmacology (of which Goldstein was a leading member) collaborated on teaching about the kidney, and, finally, how a previously disparate course in neurological sciences had now become unified. Based on this evidence, Goldstein urged that Fuhrman's proposal be rejected. "We should recognize," he concluded, "that radical curricular changes have been accomplished in a short time, most of them probably beneficial, some of them possibly detrimental." He asked the committee to "reaffirm that integration and interdepartmental teaching are among the many methods that may be appropriate for implementing the [Five-Year Plan]." The committee endorsed Goldstein's position. Professor Fuhrman soon resigned as director of the integrated course.[35]

Growing student dissatisfaction with the teaching of basic medical sciences and, in particular, the integrated "Cell Structure and Function" course gave substance to Fuhrman's criticisms. The faculty not only abolished the committee; they also abolished required courses.

In 1968, a year in which the university was in civil turmoil and a major report recommended abandoning general education requirements for undergraduates, the medical school faculty swept away all required core courses, leaving to each department and the newly created Curriculum Committee on Courses (CCC) the determination of what electives would be taught in which year. In making these decisions, the faculty ended the first and only major challenge to the traditional 2×2 medical school organization of curriculum and teaching in this century. The faculty decision was made in the absence of any formal evaluation of the Five-Year Plan to determine if the curricular and instructional reform had ever satisfied the often competing SUSM ideals of graduating both first-rate medical researchers and humane physicians.[36]

With an all-elective curriculum, advising of students and assuring that the quality of graduates remained high became key items on the faculty agenda. For the first time, faculty paid direct attention to the matter of advising. They established teams of professors to assist students in choosing courses and added graduation requirements to insure that students would meet minimum standards. All students, for example, had to take the National Board of Medical Examiners (NBME) test and score at least 75% on Part 1 and an overall 75% on the exam. The faculty assumed that students would learn the factual knowledge called for on the test through the electives they took and in preparing for exams; the test would serve as a safety net for students to acquire minimum medical knowledge.[37]

Even though the all-elective curriculum theoretically gave students a blank check to take any preclinical courses they desired, the CCC provided guidelines for which classes students should take. In the next decade, students ended up largely taking the traditional array of preclinical courses that their predecessors had taken in the 1940s and 1950s (before the Five-Year Plan). Nonetheless, a faculty nervous about students' choices of courses, by the mid-1970s, had reintroduced required courses. These changes, then, ironically resulted in a revised official curriculum that hewed closely to the familiar 2×2 model.[38]

Teaching Anatomy Under the All-Elective Curriculum

Abandoning required courses in 1968 and returning to full departmental autonomy in determining what should be taught defused much faculty and interdepartmental conflict but not misgivings over the teaching of anatomy. Student dissent coalesced into a series of unusual protests over the quality of teaching in the early 1970s.

Under the all-elective curriculum, virtually all entering medical school students still chose to take anatomy courses. In early 1970, the entire 1st-year class wrote to the faculty expressing their dismay over the introductory gross anatomy course. The first-quarter course had consisted of 10 lectures, 10 handouts, a few demonstrations, and 68 hours of dissection. Three of the lectures, the students said, repeated text material, two were clinical correlations "with little anatomical relevance," two were radiological anatomy, and only three lectures helped students learn anatomy by any method other than memorization.[39]

The students didn't ask professors to abandon lectures; they wanted better lectures.

> Descriptive lectures in the same style as the text are a waste of both students' and instructors' time. . . . Other types of lectures, however, are desirable. A lecture on anatomy that demonstrates the clinical importance of structures helps the student judge which material to emphasize. . . . Lectures which demonstrate the functional significance of structures, as did Miss Kent's lecture on gaits, are useful for the same reason. . . . Lectures which take advantage of films, models, prosections, and other visual aids . . . are appropriate.[40]

The students were well aware that teaching involves more than lecturing. They were sharply critical of what they saw as a lack of guidance about what they should select out of the massive amount of factual detail on the human body.

> There was absolutely no effort on the part of the anatomy department to help the student decide which parts of the vast body of knowledge about anatomy should be emphasized—despite numerous requests for such advice from frustrated students. Requests were met with such answers as "I had the same trouble when I took anatomy 39 years ago," or "you can never tell what you might need to know."[41]

Dissecting also came in for much criticism.

> The cadaver is a cheap and willing teacher, but it cannot replace a good instructor. . . . Since the main purpose of laboratory is to provide a visual aid for learning, it is not necessary for each student to spend hundreds of hours dissecting his own cadaver. Prosections . . . could be used to spare students most of the work of dissection and thus give them more time for lectures and study.[42]

The students concluded that the course was "unsatisfactory."

> Although anatomy has always been taught this way, the rapid expansion of the basic medical sciences has made it necessary for the medical student to devote a decreasing percentage of his time to anatomy. He can no longer afford to learn anatomy in the revered but time consuming and frustrating manner of his forefathers. . . . The cadaver and text can no longer be the core of the course.[43]

A month later, at a CCC meeting, the professor heading the faculty committee on the anatomical sciences told his colleagues,

> The primary problem in gross anatomy teaching appears to be rigid adherence to traditional methods of teaching anatomy and a lack of coordination between the department faculty. There has been no significant attempt by the faculty to adapt the teaching to the reduction in hours incurred in 1968, very little effort towards increasing the relevance of anatomy to the needs of the students, very limited use of prosection and visual aids, and only timid exploration of the use of advanced students as teaching assistants.[44]

The point about "lack of coordination" may be unclear to readers. Medical school lecture courses were organized as cameo appearances by experts in the field. Usually a faculty member would be "course director" and schedule different experts to lecture on assigned topics. In some anatomy courses, students might listen to a half-dozen different lecturers. In other preclinical courses, the number of different lecturers might exceed 15. Seldom would a course director assemble the different lecturers to try to diminish redundancy or fill gaps that needed attention. Thus, student complaints about flawed coordination meant that some lecturers spoke on topics that students had not been prepared for or spoke on topics that previous lecturers had dealt with or variations of both. Although the CCC discussed "solutions" to this problem, no action was taken at that time.

In 1971, student evaluations of the gross anatomy courses—there was a 100% return—rated them from 1.9 to 2.9 (very bad to poor) on a 5-point scale; these were the lowest ratings, save one, among the entire offerings of preclinical courses that year.[45]

Students, however, were quick to compliment what they felt was effective teaching. In *The Organ,* a student-written publication, five kudos for "Teacher of the Week" went to anatomy instructors within a 14-month period. One professor was commended "for his relaxed and lucid teaching style and his many extra hours in review sessions."[46]

An external visiting committee concluded in 1972 that "the Department of Anatomy had been allowed to disintegrate." The reduction from 11 full-time faculty in 1961 to 8 in 1965 and to 7 by the time the committee inspected the SUSM revealed the gradual marginalization of anatomy within the school. Leaving the influential chair of the department vacant for long periods of time further marked the administration's and faculty's benign neglect of this basic medical science.[47]

The faculty finally acted. Under the leadership of Robert Chase, who chaired the Department of Surgery, the Department of Anatomy moved to fulfill a service function within the medical school. Faculty members who had strong teaching skills were added to the department. The anatomy faculty compressed the four-quarter sequence of gross anatomy courses into two quarters. More attention was paid to coordinating lectures, making clinical applications, and adding teaching assistants to labs. Films and other materials were made available to students. By the late 1970s, student opinion on gross anatomy courses markedly improved. At a meeting between the CCC and 16 students to discuss the basic science courses, gross anatomy was given high marks for the quality of teaching and the clear attempt to make clinical connections to lectures and lab work.[48]

Robert Chase pointed out that in these years he sought temporary faculty who were known for their teaching and were less interested in research. He expressed pride in how many of his professors of anatomy won teaching awards. This strategy of seeking out teachers, not researchers, as faculty "has brought relief to our own structural biologists whose research is at the biochemical and ultramicroscopic level from the irrelevant burden of teaching Human Gross Anatomy."[49]

Increased student satisfaction with teaching aside, by 1980, administrator and faculty actions had already downsized the Department of Anatomy in faculty billets, status, and time scheduled for teaching traditional subjects. In that year, the Department of Anatomy was reduced to a division and placed in the newly created Department of Structural Biology only to be transferred to the Department of Surgery in 1983. These organizational changes marked the end of the cyclical tensions over the teaching of anatomy. Viewing the subject as a site of research (shifting the division to the Department of Structural Biology) or as a site to prepare medical students to become practitioners (moving the division to the Department of Surgery) had been finally resolved organizationally. Service to the medical school through teaching now dominated the division. The increasing use of self-instructional and computer-based anatomy software and the hiring of faculty whose major task was to teach suggest strongly that the persistent struggle for direction in the subject had ended.[50]

REQUIRED COURSES REDUX: 1981–1990

Beginning in the mid-1970s, a small but vocal faculty group began criticizing students' choices of courses, worrying about occasional declines in NBME scores and fearing that students were missing essential knowledge and research experiences in medical school. A faculty committee evaluating the all-elective curriculum reported in 1978 that most students were opting for a 4 instead of a 5-year curriculum and failing to exploit Stanford's small student body, high faculty-to-student ratio, and talented faculty. This meant also "that students have had less time to pursue scholarly investigative efforts."[51]

Calling these outcomes "unfortunate," the committee recommended changing the number of quarters for which students would pay tuition to enable students to stay for the entire period. After wending its way through the faculty, dean, and university administration, the university's board of trustees adopted this revision.

Yet available data on students' course-taking contradicted these "unfortunate" outcomes. One group of visiting university officials in 1977, for example, concluded that "students with a sense of responsibility for their education, and a fear of missing important components, complete a curriculum on the elective basis which with certain exceptions is essentially the same as that in more rigidly structured schools."[52]

Moreover, data about student-generated research projects and joint faculty-student investigations contradict these criticisms. The Liaison Committee on Medical Education survey in 1974 reported that 48 of 76 M.D. recipients "participated in some research activity at some time" while at SUSM. Also, of those 76 graduates, 29 had "authored or coauthored or had a substantive role in a published work." Moreover, in the early 1970s, a new program specifically geared to graduate M.D.'s in research was established; by 1975, the Medical Science Training Program enrolled 27 students.[53]

What probably elevated faculty anxiety, especially for those professors in the preclinical sciences, was that certain enrollments had fallen drastically. For biochemistry, 83% of graduates in 1973 had taken it, but in 1979 only 15% enrolled. For immunology, 85% of graduates in 1973 had sat in its classes and labs; yet of 1979 graduates only 18% had.[54]

Such data concerned those faculty who saw their mission as preparing graduates for medical research careers. They pressed for constraints on students' choices and a return to required preclinical and clinical experiences. For example, in 1980, the clinical faculty had become upset enough with students' failing to choose particular clerkships in their last 2 years of medical school to convince the entire faculty to accept the reestablishment of five mandatory experiences in surgery, medicine, obstetrics/gynecology, pediatrics, and psychiatry.[55]

Key preclinical faculty also sought similar ends. Avram Goldstein, one of the strongest advocates of the Five-Year Plan and an increasingly vocal critic of the changes in 1968, campaigned among faculty for required preclinical courses. In early 1979, Goldstein circulated to the faculty a statement that a large number of professors signed. A few paragraphs suggest the tenor and direction of faculty sentiment:

> If we had set out deliberately to lower our academic standards and the performance of our students, here are some of the things we might have done:
>
> • Institute a totally elective curriculum, without structure and without required sequence . . . with no obligation for the student to demonstrate competency in any of the basic subject areas of medical science.
> • Abolish letter grades. . . .

- Refuse to acknowledge that the unique primary mission of this medical school—what our faculty is best equipped to do—is to train the next generation of clinical investigators, basic medical scientists, and academicians.

As we have sown, so have we reaped.[56]

A few months later, Goldstein wrote to the influential Committee of Five—established in 1968, it was the steering committee for the entire SUSM Faculty Senate—and urged them to come before the faculty with a list of proposals, including "a required set of *core subjects* [original emphasis], a new compulsory course that teaches the philosophy, methodology, [and] pitfalls" of research, and the introduction of small-group teaching in preclinical subjects and possible reestablishing of lab courses in particular subjects.[57]

After being elected chair of the Faculty Senate in the spring, Goldstein wrote to a supportive colleague,

The thing that disturbs me is that although through a lot of perseverance and hard work we are making progress, the opposition [to required courses] is vocal whereas the supporting claque . . . is pretty silent. That is how we gave the place away ten years ago—and I was as guilty as any of us. If we want it back again, we're all going to have to dirty our hands and waste some time in politics.[58]

In October of the same year, Goldstein reported the results of a faculty survey (81% responded) on the all-elective curriculum. One-quarter of the faculty were "seriously displeased" with the degree of electivity in the current curriculum; 16% endorsed students choosing all of their courses; three-quarters of the faculty wanted the issue studied by a committee.[59]

Students also expressed their opinions in *The Organ* over the changes. One 3rd-year student viewed the struggle over electivity as a fundamental conflict between two irreconcilable camps over the school's goals on what kinds of doctors to graduate.

[The two camps are] the 'zebras' who believe that lab science is the only real source of medical progress, and the 'horses' who for many and diverse reasons distrust that conviction. Most professors, of course, were hired to be zebras . . . while most students are horses . . . [who] are overwhelmed to find an institution that embodies the zebra philosophy. Stanford Medical Center is built on DNA replicas . . . and heart transplants, on professors' convictions and graduate students' work. . . . Patient care was of secondary importance in this kind of scheme, and the production of practicing doctors was little more than an afterthought. . . . And what is one to do? At Stanford, if one is not a zebra, one is a horse; there is no other choice. As a zebra, one is worked to death but coddled with praise and glory and tenured positions. As a horse, one is merely tolerated, educated, and sent away.[60]

By 1981, those preclinical faculty seeking required courses had triumphed. The SUSM Faculty Senate asked the CCC to develop a core curriculum in the basic medical sciences and, a year later, approved the CCC's recommendations that all students entering in 1984 had to take required preclinical courses.[61]

However, turmoil over reestablishing required courses lasted throughout the decade. In 1988, after growing student criticism of particular courses combined with faculty inaction, a group of medical students, like their peers in the 1960s and 1970s, organized Students for an Improved Curriculum. The CCC decided at about the same time to go forward with a curriculum review since such an examination had been mandated 5 years earlier when the all-elective curriculum had been finally dismantled.[62]

Quietly released to the faculty in the fall of 1990, the report of the Curriculum Review Committee sought to establish whether the shift to required courses in the early 1980s "was meeting the goal of providing Stanford medical students with the fundamental knowledge needed for a medical career." Few such program evaluations had occurred in SUSM. None had been undertaken for the Five-Year Plan (1959–1968) or for the all-elective curriculum (1968–1982). The report's conclusions were based upon the results of an Association of American Medical Colleges student questionnaire, a faculty survey, scores on national tests, and information gathered from students and faculty in clinical clerkships. What the faculty committee found might have discouraged ardent advocates of prescribed courses.

- The introduction of the required curriculum "seems to have had little or no impact on our graduates' perception of the strengths and weaknesses of . . . the medical school."
- Fifty percent of the faculty respondents have not altered their preclinical courses, as they were expected to, in response to the required courses; 59% of the basic sciences faculty "think there is insufficient coordination between required preclinical courses."
- Students "have concluded that good teaching is not a high priority of the medical school and that good teachers are not adequately rewarded."
- "There has been no significant change in student performance during the time the new curriculum has been in force."

Overall, the report found that even in the light of these shortcomings, "neither the faculty nor the students want to discontinue the required curriculum." The responses of both faculty and students, the report concluded, "suggest that what is needed in . . . the Stanford Medical School is more in the nature of a tune-up than a major overhaul of the system."[63]

Changes in the Teaching of Anatomy During the 1980s

In returning the teaching of anatomy to the Department of Surgery, the faculty considerably reduced a century-old department's power and status within the medical school. Those clinically oriented faculty who taught anatomy courses broadened the use of teaching aids to include computer graphics, more prosections, and increased access to videos. Professors spent more time linking gross anatomy to physiology and cell structure courses offered in the 1st year of medical school. Instructors stressed clinical applications both in lectures and in dissections. Pedagogy became more complex. Each cadaver, for example, was assigned to seven students. For 2 hours daily, two of the seven students would dissect. The other five joined another group of five to work in a regularly scheduled discussion with faculty on surface anatomy, on developing physical examination skills, and in demonstrations of prosections. Individual and small-group self-study was another option, which included interactive computer lessons, case studies, and radiology displays on the region of the body being studied.[64]

Throughout the 1980s, 1st-year medical students registered their satisfaction with the content and teaching of the gross anatomy course by giving it high marks (between 5.6 and 6.1 on a 7-point scale with 7 being excellent). On one student-drafted review of the human anatomy course, there were many suggestions for improvement, yet there was also overall admiration for the course's organization, quality of lectures, review sessions, clinical applications, and instructors' accessibility. One suggestion from students was to have more written self-quizzes and reviews. "All of this supports," one student wrote, "the oft-expressed opinion that 'repetition is the key to learning anatomy: tell 'em, tell 'em again, ask 'em and then tell 'em again.'" [65]

WHY HAS STANFORD'S CENTURY-OLD MODEL OF MEDICAL EDUCATION BEEN SO DURABLE?

There have been moderate and minor changes to the content and structures in the official and taught curriculum since 1908. Most of the highly touted reforms (e.g., Five-Year Plan, all-elective system) lasted about a decade with occasional key features surviving to the present (e.g., students' choice in determining how much time to spend in the preclinical years). In 1994–1995, for example, entering medical students took 30 required preclinical subjects. Current Stanford students spend 2 or 3 years on these preclinical subjects, supplemented by innovative courses to prepare for the clinical years in which they serve in required and elective clerkships. Turn-of-the-century reformers, including Abraham Flexner, would have found these requirements in the official curriculum familiar. They might have needed some help in recognizing some of the other preclinical requirements: biostatistics, health research and policy, psychiatry, and behavioral sciences. Thus, few of the recurring curricular changes that I have documented have substantially modified the core curricular structures in the established 2×2 model of medical education introduced at Stanford almost a century earlier.

Embedded in that century-old model is a vision of a first-rate doctor: a technically proficient, specialized physician who is humane, serves the public, stays abreast of new knowledge, and investigates puzzling questions in medicine. Within a university-based medical school, successive generations of Stanford faculty found this vision to be filled with conflicting values. Some chose to strengthen portions of it; others chose to alter parts of it. Driven more by the research imperative common to graduate schools than by the teaching imperative, neither faculty nor administration substantially changed it—except in the Anatomy Division, which had abandoned research as a priority by the late 1970s. Instead, across departments, faculty negotiated political compromises in curriculum and pedagogy that maintained the view that the best doctors were those who were medical researchers.

With such a dominant view of research as all-important, it is unsurprising that teaching was subordinate. Only a few shifts in teaching practices in all preclinical subjects occurred (see Figure 4.2). Laboratory time had declined and lecturing had increased, a pattern that also describes what had occurred in the teaching of anatomy with one slight difference. While laboratory and dissection time continued to dominate instruction, anatomy faculty had broadened the repertoire of teaching practices to include far more small-group work and technological aids than in most other preclinical courses.

Obviously, there have been many modifications in the organization of the preclinical curriculum and uses of different teaching methods since Stanford established its medical school prior to World War I (see Figure 4.3). These changes, however, have not substantially replaced

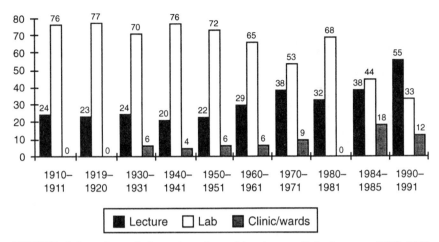

FIGURE 4.2 — Intended modes of teaching in preclinical years, 1910–1990 (percentage).

the basic 2×2 model at SUSM or, for that matter, in 95% of the medical schools in the nation; the sturdy turn-of-the-century form of medical education thrives in the face of repeated change.[66]

Why has this model of medical education remained vigorous and sturdy at Stanford? From this historical analysis of the medical school, I offer a tripartite answer. First, the 2×2 model introduced at the turn of the century worked. That is, administration, faculty, and students have largely viewed this way of organizing medical education a success. It may have flaws, inefficiencies, and, occasionally, for some students and faculty it may work ineffectively. But overall, this form of medical education has succeeded in turning out both practitioners and academic researchers. Such overall faculty and student satisfaction gave ardent reformers (at least by the 1980s) little ground to plow for making major changes. Recall the 1990 report of the Curriculum Review Committee, which concluded that even with many familiar concerns raised by both faculty and students neither group "wants to discontinue the required curriculum."[67]

Evidence of SUSM's success, advocates for stability would have argued, can be found in the highly productive faculty at Stanford who carried out biomedical research, published their findings, and garnered research funds. Advocates also pointed to the evidence found in the large pool of bright students who competed for the limited slots in each year's entering class. Stanford medical students' performance on

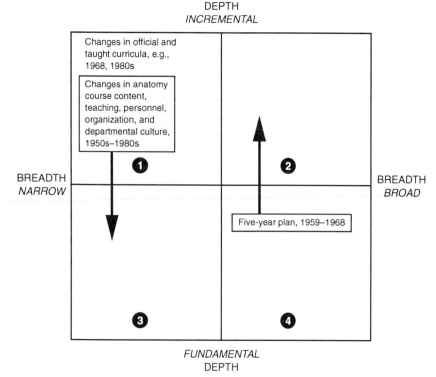

FIGURE 4.3 — Changes in the School of Medicine, 1908–1990.

national exams after their 1st year has ranked among the top in the nation. Finally, there is the prestige of Stanford as a world-class medical school known for its capacity as a research institution to produce first-rate academic scientists.

All of these points suggest strongly to faculty, students, and administration that the program has worked well. Yes, faculty would say, there is always room for improvement but no compelling need for us to seek an alternative to a program that is doing so well. It is these shared beliefs that form the foundation for the stability of the 2×2 model.[68]

Surely, those who would question this line of argument could have pointed out that sorting out the best and brightest students and faculty from the effectiveness of the program is virtually impossible. The value-added portion of the 2×2 model, in other words, is most difficult to determine not only for Stanford but for most other medical schools. Few skeptics, however, publicly challenged this dominant theme of success.

Second, no viable alternative to the historical model of medical education ever emerged and survived at Stanford, except for a brief period between 1959 and 1968 with the Five-Year Plan. This effort to introduce interdisciplinary courses and team teaching of organ systems foundered in professorial and departmental autonomy within a climate of growing student dissent over the quality of teaching. Since 1968, no overarching alternative to the existing form of medical education has been proposed and seriously debated by faculty or administration.

There have been, of course, other models of medical education that substantially revised the conventional way of educating future physicians. The "organ systems" approach to reorganizing the curriculum and instruction, which was tried for a short time at Stanford, has survived at Western Reserve Medical School, the site of the reform in the early 1950s, and had been tried at other medical schools. Similarly, McMaster University Medical School (Canada), University of New Mexico Medical School, Michigan State University, Harvard University, and other institutions have revised their traditional 4-year curriculum by adopting problem-based learning, a model of medical education that stresses fundamentally different roles for faculty and students in teaching and learning.[69]

Such changes roiling the world of medical education did influence Stanford. Administrators and faculty suggested improvements to various segments of professional training. What has occurred has been largely ad hoc incrementalism rather than any substantial shift to an alternative model of preparing students to be doctors. One example may suffice. In 1988, Harvard University Medical School adopted "New Pathways," a problem-based learning program, for all of its students. In effect, Harvard adopted an alternative to the traditional 2×2 way of training medical students. At Stanford, there was much debate over what changes to make in its program. What eventually emerged was a new course called "Preparation for Clinical Medicine" that was taught in the 2nd year of preclinical courses. It is an imaginative blending of problem-based learning, multiple-station exercises, preceptor-student exchanges, and small-group work that has gained strong support from students since it was introduced in 1993. There have been, however, no faculty-wide committees, over-arching designs, or overall comprehensive plans to overhaul the present system of training.[70]

The absence of any serious alternative to the existing program being implemented beyond individual courses at Stanford strongly suggests a basic acceptance of the 2×2 model and a negotiated political compromise over conflicting medical faculty, university administration, and student interests. The third part of my answer, then, to the question of sturdiness of the model is that political bargains were struck to harness competing interests over what kinds of doctors to prepare, over departments finding room in the curriculum for new fields, over research-oriented faculty being expected to teach introductory courses to 1st- and 2nd-year medical students. These negotiations and treaties reduced levels of conflict by creating a rhetoric of reform and tradition of curricular change that ultimately strengthened the customary medical education offered at SUSM.[71]

To drive home this last part of my tripartite answer to the question, I need to elaborate how faculty factions, shuttling back and forth between highly prized but competing values (doing research; preparing humane and competent practitioners), found it hard to fashion a lasting reconciliation, a consensus over an alternative to the 2×2 model.

The evidence for these lasting ideological tensions over faculty's competing visions for graduates surfaced in the career choices Stanford M.D.'s made when they left school. Between 1978 and 1987, for example, 4th-year Stanford medical students replied to a national questionnaire (response rates varied between a low of 54% in 1980 to a high of 93% in 1985 with a median of 75%). For first choice in a career in this decade, a median of 59% chose academic medicine; 41% opted for careers as practitioners. In 1987, for medical schools across the nation, 28% of the graduating students chose academic medicine and 72% sought to enter clinical practice. The high percentages of Stanford graduating medical students seeking academic medicine comes as little surprise since the faculty had admitted students who were interested in research and had offered numerous opportunities for students to participate in publicly and privately funded projects and to publish papers. Between 1982 and 1984, to cite one example, 73% of Stanford graduates had participated in research projects; the national average was 35%.[72]

But what happened to the graduates after they left Stanford and settled into a career? How many M.D.'s ended up as professors doing research and teaching in medical schools? Such data is far harder to extract from archival sources. What limited evidence I could find suggests that most Stanford M.D.'s became practitioners, largely as specialists. A minority of graduates entered full-time academic medicine. In a survey of physicians trained at Stanford before the 1959 merger (classes of 1952–1956) and of those trained after it (classes of 1960–1972), Lawrence Horowitz, himself a Stanford M.D., reported the data shown in Table 4.2 (87% of the alumni responded).

Horowitz's article in the *Stanford M.D.,* an alumni magazine for Stanford physicians, concluded that the contradiction between the goals, curriculum, and pedagogy (preparing students to be researchers) and what graduates did after completing their training (working mostly as practi-

TABLE 4.2 — *Career Choices of Stanford Medical School Graduates*

	Pre-merger alumni	Post-merger alumni
1. Do no research at all	84%	52%
Do some research (more than one-quarter time)	16%	48%
2. Full-time academic medicine	6%	20%
Part-time academic medicine (i.e., teaching and doing research in a medical school)	23%	15%

Adapted from Lawrence Horowitz (1978), "Stanford School of Medicine: A Question of Identity." *Stanford M.D., 17*(1), pp. 2–4.

tioners) was self-evident. Although the article triggered angry responses from fellow alumni, none of the responses could reanalyze Horowitz's data as anything other than revealing the gap between the direction in professional training and the eventual career choices. These patterns suggest, but are far from conclusive, that most graduates went into specialty practice while a sizable minority of graduates pursued academic medicine.[73]

The 1994–1995 Stanford University catalogue continues to include the competing visions that so concerned President Ray Lyman Wilbur in 1922 of preparing medical students to be medical scientists and practitioners:

> To develop in all students the capacity for leadership in the clinical practice of scientific medicine and to provide them with opportunities to prepare themselves for careers in research and teaching in the various branches of basic, clinical, and social medicine.[74]

Although the consensus over preparing students to practice academic medicine seems secure in the official curricula, the ideological tension over what kinds of doctors to graduate, amid the familiar constraints of limited time and funds, still persists in the waning years of this century. The research-driven mission of the medical school remains harnessed to institutional beliefs, rules, and organization. The research imperative is embedded within departmental priorities, curricular subject matter, and faculty autonomy to seek funds and use those monies for research and teaching. Such autonomy, of course, also encourages friction within SUSM because some departments (e.g., family practice, pediatrics) and individual professors continue to seek different values in preparing medical students to become doctors.

Thus, the historic 2×2 model of medical education, persisting through political bargaining, intersected neatly with the university's research imperative. The university's reputation hinged not upon the faculty's teaching skills but upon their published scholarship and their entrepreneurial skills in generating research grants. The university's structure of departments, academic rank, tenure and promotion criteria that stressed research productivity, and emphasis on graduate programs quietly supported and enhanced medical investigation. The center of gravity, then, within the 2×2 model was to blend research and teaching, to cultivate a spirit of inquiry within doctors-in-training while offering them the latest research findings. In short, the reform that was introduced a century ago as a 4-year university-based medical education was then (and is now) thoroughly wedded to the research imperative, which drives the university's official curriculum, instruction, and political compromises. The model was viewed as a success by its key stakeholders. Viable alternatives emerged in this century to challenge the conventional preparation program, and Stanford tried to incorporate some of these changes, but none seriously challenged the 2×2 model. Hence, change without reform.[75]

Abraham Flexner once said that "medical education is, after all, not medicine but education." If that is the case, as I believe it is, then the faculty's transforming of major changes in SUSM's curriculum and pedagogy into modest ones mirrors a frequent pattern observed by researchers who have often noted how other organizations, in surviving over time, adapt changes to fit, rather than alter, their basic structures.[76]

If converting major changes into modest ones has been the pattern for the medical school, how does what happened there compare and contrast with what happened in the history department? A professional school anchored in the medical sciences and a department rooted in both the humanities and social sciences offer dissimilar venues for change. To what degree did faculty actions in curriculum, pedagogy, advising, handling of dilemmas of purpose, and implementing strategies for change within two dissimilar venues converge and diverge? In the next chapter, I explore similarities and differences in Stanford's Department of History and School of Medicine and try to explain the surprising similarities that emerged over the last century.

HOW RESEARCH TRUMPED TEACHING IN HISTORY AND MEDICINE

On a cold winter's day, a group of porcupines squeezed very closely to each other, using their mutual warmth to avoid dying of cold. Soon, however, they felt each other's quills, which once again made them draw apart from one another. But the need for warmth brought them together again, only for the problem to repeat itself, so that they found themselves driven to and fro between the two sufferings until they found finally an intermediate distance affording them the most comfort possible.

—Arthur Schopenhauer[1]

IN THIS CHAPTER, I examine the similarities and differences between the Department of History and the School of Medicine in subordinating teaching to research. I also take up the question of whether the patterns that emerged at Stanford were echoed in universities across the nation.

DIFFERENCES AND SIMILARITIES OF THE DEPARTMENT OF HISTORY AND THE SCHOOL OF MEDICINE

Within Stanford University, the Department of History and the School of Medicine (SUSM) appear to be very different. In 1990, there were 49 professors of history (including lecturers and instructors) versus 711 on the medical faculty (including adjunct professors). Numbers of students (both undergraduates and graduates) were also dissimilar:

165

402 history majors, masters, and doctoral students versus 752 in the School of Medicine.[2]

Apart from size of faculty and student body, what seemingly further separates the department from the school are their missions and financing within the university. The history department provides general education courses as part of distribution requirements and a departmental major to undergraduates, while preparing graduate students to be historians. Because they are in a department within the School of Humanities and Sciences, history professors depend upon university funding for their billets and staffing.

The School of Medicine's mission is to prepare only graduate students to be both medical researchers and clinicians. As a professional school lodged within the university, funding the dual mission of preparing future practitioners and researchers is complex. Where the Department of History is almost entirely funded by the university, SUSM is expected to be self-supporting. Monies do come from the university, but SUSM depends upon revenues from affiliated hospitals and research grants from federal agencies, private foundations, and corporations. Such differences in mission and funding make the medical school far more sensitive than the Department of History to state and national medical licensing agencies, the exigencies of rising and falling sources of federal and private medical research funding, and changes in national health care policies.[3]

Finally, there are disciplinary differences between the life sciences and the humanities. Researchers have categorized these differences into *hard* disciplines—fields such as the physical, natural, and life sciences in which there is a relatively high degree of consensus on important theories, questions, and methods—and *soft* ones such as the humanities, including history, in which scholars possess far less agreement on these matters.[4]

Hard and soft distinctions in disciplines also characterize how scholars work in each field. For example, collaboration is especially strong among biological scientists because they are accustomed to working together on laboratory research projects and publishing jointly authored articles (but seldom books) of their investigations. Frequent interaction among senior and junior faculty and between professors and graduate students around common interests leads to coauthored proposals for external funds and conference papers. In history, a soft discipline, the norm is independently (often done in isolation from colleagues) gathering and interpreting sources and writing a book. The book, usually a monograph or a synthesis of literature on a specialized topic advancing an explanation that either strengthens or departs from a mainstream opinion, is seldom coauthored. Few collaborative research projects emerge from the field of history. The daily work pattern of historians encourages privacy and the norm of independent work.[5]

A second dimension that researchers have found in categorizing disciplines is *pure* versus *applied,* or, the differences between studying liberal arts and preparing to become a lawyer, social worker, superintendent, or doctor. History fits the liberal arts, or pure dimension, in large part because at the undergraduate level it has little direct connection to an occupation, although at the graduate level securing a doctorate in history is, indeed, vocational preparation for becoming an historian. The School of Medicine clearly fits the applied category in that it prepares graduate students to become both medical scientists and specialized practitioners.

By now, the reader may have sensed some complications arising from these distinctions. In SUSM, the *hard* biological sciences are taught in an *applied* setting. Historians, practicing in a *pure* field, vocationally prepare doctoral students to be professors who teach, inquire, and write. Hence, what appears at first glance as differences between the School of Medicine and the Department of History in size of faculty, enrollments, and discipline subsequently become less dramatic.

When I step back to judge the magnitude and significance of these differences, it is the commonalties rather than the contrasts between the history department and SUSM that strike me as being more important. Commonalities in ad hoc incrementalism in changing curricular content and structures, constancy in teaching practices, protecting departmental and professorial autonomy, and struggling with irreconcilable dilemmas arising from the university-college hybrid, I argue, have bound together two separate units within the university in ways that go well beyond obvious differences. Furthermore, when a century is examined rather than a few years or a decade, these similar features reveal unmistakably how research trumped teaching at Stanford.

ADAPTATION IN THE CONTENT AND STRUCTURES OF THE OFFICIAL CURRICULA

There is little question that the subject matter professors have conveyed to students over the last century has changed. In the history department, Americanists and Europeanists were joined over the decades by Latin-American, African, Soviet, and Asian specialists. Stanford's academic historians mirrored a national movement in the discipline to go beyond the conventional constitutional, political, and military histories to incorporate social, economic, and cultural histories.[6]

   Similarly, new medical specialties were added to SUSM. When the Department of Medicine became the School of Medicine in 1913, there were 10 departments; in 1990, there were 22 departments, each having many divisions or subspecialties. As in other medical schools across the country, both mandated and elective courses expanded as each department sought time slots in the schedule.[7]

   These improvised changes in course content within the School of Medicine and Department of History at Stanford and elsewhere stemmed from both external and internal factors. Obviously, the exponential growth of specialized knowledge in each of these fields explains many of the content changes. Also, as different students (women, minorities, war veterans) attended Stanford, courses changed (e.g., education, nursing, war issues between 1919 and 1921, ethnic studies in the 1960s). Commitments of university presidents and faculties to electives as a core principle of curricular organization since 1891 would, in of itself, yield change and growth in courses as professors who passionately pursued specialized research agendas entered and exited disciplines that themselves were undergoing changes in what knowledge had accumulated and how it was used. Consider that oncology and women's history were unfamiliar to SUSM faculties and historians two generations ago.

   Moreover, changing state and national licensing requirements in medicine, national and regional job markets for historians and physicians, and availability of external funding slowly reshaped in small ways what professors taught and the way they organized the official curriculum. During World Wars I and II and the Vietnam conflict, for example, the official School of Medicine and history department curricula—as with sister institutions in the nation—reflected both faculty-student patriotism and divisiveness, as new funds for research and training poured into the university.

   Adaptation to larger social, economic, political, and demographic events, however, seldom came conflict-free. Tremendous growth in knowledge in both history and the life sciences produced strong pressures among faculties at Stanford, Harvard, Chicago, and elsewhere to deal with an increasingly crowded and fragmented official curriculum, one that could not expand infinitely. During the 1950s, many reforms for instituting general education emerged at Stanford and elsewhere. The Stanford Study of Education (1954–1956), SUSM's Five-Year Plan (1959), and frequent revisions of requirements for history majors and doctoral students were deliberate efforts to cope with changing social, economic, and political conditions in the larger society and growing curricular incoherence as more and more subjects were squeezed into an already constrained official curriculum. Negotiated compromises between departments over allocation of time in the curriculum produced incremental rather than fundamental changes in how the curriculum was organized, as the modest revisions in requirements for history majors and doctoral students and the 2×2 SUSM curriculum have revealed.[8]

What has occurred, over time, then, has been numerous changes in how the SUSM and history faculties, mirroring similar changes in universities across the country, organized their curricula and the subject matter that professors taught. Did pedagogy also change?

CONSTANCY AND CHANGE IN TEACHING PRACTICES (INCLUDING ADVISING)

Since the introduction of major teaching innovations (e.g., labs, seminars) in the late 19th century, classroom practices have largely remained stable with small reductions in the incidence of lecturing and the slow growth of small-group teaching. The one form of teaching that has continued to dominate mainstream practice is lecturing. Lecturing absorbs at least one-half to two-thirds of teaching duties in SUSM preclinical courses and in the Department of History, with the remainder of formal instructional time being spent in leading seminars, laboratory work, discussion sections, and directed research with individual and small groups of students. This pattern in teaching permeates the rest of the campus, with some variation by departments, and is similar to other American universities.[9]

Over the century in SUSM and the Department of History, small-group teaching and students' independent work slowly spread from their original home in graduate school (for early-20th-century doctoral students and medical students in the clinical phase of their work) to the final 2 years of an undergraduate's career and the initial preclinical courses for entering medical students. Such changes in teaching approaches have lessened the impersonality of lecturing to hundreds in cavernous auditoriums. Yet even with the mild decrease in lecturing over the century and the increase in small-group teaching, the lecture still dominates preclinical instruction in SUSM and undergraduate history courses.

For the rest of the university in the 1990s, this teaching repertoire remains steadfast. Two surveys revealed sharply that most faculty still depend upon lecturing to undergraduates; few use nontraditional methods (e.g., information technologies, case studies, simulations), and those that do are a tiny fraction of the Stanford professoriate, a pattern generally applicable to most American universities.[10]

With so much instructional time still devoted to the lecture, it is no accident that lecturing has become equated to teaching. What forged the linkage even tighter in this century were faculties' core beliefs about the role of subject matter in teaching. Many history department and SUSM faculty have believed that the central purpose of teaching is to transmit disciplinary knowledge to students. According to faculty, undergraduates must gain an elementary grasp of the field before advancing to higher levels of disciplinary knowledge. Hence, the dominant teaching role is that of content-disseminator. Because it is more efficient to convey subject matter and the essentials of a discipline to large groups, the lecture prevails and the role of professor as platform performer forges a linkage with the role of disseminating content. Pedagogy is no more than delivering knowledge clearly and coherently: Those who know can teach.[11]

Yet some faculty have had (and continue to have) counter-beliefs. Teaching for student understanding rather than factual coverage has motivated many professors to practice their craft differently than their colleagues. Such beliefs drive some professors to understand how students learn, figure out the issues that confound novices in a field, and teach content in ways that unravel what students find difficult. In teaching calculus to undergraduates, for example, some math professors have restructured their courses to teach the subject through using problems that are connected to students' lives. For teaching approximations, a professor would ask students to graph the rising temperature of a yam put into a hot oven and estimate the time at which the temperature of the yam would be 150 degrees. Such professors probe and guide students in learning conceptual structures of a discipline; they seek to help students learn how to think as mathematicians, historians, or medical clinicians.[12]

In SUSM, for example, those faculty that advocated integrated preclinical courses that drew from different disciplines in the Five-Year Plan during the early 1960s worked from a different set of assumptions about content and pedagogy than prevailing faculty beliefs. Similarly, the new preclinical course, "Preparation for Clinical Medicine," designed in the early 1990s, began with beliefs that students could learn essential clinical knowledge and skills through small groups with preceptors (rather than lecturers) by concentrating upon common problems faced by practitioners. Professors seeking student understanding see the close intersection between subject matter and pedagogy. The two are entangled and need to be worked on simultaneously. Those who know both content and how students learn marry their pedagogy to that knowledge. To such faculty, there is no divorce between subject matter and teaching; they are one and the same.[13]

What complicates the conceptual map of pedagogical beliefs and practice among professors is simply that some faculty hold both prevailing and counter-beliefs simultaneously, enacting each in different settings. Consider historians such as David Potter and David Kennedy who taught both lecture courses and seminars. In each venue, students have described how the professors were engaging platform performers as lecturers and, in advanced seminars, using analogies and metaphors to represent complex ideas while prodding individual students to think like historians. Those who understand both content and pedagogy can teach well.[14]

What emerges, then, from the repertoire of teaching practices over the last century and the beliefs that undergird them both at Stanford and other universities is a distinct pattern of stability following the late-19th-century introduction of innovative pedagogies. Once established, seminars, lab work, and independent study became fixtures in professors' classrooms, supplementing the reliable (and dominant) practice of lecturing decade after decade. What did change over time was the slight reduction of lecturing and a gradual spread of graduate teaching practices, such as small-group work into history colloquia, seminars for juniors and seniors, and periodic SUSM efforts to include similar experiences in preclinical courses. For most faculty, however, knowing one's subject and the craft of teaching remained distinctly separate activities.

When one turns to that form of informal teaching known as advising, results have been consistently dismal. From the introduction of the major-professor system in 1891 to its dismantling in 1920, and in repeated efforts to improve advising between the 1950s and 1990s (it continues into the final years of the century with the recommendations of the 1994 Commission on Undergraduate Education report), both administration and faculty across the university have bemoaned the sad state of affairs. The long-term trend in advising was clearly evident by the 1990s: The task of advising students has moved steadily, even inexorably over the last half-century, from a faculty responsibility to a task discharged by an especially hired staff.

In SUSM, for example, the ambitious plan for faculty advising teams that arose from the all-elective system (1968) that sought to reform the Five-Year Plan dissolved through neglect within 2 years. By 1974, SUSM's Office of Student Affairs had hired professional staff to advise medical students. Similarly, in the history department, alumni and senior surveys registered mild to strong disappointment with faculty over their inaccessibility as advisers. Overall, the university responded to these complaints by recruiting staff whose primary task was to provide academic advising. Thus, there have been many efforts to improve this aspect of informal faculty teaching over the last century.[15]

Changes have indeed occurred in the conduct of advising, but no reform intended to cement academic ties between professor and student has lasted. Perhaps one professor, speaking in 1995 about yet another effort aimed at securing more professors to advise undergraduates, best summed up a general faculty belief about advising at Stanford.

> I think we have to keep advising in the large picture of perspective and priorities. Advising will never be perfect. It is not as important as the teaching and research that happens in the University. It is not what the University exists for. Good teaching and good research are the most important things.[16]

These patterns of change and constancy in curriculum and teaching practice (including advising) in SUSM and the Department of History—as well as the larger university and its sister institutions across the nation—are notable when viewed over a century. What has helped to shape these patterns of curricular and pedagogical adaptations and continuity is the strong influence of professorial and departmental autonomy that favored disciplinary-driven research agendas over teaching.

DEPARTMENTAL AND PROFESSORIAL AUTONOMY

Stanford began with professors as the individual building blocks for a great university. Within a few years, however, it became clear that professorial freedom had led to certain obligations, such as advising students, going unfulfilled. President Jordan then turned to departments for discharging these responsibilities. Department chairs determined who would teach what, decided when time off could be taken to do research, and recommended individuals for appointment and promotion. The autonomous and decentralized department, over time, came to stand between the professor and top administrative officers, not only at Stanford but at virtually all American universities.[17]

As a consequence of this freedom, Stanford departments, through their influential executive heads (Ephraim D. Adams and Edgar E. Robinson in the history department and Ray L. Wilbur in the Department of Medicine), became powerful engines that have driven both disciplinary and professorial norms to favor research over teaching, advanced over introductory courses, and graduate students over undergraduates. In short, both the Department of History and SUSM developed strong research and weak teaching cultures. A few examples from the Department of History and SUSM elaborate the potent political authority that individual professors and departments exerted within the university to account for the makeshift adaptations in the official curriculum and teaching practices, including advising.[18]

Within the Department of History, the social structure of the discipline, with its norms of scholarly independence, permitted faculty to avoid, where possible, joint planning of either undergraduate or graduate courses and team-teaching. The value of professorial autonomy heightened an already vigorous sense of individualism. Except for the "Problems of Civilization" (1921–1935) and "Western Civilization" (1935–1968) courses, both of which were directed by members of the department, the dominant norm in departmental teaching was giving solo lectures and leading seminars. Even in the jointly planned undergraduate courses mentioned above and in colloquia on historiography, specialists made separate appearances without much preplanning or debriefing. One professor expressed dismay with university efforts that encouraged interdisciplinary courses. He claimed that the department had done quite well in its scholarship and teaching without any interdepartmental collaboration.[19]

Also the singular preference for teaching one's specialty to graduate students rather than teaching introductory courses to undergraduates underscored the powerful norms supporting research within the department. In 1969, for example, in the aftermath of recommendations from the Study of Education at Stanford to offer more small-group courses to undergraduates, David Potter—a professor whose appreciation and practice of the art of teaching was admired by colleagues—pointed out to his colleagues that teaching two colloquia to history undergraduates and two seminars to doctoral students would have to change so that some faculty would have to offer more colloquia: "I, for one, would be unwilling to have such a disproportion ... between my undergraduate and graduate teaching loads." Such decisions about team-teaching, collaboration with other departments, and allocating teaching assignments were made through faculty bargaining among themselves within the department, honoring the norm of professorial autonomy. With such a weak departmental culture in support of teaching, invariably intrafaculty bargaining sacrificed pedagogical concerns.[20]

At SUSM, the disciplinary norms in the life sciences supported joint planning of courses, which seemingly would signal strong support for collegiality in teaching. But as the courses were implemented, concerns for the quality of teaching became secondary. Course directors would line up a series of colleagues to lecture on prespecified topics to students, say, in biochemistry or neuroanatomy, and the professors would

arrive in the amphitheater, deliver the lecture with appropriate technological aids, and, after answering student questions, exit. Student complaints about certain preclinical courses, beginning in the mid-1960s and
continuing through the 1980s, pointed out the duplication of content in
lectures and lack of coordination among visiting lecturers.

As in the history department, SUSM had a weak teaching culture.
Yes, there were awards for excellence in teaching within SUSM. And, yes,
there were individual faculty members who were admired by colleagues
for the passionate quest to improve their craft. But the daily and weekly
routine work of medical education found few discussions about teaching that animated the Faculty Senate and few departments that made
more than occasional references to too much (or too little) lecturing in
preclinical courses. Except for occasional discussions in the curriculum
committees, school-wide debates about the quality of teaching and its
improvement arose only when students complained and individual
departments could no longer contain the grievances, as occurred in the
1960s with the teaching of anatomy.

What transpired with the anatomy department in the mid-1970s
through the early 1980s under the leadership of Department of Surgery's
Robert Chase threw into bold relief the flimsy support for teaching at
SUSM. In the division of anatomy, faculty leaders had created a genuine
culture supportive of teaching. Chase recruited faculty who were committed to teaching gross anatomy to medical students within a clinical
framework while assuring that the latest technologies were enlisted to
help students master the myriad facts that had to be absorbed.

The closest that SUSM faculty came to constructing strong norms
that supported teaching was when the Five-Year Plan produced cross-
departmental integrated courses in organ systems and lab work in the
early 1960s. The dean and faculty turned to subject-matter committees
that drew from various departments in SUSM, but at no point were these
new committees seen as superseding departmental authority to allocate
funds for teaching or to make appointments. By the mid-1960s, the committees had dissolved and the embryonic culture of teaching that had
supported school-wide discussions of pedagogy and content disappeared. What remained was a strong research culture anchored in
departmental and individual autonomy.[21]

Departmental politics and bureaucratic procedures ruled large units
in the medical school. University funds, for example, flowed into the
medical school budget—in 1982 it was $138 (rising to $168 in 1987) per
student per unit—and were redistributed to departments within the
school depending on course enrollments. Beginning in 1981, the Curriculum Coordinating Committee (CCC) argued that this formula favored

those departments offering lecture courses with large numbers of students and disadvantaged small-group courses, such as labs, clerkships, and seminars, "even though that is the type of teaching that the CCC would like to see encouraged."[22]

Interdepartmental disagreements over formula-derived funds for teaching reflected opposing views over the best types of teaching in medical school. In an unusual survey given in 1973 to medical school faculty, 60% of the faculty (141 professors replied) wanted lecture courses in the basic medical sciences; the remainder voted for small-group experiences. Not until 1981 did the CCC identify teaching approaches and funding formulas as an issue. It was still unresolved by 1990. In that year, a faculty self-study, prepared for an accreditation visit, found that 70% of preclinical classroom hours were devoted to lectures, 13% in conference, and 17% in laboratory exercises. This suggests that faculty preferences for small-group teaching over large-group lectures were ignored because of bureaucratic rules established many years earlier that favored one form of teaching over another. Departmental treaty-making among heads of departments within SUSM had retained a formula that favored lecturing for almost 2 decades.[23]

The departmental tilt toward offering large-group lectures over small-group courses and faculty preference for seminars over survey courses is no accident at Stanford. For both SUSM and the history department, large classes for 1st- and 2nd-year students, and small classes and independent work for majors and advanced medical students permitted departments to subsidize professors' research agendas by paying inquiry-oriented graduate students to assist professors who taught introductory courses. Such compulsory survey courses, originating in the 1920s and extending into the 1990s (except for a brief hiatus with the all-elective curriculum), resulted from faculty decisions prescribing general education courses. In doing so, the faculty forged modest compromises with the elective principle in organizing the official curriculum. Thus, over the century, these compromises have ensured large lecture courses for the first 2 years and smaller classes for the last 2.

Finally, university and departmental decisions to reduce teaching loads over the decades left more time for research. Both the history department and School of Medicine, over the century, responded to university initiatives by steadily reducing the number of courses and weekly hours of teaching that professors were expected to offer. Reductions in teaching loads, creation of large-group lectures in introductory courses for undergraduates, faculty autonomy to teach and investigate what each professor desires, and university structures such as academic rank and publication-driven criteria for granting tenure and promotion have accumulated quietly for decades to create strong departmental cultures favoring research over teaching. Not without discord, however.

Periodically, student outbursts over, for example, an assistant professor who had received awards for excellence in teaching being denied tenure on the basis of scholarly criteria dredged to the surface the continuing tension between publishing research and teaching. On such occasions, the importance and quality of teaching was sounded vigorously, and often eloquently, by Stanford president after president. At different times, administrative and faculty initiatives recognized teaching and thereby sought to elevate its status through awards (The Gores award in 1971; The Bing award in 1992), the creation of new units such as the Center for Teaching and Learning (1975), and Faculty Senate committees that focused on the improvement of teaching through evaluation (1970s and 1990s).

The pervasive influence of departmental and professorial autonomy, however, permitted research to thrive in the university. The structural mechanisms and cultural norms mentioned above buffered faculty from the inexorable social, economic, and demographic changes within the larger society while allowing the research imperative to dominate teaching, but not without faculty and presidential angst over the importance and quality of teaching. The pervasive and persistent tensions between teaching and research have endured, then, because they are rooted in intractable dilemmas that have faced the university and permeated both the Department of History and SUSM (see Figure 5.1 for a summary of changes at Stanford).

STRUGGLING WITH INTRACTABLE DILEMMAS

The tensions that have appeared and reappeared in these chapters have emerged from value conflicts in institutional purposes. These multiple and competing purposes have shaped the growth and ultimate identity of universities in the United States. Not unlike those cold porcupines rustling closer and closer until quills in eyes and bellies drive them apart only to return again for warmth until again repelled, Stanford and its sister institutions have experienced repeated tensions over these purposes and sought a balance between unlimited possibilities and inexorable limits. Such situations are dilemmas where two or more conflicting values cannot be reconciled because of constraints of time, money, people, and other resources. Therefore, unattractive choices must be made between competing, prized values. What results are not solutions

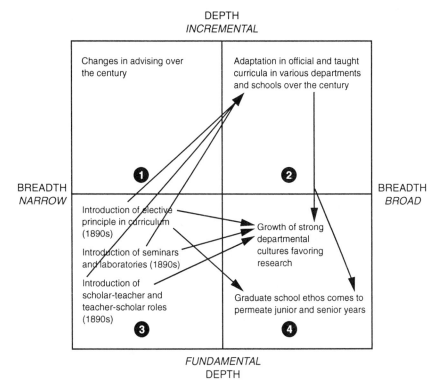

DEPTH
INCREMENTAL

Changes in advising over the century

Adaptation in official and taught curricula in various departments and schools over the century

BREADTH
NARROW

BREADTH
BROAD

1

2

Introduction of elective principle in curriculum (1890s)

Introduction of seminars and laboratories (1890s)

Introduction of scholar-teacher and teacher-scholar roles (1890s)

Growth of strong departmental cultures favoring research

Graduate school ethos comes to permeate junior and senior years

3

4

FUNDAMENTAL
DEPTH

FIGURE 5.1 — Summary of changes at Stanford, 1891–1990.

but compromises that, over time, can be, and often are, reshaped to give salience to a value that was given less attention at an earlier time. However the compromises are negotiated and temporarily reconciled, the dilemmas themselves remain. Dilemmas are not solved; they are managed.[24]

Is Stanford a university dedicated to creating knowledge or a college devoted to teaching undergraduates what their intellectual, moral, and civic duties are to their community and country? Are professors expected to be exemplars of moral and intellectual behavior in what and how they teach? Should the School of Medicine give priority to preparing scientists or practitioners? Should Stanford historians be teacher-scholars working to help undergraduates understand history or scholar-teachers geared to preparing the next generation of academics? And, finally, should research take precedence over teaching at Stanford, as it clearly has done?

The temptation to counter these questions with the rebuttal that these values are not mutually exclusive or dichotomous is strong. One could claim that both values can be fulfilled. If they could, I argue, they would have and the tensions would have dissolved. Constraints of time and money and the strongly stated preferences on the part of participants, however, have produced conflicts time and again. Thus, answers to these questions offer insights into these durable contradictions that have been so evident at Stanford and the nation's universities.

Dilemmas of Purpose: The University-College

From the very origins of universities in the waning decades of the 19th century, research was a "fundamental goal." After all, Johns Hopkins University (1876) and Clark University (1887) were founded as graduate schools wholly committed to the Humboldtian tradition of the research university, catering to only the most serious of students who worked closely with professors who conducted original research. Most historians charting the development of research-driven universities between 1870 and 1920 included Stanford.[25]

Since the 1885 Founding Grant, Stanford's explicit mission has been to advance knowledge through systematic inquiry and disseminate that knowledge through published scholarship, teaching, and public service. Its motto of *Die Luft der Freiheit Weht* (The Winds of Freedom Blow) embraced the German *lehrfreiheit* and *lernfreiheit* that so enraptured its young president in 1891. David Starr Jordan's belief in the centrality of research led to his "brashly"—it is historian Laurence Veysey's word—publishing annual reports that listed faculty's publications.[26]

Yet Stanford was also a college that accepted 17-year-olds and sought—through the liberal arts, sciences, and extracurricular activities—to turn teenage undergraduates into young mature men, within 4 years, who knew their responsibilities to their community and nation. This transformation was in the hands of professors who could teach with verve, enticing students into the life of the mind, and be exemplars of character that students would admire. If the production of value-free knowledge encased in the research imperative drove the university, then the value-laden teaching imperative fueled the college. "The American university," Jordan said in 1906, "is emphatically a teaching university." After 4 years in such a place, graduates would enter the world as well-proportioned citizens of high moral character who would eventually give business, cultural, and civic leadership to their communities. Like Harvard, Yale, Columbia, and Chicago, Stanford slowly evolved a compromise that became a hybrid structure serving two distinct traditions in higher education: the university-college.[27]

Commitment to blend the traditions, however, proved difficult in light of limited university resources, students' varied high school preparation, and constraints upon faculty's capacity to satisfy both values. At Harvard, for example, after Charles Eliot's 40-year presidency, in which he fashioned a national university anchored in the elective system, his successor, A. Lawrence Lowell, sought to restore the undergraduate college to its former stature by increasing required courses and renewing its focus upon teaching while reducing emphasis on graduate education. After decades of this refocusing upon undergraduates, English professor Bernard De Voto pleaded with the president in the 1930s: "Let the College rest awhile; it is time to give us back the University."[28]

At Stanford, Presidents Jordan and Wilbur repeatedly brought to the trustees plans for splitting off the initial 2 years of undergraduate work in introductory courses and letting the high school or newly emerging junior colleges perform the task. And just as repeatedly, the trustees rejected these plans for resolving the tensions between the morally laden teaching imperative nested in undergraduate education and the research imperative anchored within graduate education. In 1992, newly installed President Casper, for reasons more closely associated with the rising costs of a Stanford education, advertised the possibility of reducing the 4-year undergraduate career to 3 years. The subsequent 1994 Commission on Undergraduate Education report dismissed the proposal, condemning it to the same fate that earlier examinations of bisection encountered decades earlier.[29]

These tensions over purpose, uneasily reconciled in the university-college compromise, arose repeatedly over the century in various local and national debates over university curricular breadth versus depth, general education versus vocational specialization, and the growing imbalance between research and teaching in the explosive growth of graduate schools.

Consider the medical school, where its mission as a professional school was to prepare physicians who could combine the mind-set and skills of being a medical scientist, clinical researcher, and practitioner serving patients. The chapter on the SUSM detailed the conflicts that arose from these competing goals in anatomy and in the rest of the preclinical curriculum. Faculty members were divided over these goals, and attempted reforms moved back and forth in this century between electivity and prescription. Occasionally, a faculty member would tell students bluntly why they were in medical school. At a 1988 forum convened by a medical student group to discuss medical education at Stanford, Dr. Paul Berg, chair of the Department of Biochemistry, told the assembled students his view of SUSM's mission:

> I thought you all came here because you all wanted to learn how to become well-educated doctors; that doesn't mean just practitioners, it means learning the basis for contemporary medicine and preparing yourself for the medicine of the future, not the medicine of today.... I think we are all in agreement that our goal is to train you to be medical scientists. If you didn't have that in mind, then you may be in the wrong place.[30]

Of course, colleagues and students at that forum disagreed with Berg, revealing yet again the ambivalence over seeking highly prized but competing values within SUSM. The turn-of-the-century consolidation of the university-college failed to rid the institution of conflict over institutional purpose; it bubbled up time and again in professional schools and departments.

For departments, the university-college hybrid prompted hard professorial decisions over the nature of academic work: How much time to set aside for teaching undergraduates? How much time for advising? How much time for research? How much time for preparing students to be historians and physicians? In short, the historic university-college compromise has repeatedly driven Stanford academics to and fro, like those chilled porcupines, in coping with the tensions arising from curricular and teaching policies that sent mixed signals to those seeking the double glory of being first-rate scholars and teachers. The structures of the blended university-college kept the strain alive between teaching undergraduates and pursuing individual research agendas with graduate students.

Research Versus Teaching

Posing research and teaching in tension with one another may annoy many academics, particularly deans and presidents, and even some readers. It may be irritating to many because a prevailing, often-expressed belief is that each strengthens the other and to fulfill the duties of being an effective professor one must be a winner in each category. Yet, there is much evidence that the two central tasks of academic work compete for the professor's time and are, indeed, in conflict with one another. The dominant belief that professors can play starring roles both in the classroom and in a scholarly discipline has become a surrogate battlefield for reconciling the inherent dilemmas within the university-college hybrid and the mixed purposes of the professional school. This section explores both the well-publicized but much-less-articulated relationship between teaching and research in universities.[31]

Framing the competing values as being essentially compatible and mutually reinforcing was, to many faculty, embodied in the School of Medicine's mission of producing both medical researchers and practitioners, establishing university and medical school awards for excellence in teaching since the 1960s, and securing abundant federal and private grants to conduct research. That the faculty saw the two as compatible was echoed by Assistant Professor of Medicine Charlotte Jacobs who told students in a 1982 interview: "I am very satisfied with a career in academic medicine because it allows me to pursue the three aspects of medicine I enjoy most—teaching, patient care, and research." Seasoned faculty in the medical school and other professional schools, nonetheless, quietly cautioned junior colleagues that while teaching may be important, what enhanced one's chances for tenure were publications.[32]

Similarly for the Department of History, there were many words from senior faculty and executive heads about how professors could seamlessly combine scholarship and teaching. David Kennedy named six colleagues who he considered first-rate teachers. They were also highly productive scholars who were nationally and internationally respected in their fields. In an earlier chapter, however, I described how Ephraim Douglass Adams, Mary Sheldon Barnes, Edgar E. Robinson, and Thomas A. Bailey constructed compromises to competing values in becoming either teacher-scholars or scholar-teachers. Presidential messages to the history department's earliest executive heads were patently clear: What mattered for advancement to tenure and full professorships were scholarly publications. Furthermore, institutional norms of autonomy and beliefs about teaching diverted collective attention from the craft of teaching in departmental meetings, save for those few professors who enjoyed the intricacies of lecturing, leading seminars, and figuring out how to convey complicated ideas to undergraduates. Thus, the faculty came to see—as their peers across the country did in the early 1970s (driven in great part by the unforgiving job market for historians)—that doctoral programs in history had to produce academics who had to teach. This realization, albeit a tardy one, led finally to the department's requiring doctoral candidates to teach prior to receiving the Ph.D. and, by the 1990s, to attend voluntary workshops and seminars specifically geared to preparing neophyte academics to design syllabi, grade papers, deliver lectures, and lead seminars.[33]

The patterns of academic work in the history department, as in the SUSM, were unmistakable: In the daily life of university professors, where freedom competed with obligations and where limited time and monies constrained autonomy, unattractive choices had to be made among highly prized values such as research and teaching. For both historians and medical faculty at Stanford and elsewhere, strong university, departmental, and individual norms dictated that research came first. So newly hired and tenured professors learned to live with the angst-ridden contradiction that flowed from the university-college: They were hired to do research but paid to teach; then they were retained or fired on the basis of publications.[34]

Yet the bulk of the words, written and spoken, about the two central tasks of the university-college at Stanford and elsewhere in this century unambiguously pronounced the two as mutually reinforcing, even synergistic, rather than in deep conflict with one another. Let me now examine in more detail both the dominant and less-favored formulations at Stanford.

Research and Teaching Are Compatible

This is the Humboldtian ideal imported from 19th century Germany by American academics who had studied there.[35] Among Stanford faculty and administrators, it has reigned as the dominant way of framing the issue. A sampling of this prevailing view follows.

- President David Starr Jordan (1906): "The university is a school of instruction through investigation. . . . To the university teacher, individual research is the breath of life."[36]
- Economist Thorstein Veblen (1918): "The work of teaching properly belongs in the university only because and in so far as it incites and facilitates the university man's work of inquiry. . . . [T]eaching, as a concomitant of investigation, is distinctly advantageous to the investigator."[37]
- Norman K.Wessells, Professor of Biological Sciences (1973): "I view the so-called teaching versus research dichotomy as an immense red herring built on false premises. All of our regular faculty should be both creative scholars and teachers."[38]
- Gordon Craig, Professor of History (1992): "Everybody who was doing this . . . teaching . . . was a first-class scholar. It was impressed upon us when we came that we were supposed to be teacher-scholars. Nobody found this at all alarming or unusual. . . . Why? Simply because we all had a pretty good idea that we couldn't be good teachers unless we were working actively on research in the field in which we were teaching."[39]
- Commission on Undergraduate Education (1994): "In his preface to his classic treatise, *The Idea of a University,* John Henry New-

man wrote: 'To discover and to teach are distinct functions; they are also distinct gifts, and are not commonly found united in the same person.' Universities like Stanford are based on the conviction that Newman was wrong, that discovery and teaching are mutually enriching activities, and that it is possible to pursue excellence in both."[40]

From presidents to professors to special commissions, the public message is the same: Research and teaching are not only compatible, they enhance one another. The belief, maturing over the century into mythic proportion, was (and is) publicly stated at ceremonies honoring professors' achievements and in formal statements from university officers. That there were a small number of star performers who were highly esteemed locally as teachers and nationally as world-class scholars only gave further credence to the widely shared belief.[41]

Indisputable facts, however, challenge both the words and the belief. These facts, also derived from professors' testimony and supplemented by numerous faculty surveys, account for a second, less popular, formulation of the relationship between teaching and research.

Teaching and Research Are Inherently in Conflict

They are inhospitable to one another because of the constraints of time, energy, and resources in a professor's life. These externally imposed limits upon a professor force academic historians, biologists, anatomists, and economists to choose where to spend their time: advising the distraught student, preparing a new lecture, leading a discussion section, reading the latest journal articles in the field, completing the chapter promised to a colleague, going into the lab in the evening to work with graduate students, spending time with the family, and so on. This formulation underscores the pervasive and inexorable stress arising from fulfilling obligations one may have inadequate preparation for—teaching—and having insufficient time to complete research projects. A variation on this formulation goes beyond role-conflict and asserts that teaching and research are essentially incompatible because each activity demands very different capabilities, dispositions, and skills.[42]

Not until the mid-1950s did a direct challenge to the core belief in compatibility at Stanford openly surface. In the Stanford Study of Undergraduate Education, the authors of the summary volume concluded:

> It is clear that teaching and research skills are not always present in high degree in the same person, with the consequence that a faculty chosen and promoted largely because of its research ability may offer the

student, on too many occasions, little more than second-rate instruction. Moreover, a faculty member with exceptional teaching skills may neglect his courses and spend little time with students if he comes to believe that promotion depends upon publication. The university's problem and the faculty member's dilemma thus center about the university's multiple obligations to undertake undergraduate instruction, graduate instruction, and research.[43]

For the first time, a university publication explicitly noted the conflicting choices faculty faced. Beyond suggesting that teaching be formally evaluated, nothing was done to further challenge the belief that teaching and research enhance one another.

A decade later, however, in the midst of campus turmoil, a far stronger case for inherent conflict was made by the subcommittee on teaching and research in *The Study of Education at Stanford*. Faculty surveys and interviews provided further evidence that the tensions between the two activities were real and should be taken quite seriously by the university. One staff member interviewed 100 faculty in the School of Humanities and Sciences on their perceptions of how university rewards for teaching and research were distributed and how they should be allocated. Three of every four faculty viewed research and scholarship as being very influential in determining academic rewards. In another set of 115 interviews, emeritus faculty asked a "representative sample" of the entire faculty questions about the different pressures that they felt. To the first prompt, "Do you have the sense that you can never quite get caught up?" 90% of the respondents answered "yes." In answering what keeps professors from feeling that they "never get caught up," 43% said "obligations . . . to do too much writing" and 35% said that they had "too heavy a research load." Only 20% responded with "too heavy a teaching load."[44]

Such data strengthened the claim that teaching and research conflicted not only because academics faced competing demands on their limited time but also because the university communicated to its faculty that both teaching and research should be done well yet it richly rewarded research-based scholarship rather than effective teaching and advising. The study's staff, concerned over such data, sought to prove the compatibility of both academic tasks by scouring the educational literature for clear, compelling evidence of a positive correlation between research productivity and teaching effectiveness. They found none.[45]

In acknowledging the deep-seated conflict, the faculty authors of the report were uncommonly candid in their conclusions and recommendations. "There is little likelihood," they said, "that Stanford's great emphasis on research will be reduced for the sake of improving teaching." Instead, ways have to be found to improve teaching in the face of this obvious tilt toward research. They recommended creating "a counter-vailing force in favor of devotion to teaching" through systematic student rating of teaching (and using those ratings to make appointments and promotions) and university-subsidized efforts to improve teaching.[46]

Since 1968, continuing evidence drawn from dissertations, reports, and surveys further strengthens the intrinsic conflict thesis. A mailed survey on improving teaching at the university sent in 1985 to a random sample of 398 Stanford faculty yielded a 53% return. As with the earlier survey and interviews in 1968, faculty (46%) found that university rewards for teaching were low. The perceived rewards for good teaching varied by school: For the Graduate School of Business, 43% of faculty ranked the recognition for teaching high; 35% did the same for the School of Law. But for the School of Medicine, 62% of faculty ranked the recognition and rewards for good teaching as low—offering additional evidence of the weak support for teaching in SUSM's overall academic culture. For efforts to improve teaching, business and law schools again ranked the highest in both effort and practices, while social sciences and education, natural sciences and math, arts and humanities, and medicine ranked the lowest.[47]

One doctoral student interviewed six winners of the Gores Award for excellence in teaching. While some of their comments notably display that teaching and research are in sync, there were equally as trenchant points made that "teaching is seasonal" while research is an annual, on-going activity in quiet competition with the classroom. As one professor put it, "To really do my best in teaching it takes a lot of time, to do the best of my research, it takes full time. I find I really like to do them alternately." And another said, "I found I am very distracted during those two quarters when I teach. So during that time, my research suffers. It just does not get the same kind of attention as I would like to give, but I cannot help that."[48]

In one national survey of faculty opinion about research and teaching, which contained 250 Stanford professors' responses (representing a 41% return of the 608 sent out), Stanford faculty rated their research slightly more important than teaching undergraduates; when they were asked how important both were to colleagues, deans, and administrators, professors replied that research was far more important than teaching (the rankings for research over teaching almost doubled).[49]

Carol Colbeck's investigation of 12 professors in two departments at two large West Coast institutions, one of which was a *Research I* university, found both integration (i.e., compatibility of research and teaching) and fragmentation (i.e., conflict between the two) in academic work. She reported that her 12 professors from two universities in physics and English integrated their many daily work activities just over one-third of the time. Two-thirds of their time, however, was fragmented, meaning that their tasks and time were split between teaching and research activities without much overlap.[50]

Between these surveys, personal accounts, and dissertations, there is sufficient evidence to question the dominant belief at Stanford and similarly situated universities that teaching and research were inherently compatible. The internal conflict that arose in professors from juggling multiple obligations and the strong perception that the university rewards research more handsomely than teaching gave much weight to the belief that the two highly prized tasks were in conflict.

The prevailing belief among both Stanford academics and those at other institutions that research and teaching strengthen one another competed with a contrary view, also strongly held among faculty, albeit less publicly voiced. Professors working in undergraduate and graduate programs were torn by their conflicting duties. Both formulations of the research-teaching dilemma were anchored in the strain between competing values within the university-college hybrid.

HOW DID RESEARCH OVERWHELM TEACHING IN TWO VERY DIFFERENT PARTS OF THE UNIVERSITY?

After comparing and contrasting the Department of History and the School of Medicine, I found distinctive commonalities that overrode the obvious differences in size, mission, funding, and disciplines. In both settings, since the turn of the century, there have been changes in the subject matter and organization of the curricula. What historians and medical faculty taught a century ago and what they teach now has changed considerably, although there is a constancy in particular historical topics and medical subject matter in preclinical courses. Curricular structures also changed incrementally. To reconcile the competing values of depth and breadth in undergraduate studies, faculty repeatedly modified time schedules, units assigned to courses, hours of instruction, distribution requirements, and the total number of courses needed for majors in a department or for graduation. These changes were made again and again in this century without dislodging the fundamental core value driving the official curriculum: the elective principle.

Turning from the content and structures of curriculum to instruction in history and medicine, the initial fundamental changes in expanding the faculty's teaching repertoires (seminars, labs, etc.) that occurred with the founding of the university were followed by a durable stability in using a finite range of classroom practices: lectures for introductory courses; small-group discussions, seminars, labs, and independent work for advanced students. This durable constancy in the core set of teaching practices during this century was slightly modified by three associated trends. There was a small reduction in the numbers of lectures in the Department of History and the School of Medicine—as compared to turn-of-the-century practices—and a moderate increase in small-group work in both settings. Finally, SUSM faculty used far more technology in classrooms than the Department of History.

For advising—informal teaching—the pattern was easily observable: indifference to the task, followed by student and faculty complaints leading to changes that transferred responsibility for advising from professors to specially trained staff. Over the decades, allowing for the inevitable variation that existed among professors, most faculty viewed advising as a task divorced from teaching.

What stitches together the two units' commonalties of constancy and change in curriculum and instruction has been the existence of persistent, unresolved core dilemmas. The irreconcilable dilemma embedded in the university's many purposes—of creating knowledge, disseminating it to scholars and undergraduates, preparing students to be professionals, and serving the public—produced at Stanford (as with other similarly situated institutions) the university-college. These hybrid structures were compromises between the value-laden teaching imperative rooted in the undergraduate college and the value-free research imperative equally as rooted in the idea of the university, especially the graduate school.

That core dilemma cemented within Stanford's university-college became a practical matter as it evolved into a recurring, century-long debate over the relationship between research and teaching. The compromise of the university-college failed to resolve permanently the entrenched conflict between competing purposes within the overall mission. What the compromise structure did was to transfer the conflict to curricular debates among faculty over breadth and depth of knowledge that undergraduates should have and individual professors' tensions over their choices in allocating time to those highly esteemed tasks of teaching and research.

Academic norms of professorial and departmental autonomy that permeated the history department and the School of Medicine made the dilemma a routine matter that had to be negotiated constantly. Decentralized in authority at Stanford, faculty in departments and professional schools valued the freedom they had to organize activities in the history department, SUSM, and similar units across the campus in order to advance their individual research agendas. In making decisions about teaching loads, who teaches what, who will be recommended for tenure and promotion, and what academic requirements undergraduate and graduates will be expected to fulfill, departments both protected their corporate autonomy as disciplines and the cherished value of professorial freedom to inquire. Departmental discretion, strengthened by the university's existing mission, structures, and dominant norms, inevitably favored research over teaching. The aggregate influence of the university's elective system of curricular choice (for both students and faculty), research-driven criteria determining tenure and promotion, allocation of sabbaticals, growth of graduate education, and reduction of teaching loads over the century gave each department sufficient latitude to develop strong research and weak teaching cultures. While the Department of History and SUSM varied in the value they placed on teaching, there was little doubt that research was the highest priority.

In coping with this dilemma of academic work, two formulations of the linkages between research and teaching have emerged at Stanford in the last century. The popular belief among presidents and administrators sees the two tasks as essentially compatible; the less-popular one, seldom voiced publicly, sees the two as competitive. No body of evidence convincingly shows that first-rate researchers are also (or are not) first-rate teachers or that one task undermines the other, leaving no firm basis for either belief to carry weight beyond the person expressing the sentiment and the anecdotes about those few professors who shine as scholar-teachers.[51]

There are, of course, other ways to reframe the relationship between research and teaching. One way would be to say that each task requires different individual capabilities and skills. At Stanford, for example, there are specific nontenured positions that have *teaching* or *research* labels, which means that, for a contracted period, the person specializes in one or the other activity. Also recall that the anatomy department (and later division), under Robert Chase, accepted the teaching role and hired the best cadre of instructors it could find.

Another way to frame the relationship is that teaching is a form of scholarship with tangible and measurable products that can be included within the criteria used to hire, tenure, and promote professors. President Donald Kennedy's initiatives in the early 1990s embraced that view but, as the decade closes, have made little headway other than in an occasional department or professional school.

The relationship between research and teaching can also be seen as a matter of level: The two functions are more compatible with doctoral students than with undergraduates. The perennial "bisection" movement in the early decades of this century motivated this view. A fourth view is that some disciplines, such as molecular biology or one of its subspecialties, offer more promise of tighter coupling between research and teaching than others. Even another view is that different stages in a professor's career offer more convergence in these tasks. Stanford and most other universities have not given this developmental view of a career serious attention. Finally, one could frame the relationship as some combination of these different factors. Whatever the case, this angst-ridden dilemma, as currently defined, remains firmly implanted in the structure of the university-college.[52]

To the degree that faculty research and displays of scholarship were (and are) considered essential for attaining national reputation, little impetus to correct the imbalance could be generated beyond a brace of awards and fulsome words for attending to the quality and importance of teaching. To the degree that Stanford was viewed by key constituencies (alumni, funders, faculty, parents, and students) as a premier research-driven institution, there could be little incentive to alter the imbalance. Why change what works?

When tuition costs have risen in selective universities to unimagined heights and stories of large undergraduate classes taught by doctoral students have angered parents, pressures on university presidents and faculties to improve teaching have produced surges of new initiatives for teaching improvement. However, few substantive changes in redefining research, criteria for tenure and promotion, and pedagogy (or advising) have lasted. I have already suggested that departmental and professorial autonomy helps to explain this posture toward teaching, and so, in part, does the unresolved linkage between the insistent imperatives of teaching and research embedded in undergraduate and graduate work. The dominant belief that a first-rate professor combines stardom in both teaching and research (annually reinforced by awards to those singular few who achieve that status) belies the equally as strong but unpublicized belief that the two are inherently in conflict. It is the unrelieved tension between the two priorities that causes internal conflict among so many faculty and within departments.

The persistent strain has often shifted attention from focusing on an intractable issue to doing what can be done: curricular adaptation. Changing the content of courses or the mechanics of curricular organization is far more concrete and permits victories to be announced. Yet such tangible actions often end up strengthening the research imperative through adding advanced seminars for undergraduates, counting units for doctoral research, and independent laboratory projects rather than attending to the substance of pedagogy.

In analyzing how teaching has become secondary to research, I have yet to assess whether these and current incremental changes within Stanford and similar universities can add up to a fundamental shift in the balance between research and teaching. The final chapter makes that assessment.

══ 6 ══

SCHOLARS OR TEACHERS

How Much Change Is Possible?

SINCE THE MID-1500s in the Western world, there have been 66 institutions that have survived and can be easily recognized today. They are the Catholic and Lutheran Churches, the Parliaments of Iceland and the Isle of Man, and 62 universities. The stunning resiliency of universities over the centuries prompted the Carnegie Council for Policy Studies to conclude:

> Universities in the past have been remarkable for their historic continuity, and we may expect this same characteristic in the future. They have experienced wars, revolutions, depressions, and industrial transformations, and have come out less changed than almost any other segment of their societies.[1]

Over the last century, the 100-plus American elite research-driven universities have displayed a similar suppleness in their mission and work. Of the 14 institutions that formed the Association of American Universities in 1900, for example, all have reached the 21st century. Their longevity has demonstrated malleability to shifting circumstances. The emergence of the university-college—itself an adaptation intended to finesse highly prized but conflicting values (the moral mission of teaching undergraduates while creating value-free knowledge)—meant that the nature of academic work changed also.

Charles Eliot's experience as president of Harvard University for over 4 decades underscores such a shift. In his inaugural address in 1869, Eliot said that the "prime business of American professors must be regular and assiduous class teaching." Almost 40 years later, as he prepared to retire from the presidency, Eliot said that appointment and

191

promotion at Harvard depended as much on professors' "success as investigators" as on their teaching. Eliot's conflicting words, bracketing the closing and opening decades of the century, display the evolving supremacy of the research imperative between the end of the Civil War and 1900 in a small group of American universities. That advancing knowledge would turn out to be the path to an elevated national reputation in the keenly competitive arena of higher education was what Harvard, Yale, Johns Hopkins, Berkeley, Michigan, and scores of other private and public universities learned during the 20th century. And so it was for Stanford. The story of constancy and change in teaching and curricular content and organization at Stanford and its sister institutions reveals how deeply entangled curricular and pedagogical reform were with the triumph of research over teaching.[2]

THE BASIC ARGUMENT

In previous chapters, I have argued that Stanford's presidents and faculties, like others in similar institutions, believed so deeply in the mission of creating new knowledge that they adjusted to larger social and economic changes over the last century in order to preserve that ideal while seeking a prestigious niche within the sharply competitive university market. In admitting undergraduates, these research-driven universities contended with the moral mission of the undergraduate college, which was committed to molding student character and building citizens. Facing this dilemma of reconciling conflicting ideals, presidents of these turn-of-the-century institutions pursued different compromises, from splitting off the initial 2 years of undergraduate college to hiring cadres of special teachers. None of these compromises survived for long.[3]

What seemed to work at Stanford and its sister institutions in the early 20th century was the hybrid invention of the university-college. This restless détente of institutional ideals permitted presidents and professors to strike a balance between conflicting, highly prized values of teaching and research while striving for higher institutional prestige.

The precarious balance between the teaching imperative buried within the college and the research imperative within the graduate school went awry as decades passed. The "academization of the undergraduate curriculum," or spread of the research-based graduate school culture to undergraduates, tilted more toward specialized study than building citizens. In constructing this early-20th-century compromise of the university-college, then, the jerrybuilt hybrid generated new contradictions that have accompanied it ever since.[4]

In curriculum, faculty debated again and again the same question: How much breadth and depth of liberal arts should undergraduates attain within 4 years? The core elective principle of students choosing courses to take and professors choosing what they will teach meant that answering the question became increasingly more difficult as specialized knowledge accumulated and pressures for preparing undergraduates for careers accelerated. Surges of interest in general education, often mirroring pervasive social changes spurred by wars and economic depressions, stirred faculties to reexamine the drift toward academic specialization and question its embrace as the principle of choice. The faculty-designed curricular reforms required undergraduates to take new courses and choose other courses in related fields of knowledge. But champions for general education reform, losing their enthusiasm over time, watched the decline of mandated undergraduate courses as faculty renewed their fervor for the elective principle. The conundrum of breadth versus depth of knowledge for undergraduates, then, was inherent in the structure of the university-college. The invention of the university-college, however, yielded another paradox facing inquiry-oriented professors who had to teach both introductory general education courses and their specialties to both undergraduates and doctoral students: They were "hired to teach but paid to publish."[5]

The contradiction of being employed to teach but being rewarded for scholarship gained public exposure each time assistant professors renowned for teaching excellence were denied tenure and dismissed for lack of star-quality scholarship. The elaborate university structures and academic norms that grew throughout this century of requiring the Ph.D. degree to become a professor, hierarchical academic rank, and the awarding of tenure and promotion to those who excelled in research rather than teaching were anchored in a core belief in the essential compatibility of research and teaching. For those presidents and professors who believed that the two tasks were intertwined, there was no contradiction. Yet, as I have argued in this study, the deep tensions that faculty have experienced at Stanford and elsewhere in managing the allocation of their time strengthened the view, as former Stanford President Donald Kennedy put it: "The constant tension between research and teaching . . . is now the single greatest problem facing the professoriate."[6]

This contradiction, arising from the turn-of-the-century invention of the university-college to reconcile conflicting ideals, helps to account for the importance of the elective principle in curricular organization, departmental structures, deeply entrenched cultures, and pervasive beliefs about teaching and research, which have become easily recognized features (and targets of criticism) within the modern university.

As surges of reform swept over higher education in this century, these institutional paradoxes within the university-college provided the framework for Stanford faculty, including historians and medical scientists, to improvise in curriculum content, organization, and pedagogy. University-colleges, then, have been places where century-old contradictions produced an enduring stability in beliefs, structures, and cultures that have enabled faculties to design again and again many symbolic curricular and pedagogical changes but sustain few deep and lasting reforms.

Institutional beliefs, structures, and academic culture, however, seldom produce uniformity. Within private and public and small and large bottom-heavy universities there has been sufficient slackness generated by professorial autonomy and departmental organization to permit variation in how much teaching and advising is honored. Certain departments at Stanford and many individual professors have experimented with nontraditional forms of teaching and have been recognized by students as first-rate advisers. But they are a distinct and small minority among those faculty members who have entered and exited Stanford classrooms in this century. Why, then, has there been this stunning continuity punctuated by modest recurring changes in teaching and curricular organization at Stanford and other universities? Does the existence of the dilemma-laced university-college explain it all? Hardly.

The argument I have offered thus far is incomplete. It is inadequate just to identify the innovative university-college and suggest that the hybrid's interior conflicts at Stanford and other similarly situated institutions fully explain a curricular and pedagogical stability periodically strengthened by makeshift changes. Nor is it enough to point out that the nation's research-driven universities comprised an organizational collectivity in which presidents and faculties, sensitive to larger social beliefs and expectations for what they had to offer students, parents, and alumni, copied one another to retain their competitive edge.

Although I do find this explanation persuasive in understanding universities' adaptive powers and the strong similarities among them, what bothers me about it is its premise of environmental determinism: The larger society with its unpredictable changes, dominant beliefs, and available resources drives universities to secure legitimacy, prestige, and predictability. While institutional contradictions of ambition and mimicry do help to explain why, at certain times, periodic waves of curricular reform ebb and flow among universities, what goes unexplained is how universities end up changing reforms to maintain stability. An institutional view credibly explains how the university adopts reforms but not how or why universities end up incrementalizing, marginalizing, and enclaving reforms. What is missing from this explanation is an understanding of how the political process accounts for changes in reforms and for maintaining continuity.

HOW UNIVERSITIES CHANGE REFORMS

In Chapter 2, I had outlined how Stanford presidents and faculties had responded to social and economic changes by altering the direction, scope, and content of intended major reforms, such as the School of Medicine's Five-Year Plan and the evaluation of teaching—to cite two examples. In establishing a tradition of reform, faculties and administrators retained those portions of proposed changes that enhanced the stability of the university-college, including its linkages to the elective curriculum and the freedom that professors and departments so dearly sought to keep. Universities were hardly soft waxes that reformers stamped. University administrators and faculties tamed reforms.

Professors and presidents, depending upon shared beliefs, a common rhetoric, existing structures, and political processes, refashioned reforms to preserve the delicate balance among competing values while enhancing their institutional reputation. Recall the case study of the Stanford School of Medicine in this century, particularly what occurred with the teaching of anatomy. The case displayed in sharp relief how the medical faculty's vested interests were intertwined with curricular and instructional innovations and shaped the direction that those changes took between the late 1950s and the present. In this struggle for power and prestige, initiatives from a SUSM dean or Stanford president that threatened the medical faculty's prerogatives in deciding academic matters of curriculum and pedagogy were often brushed aside or marginalized to protect professorial privileges. Tenured faculty, like any group of political stakeholders in an institution, sought to protect their interests. Here, again, ad hoc incrementalism became the strategy of choice in maintaining the existing structures and academic culture, which esteemed research.[7]

In wedding an institutionalist explanation to the political bargaining at work among university stakeholders, I can account for both the entry, spread, and change of reform as it melded into university routines. Yet the political explanation remains incomplete without attention to administrators' and faculties' abiding satisfaction with the university's success, their fierce desire to maintain that triumph, and a perceived lack of a viable alternative to the university-college.

Basic Satisfaction With the University's Success

If a university-college such as Stanford or Harvard or Berkeley is viewed as nationally prestigious, attracting star-quality professors, valedictorians, and ample resources, why should ambitious administrators and satisfied faculties make major changes in what presumably works? Being reputed as successful among research-driven universities has been historically linked to high rankings on published lists of doctoral-granting institutions. To rank at or near the top of such lists is to be defined as successful and of major importance to fundraising and political support in the larger community. Again, why tamper with what already works?

Although criteria for success and therefore prestige on these lists have shifted considerably over time, scholarly productivity and perceived quality have been constants. The first national ranking in 1910 had peers rate the top 1,000 men in science and then listed the colleges and universities from which they graduated. Most reputational surveys in the 1980s also used peer judgments of scholarly quality for graduate departments in doctoral-granting institutions. Listings in popular magazines have included scholarship but also used many other measures: facilities, numbers of doctorates graduated; faculty-student ratios, endowment, research funds acquired, and so on. Yet the gold-standard for quality has persisted in peer-evaluated research.[8]

Note that the criteria used and indicators of success concentrate on faculty, funds, and facilities—"inputs" in the vocabulary of some researchers. Student "outputs" after 4 years of university-college are far more contentious as a measure of success. Studies over the last half-century have been circumspect in claiming that 4 years of attendance at colleges and universities has added a great deal to graduates' critical thinking, analytic skills, intellectual flexibility, and values.[9]

Almost 2 decades after its founding, upwardly mobile Stanford had already found a place on the first national list. Over the years, Stanford climbed in the rankings, gaining prestige, particularly in the 1960s and since, to make Wallace Sterling's dream of becoming the "Harvard of the West" a reality, although few on the Quad or in campus publications in the 1990s would be gauche enough to publicly proclaim such a comparison.

The competition to get higher national rankings has driven university presidents, such as Sterling, to raise endowments, lure star researchers away from sister institutions, build bigger and better science laboratories and libraries, and attract budding student scholars. Observing the intensity of institutional ambition for "a place at the head table of academic respectability," Clark Kerr labeled the perennial contest as the "new race to be Harvard, Berkeley, or Stanford."[10]

For those universities that reached for higher status in national rankings, the competition with rivals for faculty, students, and research funds has, to be sure, prodded innovation. Similarly, when the country stirred (e.g., war, economic boom or bust, broader student pool seeking admission) and the sources of political and economic support were realigned, presidential and faculty risk-taking rose perceptibly to maintain institutional prestige and ward off competitors' attempts to attract renowned faculty and able graduate students. Evidence for that risk-taking surfaced in the Stanford experience of the 1950s and 1960s as science faculty sought and acquired federal funds for research and Provost Terman implemented a "steeples of excellence" strategy for securing faculty and improving departments.

But once the university settled into the top ranks, the university presidents' and faculties' passion for high- or even moderate-risk major innovations in curriculum and pedagogy often declined while their efforts to preserve their hard-earned status through incremental changes gained ascendancy. Again, the record of attempted changes at Stanford overall and in the history department and medical school in the 1970s through the 1990s documents a deep reluctance to gamble on either high-risk innovations or reach for fundamental changes. In short, the remarkable climb of Stanford into the top-ranked universities in the nation (and world) has had the glow of success—as conventionally defined in peer-rated national ranking—surrounding it. In such institutions, incremental and symbolic changes in curricular organization and instruction are politically astute responses to externally driven crises or internally defined problems. Preserving success accompanies gilt-edged status in higher education.

Perceived Lack of a Viable Alternative to the University-College

Since 1900, university presidents and faculty have explored different ways of finessing the contradictions embedded in the university-college. None have lasted. Founded as research institutions, Clark and Johns Hopkins Universities initially sought to exclude undergraduates. They failed. Within a short time, both created 4-year colleges. David Starr Jordan, William Rainey Harper, and other university presidents advocated separating the initial 2 years of college from advanced academic work. They failed. Creating separate colleges that honor the liberal arts and avoid preparing undergraduates for doctoral work also have been tried since Alexander Meiklejohn's experimental college at the University of Wisconsin in the 1920s, Robert Hutchins's college at the University of Chicago in the 1930s and 1940s, and a host of alternative colleges within the

University of California (at Santa Cruz and at Berkeley itself) in the 1960s and 1970s. Some have survived as enclaves; most have disappeared. The 4-year college and graduate school still dominate university-colleges in the Ivy League and at Chicago, Michigan, Wisconsin, Berkeley, and Stanford.

The warring ideals embedded within the university-college and the insistent imperialism of the graduate school plunging down into 1st- and 2nd-year coursework have frustrated reformers seeking a practical alternative—a creative compromise—to the hybrid invented at the turn of the century. The department as the core organizational unit in the decentralized university has remained dominant. Interdisciplinary programs have spread in universities, but the department remains the powerful institutional unit it was a century ago. No viable alternative to the department and the university-college has been proposed, adopted, implemented, and institutionalized sufficiently to convince presidents and faculties that there is another, low-risk, economically efficient way of combining the teaching mission of building future citizens with the missions of increasing knowledge and maintaining high-prestige. Lacking any appealing alternatives, ad hoc incremental changes to remedy inefficient aspects of the existing curricular organization and instruction have been found to be pragmatic and credible responses.

That has been the argument offered in preceding chapters. Of what significance is such an argument, considering the evidence that I have mustered and the explanations for how research has overwhelmed teaching in universities and preserved that asymmetry?

I can begin by saying that this study is *not* a case of how the research imperative has ruined universities by ignoring teaching. Popular critics have made that claim often in the last 2 decades (repeating similar charges made since the turn of the 20th century) prior to offering their pet solution. What critics and researchers have failed to understand is *how* research trumped teaching in universities. If anything has emerged from this study, it is documenting that teaching and researching, so valued by Stanford presidents and professors, became entangled with other entrenched beliefs, emergent traditions, and commonplace structures that have quietly and steadily subordinated one ideal to the other. Conflicting beliefs about the mission of the university that were embedded in the structure and practices of the university-college have led to faculty compromises initiated and supported by administrators who clearly favored research over teaching. Thus, Stanford tamed highly touted curricular and teaching reforms to preserve the research imperative. Such actions have produced noted strengths for the research enterprise in American universities, which have become the envy of the world since 1945. Teaching *is* valued symbolically at Stanford and among sister institutions. Students laud their best teachers.

Administrators, faculty, and students give recognition and cash awards for excellence in the classroom.

Yet, having made that important point, the core contradictions in the beliefs, structures, and processes remain at Stanford and elsewhere: Professors are rewarded far more handsomely for being researchers than for their classroom performance. The university's structures and norms converge to strengthen the research imperative. It is in those dramatic instances of a faculty, provost, or president denying tenure and dismissing an assistant professor known for teaching excellence that the paradox surfaces to underscore the point that advancing knowledge remains far more important than effective pedagogy.[11]

Thus, the Stanford case reveals the enduring dilemmas faced in an institution's efforts to reconcile contradictory values. Favoring research over teaching is not some conspiracy of security-minded faculties aided by administrators who fear conflict, as some critics allege. Concentration on research flows from durable compromises made over the century to deeply embedded value-conflicts in the university's mission and a keen ambition to remain on the top rungs of the prestigious ladder. Furthermore, the high-status accorded to research-produced knowledge by profit-driven corporations, all levels of government, and popular opinion strengthens presidents' and professors' commitments to advancing knowledge.

The case of Stanford illustrates the ebb and flow of the tensions surrounding the research and teaching imperatives. The university's beliefs, structures, and cultures sustained the core paradox facing professors, thus revealing how difficult the task is of realigning research and teaching in an elite institution. Announcements of major reforms in curriculum and teaching often led, over the years, to modest, if not symbolic, alterations.

Is this study, then, a case of failed change? Not at all. I have noted numerous curricular and pedagogical changes that have occurred at Stanford and other universities. Distinguishing between fundamental and incremental changes helps to clarify that a complex institution can be both stable and change-prone simultaneously. If anything, the study reveals how difficult it is to make deep, broad, and lasting changes in beliefs, structures, and cultures. Making fundamental changes in long-lived institutions is, to restate the obvious, a rare event.

MANAGING DILEMMAS

What this study offers is an historical glimpse into the actions of one university's faculty, presidents, and boards of trustees, all of whom expressed interest in altering in either modest or major ways the priorities invested in the university-college, especially in heightening the importance and quality of teaching.

The picture presented here will hardly excite reformers. The argument and evidence offered from one private elite university offers a strong caution to those reformers who are eager to elevate teaching to equal or superior status over research. Faculty beliefs and actions wedded to the university-college's structures, academic norms, and traditions of reform that have evolved over the century have displayed time and again resiliency in adjusting to strong external pressures for major changes. Stanford's structures and cultures have adapted time and again to internal constituents to maintain its prestige among top-ranked rivals while responding to the changing agendas of those external groups whose financial and political support it had to have in order to survive.

Such a picture of an independent, paradox-ridden institution is not meant to portray arrogance; it is meant to portray a notable flexibility in the face of a turbulent, unpredictable environment. It is also meant to warn reformers that changing professors' behavior in and out of classrooms goes beyond administrators establishing more awards for teaching or exhorting faculty to pull up their socks and teach more classes. William Arrowsmith put the point vividly: "At present [1966] the universities are as uncongenial to teaching as the Mojave Desert to a clutch of Druid priests. If you want to restore a Druid priesthood, you cannot do it by offering prizes for Druid-of-the-year. If you want Druids, you must grow forests. There is no other way of setting about it."[12]

This study suggests strongly that a new law, a new policy, a new program, a new president, a new technology are not the "forests" that have to be grown. To be blunt: There are no magical programs, awards, or charismatic leaders that will solve age-old dilemmas. There are, however, better compromises that can be constructed and managed.

Reformers need to recognize that institutional contradictions seldom succumb to rhetoric or innovative designs; they need to acknowledge that self-interest and enjoying the transient pleasures of prestige often reduce presidents' and professors' appetites for redesigning institutions. Reformers need to see clearly that the university-college itself was a structural compromise to cope with competing values embedded in the university's mission. This historic compromise is held in place by a web of social beliefs, departmental structures, academic ranking, cultural norms, and a larger competitive environment of rival institutions. In short, the university-college is a complex, decentralized system of governance and academic work that has had remarkable capacities to absorb and redirect changes in order to maintain continuity. Such awareness on the part of those seeking to redress the imbalance between

teaching and research becomes an important first step prior to charting directions—growing "forests"—for realigning the faculty's academic
duties in university-colleges.

There is, then, a practical significance in knowing about past efforts
of an elite institution's record in coping with its inherent dilemmas.
Understanding how previous generations of well-intentioned and shrewd
administrators and faculties managed the paradoxes they faced can both
reduce organizational forgetfulness and inform current policy initiatives
aimed at better realigning the priorities of teaching and creating knowledge. Amnesia about the options earlier generations pursued is an occu-
pational disease among reformers with Ph.D.'s. When intended fundamental changes get incrementalized or disappear without leaving a
fingerprint, reformers often blame others for the failure: If only the president. . . . If only those professors. . . . If only alumni. . . . and on and on.
More to the point, and often ignored by fervent reformers, are the *consequences* of blame and disappointment over failed ventures. Frustra-
tions arising from unsuccessful designs for fundamental changes often
clot into cynicism, making it so much harder for the next generation of
well-intentioned, but forgetful, reformers to mobilize faculty energies to
undertake the next round of curricular and pedagogical change.

Such faulty attributions and dashed hopes only further enforce the
popular conclusion that universities seldom change, a statement that I
have shown to be false. Universities do change. The changes, however,
have often strengthened existing beliefs, structures, and processes.
Reformers, then, must inform themselves about past compromises and
the outcomes to cope with enduring dilemmas in correcting the imbalance between the university-college's unchanging charges to faculty to
inquire and teach.

Reformers might also be clear on why the historic imbalance
between teaching and research imperatives *should* be realigned. In this
study, I have assumed that teaching is essential to the mission of any
university. That cardinal assumption came from my quarter-century of
experience in public schools and fed my frustration with the university's
inattention to the art and science of teaching. This study and others
have established that universities' structures, cultures, and processes,
built up over a century, subordinate teaching (and advising) to the
research imperative. Fundamental realignment will hardly come without struggle. But should it?

I believe it should for the following reasons. The basic assumption
motivating university teaching is that professors will inspire the young
to use knowledge creatively and constructively. David Starr Jordan,
Charles Eliot, and other 19th- and early-20th-century university

presidents preached the importance of professors as agents for making society a better place than it has been. It is an assumption that I embrace.

Too often, however, the act of teaching has been divorced from who one is as a human being as much as from knowing one's discipline and publishing scholarship. Pedagogy and subject matter are as connected in the lecture hall and seminar as they are in finding just the right word to convey a thought in a journal article. To teach is to model character as much as intelligence. To teach is to convey unveiled enthusiasm for ideas, for inquiry, as it is about the details of a lecture or a response to a student's question in a seminar. Too often, teaching has been stripped of it artistic and human dimensions and made into a series of technical moves that can be swiftly learned and put into practice by anyone of average intelligence.

Many undergraduates and doctoral students, however, seldom divorce pedagogy from content. They are (and have been) acutely sensitive to the convergence of teaching and knowledge of a discipline. They will seek out as exemplars those professors who integrate, rather than separate, the two. Teaching undergraduates and doctoral students, then, is entering into a relationship and displaying a form of moral behavior of critical importance to the mission of the university-college, but this is too often discounted.

Moreover, I believe that the imbalance should be corrected because most professors seek to teach well. Survey after survey has revealed that most professors relish the satisfactions that flow from teaching yet are hindered by factors documented in this study and elsewhere from pursuing the craft of teaching. It is for these reasons that I have argued for a balance between the teaching and research imperatives.[13]

Suppose, then, that those presidents, professors, and others who style themselves as reformers embrace this assumption and know well the history of how their hard-working, fervent predecessors managed these dilemmas inherent to the university-college. Were they so inclined, could they make fundamental changes in the priorities of teaching and research at places such as Stanford? Were major events to occur in the larger society, such as a full-scale war, a severe and protracted economic slump, or similar shocks, the chances of reformers taking advantage of such deep shifts might occur. The resiliency of universities over the last 500 years in the face of similar catastrophes has displayed impressive instances of presidents and faculty making major changes during and after such trauma.

Short of such major external jolts to the society, however, the prognosis for a radical realigning of the asymmetry between teaching and research is unpromising. Given the larger, ever-changing environment in which universities compete for resources and prestige, and given the strength and deep acceptance of the existing core beliefs (e.g., that effective teaching and first-rate research go hand-in-hand), structures (e.g., university-college, academic rank, tenure criteria, departmental organization), and academic norms (e.g., professorial autonomy to teach and investigate), I doubt seriously whether designing and launching major reforms seeking systemic change will yield intended results. One example of an emerging trend may illustrate the difficulties of realigning the balance between teaching and research.

With reductions in federal grants to research universities and the ever-intense search for new revenues to maintain existing operations and high reputations, many universities in the last 2 decades have turned increasingly to joint commercial ventures with corporations. Entrepreneurial administrators and faculty have found venture capital or entered into agreements with private corporations to underwrite research with immediate application to engineering and medical problems while improving existing technologies. Federal legislation in 1980 permitted universities to receive royalties from patents. Universities established policies permitting individual professors to take out patents for their inventions and create private companies and, in joint-venture deals, to profit from the proceeds of their new device, process, or pill.[14]

The commercialization of academic research, as critics have labeled the trend, has raised serious issues about ownership of intellectual property, faculty profit-taking, and professorial conflicts of interest, much less conflicts in their commitments to inquiry and teaching. When professors in the physical and life sciences get rich from patents or start-up companies, for example, their objectivity as researchers comes under a cloud of suspicion. Moreover, professors' division of time devoted to university duties and private financial gain becomes suspect. Since the early 1980s, universities have created elaborate rules to separate professors' academic responsibilities from private financial gain and ownership of intellectual property involving graduate students and their mentors. These rules have helped sort out the conflicts of interest over institutional and individual financial rewards from conflicts in commitments to academic duties. But differentiating the conflicts have not reduced their potential impact upon the changing mission of the university.[15]

Creating and disseminating knowledge has been the primary mission of universities for centuries. Exactly what the long-term effects will be of patenting devices and processes within a university culture of sharing broadly new knowledge or of more and more professors seeking financial gain and cutting back on their teaching duties is difficult to predict. New and revised rules are incremental changes that may well combine, over time, into a quiet fundamental change in the university's historic ideals. One does not have to be a prophet, however, to guess that the commercialization of academic research will yield few gains for those seeking a better realignment between inquiry and teaching.

Thus, restoring a balance between research and teaching requires going well beyond a magic-tinged solution (e.g., a new president, a larger endowment, more revenue from commercial ventures) that can miraculously alter the entire system. It requires a deep understanding of the American university structures and processes, the larger socioeconomic and political arena in which it exists, and a blend of different approaches that seek to achieve incrementally a major realignment.

Nonetheless, assume that a few boards of trustees, university presidents, administrators, and faculty seek systemic change to restrike a better balance between research and teaching within their institutions. What could they do?

Altering this very complex university system requires these would-be reformers, initially, to map the interactions between dispersed powers contained within university governance and to acknowledge openly the strong commitment of the institution to decentralized departmental organization, the faculty's entrepreneurial autonomy, and the competitive market in which universities seek prestige. A second ingredient would be to find a president and provost of uncommon political will, astuteness, and determination to persist for 5 to 10 years on this task. A third ingredient would be the leaders' mobilization of a critical mass of administrators and faculty to support a strategy of incrementalism to correct the imbalance. The incremental strategy that I suggest is not the *ad hoc* incrementalism I have described earlier—those changes aimed at defusing conflict while maintaining existing structures. What I propose is *strategic* incrementalism or short-term tinkering toward a defined long-term purpose of redesigning university structures, processes, and cultures. The kind of leaders I refer to are those who resist hunting boulders to crush the opposition and rather search for pebbles to make a path toward respecting and admiring teacher-scholars.

Creative tinkerers working within resilient decentralized institutions might consider a series of small but high-profile improvements: establishing interdisciplinary programs that cross departmental boundaries and whose billets come from the university, not departments; recruiting a cadre of tenured professors who want to teach undergraduates and whose salaries and recognition will compare favorably with colleagues but whose home base will be the university, not the department; rewarding departments that carefully evaluate professorial instruction through combinations of student and peer ratings; redirecting alumni gifts toward endowing a faculty development fund; and reinterpreting the criteria for research to include the products of teaching (e.g., textbooks, case studies, publications about teaching subject matter, a new curriculum).

Careful readers may have noted that many of these suggested incremental changes have either occurred or have been proposed at Stanford in the last quarter-century. Commonly, these improvements appeared episodically in scattered departments and schools (e.g., the growth of interdisciplinary programs, the practice of the Graduate School of Business to include the creation of teaching products in tenure decisions, the cadre of teachers hired in the anatomy division of the Department of Surgery within the School of Medicine). Or, the changes were ad hoc and symbolic reactions to crises that erupted outside or within the university (e.g., the adoption of an instrument to evaluate professors in the early 1970s; the hiring of junior faculty and graduate students to staff proliferating discussion sections for the "Problems of Civilization" course in the 1920s, "Western Civilization" courses in the 1930s, "Western Culture" in the 1980s, and "Cultures, Ideas, and Values" in the 1990s). This is unfocused, symbolic incrementalism aimed at reducing conflict and preserving stability.

Advocates for strategic incrementalism, to pose the alternative, see, for example, the heavier weighting of teaching performance in tenure decisions as an important tactic in a long-range effort. They see the spread of interdisciplinary programs subsidized by the university, particularly in the humanities and social sciences, as a way of enhancing the importance of teaching. Some researchers have found that there is more openness to trying different forms of teaching and collaboration in interdisciplinary programs. In getting faculty to collaborate across disciplinary borders and thereby curb departmental powers that have historically diminished both teaching and advising, this tactical move, as part of a long-term strategy, also offers promise.[16]

Will strategic incrementalism toward redesigning university structures and processes redress the imbalance between the teaching and research imperatives? I do not know. I am uncertain that an aggressive policy directed at better managing the paradox of teaching and research within a university-college can be designed and carried out in a competitive, ever-shifting, unpredictable environment where short tenure in presidential office is common, the quality of faculty leadership varies from inspired to self-protective, and the unrelenting search for funds has drawn universities increasingly toward commercializing research.

Part of me regrets ending this study on a pessimistic note. As a former public school teacher and administrator for a quarter-century and as a professor for 2 decades, I seek an optimistic ending that includes an uplifting flourish with a tidy solution to the thorny problems that I have analyzed. Yet, the simple framing of problems and offering of equally simple solutions is inappropriate for institutional paradoxes. Modest language, as in "managing dilemmas" and "refashioning compromises," is, in my judgment, more appropriate even if some readers may conclude that my humility is no more than a killjoy at work.

I end this book realizing that universities such as Stanford survive as institutions because they adapt to changing circumstances and mirror the larger society's values. Elite universities in America have been (and are) institutionally ambitious, upwardly mobile, entrepreneurial, competitive, maximizers of individual choice, and seekers of freedom from governmental authority—values most Americans prize.

But universities are not mere extensions of the larger society in either mission or action. They are different. Nor are they helpless in the face of societal constraints or intractable dilemmas. In reflecting the larger society's values for over a century, university presidents and professors have nonetheless used political bargaining, bureaucratic structures, and organizational strategies in having research trump teaching. And they have succeeded in making these research-driven institutions the envy of the world. If there is institutional inertia, there is also institutional agency. Surely, these presidents and professors have been deeply influenced by their unique histories and surroundings in choosing ad hoc incrementalism as a way of strengthening the research imperative.

Yet it is not pessimistic to expect very few fundamental changes in universities that will reverse permanently these priorities. It is realistic. It is not pessimistic to state that incremental changes targeted toward enhancing teaching, uninformed by a clear understanding of institutional contradictions and history and without sustained presidential and faculty leadership, will result in little more than rhetorical praise and episodic surges of recognition for teaching. It is realistic.

But is it realistic, then, to ask university-colleges to recognize and increase the numbers of teacher-scholars on their faculties? I believe so. It can be done—if the deliberate choice is made to pursue a policy of strategic changes. Fatalism—nothing can be done—is popular but forgetful about past changes that have made university-colleges selective and envied. It is realistic, I believe, to ask these universities, which exert much influence in higher education, the economy, and among national policymakers, to pursue a strategic incrementalism geared toward realigning the imperatives to teach and to do research. Were it to occur, universities could finally step beyond cultivating cherished myths and indulgent rhetoric to realize fully their ideals.

NOTES

INTRODUCTION

1. Both quotes are cited in Derek Bok, *Higher Learning* (1986), p. 160. Bok's observation is on p. 161. Of course, there are many variations of these views. Historian Frederick Rudolph (1962/1990) says categorically: "Resistance to fundamental reform was ingrained in the American collegiate and university tradition, as over three hundred years of history demonstrated" (*The American College and University: A History*, p. 491). Abraham Flexner (1930/1994) viewed European and American universities differently: "Very different indeed is the Harvard of which Mr. Eliot became president in 1869 from the Harvard which he left on his retirement in 1909. Historians have traced certain aspects of this evolution in detail...made in the course of centuries by institutions usually regarded as conservative, frequently even as the stronghold of reaction. I say then that universities in most countries changed" (*Universities: American, English, German*, p. 5).

2. I borrow the phrase "steady work" from Irving Howe's collection of political essays, *Steady Work* (1966). The title comes from the fictitious eastern European village of Chelm where a gatekeeper complained about the low pay he received to wait for the Messiah. The village elders agreed with the man that the pay was low but said that the work was steady. The phrase is also the title of Richard Elmore and Milbrey McLaughlin's study of school reform (1988).

For the constant changes in universities since World War II, see Clark Kerr, *The Uses of the University* (1982), pp. 94–123. For the current ferment in universities, including criticism and response through reforms, see Francis Oakley, "Historical Perspectives and Our Current Educational Discontents" (1996); Gerald Graff, *Beyond the Culture Wars: How Teaching the Conflicts Can Revitalize American Education* (1992); and Lawrence Levine, *The Opening of the American Mind* (1996).

3. Historical studies that have examined, in part, these issues include Laurence Veysey, *The Emergence of the American University* (1965); Gerald Grant and David Riesman, *The Perpetual Dream: Reform and Experiment in the American College* (1978); Hugh Hawkins, *Between Harvard and America: The Educational*

Leadership of Charles Eliot (1972); Julie Reuben, *The Making of the Modern University* (1996); Richard M. Freeland, *Academia's Golden Age: Universities in Massachusetts, 1945–1990* (1992); and Frederick Rudolph, *Curriculum: A History of the American Undergraduate Course of Study Since 1636* (1977).

4. The labels *Research I and II* come from a Carnegie-funded taxonomy of higher education institutions; see Carnegie Foundation for the Advancement of Teaching, *A Classification of Higher Education* (1987), pp. 3–4, 7–8. The classification scheme was changed in 1994, and the number of Research I and II institutions increased from 104 to 125. See Jean Evangelauf, "A New 'Carnegie Classification'" (1994, April 6); Roger Geiger, *To Advance Knowledge: The Growth of American Research Universities* (1986); and Clark Kerr, *Troubled Times for American Higher Education: The 1990s and Beyond* (1993).

5. Reuben (1992), pp. 61–87; Mary Ann Dzuback, *Robert M. Hutchins: Portrait of an Educator* (1991), pp. 109–135; Daniel Bell, *The Reforming of General Education* (1966), pp. 12–68; and Freeland (1992), pp. 123–130.

6. Joseph Ben-David, *American Higher Education* (1972), pp. 87–109; Patti Gumport, "Graduate Education and Organized Research in the United States" (1993); Hugh Hawkins, "University Identity: The Teaching and Research Functions" (1979); James S. Fairweather, *Faculty Work and Public Trust* (1996), pp. 186–187. In 1966, Alan Cartter, who had just completed his study of graduate schools in the nation, summed up dominant opinion of the time when he said, "The selective liberal-arts colleges of the future must become first-rate preparatory colleges for graduate education"; cited in Alvin C. Eurich, *Campus 1980: The Shape of the Future in American Higher Education* (1968), p. 127.

7. Donald Kennedy, "Learning, Thinking, and Believing" (1990, June 13) and "The Improvement of Teaching" (1991, March 11); Stanford University, Faculty Senate, *Toward Greater Excellence in Teaching at Stanford* (1995, April).

8. Kelly Skeff and Nel Noddings, "Teaching Improvement in the University: The Views of Faculty" (1985, September); Nira Hativa, "What Are the 'Cultures' of Teaching of University Professors?" (1995, July); Larry Cuban, *How Teachers Taught: Constancy and Change in American Classrooms, 1880–1980* (1984).

9. Hawkins (1979), pp. 285–312; Burton Clark, *The Academic Life* (1987), pp. 69–104; Martin Finkelstein, *The American Academic Profession* (1984), pp. 43–154.

10. Logan Wilson, *American Academics: Then and Now* (1979), pp. 210–233.

11. See Geiger (1986), Kerr (1982), Veysey (1965), Clark (1987), and Reuben (1996) for historians and social scientists who studied groups of research-oriented universities and included Stanford as one of their cases. Many historians have drawn from Stanford's archives. W. B. Carnochan has written about the long-term curricular struggle over a liberal education (with little mention of the accompanying pedagogy) in *The Battleground of the Curriculum* (1993). Rebecca Lowen concentrated upon Stanford and its rise to prominence following World War II. Using the papers of Provost Frederick Terman and President Wallace Sterling, Lowen argued in *Creating the Cold War University* (1997) that the transformation of Stanford came largely as a result of administration initiatives in securing federal and private funding during and after World War II.

CHAPTER 1

1. Beginning in the mid-1980s, presidents and provosts of research universities, responding to the growing public unease over research overshadowing undergraduate teaching, spoke and wrote about the dilemmas inherent to the discovery, communication, and application of knowledge. See, for example, Derek Bok, *Higher Learning* (1986); Bartlett Giamatti, *A Free and Ordered Space: The Real World of the University* (1988); Henry Rosovsky, *The University: An Owner's Manual* (1990); Jonathan R. Cole, Elinor Barber, and Stephen R. Graubard (Eds.), *The Research University in a Time of Discontent* (1994).

There were also strong critiques of professors who taught infrequently, ignored undergraduates, and generally did as they pleased. See Charles Sykes, *Profscam: Professors and the Demise of Higher Education* (1988); Bruce Wilshire, *The Moral Collapse of the University* (1990); and Page Smith, *Killing the Spirit: Higher Education in America* (1990).

2. Stanford Alumni Association, *The Stanford Century* (1991), p. 215. Burton Clark points out the two imperatives in *The Higher Education System: Academic Organization in Cross-National Perspective* (1983), p. 191.

3. Orrin L. Elliott, *Stanford University: The First Twenty-Five Years* (1937), p. 24. Elliott was registrar of the university between 1891 and 1925. His history combines contemporary accounts, personal observations, and original documents.

4. David Starr Jordan, *The Days of a Man: Being Memories of a Naturalist, Teacher, and Minor Prophet of Democracy* (1922), Vol. 1, pp. 493–510; Elliott (1937), pp. 3–64, 81–92; and Edith R. Mirrieless, *Stanford: The Story of a University* (1959), pp. 13–51. In writing this chapter on one aspect of Stanford's history, I have used first-hand accounts, informal histories, memoirs, doctoral dissertations, and official documents.

5. Luther Spoehr, *Progress' Pilgrim: David Starr Jordan and the Circle of Reform, 1891–1931* (1975), pp. 8–19.

6. Elliott (1937), pp. 39–49; Spoehr (1975), pp. 20–50. Jordan (1922), pp. 106–120; Jordan, *The Trend in the American University* (1929), p. 82.

7. Jordan (1922), pp. 293–297; Elliott (1937), pp. 70–74. Frederick Rudolph (1977) points out that George Ticknor and others had brought from Germany in the 1820s the idea of a major but it was not until the 1880s and 1890s that it reemerged in concert with electives (p. 228). Also see David Tyack, *George Ticknor and the Boston Brahmins* (1967). One frequent objection to an elective curriculum was that many students would need help in making choices. Thus, the idea of professor as adviser became an important prop to support such a curriculum, combining the older college concern for the professor as a moral model in building student character and mind with the newer university spirit of professors giving only academic and career advice. In the mid-1870s, at Johns Hopkins University, an hour a week was set aside for students to meet with their advisers. The professor's duty was "to establish relations of friendliness and confidence with the students assigned to his care." Cited in Hugh Hawkins, *Pioneer: A History of the Johns Hopkins University, 1874–1889* (1960), p. 248.

8. Elliott (1937), pp. 65–74. For photo and names of original faculty, see p. 63.

9. For history, see Edward Kriehbiel, "History Courses at Leland Stanford" (1910, October), pp. 29–30; and Stanford University, *Register* (1894–1895). For mining engineering, see E. E. Slosson, *Great American Universities* (1910), pp. 131–132. The figures for enrollments are in Slosson, p. 147.

10. Spoehr (1975), p. 164; Elliott (1937), p. 50.

11. Elliott (1937), p. 362; Jordan (1922), p. 298. Jordan's strong belief, and those of his colleagues at other universities, in the moral imperative embedded in teaching was later captured in the 1915 *Report on Academic Freedom and Tenure* of the American Association of University Professors: "It is not only the character of the instruction but also the character of the instructor that counts; and if the student has reason to believe that the instructor is not true to himself, the virtue of the instruction as an educative force is incalculably diminished. There must be in the mind of the teacher no mental reservation. He must give the student the best of what he has and what he is." Cited in Richard Hoftstader and Walter Metzger, *The Development of Academic Freedom in the United States* (1955), p. 408.

12. As a technique commonly used in 19th century colleges, university recitations in these years usually meant a scheduled hour in which professors would ask undergraduate students to repeat portions of the text, recall key points from lectures, or, in general, display that they had memorized subject matter. The format was that of professors asking questions and students answering, with professors pronouncing judgments on the accuracy of the responses.

For the universality of lectures, laboratory work, and seminars as university teaching approaches in the late 19th century, see Hawkins (1960), pp. 220–232; Rudolph (1977), pp. 232–234; Veysey (1965), pp. 153–156, 221–232; and Hawkins (1972), pp.273–277.

13. *Daily Palo Alto,* November 14, 1895, p. 2; see also February 27, 1895, p. 2.

14. Ibid., September 26, 1895, p. 2.

15. See Stanford University's *Register* for any of the years in the 1920s.

16. Edwin Smith, "Conceptions of Leading Nineteenth Century Educators Concerning the Relationship of Teaching and Research" (1949), p. 220–221; "Opening Day Speech, October 1, 1891," in Jordan (1922), pp. 688–690; Robert Bersi, *Five Stanford Efforts to Drop The Freshman and Sophomore Years* (1966), p. 49; E. E. Slosson (1910), p. 117.

17. Stanford University, *Annual Report of the President* (1915), p. 16, for chart of student enrollments 1891–1915; for faculty counts, see *Annual Reports* for the years cited. Note that students paid no tuition from the founding of the university until 1919 when Stanford charged $40 per quarter to attend.

18. Jordan quote on teaching cited in Smith (1949), p. 220. The data on teaching load comes from a 1906 study funded by the Carnegie Foundation for the Advancement of Teaching. The average weekly number of hours across departments in seven universities (including Stanford) was between 8 and 10. For seven colleges that also participated in the study, the average across depart-

ments ran from 15 to 18 hours a week. This study, however, failed to ask those responding to their questions how many hours a week were spent preparing for lectures, recitations, and laboratories or the time spent in grading papers or preparing syllabi for new courses. See Carnegie Foundation for the Advancement of Teaching, *Third Annual Report of the President and Treasurer* (1908), p. 136. Jordan quote on advising is in Elliot (1937), p. 449.

19. Elliott (1937), pp. 509–511.

20. Harper is cited in Rudolph (1962/1990), p. 446. See also Hawkins (1972), p. 272.

21. Bersi (1966), pp. 57–75; Jordan (1922), pp. 171–172; J. Pearce Mitchell, *Stanford University, 1916–1941* (1958), pp. 69–70; Elliott (1937), pp. 518–533. For other universities, see Veysey (1965), p. 338.

22. See Laurence Veysey, "Stability and Experiment in the American Undergraduate Curriculum" (1973), pp. 9–14.

23. Edgar E. Robinson and Paul C. Edwards (Eds.), *The Memoirs of Ray Lyman Wilbur, 1875–1949* (1960), chaps. 5–7; Bersi (1966), pp. 76–78.

24. Reuben (1996), pp. 237–244. George Nash, *Herbert Hoover and Stanford University* (1988), pp. 52–54. Unknown to Wilbur, years earlier Hoover had paid for a scholarship to help the struggling medical student complete his studies (Nash, p. 25).

25. Mitchell (1958), pp. 57–59; Frank Medeiros, *The Sterling Years at Stanford: A Study in the Dynamics of Institutional Change* (1979), pp. 48–51. In reputational rankings of graduate schools in 1924 and 1934, Stanford placed 14th and 13th, respectively, out of 24 schools. See Clark Kerr (1994), pp. 168–169.

26. Robinson and Edwards (1960), p. 281; Gilbert Allardyce, "The Rise and Fall of the Western Civilization Course" (1982), pp. 695–743; Veysey (1973), pp. 9–14. For the wartime activities of universities and professors, see Carol Gruber, *Mars and Minerva: World War I and the Uses of the Higher Learning in America* (1975).

27. The quote nicely captures the same sentiment about a residual moral mission in educating undergraduates that Jordan and other university presidents expressed in the decades bracketing World War I; see Reuben (1996), pp. 164–167.

28. Stanford University, *Annual Report of the President* (1920), Stanford University Publications, No. 36 pp. 11–12.

29. The reemergence of interest in breadth of knowledge and "liberal education," as defined in post–World War I terms, was not the same as the pre–Civil War college curriculum of 3 or 4 years of required subjects. See Rudolph (1977), chap. 3. For the complexity of the phrase *liberal education* and the beginnings of *general education* and its changing meaning over the last 2 centuries of use in higher education, see Bruce Kimball, *Orators and Philosophers: A History of the Idea of Liberal Education* (1986); Carnochan (1993); and Bell (1966).

30. Stanford University, *Annual Report* (1920), p. 19.

31. Ibid., p. 18. The reference to "strange doctrines" is to the deep concern of national and local leaders over the "Red Scare" of 1919 and efforts of radical labor, political, and educational organizations to challenge established leadership. See Carnochan (1993), pp. 77–79.

The renewed vigor of the moral mission of the university in educating undergraduates accounts, in part, for the introduction of the Honor Code in 1921 when the Academic Council, at the request of students, and with President Wilbur's approval, agreed that students would be honor-bound not to cheat on examinations or plagiarize papers or help others do so and report those who do. No longer would faculty proctor exams or create situations that might tempt students to violate the code. See Stanford University, *Courses, Degrees, and Information, 1994–1995* (1994), p. 806.

32. Mitchell (1958), pp. 65–66, 70–71.

33. Robinson and Edwards (1960), p. 287.

34. Wilbur quoted in Bersi (1966), p. 84.

35. Ibid., p. 83.

36. Robinson and Edwards (1960), p. 286. For the activities of national associations to improve the quality of teaching in universities, see Chester Robinson, *The Work of Eight Major Educational Associations Toward the Improvement of College Teaching, 1920–1940* (1950). Also see Reuben (1996), pp. 247–252.

37. *Quad, 1929,* quoted in Stanford Alumni Association (1991), p. 103. For common methods of instruction at Harvard, Columbia, and Chicago in these years, see Bell (1966), chaps. 2 and 5.

38. E. D. Duryea, *Background and Development of Stanford Curricular Organization* (1948), pp. 162–163, 166. For changes in the "quiz" section, see "Conference of Instructors in Citizenship" (1923, October 10).

39. "Problems of Citizenship" (1925, April 15).

40. *Report of the Committee of the School of Social Sciences upon the Course in Citizenship* (1935, February 7); letter from Edgar E. Robinson to Ray Lyman Wilbur on May 25, 1935 (in Stanford University, Special Collections, SC29, Box 5, folder 127).

41. *Report of the Committee of the School of Social Sciences* (1935, February 7), pp. 163–167.

42. Stanford University, *Annual Report* (1920), p. 23.

43. In three national reputational surveys of graduate school rankings (data collected in 1957, 1964, and 1969), Stanford placed 13th, 5th, and 3rd; see Kerr (1994), pp. 168–169.

44. Edwin Kiester Jr., *Tresidder* (1992), p. 65.

45. Mitchell (1958), pp. 141–147; Medeiros (1979), pp. 8–24.

46. Kiester (1992), pp. 58–59, 85–88; Lowen (1997), pp. 75–94.

47. Hoover quoted in Medeiros (1979), p. 54. For Sterling's career, see Medeiros (1979), pp. 52–55. See also Nash (1988), p. 124.

48. Stanford Alumni Association (1991), p. 138. National aspirations for Stanford did not begin with President Sterling. David Starr Jordan acted as if Stanford were in the small group of universities that were imprinting higher education. In 1900, he chaired the committee that created the Association of American Universities, an organization including the University of California, Chicago, Clark, Columbia, Cornell, Harvard, Johns Hopkins, Michigan, Princeton, Virginia, Wisconsin, and Yale. See Jordan (1922), Vol. 2, pp. 1–2. In a 1906 ranking of the top 15 universities from which the top 1,000 men in science were affiliated, Harvard was 1st, followed by Columbia and the University of Chicago. Stanford was 12th. See Geiger (1986), pp. 38–39.

49. Stanford Alumni Association (1991), pp. 101–190. Sterling succeeded in expanding the university endowment and attracting public and private monies. In 1950, Stanford received from federal contracts and grants about $1.4 million; in 1959, the figure was $10.6 million. In 1962, the federal government built the Stanford Linear Accelerator for $114 million, the largest single research facility in the nation at that time. From corporations, Stanford received $158,000 in 1951, and a decade later, $1.7 million. From the Ford Foundation alone, Stanford received $100,000 in 1950; by the end of the decade, Stanford had received just from this foundation almost $10 million (pp. 104, 107, 116–117). For further elaboration of Sterling's work with the board of trustees in land development and Terman's efforts to raise funds from federal agencies and industrial corporations, see Gary Matkin, *Technology Transfer and the University* (1990), pp. 36–38, 257–258; and Lowen (1997), pp. 73–75, 80–81, 157–177. For growth of post–World War II federal investments in sciences, see Roger Geiger, "Organized Research Units—Their Role in the Development of University Research" (1990).

50. Conant quote cited in Freeland (1992), p. 54. Terman quoted in Medeiros (1979), p. 125. Note that faculty "steeples" are experts renowned for their scholarship. Achievements in teaching go unmentioned. Using the Terman and Sterling archives at Stanford, Rebecca Lowen (1997) argues that Tresidder, Terman, and Sterling centralized power in the president's and provost's posts, moving Stanford into closer ties with the federal government and corporations. She attributes Stanford's success in securing federal contract money, foundation support, and noted scholars to the aggressive efforts of Sterling and Terman (pp. 147–190).

51. Robert Hoopes and Hubert Marshall, *The Undergraduate in the University: A Report to the Faculty by the Executive Committee of the Stanford Study of Undergraduate Education, 1954–1956* (1957), p. 4. For Harvard's curricular reform, see Freeland (1992), pp. 109–110.

52.Hoopes and Marshall (1957), pp. 120–125.

53. Ibid., pp. 84–116, 128–129; Stanford University, *The Study of Education at Stanford: Report to the University* (1968), Vol. 2, pp. 3–8. In the Hoopes and Marshall report of the 1954–1956 study, one required course received rave reviews from seniors (in 1955) and members of the study's student committee: "Western Civilization." Over 80% of the seniors said that this course (1 of 30 listed) was of great or considerable value to them, a figure no other course even approached (see pp. 96–97).

54. Hoopes and Marshall (1957), p. 37.

55. Cited in Robert Blackburn and Janet Lawrence, *Faculty at Work* (1995), p. 178.

56. Ibid., pp. 177–181.

57. Hoopes and Marshall (1957), p. 43. Without reliable knowledge of how professors have taught for over a century and why they have taught as they did, I find little comfort or help in reading about how professors ought to teach—the most popular form of literature about pedagogy in universities. For those undergraduate colleges that have specified the goals and outcomes of teaching, see Bok (1986), pp. 60–64. For divergent views of teaching over the centuries, see Finkelstein (1984), pp. 106–109; and Philip Jackson, *The Practice of Teaching* (1986). For the history of researchers' efforts to establish what is effective teaching, see Wilbert J. McKeachie, "Research on College Teaching: The Historical Background" (1990); and Robert Dubin and Thomas Taveggia, *Teaching-Learning Paradox: A Comparative Analysis of College Teaching Methods* (1968).

58. Hoopes and Marshall (1957), pp. 46–47.

59. Ibid. The executive committee also considered another alternative to elevate the importance of teaching and improve its practice. They discussed creating a cadre of undergraduate teachers, such as those at the University of Chicago while Robert Hutchins was president, whose primary duty was to teach. That was briefly discussed and then disappeared from the agenda. Such a proposal to divide professors into those who teach and those who do research had been offered many times before by presidents, deans, and faculty but was dismissed. David Starr Jordan in 1906, for example, said, "We cannot divide our men into research professors and teaching professors. It is not good for the universities that among its varied helpers we should recognize distinctions of caste, nor should we try to develop one group of professors as higher than another or apart from it" (quoted in Bersi [1966], p. 52).

60. Hoopes and Marshall (1957), pp. 51–53. Of course, external factors come into play also in trying to explain this emergence of concern over the quality of teaching. The G.I. Bill generated higher enrollments in post–World War II universities of older undergraduates. The Harvard *Red Book* that called for a renewal of general education (1945) slowly permeated like-minded campuses and led to intense discussions of curriculum, teaching, and their relationship to research across the country. See Veysey (1973), pp. 14–16; Christopher Jencks and David Riesman, *The Academic Revolution* (1977), pp. 497–501; and Allardyce (1982), pp. 716–718.

61. Hoopes and Marshall (1957), pp. 114–115.

62. Quoted in Lowen (1997), p. 232.

63. Quoted in Medeiros (1979), p. 211. Rankings come from Kerr (1994), pp. 168–169. Also, for rankings, see Hugh Davis Graham and Nancy Diamond, *The Rise of American Research Universities* (1997), pp. 34–40.

64. Events taken from chronology in Stanford Alumni Association (1991), p. 216C.

65. Ibid., p. 216D; Richard Lyman, "Student Revolt and Campus Reform in the 1960s: The Case of Stanford's Judicial Charter," (1996); Larry Liebert, "Years of Hope, Days of Rage: Twenty-Five Years Later" (1995). The phrase that Lyman quoted comes from Todd Gitlin, *The Sixties: Years of Hope, Days of Rage* (1987). Lyman also points out in his article that while student activists were the subjects of media attention, most students opposed activist peers taking over offices and buildings. Almost 4,000 students voted in favor of a resolution, calling the forcible occupation "unacceptable behavior"; about 1,700 voted against resolution. The faculty, on the other hand, voted to give amnesty to students who had taken over a building; 284 voted in favor of amnesty; 245 voted against it. See Lyman (1996), p. 118.

66. Enrollment and faculty figures come from the chronology in Stanford Alumni Association (1991), pp. 216A–D; and Stanford University, *Annual Report,* for years indicated; see also Joan Hamilton, "A Cue from the Past" (1994), p. 50.

67. Hamilton (1994), p. 51.

68. Medeiros (1979), pp. 231–234.

69. The statements about the distribution requirements for 1956–1968 are drawn from Stanford University, *Study of Education* (1968), Vol. 2, pp. 8–10.

70. Ibid., p. 10.

71. Ibid., pp. 11–17. Quote on "impracticable" is on p. 24. For one participant's view of what occurred at Stanford in dropping the "Western Civilization" course, see Allardyce (1982), pp. 720–724.

72. Stanford University, *Study of Education* (1968), recommendations in Vol. 2, pp. 50–55, quote in Vol. 1, p. 14.

73. See Carnegie Foundation for the Advancement of Teaching (1908) for weekly hours of teaching at universities. For national statistics on teaching load, see Clark (1987), pp. 74–77.

74. Stanford University, *Study of Education* (1968), Vol. 8; Hugh H. Skilling, *Do You Teach? Views on College Teaching* (1969). For the introduction of computers to Stanford, see Jacqueline Ann Schmidt-Posner, *Electronic Ivory Towers: Organizational Approaches to Faculty Microcomputing* (1989). For the national picture of uses of educational technology in the 1960s and 1970s, see Lewis B. Mayhew, *Legacy of the Seventies* (1977), pp. 168–214.

75. Stanford University, *Study of Education* (1968), Vol. 8, pp. 6–8; Burton Clark, *Places of Inquiry: Research and Advanced Education in Modern Universities* (1995), p. 21. Also see Hawkins (1979), pp. 285–312. *Lehrfreiheit* and *lernfreiheit* were part of the original Stanford motto chosen by David Starr Jordan.

76. Stanford University, *Study of Education* (1968), Vol. 8, pp. 115–123.

77. Ibid., pp.72–73. Across San Francisco Bay, colleagues at Berkeley had struggled a few years earlier with many of the same issues, including the linkage between research and teaching. The 1966 report of the Academic Senate's Select Committee on Education contained a "Homily on the Importance of Teaching." The recommendations in the report included using teaching performance in tenure decisions, experimenting with student evaluations, identi-

fying alternatives to lecturing, creating smaller classes, and having senior colleagues teach undergraduates. See University of California, Berkeley Academic Senate's Select Committee on Education, *Education at Berkeley* (1968), pp. 39–63.

78. Stanford University, *Study of Education* (1968), Vol. 8, pp. 123–127. The study's staff conducted a pilot project that collected student opinions about 98 instructors (59 of whom taught Western Civilization and Freshman English) and returned confidential summaries of student responses to faculty (see pp. 134–135). See Hoopes and Marshall (1957), pp. 46–48 for earlier recommendation on determining teaching effectiveness.

In 1968, a doctoral student interviewed Stanford faculty on evaluating teaching and research. Robert Hind questioned 100 randomly chosen professors in the humanities and sciences at each level of the professoriate and found that faculty perceived evaluations of research far more influential in their career than those of teaching although the interviewees wanted teaching to have more influence in formal university rewards. These findings underscored the conflict professors experienced over what the university expected regarding teaching and what the institution rewarded regarding tenure and promotion. Robert Hind, *Evaluation and Authority in a University Faculty* (1968), pp. 76–78, 86–98, 142–146, 168.

79. Stanford University, *Study of Education* (1968), Vol. 5, p. 12.

80. Ibid., p. 32. Advising students at Berkeley in these years was little better than was reported at Stanford. In a study that sampled student and faculty opinion about interaction with faculty inside and outside the classroom, the data showed infrequent contact and much social distance between Berkeley professors and their students.

81. Of the four that I could find, only one dealt explicitly with the quality of teaching; it involved Henry Rolfe in the classics department. I included Edward Ross (economics) who was fired for his political opinions and Earl Barnes (education) who had committed adultery and was asked by Jordan to leave. I do not include Thorstein Veblen (economics) whose illicit affairs ultimately led to his resignation, although his dismissal was imminent. See Spoehr (1975), pp. 148–150, 166–248. These dismissals illustrate, in part, the deep belief on the part of the administration that unsullied faculty behavior inside and outside the classroom was linked to developing unblemished character in undergraduates. Julie Reuben (1996) points out that the original religious mission of the college had become distilled by the early 20th century into a heavy emphasis on the value-laden tasks of teaching and advising. Engaging in what was defined as immoral behavior for the times endangered the morally loaded role that professors had to play in the classroom (pp. 245–253).

82. Stanford University, *Study of Education* (1968), Vol. 8, pp. 89–91.

83. Information on the Gores award and the Center for Teaching and Learning comes from Michele Fisher (Ed.), *Teaching at Stanford: An Introductory Handbook* (1985), pp. 4, 31; and Stanford University, Provost Office, *Faculty Handbook* (1993), p. 19.

84. *Report of the Committee on the Professoriate at Stanford* (1974, February), p. 64.

85. Ibid., pp. 64–65.

86. Mervin Freedman, *Academic Culture and Faculty Development* (1979), pp. 39–44.

87. Stanford University, Faculty Senate, "Faculty Senate Minutes" (1976, December 2), pp. 3–11; "Memo from Committee on Undergraduate Studies to Faculty Senate" (1979, November 28), pp. 1–3.

88. Stanford Alumni Association (1991), pp. 216–217; Stanford University, Office of the President, *Stanford Statistics* (1988, December), p. 1; Stanford University, Office of Undergraduate Admissions, "Undergraduate Students, Freshman Class, 1965–1996."

89. Richard Roberts, a Stanford professor of history, points out that much of the furor over changing the "Western Culture" course was as much anchored in faculty concerns over the narrowness of the course, displayed as early as 1984, as the more publicized student protests that began in 1986. Richard Roberts, "Teaching Non-Western History at Stanford" (1994).

90. Bob Beyers, "Broader Conception of West Is Needed, Faculty Senate Told" (1988, February 10), pp. 1, 13, 15.

91. For faculty and student criticism, see William King, Black Student Union letter to Committee on Undergraduate Studies, in *Campus Report*, April 29, 1987; open letter to campus community from Professors Barry Katz and John Perry, June 17, 1986. The charge to the Task Force on Area One Requirement is in a September 29, 1986, memo to the Task Force from Provost James Rosse. For an alternative to the Task Force's proposal, see "Memo From 23 Professors in Humanities and Social Sciences to the Faculty Senate" (1988, January 19) in *Stanford News*.

92. Bob Beyers, "Western Culture 'Great Debate' Opens in Senate" (1988, January 27), pp. 1, 12. Also see statements of professors in Beyers (1988, January 27), pp. 6–12; and Beyers (1988, February 10), pp. 1, 13–16, 21–23. For media attention, see *The Washington Post* editorial, February 23, 1988; *Newsweek,* February 1, 1988, p. 46; and *Los Angeles Times* editorial, February 1, 1988. The compromise is in the text of the legislation that the Faculty Senate approved on March 31, 1988, as reprinted in the *Campus Report.* Also see Frank Quaratiello, "A New Era: CIV Sweeps in Fac Sen" (1988, April 1).

93. "State of University" address reprinted in *Campus Report,* May 5, 1993, pp. 10–11.

94. Quotes from the chair of CUE are in Don Kazak, "Creating the Right Curriculum" (1995, April 5), p. 20. Most observers of the Stanford scene, whether from the political right, center, or left, agree that the investigation of Stanford's use of federal funds to recover indirect costs associated with underwriting research grants led to the eventual resignation of President Donald Kennedy in 1991. The allegations that federal funds were allocated to pay for tuition costs for children of faculty and staff and for personal items in the president's home became the subject of national media attention and a congressional investiga-

tion into university use of indirect costs recovered from federal research grants. Stanford, of course, was not alone in charging the federal government for indirect costs associated with the conduct of research, but the discovery by a federal auditor of certain items charged to the government by Stanford led to such close media scrutiny that Kennedy chose to resign. It was very difficult, he said in his statement to the faculty, "for the person identified with a problem to be the spokesman for its solution."

As a consequence of the federal investigation and the widespread practice of universities across the country receiving as high as 75% indirect costs (e.g., on a $1,000,000 research grant from federal agencies, the indirect costs would add another $750,000), the federal government renegotiated the indirect costs considerably downward, thereby reducing revenues that heretofore universities had expected. This led to budget reductions at Stanford and elsewhere. In this climate of scandal and fiscal retrenchment, the board of trustees in 1992 appointed its ninth president, former dean of the University of Chicago Law School, Gerhard Casper. See Joel Shurkin, "Congressional Committee Criticizes Stanford's Accounting Procedures, Suggests Some Employees May be Guilty of Fraud in Indirect Cost Issue" (1991, March 14); John Wagner, "House Subcommittee Lambasts Stanford" (1991, March 14); Donald Kennedy, "Statement on Indirect Costs" (1991, January 8); Jeff Gottlieb, "U.S. Probe of Stanford May Cost Other Schools" (1991, January 22); and "Chronological Guide to Indirect Costs at Stanford" (1992, May 28). Also see Rosenzweig (1998), pp.79–80. Donald Kennedy describes these events in *Academic Duty* (1997), pp. 167–175.

95. *Report of the Commission on Undergraduate Education* (1994), pp. 7–8; Casper (1997, July 31).

96. I use the word *culture* to mean the beliefs, formal and informal rules, and rituals shared within a university and its many schools and departments. While a university has a campus-wide culture that permeates its many units, those units also have subcultures anchored in the different disciplines that vary among themselves in rules, beliefs, and rituals. Hence, I use the concept of culture as a variable in my analysis rather than as a metaphor. See Linda Smircich, "Concepts of Culture and Organizational Analysis" (1983). For an application of using culture as a variable, see Diane Vaughn, *The Challenger Launch Decision* (1996), pp. 64–68, 209–215. For departmental cultures in universities, see Kathleen Quinlan, *Collaboration and Cultures of Teaching in University Departments: Faculty Beliefs About Teaching and Learning in History and Engineering* (1996), chap. 5. Quinlan studied cultures in history and engineering in two Research I institutions.

97. Many of these examples come from Stanford University, Faculty Senate (1995, April), appendix B, p. 21; see also Weisberg, R. (1995, December 5). Memo from Robert Weisberg, vice-provost for faculty recruitment and development, to chairs of departments (Provost's Officer, December 5, 1995).

98. Jett Pihakis, *Teachers Rethinking Teaching: A Peek Inside the Black Box of Instructional Consultation* (1996), p. 214.

99. Ibid., p. 214.

100. Weisberg (1995, December 5), p. 1. Here, again, is another effort to shrink the margin of difference between recognition and rewards for teaching and for those of research not to alter the asymmetry but to reduce the obvious discrepancies.

101. Wagner Thielens Jr., *The Disciplines and Undergraduate Lecturing* (1987). For other national studies of teaching practices in universities and colleges that show lecturing as the dominant approach, see Robert Blackburn, Glenn Pellino, Alice Boberg, and Colman O'Connell, "Are Instructional Programs Off-Target?" (1980), pp. 32–48; and Educational Testing Service, *Student Instructional Report: Comparative Data Guide for Four-Year Colleges and Universities* (1979).

102. Hativa (1995). Hativa points out that the low response rate is typical of faculty returns to questionnaires—the range is between 13 and 25%. She found, however, that those who did respond were representative of the entire faculty (see p. 12).

103. *Report of the Commission* (1994). Survey results are in the appendix.

104. Senior surveys for the years, 1986, 1988, 1990, 1992, and 1994 were prepared by the Office of the Registrar, Institutional Research Unit, and carry the title Stanford University, Office of the Registrar, *Statistical Summary of Senior Survey* for the particular year. The response rates of graduating seniors ranged from a low of 25% in 1994 to a high of 52% in 1990 with the modal rate 37%.

105. Diane Manuel and Marisa Cigarroa, "A Tangible Commitment" (1996, July/August), p. 28.

106. *Report of the Commission* (1994), p. 42. Commission members had access to senior surveys for the late 1980s and early 1990s. For example, for 3 straight years almost 70% of the seniors rated "general advising" from faculty as "fair" to "poor." See *Statistical Summary of Senior Survey* for 1986–1988.

At a university-wide committee meeting discussing departmental policies, a social science colleague burst out that he was assigned 15 majors to advise, has hardly any time to see them, and few of them show up during his office hours. He was upset because in writing recommendations for advisees who are seniors and with whom he has had virtually no contact, he has to meet with each one to find out enough information to write a few paragraphs. See Stanford University, "Faculty Senate Committee Meeting" (1997, February 12).

107. *Report of the Commission* (1994), pp. 42–44.

108. For evidence of Presidents Kennedy and Casper's commitment to the desired linkage of teaching and research, see Kennedy (1991, March 11), p. 16; and Gerhard Casper's remarks as newly inducted president in the *Campus Report* (1992, April 1), p. 10.

109. Sykes (1988), pp. 51–54. Donald Kennedy's story is in his speech to the Stanford community (1991, March 6).

110. Carolyn Mooney, "Professors Feel Conflict Between Roles in Teaching and Research" (1991, May 8), pp. A15–A16; also cited in John Centra, *Reflective Faculty Evaluation* (1993), p. 3. Also see Carol Colbeck, *Weaving Seamless Lives:*

Organizational and Disciplinary Influences on Integration and Congruence of Faculty Work (1996), chap. 1. Colbeck documents the long history of beliefs about the compatibility and tensions between research and teaching.

111. Kelley Skeff and Nel Noddings (1985), pp. 13, 21–22, 35, 41.

112. Hativa (1995), pp. 22–25.

113. Stanford University, Faculty Senate (1995, April). The report built upon the concerns of university presidents, provosts, and higher education associations over the diminished importance and quality of teaching that critics had identified in the 1980s. The report also took ideas articulated earlier by Don Kennedy and endorsed by Gerhard Casper and converted them into formal recommendations. See Ernest Boyer, *Scholarship Reconsidered: Priorities of the Professoriate* (1990).

114. Stanford University, Faculty Senate (1995, April), pp. 10, 15–16. The report offered illustrations of particular departments that had institutionalized practices of colleagues visiting and discussing one another's classes. Peer review had been initially suggested in the *Report of the Committee on the Professoriate at Stanford to Faculty Senate* (1974, February), pp. 64–65.

115. Hoopes and Marshall (1957), pp. 46–47.

116. Stanford University, *Study of Education* (1968), Vol. 8, pp. 123, 126.

117. In California, only 7% of the faculty used services such as CTL at universities in the 1980s. Paul Berman, J. Intilli, and Dan Weiler, "Exploring Faculty Development in California Higher Education" (1987), cited in Nira Hativa, *The Department-Wide Approach to Improving Faculty Instruction in Higher Education: A Qualitative Evaluation* (1993, April), p. 3.

118. Don Kennedy (1991, March 11).

119. Jencks and Riesman (1977); Jonathan R. Cole, "Balancing Acts: Dilemmas of Choice Facing Research Universities" (1994); Don Kennedy, "Making Choices in the Research University" (1994).

120. W. Bliss Carnochan, "The Paradox of the University: 1906, 1997" (1997, April 16).

121. In 1994–1995, breadth of knowledge at Stanford meant that students took 11 courses in 9 areas (distribution requirements) for at least 33 units (180 were required for graduation). Depth of knowledge was left to the major. According to university policy, a major must be at least one-third of a student's program but can be no more than two-thirds "to ensure the values of breadth." Departmental requirements vary, but these are the lower and upper limits of pursuing depth of knowledge. Stanford University, *Courses, Degrees, and Information* (1994–1995), pp. 28–33. Don Kennedy quote is from his comments reprinted in the *Campus Report* (1992, April 29), p. 12.

122. Lee Shulman, "Those Who Understand Teach: Knowledge Growth in Teaching" (1987). Such a divorce while common to most universities is not, however, uniform across Stanford departments and professional schools. For example, the case-method approach to teaching students in law, graduate business

school, and public policy display a marriage between content and pedagogy at Stanford and elsewhere. In medical education, problem-based learning (PBL) as a way of both teaching and learning has been adopted in many schools. See Russell L. Weaver, "Langdell's Legacy: Living with the Case Method" (1991); Steven Schlossman, Robert Gleeson, Michael Sedlak, and David Allen, *The Beginnings of Graduate Management Education in the United States* (1994); Mark Albanese and Susan Mitchell, "Problem-Based Learning: A Review of Literature on its Outcomes and Implementation Issues" (1993).

123. Reuben (1996), pp. 62–66.

124. Note that with student and faculty choices being salient, determining what constituted a "course" with units corresponding to how many times the professor and students would meet weekly became essential. The standardization of courses with numbering systems, allocation of units, and how many times weekly class would meet, became fixtures in universities by the turn of the century. See Veysey (1973), pp. 23–26.

125. Bok (1986), pp. 39–46; Jencks and Riesman (1977), pp. 492–504; Veysey (1973), pp. 1–21; Carnochan (1993), pp. 68–99.

126. One obvious exception is the few colleges and universities committed to a *great books* curriculum where small-group discussions are intimately tied to the curriculum's ideology. See Reuben (1996), pp. 62–66.

127. William James, *Memories and Studies* (1934), p. 337. Attacks upon the Ph.D. have been a cottage industry since James. Recent critiques of this degree come from David Damrosch, *We Scholars* (1995); and Louis Menand, "How to Make a Ph.D. Matter" (1996, September 22). For doctoral dropouts, see William Bowen and Neil Rudenstine, *In Pursuit of the Ph.D.* (1992); and Damrosch's (1995) discussion of these findings, pp. 143–147.

128. Hawkins (1979), pp.292–293.

129. Edward Shils, "The Order of Learning: The Ascendancy of the University" (1979), pp. 28–29. In a letter from Thomas A. Bailey to H. Stuart Hughes on July 12, 1954, Bailey echoed what Max Savelle, then head of the "Western Civilization" course, had said a decade earlier to the same suggestion: "I certainly would not for a moment consider being the chairman of a course being taught by a group of older men who had no interest in what they were doing." Savelle's comment was in a confidential letter from Savelle to E. E. Robinson, March 16, 1944. Both of these are located in "Thomas A. Bailey Papers" in Stanford University, Special Collections (SC54).

130. Geiger (1986), pp. 20–38; Hawkins (1979), pp. 293–294; Veysey (1965), pp. 320–324. The German influence upon American professors and presidents in the ideals of specialization, the pursuit of truth through scientific methods, the departmental organization, and the model of the research-oriented professor are noted in these sources. Also see John Higham, "The Matrix of Specialization" (1979); and Hawkins (1979), pp. 291–294.

131. Freeland (1992); Veysey (1973), pp. 17–18; Jencks and Riesman (1977), pp. 501–503; and Gumport (1993).

CHAPTER 2

1. For these distinctions about change and the common charge that schools and universities seldom change, I have drawn from my earlier work. See Larry Cuban, "A Fundamental Puzzle of School Reform" (1988) and "Reforming Again, Again, and Again" (1990). Much of my thinking then was influenced by Paul Watzlawick, Richard Frisch, and John Weakland, *Change: Principles of Problem Formation and Problem Resolution* (1974). Since then, I have broadened my initial framework that was geared to public schools in the United States to include higher education by drawing from Gerald Grant and David Riesman, *The Perpetual Dream: Reform and Experiment in the American College* (1978); Clark Kerr, *The Uses of the University* (1982); Arthur Levine, *Why Innovation Fails* (1980); Burton Clark (1983, 1984, 1987); John Meyer and Brian Rowan, "The Structure of Educational Organizations" (1978), pp. 78–109; and Paul DiMaggio, "Interest and Agency in Institutional Theory" (1988), pp. 3–22. I am especially grateful for the formulation of Ladislav Cerych, "The Policy Perspective" (1983), which pulled together strands of my thinking that had been previously disconnected.

2. See James G. March, "Three Lectures on Efficiency and Adaptiveness in Organizations" (1994); and Kathleen O'Toole, "Efficiency in Higher Education Poses Problems, March Argues" (1995).

3. Cerych (1983), pp. 248–253.

4. I have drawn from several sources for what I mean by structures, cultures, and processes. See W. Richard Scott, *Organizations* (1987); Clark (1987); and H. M. Trice and Janice Beyer, *The Cultures of Work Organizations* (1993).

5. Neither kind of planned change is inherently superior to the other. As a result, I have chosen neutral words to steer away from making value judgments about whether incremental or fundamental changes are better or worse than the other. Researchers and reformers often signal their biases by their choice of words. Those favoring incremental change often use words such as *improvements, enhancements, worthwhile additions,* and so on. Those who oppose plans for incremental changes call them *piecemeal, tinkering, superficial,* or *fragmented.* Advocates for fundamental change use such words as *real, systemic, deep,* and *comprehensive.* Those opposed to fundamental changes use such words as *utopian, escapist,* and *impractical.*

6. The commonly used word *innovation,* or a planned change new to the host organization, can refer to either an intended incremental or fundamental change. The determination depends upon the intent of the innovation's designers for depth of change and its subsequent implementation.

7. See David Tyack and Elisabeth Hansot, *Managers of Virtue* (1982); Robert Nisbet, *History of the Idea of Progress* (1980), pp. 56–59; and Warren Susman, *Culture as History: The Transformation of American Society in the Twentieth Century* (1984). In his essay "The Persistence of Reform," Susman underscores the perennial impulse within Americans to improve themselves and institutions (pp. 86–97).

Most popular and scholarly writers in education seldom make the distinction between incremental and fundamental change and use the words *change* and *reform* as equivalent terms. Examples in the academic literature where *reform* and *change* are used interchangeably can be found in Arthur Levine and John Weingart, *Reform of Undergraduate Education* (1973); J. B. Hefferlin, *Dynamics of Academic Reform* (1969); and Jencks and Riesman (1977). In *The Perpetual Dream* (1978), Grant and Riesman distinguish between "telic reforms," which aim to create undergraduate institutions that have very different goals than the multiversity, and "popular reforms," which create a "loosening of the curriculum" (p. 15). They are among the few scholars who seek to make a distinction between magnitude of changes and what I call fundamental and incremental changes.

For others who have used the distinction that I offer here, see Ernest House, "Technology Versus Craft: A Ten-Year Perspective on Innovation" (1979); Seymour Sarason, *The Culture of the School and the Problem of Change* (1971) and *The Predictable Failure of Educational Reform* (1990); Kerr (1982), pp. 151–181; and Watzlawick, Frisch, and Weakland (1974).

8. Dzuback (1991); Grant and Riesman (1978).

9. For descriptions of problem-based learning in these medical schools, see Patricia Kendall and George Reader, "Innovations in Medical Education of the 1950s Contrasted With Those of the 1970s and 1980s" (1988); and Margaret N. Bussigel, Barbara M. Barzansky, and Gary G. Grenholm, *Innovation Processes in Medical Education* (1988).

10. One way of describing the university system is to speak of policies, programs, and processes involving the goals, funding, governance, organization, curriculum, instruction, and cultures of the institution.

11. For a description of open admissions at CUNY, see James Traub, *The School Upon the Hill* (1994). Arthur Levine (1980) describes the failed effort to transform the University of Buffalo.

12. Clark (1983), p. 115.

13. Clark (1987); Meyer and Rowan (1978); Karl Weick, "Educational Organizations as Loosely Coupled Systems" (1976).

14. Stanford University, *Faculty Handbook* (1993), p. 19. For Law School, see Stanford University, Faculty Senate, *Toward Greater Excellence in Teaching at Stanford* (1995, April), p. 21.

15. Lee Shulman and Kathleen Quinlan, *S-CEIT Focus Group Report* (1993), pp. 3–9. The phrase "countervailing force" comes from Stanford University, *Study of Education* (1968), Vol. 8, p. 122–123; see also Stanford University, Faculty Senate (1995, April), pp. 23–24.

16. For this description of Santa Cruz, I depended upon Grant and Riesman (1978), and Levine and Weingart (1973). Quote is from Grant and Riesman (1978), pp. 254–255.

17. Grant and Riesman (1978), pp. 77–134.

18. Ibid., pp. 272–273.

19. Ibid.

20. Another example of this incrementalizing of an intended fundamental change is Gerald Graff's study (1987) of the founding and spread of university interdisciplinary programs in American Studies during the 20th century. Such programs implicitly challenged the basic structure of departmental organization and sought to reorganize knowledge and to view American culture through a different lens. What Graff found was that new programs were either added to existing departments or lapsed into what he called "patterned isolation," or marginality within the institution (see pp. 209–225).

21. See Rudolph (1962/1990), pp. 460–461; and George Pierson, *Yale: The University College, 1921–1937* (1955), pp. 333–357, 400–444.

22. The reforms introduced at Columbia College in the 1920s, and at the University of Chicago by Robert Hutchins in the 1930s, and the creation of 4-year colleges devoted to the liberal arts were dedicated to reversing the clear trend toward transforming undergraduate institutions into graduate preparatory programs. See Daniel Bell, *The Reforming of General Education* (1966) and *The Idea and Practice of General Education* (1950/1992). Rudolph (1962/1990) calls these undergraduate reforms a "counterrevolution" (pp. 440–461).

The late 1970s and early 1980s attempts to revitalize undergraduate education are recounted in Harvard's case by Henry Rosovsky (1990), and in Columbia's by Robert Belknap and Richard Kuhns, *Tradition and Innovation: General Education and the Reintegration of the University, A Columbia Report* (1977).

Diane Vaughn (1996) suggests another example of unplanned incremental changes accumulating into an unwitting fundamental change, which turned out to have untoward, even devastating, effects: U.S. involvement in Vietnam, the collapse of IBM in the 1980s, and the destruction of the Challenger shuttle (p. 410).

23. Bell (1966), pp. 38–53. Bell points out that a faculty committee report in 1965 gave a scathing review of the enormous gaps in the general education program and recommended many modifications; the faculty rejected the Doty Report. See Belknap and Kuhns (1977), p. 188. For an unusual view of these courses from a journalist who had been an undergraduate in the 1960s and returned to Columbia in the 1990s to take again the humanities course, see David Denby, *Great Books* (1996).

24. Richard N. Smith, *The Harvard Century: The Making of a University to a Nation* (1986), p. 94. Hawkins (1972), pp. 263–289; the Lowell quote is on p. 283.

25. Harvard University, *General Education in a Free Society* (1946), pp. 177–247.

26. Smith (1986), pp. 160–175.

27. Rosovsky (1990), pp. 113–129.

28. The formulation around "great" comes from Bell (1966), p. 48.

29. Bell (1966), p. 26–28; Kerr (1982), p. 33. See also Dzuback (1991), p. 115.

30. This description of the program is drawn from Dzuback (1991), pp. 109–135; Bell (1950/1992), pp. 259–324; and Bell (1966), pp. 26–38. One clarification: All of these writers underscore the point that these yearlong courses were not devoted to "great books," what Hutchins and his persuasive friend Mortimer

Adler sought. While the syllabi certainly contained excerpts from many of these sources in the Western cultural tradition, the courses were neither devoted to such a canon nor to the unique teaching practices associated with *great books* courses.

31. Bell (1966), p. 193.

32. Although I have described only three institutions from the 20th century, curricular reform has been a traditional pattern in many other universities, public and private, in this century. The general histories written by John Brubacher and Willis Rudy, *Higher Education in Transition* (1976); and Rudolph (1977); and the studies of particular periods, such as Grant and Riesman (1978), Levine and Weingart (1973), and Hefferlin (1969), all underscore the pervasiveness and persistence of this type of reform.

33. Most informed accounts of higher education stress the point of universities having to respond to their ever-changing surroundings to survive. See, for example, the essays by Patrick Callan, "Government and Higher Education"; Margaret Gordon, "The Economy and Higher Education"; and Roger Geiger, "Research Universities in a New Era: From the 1980s to the 1990s" in Levine (1993). For a study of Stanford students' shifting aspirations while they were undergraduates, see Herant Katchadourian and John Boli, *Careerism and Intellectualism Among College Students* (1985).

34. See Jeffrey Pfeffer and Gerald R. Salancik, *The External Control of Organizations: A Resource Dependence Perspective* (1978); and Bok (1986), pp. 14–15.

35. For ambiguity in university purposes, see Michael Cohen and James G. March, *Leadership and Ambiguity* (1974), pp. 195–197. The multiversity point comes from Kerr (1982), pp. 1–45. For elaboration historically of university purposes, see Reuben (1996) and Veysey (1965). Also see Abraham Flexner, *Universities: American, English, German* (1930/1994). Flexner said they had become "'service' stations for the general public" (p. 45).

36. The phrase "real university" derives from institutional theory where the power of dominant social beliefs both shapes and gives stability to organizational structures and processes. See John Meyer and Brian Rowan, "Institutionalized Organizations: Formal Structure as Myth and Ceremony" (1977). Mary Metz adopted portions of institutional theory and applied them to public schools by calling the beliefs held by students, teachers, and parents about high school as the "real school"; see "Real School: A Universal Drama Amid Disparate Experience" (1990), pp. 75–91.

37. Geiger (1986), pp. 18–19. For the concept of organizational field, see Paul DiMaggio and Walter Powell, "The Iron Cage Revisited: Institutional Isomorphism and Collective Rationality" (1991).

38. Much of this institutionalist explanation is drawn from Meyer and Rowan (1977); DiMaggio and Powell (1991); DiMaggio (1988); and W. Richard Scott, John Meyer, and Associates, *Institutional Environments and Organizations: Structural Complexity and Individualism* (1994).

39. Bok (1986), p. 40.

40. Meyer and Rowan (1978); and James G. March and Johan P. Olsen, *Redis- covering Institutions: The Organizational Basis of Politics* (1989), pp. 69–94. March and Olsen describe government reorganization as a perennial activity. See also Nils Brunsson and Johan P. Olsen, *The Reforming Organization* (1993), pp. 33–47.

41. For an analysis of symbolic uses of reform language and activity as applied to public education, see John Meyer, "Innovation and Knowledge Use in American Public Education" (1992).

42. Brunsson and Olsen (1993), pp. 34–41.

43. Weick (1976); and Karl Weick, "Contradictions in a Community of Schol- ars: The Cohesion-Accuracy Tradeoff" (1984).

CHAPTER 3

1. Letter from E. D. Adams to Richard Piatt on April 26, 1922 (in Stanford University, Special Collections, SC29, Box 5, folder 117).

2. *Dictionary of American Biography* (1944), pp. 8–9.

3. Letter from Thomas A. Bailey to Diane Howell on June 2, 1947 (stored in SC54, Box 3, folder 26). In his autobiography, Bailey praises Adams's lecturing: "He brought home to me the value of the short illustrative anecdote or the pun- gent phrase, and these devices I have since then used in both my lecturing and writing" (*The American Pageant Revisited: Recollections of a Stanford Historian,* 1982, p. 71).

4. Syllabi can be found in Stanford University, Green Library, Special Col- lections, 3951, "Course Syllabi," years 1914–1928. Enrollment figures come from annual copies of the Stanford *Register* for these years.

5. I concentrated on the U.S. history syllabi for Adams's courses between 1914 and 1928 to see how much was duplicated each year that he taught the course and how much was added and deleted.

6. Nash (1988), pp. 49–50, 59–62, 75–76. Leopold von Ranke (1795–1886) is considered to be the "father . . . of modern historical scholarship." He was pro- lific—completing 60 volumes—and self-conscious about formulating a method- ology in producing scholarly work. To many Americans who studied in Germany in the post–Civil War decades, the historical seminar for advanced students to study archival sources was a Rankean innovation that was imported to the United States for newly emerging universities committed to research. See Fritz Stern (Ed.), *Varieties of History* (1956), pp. 54–55.

These intellectual positions that Adams attributed to colleagues at Stanford were widely shared among peers, especially within the American Historical Asso- ciation (AHA). See Peter Novick, *That Noble Dream* (1988), pp. 21–85.

7. Even with these competing aims, Adams had gradually fashioned a rep- utation among historians that went beyond Stanford. Adams had joined the AHA and was active in presenting papers at its annual conferences and to its many committees. He had been elected a vice-president and was slated to become

president of the association, the highest honor professional historians could bestow upon a colleague, when he died in 1930.

8. Becker quote cited in Novick (1988), p. 272. Data from Stanford University, *Register* (1917–1918), p. 184. Adams's son was taken prisoner at Metz, as noted in a letter to Mrs. Susie Light, December 18, 1918 (stored in SC29, Box 5). Adams developed and, with eight instructors, taught the "War Issues" course between 1919 and 1921, a course that directly led to the "Problems of Civilization" and "Western Civilization" courses in the mid-1920s and 1930s. "Minutes of Committee on the Course on War Issues," September 19, 1918; letter from Frank Aydelotte to Adams, September 26, 1918; from Adams to Aydelotte, October 7, 1918 (stored in SC29, Box 5, folder 119).

The dilemma also faced Yamato Ichihasi, a Japanese citizen, and then an assistant professor teaching Asian history at Stanford, who advised the Japanese delegation to the Washington, D.C., disarmament conference in 1921 and, as a consequence, came under the scrutiny of the Federal Bureau of Investigation (FBI). See Gordon Chang, *Morning Glory, Evening Shadow: Yamato Ichihasi's Wartime Writings* (1996).

9. In two peer assessments of the nation's history departments' doctoral programs (1982 and 1993) done by the National Research Council, Stanford placed eighth and seventh respectively. In teaching effectiveness, peers ranked its teaching "extremely effective." Denise Magner, "Doctoral Judgments" (1995, September 22), p. A29; Stanford University, *Stanford Observer* (1995), pp. 1, 20.

10. Obvious external influences, such as war, economic depressions, and social movements, have been noted by other historians of the curriculum in higher education. See Rudolph (1977). I will be focusing more on the organizational mechanisms that shaped the content of courses.

As a longtime member of the AHA, Adams was in frequent contact with luminaries in the field. There are letters to Charles M. Andrews at Johns Hopkins (November 15, 1909), William Dunning at Columbia (March 16, 1911), and Andrew McLaughlin at the University of Chicago (March 26, 1915) (stored in SC142). In bringing Edgar E. Robinson to Stanford from Wisconsin, where Robinson had studied with Frederick Jackson Turner, Adams knew Turner well enough to ask about Robinson and to stay in touch with him in subsequent years. See letters from Adams to Turner on April 6, 1915; and from Turner to Adams on May 11, 1917, and Adams's response on May 16, 1917 (stored in SC142, Box 1, folder 13).

11. Stanford University, *Circular of Information, No. 6* (1891), pp. 35–37.

12. Stanford University, *Register* (1901–1902), pp. 97–102.

13. Ibid., (1929–1930), pp. 418–426.

14. Ibid., (1921–1922), pp. 211–213; and (1945–1946), pp. 529–538. Also see Stanford University, *Courses, Degrees, and Information* (1965–1966), p. 298; and (1967–1968), p. 261. The expansion of geographical specialties in the 20th century occurred across both public and private universities. For a study of history curricula in 18 land-grant universities, see David J. Frank, Evan Schofer, and John Torres, "Re-Thinking History: Change in the University Curriculum, 1910–1990" (1994).

15. Stanford *Register* (1945–1946), pp. 527–528. Stanford *Courses, Degrees* (1967–1968), pp. 256–257; (1975–1976), p. 379; (1985–1986), p. 429; and (1994–1995), pp. 500. The first Stanford doctorate was awarded in 1894. In history, the first doctorate was awarded in 1910 to Payson Treat in Far East studies (he then became a faculty member in the department); 23 doctorates were awarded before 1940. In all of these cases, a student worked closely with a professor in choosing the fields of specialization, the courses that needed to be taken, the proposal for the dissertation, and the study itself. It was highly individualized and informally done prior to the 1940s. See Stanford University, *Annual Report of the President* (1915), p. 10; Stanford University, *Stanford History Newsletter,* (1966, Fall), p. 14.

16. There were a few uncommon additions to the faculty in these years. Even though academic anti-Semitism, including at Stanford, was pervasive until the 1950s Stanford did hire Frank Golder as an associate professor in 1921 with the full support of Ephraim Adams; Golder was promoted to full professor in 1928 and died the following year. Golder had written extensively about Czarist Russian expansionism in the Pacific and the revolution itself. He had helped collect, translate, and edit documents that became part of the Hoover War Library, and Adams wanted him at Stanford. See Alain Dubie, *Frank A. Golder: An Adventure of a Historian in Quest of Russian History* (1989). Adams, however, had raised questions before World War I about Golder being Jewish when the Harvard-trained historian, then teaching at State College of Washington, was seeking a post at Stanford. Adams had written to David Starr Jordan on February 17, 1911 that "he is a Jew and . . . he should be seen personally before any engagement with him was made" (in SC29, Box 4, folder 31). He was not hired at this time. For pre–World War II discrimination against Jews in universities, see Novick (1988), pp. 172–174. For instances of overt feelings about hiring Jewish professors, see Adams's letter on May 20, 1922, to a colleague at the University of Southern California about Abraham Zvenigrad; letter from Thomas A. Bailey on November 25, 1940, to Edwin Cottrell in political science at Stanford about Albert Weinberg, a candidate for a post in that department (in SC54, Box 2, folder 11).

Another anomaly was Harvard-trained Yamato Ichihasi who began at Stanford in 1913 as an history instructor, advanced to an assistant, associate, and full professor by 1931, the first nonwhite professor to achieve that rank. A Japanese citizen, Ichihasi's salary was initially paid by the Japanese government through intermediaries. Then, Stanford assumed costs for the post, creating the first endowed chair in history. In 1942, the Ichihasi family was sent to a Japanese-American relocation camp. During his internment, Stanford conveyed emeritus status on him (Chang, 1996). Dates for Ichihasi's tenure come from Stanford *Register* for those years.

17. The demographics of the department come from examining faculty names in the annual catalogue for the department, departmental reports, and minutes between 1891 and 1991.

18. The chart for Americanists shows that the mean number for courses taught and weekly hours in class is below 4 and 6, respectively. The reason is that some professors have split their duties between teaching and administra-

tion or between teaching and large research projects, which drop the mean since the number of faculty is small. I chose Americanists because these historians usually anchor most history departments in U.S. universities, as they have at Stanford.

19. Bailey (1982), pp. 76–77.

20. Interview with Emeritus Professor George Knoles on April 7, 1993.

21. Letter from Gordon Wright to David Potter on January 28, 1961 (in *David Potter Papers,* SC88, Box 3, under "Correspondence: My Teaching, 1961–1962"). Letter from Bailey to Dean P. Rhinelander on December 22, 1958 (in SC54). Also see history department files in SC29, Box 3, folder 86.

22. Interview with Emeritus Professor Richard Lyman on April 27, 1993.

23. Stanford *Courses, Degrees* (1984–1985), p. 427.

24. Senior lecturer Joseph Corn was profiled in a campus publication for his creating an online newsgroup in a class through a home page on the World Wide Web. See Marisa Cigarroa, "E-Mail, Web Sites: No More Pencils, No More Books?" (1995, September 13), p. 1. Carolyn Lougee had created software for a European history course that she taught; by 1995, historian Tim Lenoir had put courses on the Internet (as noted in a conversation with Decker Walker, School of Education, March 25, 1996). Quote is from an interview with David Kennedy on July 22, 1996.

25. Stanford *Courses, Degrees,* (1984–1985), pp. 422, 427.

26. I have compiled these estimates of seminar and lecture courses from catalogues that were available at the Stanford library. Particular years may have been missing, which accounts for the occasional unevenness of 5-year or decade sampling that I did. Also since these data are taken from catalogues, there is some slippage between what is advertised and what is actually offered. Thus, I call these estimates.

27. *The Department of History* (1953), p. 2; interview with David Kennedy.

27. See letter from Thomas A. Bailey to Gordon Craig on October 28, 1960 (in SC29a, Box 3, folder 92); letter from Gordon Wright, Executive Head, to David Potter on January 9, 1961 (in SC29a, Box 4, folder 93); and, especially, letter from Bailey to Provost Frederick Terman on April 28, 1960 (in SC29a, Box3, folder 91).

29. *Report of the Committee on the B.A. in History* (1959).

30. Ibid., p. 6.

31. Ibid., pp. 6, 11, 15.

32. Stanford University, Department of History, *Committee on Priorities and History Undergraduate Student Association: "Undergraduate Survey, 1969–1970"* (1970), p. 2. How many of the 112 students responded was omitted.

33. Stanford University, Department of History, *Revisions of the History Undergraduate Curriculum* (1991), p. 7. The chair of the committee's report was Professor Richard Roberts.

34. Letter from Bailey on January 13, 1932 (in SC54, Box 1, folder 6).

35. Letter from Bailey on May 8, 1948 (in SC54, Box 3, folder 31; and SC54, Box 3, folder 33).

36. David Starr Jordan made the connection frequently. "The ideas of *'Lehrfreiheit'* and *'Lernfreiheit'*—freedom of teaching and freedom of study, on which the German university is based," Jordan, then President of Indiana University, said in a speech in 1887, "will become a central feature of the American college system." Cited in Gerhard Casper, *"Die Luft der Freiheit Weht*—On and Off on the Origins and History of the Stanford Motto" (1995), p. 7.

37. Letter from Max Farrand to Henry Cannon on March 10, 1903; letter from Thomas Bailey to Wallace Davis on January 24, 1961 (in SC54, Box 5).

38. Letter from Adams to Ray Lyman Wilbur on January 20, 1917 (in SC29a, Box 1, folder 53); Hulme quote, March 7, 1930 (in SC54, Box 1, folder 4).

For indirect evidence of how professors learned to teach, see Hativa (1995), p. 18. While 113 professors across departments responded to the survey, the response rate was only about 20%. To the question of what contributed most to learning how to teach in the university (there were multiple options from which to choose) 85% said that a "large or very large" contribution came from trial-and-error in their teaching; 82% said it came from student feedback; 56% said it came from observing their professors when they were students.

39. Letter from Max Farrand to Adams on April 10, 1908 (in SC142, Box 1, folder 2); Slosson (1910), p. 117.

40. "The Department of History is one of the great 'service' departments of the University. While relatively few of our graduates become professors of history, the Department has over the years served the majors of other departments . . . to say nothing of the great body of Lower Division students." Cited in *A History of History at Stanford, 1932–1943*, p. 5 (in SC3950, Box 1, folder 2). In 1953, the first line of a departmental report states: "We regard ourselves as essentially a service department. We exist primarily for the purpose of helping to provide a broad cultural background for our student body" (*The Department of History*, 1953, p. 1).

41. Stanford *Register* (1917–1918), p. 184; (1918–1919), pp. 192–193.

42. Stanford *Courses, Degrees* (1994–1995), p. 498.

43. When asked what their goals were for undergraduates, 92% of 115 Stanford professors in 1995 ranked the goal of presenting "the basic body of knowledge of the domain" as "high" or "very high." On the goal of presenting "the structure and organization of knowledge in the domain," 73% rated it "high" or "very high" (Hativa, 1995, pp. 26–27).

Surveys and discussions of lecturing to undergraduates about a complex field of knowledge often miss the pedagogical decisions that professors concerned about communicating clearly to their audiences must make. Richard Feynman captured these content decisions in introductory physics succinctly: "What should we teach first? Should we teach the *correct* [original emphasis] but unfamiliar law with its strange and difficult conceptual ideas, for example the theory of relativity, four-dimensional space-time, and so on? Or should we first teach the simple 'constant-mass' law, which is only approximate, but does not involve such difficult ideas? The first is more exciting, more wonderful, and more fun, but the second is easier to get at first, and is a first step to a real understanding of the second idea. This point arises again and again in teaching physics." Cited in Marcia Linn and Lawrence Muilenburg, "Creating Lifelong Science Learners: What Models Form a Firm Foundation?" (1996), p. 18. Similar pedagogical decisions arise for historians in introducing colonial American history, the progressive movement, and the Cold War.

44. Edgar E. Robinson, *Scholarship and Cataclysm: Teaching and Researching American History, 1939–1945* (1947), p. 34. Kennedy quote taken from interview, July 22, 1996.

45. Forrest McDonald, "Charles Beard" (1969), pp. 130–132.

The differences between the work of doing historical research and teaching students history have yet to be thoroughly explored by academic historians. Where a strong beginning has been made is in comparing what historians do as scholars with what high school history teachers do. See Peter Seixas, "The Community of Inquiry as a Basis for Knowledge and Learning: The Case of History" (1993), pp. 305–324; Samuel Wineburg and Suzanne Wilson, "Subject-Matter Knowledge in the Teaching of History" (1991); and Samuel Wineburg, "Reading Historical Texts: Notes on the Breach Between School and Academy" (1991). For higher education, see Kathleen Quinlan (1996).

46. It is at the graduate level that teaching, research, and writing can merge. Harvard University historian Bernard Bailyn acknowledges that each of the tasks are "different elements but they reinforce each other." Bailyn said that everything he has written was first introduced in his classroom. "Teaching from my own research is to me fresh, experimental, and intense." He also pointed out the negative side of the convergence in the inevitable constraints on time and energy. "One can't do everything at once; and teaching, I have found—especially undergraduate teaching—is very time-consuming." Edward C. Lathem (Ed.), *Bernard Bailyn: On the Teaching and Writing of History* (1994), pp. 28–29.

47. There were 23 doctorates awarded in history between 1910 (the first) and 1940. The publication of the Department of History's *Stanford History Newsletter* (later renamed *Stanford Historian*) often listed graduates who had secured employment. In the first issue in 1966, Ph.D. alumni of the department (between 1910 and 1965) were listed. Of the 127 alumni who were identified and had responded, 80% were serving, or had served until they retired, as academic historians (No. 1, pp. 9–15); in the 1994 issue of the *Stanford Historian,* there is a section labeled, "Placement of Ph.D.s," and of the 15 placements listed, 13 are junior members of college and university departments and 2 are continuing research as post-doctorates in university departments (No. 18, p. 19).

48. Stanford *Register* (1948–1949), p. 305; Stanford *Courses, Degrees* (1967–1968), p. 257. Professor Donald Fehrenbacher wrote to colleagues David Potter and George Knoles on March 6, 1967, about his proposal to create a five-unit course in the teaching of history that would place a doctoral student in an apprenticeship to a senior faculty member who is teaching a lecture course. The proposal would, in effect, "be regarded as an essential part of Ph.D. train-

ing, like practice teaching in the School of Education. Its stated purpose should be to make sure that no Ph.D. . . . leaves Stanford without some experience on the teaching side of his profession." No such course or apprenticeship was created then. See Stanford University, *Courses, Degrees* (1965–1997), p. 303; and "History Department Minutes," January 25, 1984, and April 28, 1993.

49. Interviews with George Knoles (April 7, 1993), Richard Lyman (April 27, 1993), Don Fehrenbacher (April 20, 1993), and David Kennedy (July 22, 1996). On the disciplinary ethos in academic history, see Quinlan (1996); Tony Becher, "Towards a Definition of Disciplinary Culture" (1981); Gumport (1993), pp. 261–293.

I did find explicit discussion of teaching performance in private correspondence, copies of recommendation letters, and confidential reports from Max Savelle to E. E. Robinson on each instructor in the "Western Civilization" program. For almost a decade, Savelle chaired the program and visited each instructor's section, meeting with the group to discuss faculty lectures and ways of improving the course. He reported these deliberations to the executive head, including his evaluations of instructors' teaching performances. See, for example, his memos to Robinson on January 30, 1937; March 5, 1938; April 20, 1940; March 16, 1944 (in SC29, Box 5, folder 124).

50. Richard Roberts, "History" (1995), p. 5.

51. See "Report From the Chair" in the *Stanford Historian* (1993), p. 15. Interviews with Kennedy, Knoles, Lyman, and Fehrenbacher. I also attended three seminar meetings on teaching with 1st-year doctoral students led by Professors Richard Roberts and Nancy Kollmann between 1994 and 1996 and found their passion for teaching very evident.

52. See Quinlan's treatment (1996) of an East Coast public university's history department in which these questions were raised repeatedly in interviews and discussions.

53. For this first generation of scientific historians, I have relied upon Higham (1965); Novick (1988); Hazel Hertzberg, "The Teaching of History" (1980); Deborah Haines, "Scientific History as a Teaching Method: The Formative Years" (1977); Charles Bishop, "Teaching at Johns Hopkins: The First Generation" (1987); and Carol Baird, "Albert Bushnell Hart: The Rise of the Professional Historian" (1965).

54. Even though teaching at other universities was almost always valued in words and official statements, as at Stanford, course loads of 15–18 hours a week, advising students, and service on departmental and university committees, according to professors of the day, left little time for research and even fewer hours for writing. See Novick (1988), pp. 175–176, for discussion of teaching.

55. For descriptions of pedagogy in the humanities in the decades before and after the Civil War, see Rudolph (1977), pp. 65–90; and Veysey (1965), pp. 37–38.

56. Stanford *Register* (1900); (1906), p. 110; and (1921–1922), p. 224.

57. Cited in "Course Syllabi, 1892–1962" (in SC3951). Arley Show came to Stanford in 1893 as an instructor, 2 years after the university opened, and stayed for his entire career. He was deeply interested in the teaching of history both at the high school and college levels. See the April 1917 issue of *The History Teacher's Magazine* where a verbatim account of a conference on the teaching of freshman history, chaired by Show, was sponsored by the American Historical Association on December 27, 1916.

58. Originally, this generation of historians used the word *seminary*. It was shortened to seminar by the early 1900s.

59. I use these terms *teacher-scholar* and *scholar-teacher* less as dichotomous terms and more to describe hybrids where both tasks of teaching and producing scholarship were deemed important but one dominated the other. Both duties were performed; it is a matter of emphasis rather than either/or. The work of Lee Shulman and his students in the teaching of content subjects in public secondary schools in which the phrase "pedagogical content knowledge" is elaborated captures the distinction that I make here between types of scientific historians in this and subsequent generations. Mary Sheldon Barnes represents those few professors then and now who seek to know what historical concepts and misconceptions students bring to lecture halls and seminars and who seek to transform their special historical knowledge into analogies, metaphors, media, and instructional methods so as to convey knowledge with clarity and understanding to students. See Lee Shulman, "Those Who Understand Teach: Knowledge Growth in Teaching" (1986).

60. Herbert B. Adams, *The Study of History in American Colleges and Universities* (1887), pp. 214–215.

61. *Dictionary of American Biography* (1928), p. 632; Robert Keohane, "Mary Sheldon Barnes and the Origin of the Source Method of Teaching History in the American Secondary School, 1885–1896" (1948).

62. Keohane (1948), pp. 69–70, cites Barnes in her teachers' manual to *Studies in Historical Method* (1986).

63. "History from a Witness" (1893, January 27).

64. See *Dictionary of American Biography* (1928), p. 632; and Mary Sheldon Barnes (1896). Earl Barnes was accused of having an affair with a local schoolteacher and Jordan fired him. Mary Sheldon Barnes was told of the affair; both left Stanford for Europe. After his wife's death, Barnes applied for different academic posts and Jordan refused to give him a recommendation. See Spoehr (1975), pp. 147–148.

65. Robert De Roos, "Edgar Robinson Held Sway as Teacher, Author, Administrator" (1992), p. 10; Mitchell (1958), pp. 93–94.

66. De Roos (1992), p. 10; unpublished memoirs of E. E. Robinson (n.d.), p. 100.

67. Adams quote is in Robinson's unpublished memoirs (n.d.), pp. 10–11.

68. E. E. Robinson (1947), p. 34.

69. Robinson's unpublished memoirs (n.d.), p. 28.

70. Thomas A. Bailey, "Statement on History" (1955), and "The Obligation of the Teacher to Be a Scholar" (1949).

71. Bailey (1982), pp. 1–34; letter from Bailey to Mr. Whelan on December 25, 1949 (in SC54, Box 4, folder 14). Robinson sold his home to Bailey in 1937 (see SC54, Box 1, folder 21).

72. Bailey (1982), pp. 98–99.

73. Letter from Bailey to George Walker on December 22, 1934 (in SC54, Box 1, folder 10).

74. Bailey (1982), p. 113. Bailey submitted this example in 1941 to *Readers Digest,* which sponsored a contest soliciting "dramatic teaching methods." Over 4,000 entries were received; Bailey's was returned (in SC54, Box 2, folder 21).

75. Bailey (1982), p. 112; letter from Bailey to Armin Rappaport on July 23, 1951 (in SC54, Box 4, folder 17).

76. Letter from Bailey to George Walker.

77. Bailey (1982), p. 183.

78. David Kennedy, "Thomas A. Bailey as Textbook Author" (1984, August 17), p. 6.

79. Note from *Stanford Daily* is for February 14, 1936 (in SC54a, Box 1, folder 18). By the late 1950s, Bailey's fame as a lecturer had waned and, in the 1960s, had clearly declined insofar as students enrolled in his courses. He increasingly grew critical of the students' habits and tastes, seeing them as very different from ones whom he had taught in earlier decades. See Bailey (1982), pp. 36–37, 39–40, 204.

80. Enrollment figures come from annual Stanford *Register* for each course that is listed for the years mentioned. Enrollment in courses also meant extra money for professors. Until the 1950s, history faculty had students buy a course syllabus that contained an outline of the course, reading assignments, collateral readings, and, depending upon the professor, detailed notes. For years, it was $1 a syllabus. The money was reallocated to the faculty based upon the numbers of students that took each course and was used to purchase equipment, books, and photographs.

81. The syllabi for the diplomatic history course during these years are located in SC3951, Boxes 3–7.

82. When the announcement of Bailey's endowed chair (and chair of the department) was made in one of his large lecture courses, the students greeted him with a "congratulatory burst of applause." He dryly commented in his autobiography that the "endowed chair did not bring with it an increase in rank or salary and that the department headship involved new and onerous duties that I did not enjoy or want" (Bailey, 1982, pp. 107, 201–202).

83. Ibid., pp. 127–136, 154–161, 179–187, 207–217.

84. Ibid., p. 115. Also see pp. 127–128, 160–161, 180, 210. Repeatedly, Bailey compares the "call" to educate students and the public with the "call" to be a minister that he experienced as a teenager.

85. Ibid., p. 154.

86. Ibid., pp. 179–180. Bailey explicitly acknowledged the tension and the importance of seeking a balance in his 1949 article, "The Obligation of the Teacher to be a Scholar," p. 355.

87. David Kennedy (1984), p. 2. Bailey died in 1980. From the monies that he had earned from text royalties, he had endowed funds for the history department and libraries to purchase books.

E. D. Adams constructed a different compromise between scholarly and nonscholarly audiences during his career at the University of Kansas and at Stanford. He began writing a textbook for seventh and eighth grade students in the late 1920s—almost 30 years after he became a professor; he had prepared a manuscript and was about to sign a contract with Houghton Mifflin when he took ill and died in 1930. See letters to Mr. A. K. Allen from Adams for October 14, 1929; November 8, 1929; and February 9, 1930 (in SC142, Box 2, folder 13).

88. Quote comes from my interview with David Kennedy on July 22, 1996.

89. Ibid.

CHAPTER 4

1. Stanford University, *Annual Report of the President* (1922), p. 29.

2. For histories of reforms in medical education, see Paul Starr, *The Social Transformation of American Medicine* (1982), pp. 112–127; Kenneth Ludmerer, *Learning to Heal* (1985), pp. 72–122; William Rothstein, *American Medical Schools and the Practice of Medicine* (1987), pp. 89–116; Abraham Flexner, *Medical Education: A Comparative Study* (1925); W. C. Rappleye, *Medical Education: Final Report of the Commission on Medical Education* (1932); Peter Lee, *Medical Schools and the Changing Times: Nine Case Reports on Experimentation in Medical Education, 1950–1960* (1962); Kendall and Reader (1988); Bussigel, Barzansky, and Grenholm (1988).

For reports of national commissions that studied medical education and often recommended reforms, see L. T. Coggeshall, *Planning for Progress Through Medical Education* (1965); Citizens Commission on Graduate Medical Education, *The Millis Commission Report* (1966); Carnegie Commission on Higher Education, *Higher Education and the Nation's Health—Policies for Medical and Dental Education: A Special Report and Recommendations* (1970); Panel on the General Professional Education of the Physician, *Physicians for the Twenty-First Century* (1984); Commission on Medical Education: *The Sciences of Medical Practice, Medical Education in Transition* (1992). For a summary of commission reports on medical education, see Nicholas Cristakis, "The Similarity and Frequency of Proposals to Reform U.S. Medical Education" (1995).

3. Rothstein (1987), p. 49.

4. These descriptions of medical education in the mid-19th century come from Ludmerer (1985), pp. 9–19; Rothstein (1987), pp. 50–63.

5. Starr (1982), pp. 112–119; Charles Rosenberg, *The Care of Strangers: The Rise of America's Hospital System* (1987), pp. 202–209.

6. Starr (1982), pp. 120–121. The historiography of the impact of the Flexner report has moved from attributing medical education reform solely to the report to blaming Flexner for the alleged inflexibility of medical schools in responding to contemporary needs of American health care. The position that many historians, such as Ludmerer and Rothstein, and others take is that a vital medical education reform movement began as early as the 1st decade following the Civil War and slowly spread. By 1904, the American Medical Association's Council on Medical Education had already developed a ranking system of medical schools and had begun to privately rate schools. They then sought public legitimacy for these rankings by negotiating with the Carnegie Foundation and cooperating with Flexner. The muckraking report exposed the shoddy condition of medical training, alerting the public to the damages that accrue to a society in which profit-grounded medical education is done unscientifically. Just as important, the report and Flexner's subsequent lobbying of industrialist-philanthropist John D. Rockefeller led to the General Education Board spending almost $50 million to reform medical schools. See Thomas N. Bonner, "Abraham Flexner and the Historians" (1990); Robert Hudson, "Abraham Flexner in Perspective: American Medical Education, 1865–1910" (1972); Martin Kaufman, *American Medical Education: The Formative Years, 1765–1910* (1976), pp. 164–179.

7. See Bussigel, Barzansky, and Grenholm (1988), pp. 78–97

8. See letter from Roland Ciaranello to Robert Cutler on October 11, 1982, about the required preclinical curriculum. Appendix B contains listing of schools (in S1BA, Box 1, Binder 1).

9. Henry Jonas, Sylvia Etzel, and Barbara Barzansky, "Educational Programs in U.S. Medical Schools, 1993–1994" (1994), p. 697; Robert Ebert and Eli Ginzberg, "The Reform of Medical Education" (1988), pp. 5–120.

10. Robert Whitfield, "Historical Development of the Stanford School of Medicine" (1949); Gunther W. Nagel, *A Stanford Heritage* (1970); Stanford University, School of Medicine, *The First Hundred Years* (1959); George Blumer, *Recollections of Cooper Medical College, 1883–1905* (1964); Robinson and Edwards (1960). Flexner visited Stanford for his 1910 report; his harshest words were for the Lane Hospital in San Francisco: "Its organization at present, from the teaching point of view, is seriously defective. Records are meager; no surgical rounds are made in the wards; obstetrical work exists only in the form of an outpatient department; post-mortems are scarce. . . . The catalogue statement that the hospital is a teaching hospital is hardly sustained by the facts" (*Medical Education in the United States and Canada,* pp. 193–194).

11. Whitfield (1949), pp. 125–173. The thesis requirement was dropped in 1932. Attempts to revive it as a requirement for graduation occurred in 1969 and 1978 (see Stanford *Register,* 1932–1933). For the thesis requirement, see Stanford University, *Bulletin for the School of Medicine* (1914–1915), p. 36. Also see "School of Medicine Curriculum Evaluation Subcommittee Report" (1978, November 1), pp. 8–9. That this thesis idea lingers can be seen in a recent letter to me from

Emeritus Professor of Surgery Robert Chase, who recalled the resurrection of the thesis requirement in 1978: "If we are to continue to state that we want our medical school to be more like other graduate studies, then it seems to me that one of the things that we would want to do is to see each student produce a piece of scholarly work during their education tour with us" (personal letter, April 3, 1995).

12. See Stanford's *Bulletin for the School of Medicine* in 1913, 1963, and 1990.

13. Stanford University, *Annual Report of the President* (1925), p. 158.

14. The main sources I used to determine medical school teaching practices were the annual announcements and bulletins of courses published every year by the university since 1910. These course descriptions, schedules of classes, and other information documented the official content that was supposed to be taught and how that subject matter was to be communicated. Caution, however, is necessary in interpreting data on what the faculty intended to be taught as it may differ from what actually happened when the courses were taught. First, these documents were often published in the spring before classes met. Commonly, there would be changes in the schedule because of shifts in staffing, leaves of absence for illness, and the like. Moreover, some course descriptions and schedules omitted references to instruction, and I had to figure out how professors taught these courses from other archival sources, such as departmental reports to the university's president, student newspaper articles, course evaluations, professors' accounts of what they did in class, course syllabi, and periodic accreditation reports. These sources are lodged in the Lane Medical Library at the Stanford University School of Medicine.

Thus, I want to alert the reader that all data taken from these sources are approximations rather than exact descriptions of what occurred in classrooms. For example, some but not all professors scheduled 3 hours a day of laboratory work 3 times a week and would include lectures and occasional small-group conferences with students for portions of those hours to tell students what content and procedures would be covered that week and work through problems that they faced in the lab. Yet the bulletin listed the 3 hours as lab time with no mention of lectures or conferences. In calculating time for instruction, I allotted the 3 hours to laboratories. I assumed that unscheduled variations in teaching practices would still keep the ratio of scheduled laboratory to lecture to small-group conferences time roughly in the same proportion. Finally, it goes without saying that the use of the words "lecturing," "working in labs," "conferences," "ward rounds," and so on convey nothing about the quality of the experience that students had.

15. Blumer (1964), no page number available for quote.

16. John B. Blake, "Anatomy" (1980), pp. 42–43.

17. Charles H. Danforth, "Anatomy" (1959), p. 14. After reading this section, Drs. Joel Merenstein and Marc Nelson, who went to different medical schools in the early 1960s and the mid-1970s, respectively, independently called this type of intimidating questioning "pimping."

18. Stanford University *Annual Report of the President* (1927), p. 139.

19. Danforth (1959), p. 17.

20. This manner of teaching gross anatomy was called "dead house" anatomy. The phrase used in this external evaluation was intended as an uncomplimentary term, especially since students' examining one another in the 1930s had grown in popularity as a teaching innovation in anatomy. See H. G. Weiskotten and M. W. Ireland, *Review of Stanford University Medical School for Liaison Committee of American Medical Association and Association of American Medical Colleges* (1936, March), pp. 9–12.

21. For the origins of these different forms of lecturing, see Carl A. Hangartner, "Movements to Change American College Teaching, 1700–1830" (1955). For medical school lecturing, see Hilliard Jason and Jane Westberg, *Teachers and Teaching in U.S. Medical Schools* (1982), pp. 181–201. For a synthesis of studies on lecturing, see John McLeish, "The Lecture Method" (1976).

For the half-century since the merger of Cooper Medical College with Stanford, I could find no archival evidence of student or faculty concern over the quality or nature of anatomy lectures, laboratory work, small-group conferences, or other teaching practices apart from occasional individual complaints about particular teachers.

22. Departmental report for June 1952 in Stanford University, School of Medicine, *Stanford Medical School Council Report* (1952), pp. 1–4.

23. Blake (1980), p. 45.

24. Lyman Stowe, "The Stanford Plan" (1959); Lee (1962); Bussigel, Barzansky, and Grenholm (1988), pp. 23–26, 47–60.

25. Stowe (1959), p. 1060.

26. Avram Goldstein, "The Basic Medical Sciences in the Stanford Plan" (1961), p. 686. Minutes of the Curricular Study Committee, November 26, 1957 (stored in Lane Archives in School of Medicine, S1BB, Box 1.5).

27. Ibid.

28. Goldstein (1961), pp. 686–689.

29. Ibid. See also Stowe (1959), pp. 1061–1067. Note that an integrated basic medical sciences curriculum requires a high degree of faculty collaboration across departments, thus conflicting with the historic autonomy of these independent units within the medical school. In these years, Western Reserve University maintained its departments but created alternative structures ("organ committees") that drew faculty from the various departments. Stanford did try, for a brief time, committees such as the "Basic Medical Sciences" and others mentioned previously. These committees were dismantled in the early 1960s, and SUSM maintained its departmental structure without alternative organizational units. See Bussigel, Barzansky, and Grenholm (1988), pp. 47–60.

30. Ad Hoc Survey Team for the Liaison Committee on Medical Education of the American Medical Association and Association American Medical Colleges, *Report of the Survey of Stanford University School of Medicine* (1974, December), p. 46; quote is from Goldstein (1961), p. 686.

31. *Report from the Committee on Lectures and Curriculum, Year II Students* (1965, May); *Report from the Committee on Lectures and Curriculum, Year III Stu-*

dents (1965, May); Memo to Basic Medical Sciences Committee from F. E. Yates on "Evaluation of Quarters 1 and 2 by the Present Year I Class," April 27, 1965 (in S1BB, Box 1.10).

32. Special Minutes of the Executive Committee, December 30, 1966, pp. 1–3 (in S1BB, Box 1.11). A number of organizational changes in governing SUSM occurred in these years. The Faculty Senate had established new committees and delegated certain functions to them with oversight from the Committee of Five, itself a steering committee for the entire medical school faculty.

33. Ibid. The ad hoc decision on tests led to the establishing of "placement tests" for courses that permitted students who passed them to be exempt from taking the classes. These placement tests continued into the 1990s. See "CCC Minutes" for October 18, 1990, p. 3 (in S1BB, Box 3, folder 17).

34. "BMS Proposal Submitted to Curriculum Committee," January 24, 1962 (in S1BB, Box 1.3).

35. Memo from Avram Goldstein to members of the curriculum committee and department executives on "Curriculum Committee Action," January 24, 1962 (in S1BB, Box. 1.3).

36. Stanford University, *Bulletin for the School of Medicine* (1969–1970), Pt. II, pp. 5–15; Robert Chase, "A Program of Free Election" (1972); Spyros Andreopoulos, "May, 1970: A Peaceful Protest Against the Vietnam War" (1970); Hamilton (1994), pp. 48–53. President Sterling had already launched a major review of the education. On the 10-member steering committee were two representatives of SUSM, genetics professor Joshua Lederberg and graduate student Anne Osborn. See Stanford University, *Study of Education* (1968), Vol. 1, p. 4.

37. Stanford University, *Bulletin* (1969–1970), pp. 5–15.

38. Chase (1972); memo on advising students from the associate deans to CCC, June 5, 1974 (stored in S1BB, Box 2); Committee on Courses and Curriculum, *Joint Report and Recommendations of the Subcommittees* (1972, June 5), pp. 9–10. *Report of the Survey of Stanford University School of Medicine by the Liaison Committee on Medical Education* (1972, April), p. 16.

39. Memo from "Members of the Anatomy 201 Class to Members of the Committee for Anatomical Sciences," February 9, 1970 (in S1BB, Box 1.16).

40. Ibid.

41. Ibid.

42. Ibid.

43. Ibid.

44. "CCC Minutes," March 3, 1970 (in S1BB, Box 1.16).

45. "Course Evaluation Summary," Spring 1971 (in S1BB, Box 1.16).

46. *The Organ* (1972, November 11). When Otto Mortensen, a retired professor of anatomy from the University of Wisconsin, was appointed to teach courses at Stanford, students came to admire his helpfulness in the laboratory and the clarity of his lectures. In 1978, he received the Henry Kaiser Award for excellence in teaching, an award voted on by students. When he died a year later,

The Organ editors wrote a fond farewell to this teacher they deeply respected (1979, November 1).

47. *Report of the Survey of Stanford University School of Medicine by the Liaison Committee on Medical Education* (1972, April), p. 19. *Report of the Survey of Stanford University School of Medicine by the Liaison Committee on Medical Education* (1965, January), p. 40.

48. "CCC Minutes," May 7, 1973 (in S1BB, Box 1.17) and April 13, 1978 (in S1BB, Box 1.23).

49. Personal letter from Robert Chase to author, April 3, 1995. What Chase, Mathers, and other medical school faculty in anatomy had achieved over the years was to create a strong teaching culture in the unit.

50. "School of Medicine Curriculum Evaluation Subcommittee Report" (1978, November 1), pp. 8–9. The subcommittee is also called the "Chase Committee," after its chair, professor of surgery Robert Chase.

51. Ibid. See also Stanford University, *Bulletin for the School of Medicine* (1979), p. 37

52. Ad Hoc Survey Team, *Report of the Survey of the Stanford University School of Medicine for the Liaison Committee on Medical Education of the American Medical Association and the Association of American Medical Colleges* (1977, February 22–24), p. 23.

53. *Report of the Survey of the Stanford University School of Medicine for the Liaison Committee on Medical Education of the American Medical Association and the Association of American Medical Colleges* (1974), p. 50; William Northway Jr., "The University and the Medical School: A View of the Relationship at Stanford" (1976), p. 10.

54. *Report of the Committee on Courses and Curriculum Concerning the Required Curriculum in Basic Sciences* (1982), p. 4 (in S1BA, Box 1, binder 1). Also see John Steward and Clayton Rich, "Is the Elective Curriculum Working?" (1976).

55. Resolution from CCC to Committee of Five, November 21, 1980 (in S1BB, Box 2.6).

56. Reprinted in (April 18, 1979), *The Organ, 7*(18), p. 4.

57. Letter from Avram Goldstein to Committee of Five on November 28, 1979 (in S1BA, Box 1, binder 1).

58. Letter from Avram Goldstein to Arthur Kornberg on July 2, 1980 (in S1BA, Box 1, binder 1).

59. Memo from Faculty Senate chair Avram Goldstein to faculty on October 21, 1980 (in S1BA, Box 1).

60. David Hellerstein, "Of Horses and Zebras: The Crisis at Stanford Medical School" (1979), pp. 1, 4.

61. "Statement by the Committee of Five," October 28, 1981 (in S1BB, Box 2.7); *Report of the Committee on Courses and Curriculum Concerning the Required Curriculum in Basic Sciences,* October 11, 1982 (in S1BA, Box 1, binder 1).

In 1984, academic medicine advocates on the faculty also established the Stanford Medical Student Research Symposium, which showcased student-initiated research projects. Every year since, it has been held with classes called off for the day (see *Stanford Report*, April 24, 1996, p. 12).

62. For faculty review of required curriculum after 5 years, see "CCC Minutes" for March 7, 1988, and May 9, 1988 (S1BB, folder 3.10). (1988, May) *The Organ, 16*(9), 1, 3–8 (cited in Burns & Shen, 1988); (1988, May 24), *Stanford Daily*, p. 1 "Students for an Improved Curriculum," May 31, 1988, no author; Nat Kuhn and Nicole Calakos, *Student Report of Data Collected by the Curriculum Review Committee* (1990, October).

67. Committee of Five, *Curriculum Committee Review Report* (1990, October), pp. 1–3, 5–6, 8.

68. *Annual Report of the Division of Human Anatomy, Department of Surgery*, January 1986, pp. 5–6 (in Box S1BB, folder 3.3).

69. Quotes taken from "Student Evaluations, Winter 1983–84" (in S1BB, folder 2.17). In 1925, Abraham Flexner, in speaking about the clinical years for medical students, had this to say about repetition: "The notion that recalling or renewing facts and principles once learned is a waste of time . . . is a mistaken one. Things of importance are not learned once for all; they are . . . learned by being repeatedly recalled and in all sorts of ways" (p. 277).

70. For the statement that 95% of medical schools retain the basic 2×2 model, I relied upon the descriptions of current reforms where about 5% of medical schools have substantially converted to a different system, such as Case-Western Reserve, New Mexico University, and Harvard University's "New Pathways." Such major changes go well beyond the introduction of preclinical courses and incremental changes in the 2×2 model. See Cam Enarson and Frederic Burg, "An Overview of Reform Initiatives in Medical Education, 1906–1992" (1992); Joel Cantor, Alan Cohen, Dianne Barker, Annie Shuster, and Richard Reynolds, "Medical Educators' Views on Medical Education Reform" (1991); Stephen Abrahamson, "The Dominance of Research in Staffing of Medical Schools: Time for a Change?" (1991, June 29). For those schools that have made such changes and retained them over time while also making adaptations, see Bussigel, Barzansky, and Grenholm (1988); Greer Williams, *Western Reserve's Experiment in Medical Education and Its Outcome* (1980); Daniel Tosteson, "New Pathways in General Medical Education" (1990).

67. Committee of Five (1990, October), p. 8.

68. Data on the continued growth of medical research grants since the 1970s and particularly the 1980s can be found in *Planning in an Era of Change* (1995, December), pp. 56, A4.8.

69. For Western Reserve, see Williams (1980); and Bussigel, Barzansky, and Grenholm (1988), pp. 47–60. For McMaster and Michigan State, see Bussigel, Barzansky, and Grenholm (1988), pp. 61–96. Also see Kendall and Reader (1988) for New Mexico, McMaster, and Harvard, pp. 288–292.

70. Tosteson (1990), pp. 234–238; Stanford University, School of Medicine. "Student Orientation Packet, PCM-C" (1994). As a member of the medical edu-

cation journal club at SUSM for these years, I heard presentations from faculty about the incorporation of problem-based learning approaches in other pre-clinical courses.

71. The idea of treaty-making between different factions within schools (faculty and students, administrators and faculty) to defuse open conflict comes from Arthur Powell, Eleanor Farrar, and David Cohen, *The Shopping Mall High School* (1985).

72. Data on career choices come from Stanford University's Office for Student Affairs, "AAMC Questionnaire Study of Graduating Medical Students," autumn 1987, p. 1 (in S1BB, Box 3, binder 9). Data on research are in "Medical Student Research Opportunities and Activities: Stanford University School of Medicine," March 1985, p. 2 (in S1BA, Box 1, binder 2).

73. Lawrence Horowitz, "Stanford School of Medicine: A Question of Identity" (1978); Laurence Kedes, "Another View of the Horowitz Survey" (1978).

74. Stanford University, *Courses, Degrees, and Information* (1994–1995), p. 749.

75. The phrase "change without reform" is a variation of what I found in Samuel Bloom, "Structure and Ideology in Medical Education: An Analysis of Resistance to Change" (1988), pp. 284–306. Bloom speaks of "reform without change"—note the reversal of words—and explains the dominance of the traditional model of medical education in sociopsychological terms: He found that the structures of medical education (departments, rivalry between departments for research and teaching funds, hierarchial authority, etc.) overwhelmed the ideology of producing humane practitioners. It is the "dominance of structure over ideology" (p. 301). Surges of curriculum reform were "schizophrenic . . . defenses" of the organization to show that it shared the ideology, "while other forces actually dominate the directions of institutional process" (p. 301). The humanistic mission of medical education "is little more than a screen for the research mission, which is the major concern of the institution's social structure" (p. 294). Changes aimed at creating different kinds of graduates—he included problem-based learning—will have "little or no impact on the underlying structure of the social organization of the medical school" (p. 302).

My argument both for SUSM and for the entire university differs from Bloom in key respects. First, I distinguish between incremental and fundamental change. There have been, I have argued, many ad hoc incremental changes but no fundamental ones since—let me revert to the SUSM case—the establishment of the 2×2 model of medical training. Bloom distinguishes between *reform* and *change* by implying that the former (what I label fundamental change) is talk and the latter (what I suspect he would call fundamental change) seldom occurs because of organizational structures. Second, I distinguish between reform rhetoric—the vocabulary of those who hope for fundamental reform—and what happens to those hopes after implementation. Bloom does the same but implies that the rhetoric about wanting deep changes in medical school structures to produce caring practitioners is a cover, a pretext, or even a sham that hides the true motives of reform-minded academics: the pursuit of research. Hence, curricular

and pedagogical reforms are charades. To change medical education in fundamental ways, one must change those institutional structures.

This sociological framing of the problem of medical education represents
one line of historiographical work on the history of changes (or lack thereof) in
medical schools. The idea of stubborn social structures in medical schools has
been adopted by different writers who concentrate on the historical development of these institutional structures (Ludmerer, 1985); external factors that
shaped those structures, such as states certifying specialists and federal subsidies for medical research (Starr, 1982); and larger sociocultural beliefs, values,
and patterns of behavior that get institutionalized into organizational structures
within the medical school (Renee Fox, 1990). What I have done is to take the
Bloom phrase, reverse the nouns to stay consistent with my definition of those
terms, and apply the phenomenon to the entire university.

76. Flexner quote cited in Ludmerer (1985), p. 171. For researchers who
have pointed out how organizations absorb and redirect reforms into new goals
while maintaining customary practices (and longevity) of the organization, see
James March, "Footnotes To Organizational Change" (1981); David Rothman,
Conscience and Convenience (1980); Joseph Morrissey, Howard Goldman, and
Lorraine Klerman, *The Enduring Asylum* (1980). For universities, see Grant and
Riesman (1978); Veysey (1973). For public schools, see David Cohen, "Educa-
tional Technology, Policy, and Practice" (1987); David Tyack and Larry Cuban,
Tinkering Toward Utopia (1995).

CHAPTER 5

1. Arthur Schopenhauer, *Parerga and Paralipomena,* quoted in Jean-Loup
Amselle, "Tensions Within Culture" (1992), p. 42.

2. Stanford University, *Courses, Degrees, and Information* (1994–1995), p.
498; Data on SUSM are for 1993 and come from *School Overview* (1997) found on
the medical school's World Wide Web page (http://www.med.stanford.edu). History department figures come from Stanford University, Department of History,
History Department Statistics: Graduation Year-by-Year, 1987–1996 (1997).

3. Total amount of research awards for SUSM for 1993 was $123,699,917; see
School Overview (1997).

4. Anthony Biglan, "Relationships Between Subject Matter Characteristics
and the Structure and Output of University Departments" (1973); Becher (1984).

5. Gumport (1993); Biglan (1973); Tony Becher, "The Cultural View" (1983);
Colbeck (1996); Kathleen Quinlan (1996).

6. Higham (1965); Novick (1988).

7. Ludmerer (1985); Rothstein (1987). See also Stanford University's *Bulletin
for the School of Medicine* for 1913, 1963, and 1990.

8. R. N. Smith (1986), pp. 160–193; Jencks and Riesman (1977), pp. 492–504;
Bell (1966); SUSM, *LCME Self Study: Summary Report* (1990, November), p. 77. For

a typical realignment of what courses to teach at what times and how an associate dean negotiated departmental differences in the preclinical curriculum, see memo from Charlotte Jacobs to all preclinical medical students on August 9, 1990 (in S1BB, Box 3.17).

9. Hativa (1995); Eric Dey, Claudia E. Ramirez, William Korn, and Alexander Astin, *The American College Teacher: National Norms for the 1992–1993 HERI Faculty Survey* (1993), p. 15.

10. Hativa (1995); *Report of the Commission on Undergraduate Education* (1994) (survey results are in the appendix); Dey et al. (1993). One difference needs to be noted. The use of instructional technologies has been far more advanced in the preclinical sciences than in the teaching of history. Recall how much anatomy instruction has been enhanced by interactive software and videos since the late 1970s. Students also have access to lectures on video for certain courses. Slides are shown routinely in lectures. See Laurel Joyce, "Medical Education's Brave New World" (1991). In the history department, a few professors have created specific software programs for particular topics in certain courses. But most professors, at least by the early 1990s, had continued to use conventional means of teaching. "The slowness that [technology] penetrates this environment," historian David Kennedy noted, "is really quite remarkable" (personal interview, July 22, 1996).

11. The evidence for these statements is fragmentary and largely drawn from doctoral dissertations, Stanford faculty surveys, and interviews cited in Chapters 1–4. Thus, they are closer to inferences than factual statements. Moreover, teaching practices vary across departments and professional schools. Further strengthening the inference about beliefs concerning teaching and the importance of subject matter has been the historic absence (until recently in the Department of History and still missing in SUSM) of preparatory programs in teaching for those who seek to become academics. Finally, these pervasive beliefs about the role of teaching are seemingly shared with other academics in universities across the nation. See Clark (1987), p. 123–125.

12. Wilson (1997), pp. A12–A13. Such innovations have split departments. At Stanford, the math department began teaching calculus using different materials and methods and then abandoned the innovation after a few years. Ralph Cohen returned to the traditional format, saying, "For students who really need to know math and use it, this wasn't nearly sophisticated or rigorous enough." To Professor Brad Osgood, one of the advocates for teaching "reform" calculus, the debate over how to teach the subject and the return to the traditional format has left him so isolated that he intends to join another department (pp. A12–A13). Also see essays by Howard Aldrich, Darlene Bailey, and Karl Weick on their celebration of teaching, in Rae Andre and Peter Frost (Eds.), *Researchers Hooked on Teaching* (1997).

13. Stanford University, School of Medicine. "Student Orientation Packet, PCM-C" (1994). In the Stanford Law School and Graduate School of Business the case-method approach, as at other universities, is a staple in professors' repertoires; see Skeff and Noddings, (1985). For range of beliefs on subject matter and process of teaching, see Katherine Samuelowicz and John D. Bain, (1992).

14. See student evaluations of David Potter's teaching (in SC88, folder 10). For various courses taught by David Kennedy, see Stanford students' "Course Reviews" for 1973, 1978, and 1979 in files of Associated Students of Stanford University (ASSU). Kennedy also received the Dean's Award for Outstanding Teaching twice.

15. Chase (1972); memo on advising students from associate deans to CCC, June 5, 1974 (stored in S1BB, Box 2).

16. "Faculty Senate Report" (1995, November 15), p. 12.

17. Hawkins (1979); Veysey (1965); Geiger (1986), pp. 36–39.

18. There has been a steady, slow growth of cross-departmental (or interdisciplinary) programs at Stanford over the last 3 decades. Still, 7 out of 10 undergraduates choose departmental majors (figure is for 1992–1993). See *Report of the Commission on Undergraduate Education* (1994), p. 29.

19. "A History of History at Stanford, 1932–1943," pp. 94–95; a comparison of writing style, particularly use of vivid, even pungent phraseology, suggests that Thomas A. Bailey authored the report.

20. David Potter, "Proposals for U.S. Graduate Course Distribution, 1969–70," (n.d.), p. 1 (in SC88, folder 10).

21. "Curriculum Study Committee Meeting Minutes," March 27, 1957, pp. 1–2 (stored in S1BB, Box 1.5).

22. "CCC Minutes," September 27, 1982, p. 2 (in S1BB, Box 2.10).

23. Memo to CCC from Bernard Nelson, January 29, 1973, "Results of the Faculty Survey" (in S1BB, Box 1.18). SUSM, *LCME Self Study: Summary Report* (1990, November), p. 74.

24. This view of dilemmas can be found in Michael Billig, Susan Condor, Derek Edwards, Mike Gane, David Middleton, and Alan Radley, *Ideological Dilemmas: A Social Psychology of Everyday Thinking* (1988); Magdalene Lampert, "How Do Teachers Manage to Teach? Perspectives on Problems in Practice" (1985), pp. 178–194; Larry Cuban, "Managing Dilemmas While Building Professional Communities" (1992). For researchers who explicitly deal with dilemmas within universities, see Hawkins (1979); Claude C. Bowman, *The College Professor in America* (1938/1977); Robert McCaughey, "But Can They Teach? In Praise of College Professors Who Publish" (1993); James S. Fairweather and Robert Rhoads, "Teaching and the Faculty Role: Enhancing the Commitment to Instruction in American Colleges and Universities" (1995); Burton Clark, *Places of Inquiry* (1995); Jonathan R. Cole, "Balancing Acts: Dilemmas of Choice Facing Research Universities" (1994).

25. See Geiger (1986), p. 2–3; Reuben (1996), pp. 9–10.

26. Veysey (1965), pp. 175–176. For an interpretation of Stanford's motto, see "Inaugural Address of Gerhard Casper, Ninth President, Stanford University, Friday, October 2, 1992," pp. 3–5. For an analysis of the Humboldtian tradition, see Clark (1995), pp. 19–37. Clark's chapter on U.S. graduate schools nicely summarizes the merger between the two-and-a-half-century American college and the German import of the research-based university. Also see Fritz

Ringer, "The German Academic Community" (1979); and Flexner (1930/1994), pp. 305–338.

27. Joseph Ben-David, *American Higher Education* (1972), pp. 49–68. Jordan quote is from, "To What Extent Should the University Investigator Be Relieved From Teaching?," *Journal of the Association of American Universities* (1906), p. 24. That the ambivalence over the undergraduate mission of the university was alive and well in the 1970s, see Bayer's study cited in Bowen and Schuster's *American Professors*. The researcher found that of faculty's goals for undergraduate teaching 38% of university professors agreed that the goal of developing students' moral character is "Essential" or "Very Important." For the goal of developing "responsible citizens," 53% of the university faculty said it was essential or very important (p. 52).

28. Cited in Freeland (1992), p. 21.

29. President Casper charged the Commission on Undergraduate Education in 1993 to study the idea of undergraduates completing their student career in 3 rather than 4 years. The final report did not recommend a 3-year degree. Stanford University, *Report of the Commission* (1994), pp. 37–38.

30. Bob Burns and Janet Shen, "A Matter of Forum [*sic*] and Substance" (1988).

31. For a national faculty survey documenting professorial perceptions of conflict, see Dey et al. (1993), pp. 10, 18. In *The Organization of Academic Work*, Peter Blau (1973) explored professors' dilemmas in coping with the unattractive choices they faced in dealing with research and teaching obligations. See also Andre and Frost (1997) who have edited a series of essays written by scholars who proclaim the integration of teaching and research.

32. For Jacobs quote, see (1982, December 3) *The Organ, 11*(2), 2. For a representative study that makes the claim of compatibility of research and teaching, see Lawrence R. Jauch, "Relationship of Research and Teaching: Implications for Faculty Evaluation" (1976).

In the School of Education at Stanford, an untenured colleague who had recently joined our faculty told me the story of a senior faculty member taking her from her second-floor office to the first-floor lobby, where on one wall was a plaque that listed the names of professors who had been recognized by students as excellent teachers. He pointed out, name by name, which of the award-winning professors had been denied tenure and then, with an avuncular arm around her shoulder, made the point that such awards led nowhere; publications were everything.

33. Interview with David Kennedy, July 22, 1996.

34. Clark (1987, 1995); Gumport, (1993). Also see Colbeck (1996); this study is unusual in that it examines exactly what tasks professors actually did each day in two departments (English and physics) in a large public and private university. In shadowing professors and collecting other data, Colbeck determined how much fragmentation and how much integration of research, teaching, service, and the like occurred.

35. Clark (1995); Ringer (1979).

36. Stanford University, *Annual Report of the President, 1905* (1906), p. 17.

37. Thorstein Veblen, *The Higher Learning in America* (1918/1957), p. 12.

38. Stanford University, Office of the Dean of Undergraduate Studies, *A Stanford Education* (1973), p. 40.

39. Cited in J. E. Vader, "Are Teaching and Research Compatible" (1992), p. 34. Craig often gave a lecture to doctoral students and other professors across the university on "How To Lecture." The history department videotaped his presentation for new professors and history doctoral students (interview with David Kennedy, July 22, 1996).

40. Stanford University, *Report of the Commission* (1994).

41. Others have pointed out that the belief is essentially a myth. See Henry Crimmel, "The Myth of the Teacher-Scholar" (1984); John Hattie and H. W. Marsh, "The Relationship Between Research and Teaching: A Meta-Analysis" (1996).

42. Clark (1987); Dey et al. (1993); Everett C. Ladd Jr. and Seymour M. Lipset, *The Divided Academy: Professors and Politics* (1975), pp. 129–132, 144–145; Finkelstein (1984), pp. 120–121; 142–145.

43. Hoopes and Marshall (1957), pp. 36–37.

44. Stanford University, *Study of Education* (1968), Vol. 8, pp. 116–123.

45. Ibid., pp. 121–123.

46. Ibid., pp. 123–127.

47. Skeff and Noddings (1985), pp. 13, 34–37. Also see Robert Hind (1968), chaps. 5–6.

48. Jin He, *Positive, Negative, or Unrelated: Perspectives on the Relationship Between Teaching and Research* (1989, May), pp. 10, 12.

49. "Survey on Relative Importance of Research: Teaching Finds Faculty Perceive Peers Favor Former—Slightly" (1994, June 1), p. 8. For an earlier investigation into the tensions between bureaucratization and academic work in universities where the conflicts between research and teaching are delineated, see Peter Blau (1973), pp. 103–105, 270–272.

50. Colbeck (1996), pp. 156–188.

51. For a comprehensive analysis of the different arguments used to frame the compatibility/conflict claims, see Hattie and Marsh (1996); and Kenneth Feldman, "Research Productivity and Scholarly Accomplishment of College Teachers as Related to Their Instructional Effectiveness: A Review and Exploration" (1987).

52. Hattie and Marsh (1996) also offers varied ways of framing the relationship between effective teaching and doing first-rate scholarship. Also see Stanford University, Provost Office, *Faculty Handbook* (1997, June), 6th ed., pp. 2.7–2.8 for parenthetical positions of teaching and research.

CHAPTER 6

1. Carnegie Council for Policy Studies, *Three Thousand Futures,* cited in Kim Cameron and David Whetten, "Models of the Organizational Life Cycle: Applications to Higher Education" (1984), p. 31.

2. Eliot quotes are cited in Walter P. Metzger, "The Academic Profession in the United States" (1987), p. 135.

3. At Stanford, bisection has not been raised since the 1930s. Since the 1920s, Stanford University's practice—as in most other American universities, has been to use a corps of graduate students to teach 1st-year students in required courses. In 1996, President Gerhard Casper proposed hiring a cadre of assistant professors on term appointments to teach 1st- and 2nd-year students in seminars. See Manuel and Cigarroa (1996), pp. 28–29.

4. Freeland (1992), p. 114.

5. Crimmel (1984), p. 183.

6. Kennedy (1997), p. 29.

7. For an application of this agency theme in institutional theory, see Steven Brint and Jerome Karabel, *The Diverted Dream: Community Colleges and the Promise of Educational Opportunity in America, 1900–1985* (1989), pp. 214–220.

8. Wilson (1979), pp. 210–233; Kerr (1994), pp. 165–179; David Webster, *Academic Quality Rankings of American Colleges and Universities* (1986), pp. 3–18.

9. Ernest T. Pascarella and Patrick T. Terenzini, *How College Affects Students* (1991).

10. Kerr (1994), p. 165. Quote is from Freeland (1992), p. 357. In the mid-1980s, I was a finalist for the deanship at a large state university in the Southwest (I eventually withdrew from consideration). Part of the 2 days of interviews for finalists was spent in an interview with the president. After ushering me into his office and exchanging pleasantries, he asked me questions about where I saw the college of education moving were I to be named dean. When he asked me if I had any questions, I asked him what direction he would like to see the college of education to take in the next decade. His answer came swiftly: "I want our college of education to be ranked in the top fifteen." That university's college of education has reached that goal in the most recent rankings of university departments for schools of education.

11. Bowman (1938/1977).

12. William Arrowsmith, "The Future of Teaching," cited in Eurich (1968), p. 118.

13. For Stanford, see Hativa (1995) and Skeff and Noddings (1985); for national surveys, see Blackburn and Lawrence (1995).

14. Stanford has had a long history of close involvement with industrial firms. Initially under President Donald Tresidder in the 1940s, then under President Wallace Sterling and Provost Frederick Terman in the 1950s, joint ventures

with local corporations established profitable relationships for both the university and its commercial partners (see Matkin, 1990). For the 1980s and 1990s at Stanford and the growth of biotechnology and the thorny issues of industrial-university cooperation, see Donald Kennedy, "University and Government, University and Industry: Examining a Changed Environment" (1996), pp. 101–112; and Kennedy (1997), pp. 241–264. For the national picture of universities seeking revenues from patent royalties and partial ownership of for-profit corporations, see Harvey Brooks, "Current Criticisms of Research Universities" (1994), pp. 231–252; Walter Powell and Jason Owen-Smith, "Universities and the Market for Intellectual Property in the Life Sciences" (1998).

15. Brooks (1994); Kennedy (1997).

16. Robert C. Wilson and Jerry G. Graff, *College Professors and Their Impact on Students* (1974), pp. 55–68. Many of these suggestions are drawn from Boyer (1990); the Boyer Commission Report, *Reinventing Undergraduate Education: A Blueprint for America's Research Universities* (1998); and recent initiatives undertaken at Stanford.

REFERENCES

Abrahamson, S. (1991, June 29). The dominance of research in staffing of medical schools: Time for a change? *Lancet, 337,* 1586–1588.

Adams, H. B. (1887). *The study of history in American colleges and universities* (Bureau of Education, Circular of Information No. 2). Washington, DC: U.S. Government Printing Office.

Ad Hoc Survey Team for the Liaison Committee on Medical Education. (1974, December). *Report of the Survey of Stanford University School of Medicine.* Liaison Committee on Medical Education of the American Medical Association and Association American Medical Colleges.

Ad Hoc Survey Team for the Liaison Committee on Medical Education. (1977, February). *Report of the Survey of Stanford University School of Medicine.* Liaison Committee on Medical Education of the American Medical Association and Association American Medical Colleges.

Albanese, M., & Mitchell, S. (1993). Problem-based learning: A review of literature on its outcomes and implementation issues. *Academic Medicine, 68*(1), 52–81.

Allardyce, G. (1982). The rise and fall of the Western civilization course. *American Historical Review, 87*(1), 695–743.

Amsell, J. (1992). Tensions within culture. *Social Dynamics, 18*(1), 42–65.

Andre, R., & Frost, P. (Eds.). (1997). *Researchers hooked on teaching.* Thousand Oaks, CA: Sage.

Andreopoulos, S. (1970, May). A peaceful protest against the Vietnam war. *Stanford M.D., 9*(2), 11–17.

Bailey, T. A. (1946). *Diplomatic history of the American people.* New York: F. S. Crofts.

Bailey, T. A. (1949). The obligation of the teacher to be a scholar. *Social Education, 13*(8), 355–356.

Bailey, T. A. (1955). "Statement on History" [unpublished paper]. Available at Stanford University, Special Collections (SC54, Box 4, folder 31), Stanford, CA.

Bailey, T. A. (1966). *American pageant* (3rd ed.). Boston: D. C. Heath.

Bailey, T. A. (1982). *The American pageant revisited: Recollections of a Stanford historian.* Stanford, CA: Hoover Institution Press.

Baird, C. (1965). Albert Bushnell Hart: The rise of the professional historian. In P. Buck (Ed.), *Social sciences at Harvard, 1860–1920: From inculcation to the open mind* (pp. 129–174). Cambridge, MA: Harvard University Press.

Barnes, M. S. (1896). *Studies in historical method.* Boston: D. C. Heath & Co.

Becher, T. (1981). Towards a definition of disciplinary culture. *Studies in Higher Education, 6*(2), 109–122.

Becher, T. (1984). The cultural view. In B. Clark (Ed.), *Perspectives on higher education: Eight disciplinary and comparative views.* Berkeley: University of California Press.

Belknap, R., & Kuhns, R. (1977). *Tradition and innovation: General education and the reintegration of the university, a Columbia report.* New York: Columbia University Press.

Bell, D. (1966). *The reforming of general education.* New York: Columbia University Press.

Bell, D. (1992). *The idea and practice of general education.* Chicago: University of Chicago Press. (Original work published 1950.)

Ben-David, J. (1972). *American higher education.* New York: McGraw-Hill.

Bersi, R. (1966). Five Stanford efforts to drop the freshman and sophomore years. Unpublished doctoral dissertation, Stanford University.

Beyers, B. (1988, February 10). Broader conception of West is needed, Faculty Senate told. *Campus Report.*

Beyers, B. (1988, January 27, February 10). Western culture "great debate" opens in senate. *Campus Report.*

Biglan, A. (1973). Relationships between subject matter characteristics and the structure and output of university departments. *Journal of Applied Psychology, 57,* 204–213.

Billig, M., Condor, S., Edwards, D., Gane, M., Middleton, D., & Radley, A. (1988). *Ideological dilemmas: A social psychology of everyday thinking.* Newbury Park, CA: Sage.

Bishop, C. (1987). Teaching at Johns Hopkins: The first generation. *History of Education Quarterly, 27*(4), 499–515.

Blackburn, R., & Lawrence, J. (1995). *Faculty at work.* Baltimore, MD: Johns Hopkins University Press.

Blackburn, R., Pellino, G., Boberg, A., & O'Connell, C. (1980). Are instructional programs off-target? *Current issues in higher education* (No. 1). Washington, DC: American Association for Higher Education.

Blake, J. B. (1980). Anatomy. In R. Numbers (Ed.), *Education of American physicians* (pp. 42–57). Berkeley: University of California Press.

Blau, P. (1973). *The organization of academic work.* New York: John Wiley & Sons.

Bloom, S. (1988). Structure and ideology in medical education: An analysis of resistance to change. *Journal of Health and Social Behavior, 29,* 284–306.

Blumer, G. (1964). *Recollections of Cooper Medical College (1883–1905).* Stanford, CA: Stanford University School of Medicine.

Bok, D. (1986). *Higher learning.* Cambridge, MA: Harvard University Press.

Bonner, T. M. (1990). Abraham Flexner and the historians. *Journal of the History of Medicine and Allied Sciences, 45*(1), 3–10.

Bowen, W., & Rudenstine, N. (1992). *In pursuit of the Ph.D.* Princeton, NJ: Princeton University Press.

Bowman, C. C. (1977). *The college professor in America.* New York: Arno Press. (Original work published 1938.)

Boyer, E. (1990). *Scholarship reconsidered: Priorities of the professoriate.* Princeton, NJ: Carnegie Foundation for the Advancement of Teaching.

Boyer Commission Report. (1998). *Reinventing undergraduate education: A blueprint for America's research universities.* Princeton, NJ: Carnegie Foundation for the Advancement of Teaching.

Brint, S., & Karabel, J. (1989). *The diverted dream: Community colleges and the promise of educational opportunity in America, 1900–1985.* New York: Oxford University Press.

Brooks, H. (1994). Current criticisms of research universities. In J.R. Cole, E. Barber, & S. Graubard (Eds.), *The research university in a time of discontent* (pp. 231–252). Baltimore: Johns Hopkins University Press.

Brubacher, J., & Rudy, W. (1976). *Higher education in transition* (3rd ed.). New York: Harper & Row.

Brunsson, N., & Olsen, J. P. (1993). *The reforming organization.* London: Routledge.

Burns, B., & Shen, J. (1988). "A Matter of Forum [*sic*] and Substance." *The Organ, 16*(9), 3.

Bussigel, M. N., Barzansky, B. M., & Grenholm, G. G. (1988). *Innovation processes in medical education.* New York: Praeger.

Cameron, K. & Whetten, D. (1984). Models of the organizational life cycle: Applications to higher education. In J. L. Bess (Ed.), *College and university organizations* (pp. 31–61). New York: New York University Press.

Cantor, J., Cohen, A., Barker, D., Shuster, A., & Reynolds, R. (1991, February 27). Medical educators' views on medical education reform. *Journal of the American Medical Association, 265*(8), 1002–1006.

Carnegie Commission on Higher Education. (1970). *Higher education and the nation's health: Policies for medical and dental education—A special report and recommendations.* New York: McGraw-Hill.

Carnegie Foundation for the Advancement of Teaching. (1908). *Third annual report of the president and treasurer.* New York: Author.

Carnegie Foundation for the Advancement of Teaching. (1987). *A classification of higher education.* Princeton, NJ: Author.

Carnochan, W. B. (1993). *The battleground of the curriculum.* Stanford, CA: Stanford University Press.

Carnochan, W. B. (1997, April 16). The paradox of the university: 1906, 1997. *Stanford Report,* p. 8.

Casper, G. (1992, October 2). Inaugural address. Stanford President's Office. Stanford, CA.

Casper, G. (1995, October 5). *Die luft der freiheit weht*—On and off on the origins and history of the Stanford motto. Paper presented to the Stanford Historical Society, Stanford, CA.

Centra, J. (1993). *Reflective faculty evaluation.* San Francisco: Jossey-Bass.

Cerych, L. (1983). The policy perspective. In B. Clark (Ed.), *The higher education system: Academic organization in cross-national perspective.* Berkeley: University of California Press.

Chang, G. (1996). *Morning glory, evening shadow: Yamato Ichihasi's wartime writings.* Stanford, CA: Stanford University Press.

Chase, R. (1972). A program of free election. In V. Lippard & E. Purcell (Eds.), *The changing medical curriculum* (pp. 150–157). New York: Josiah Macy Jr. Foundation.

Chisu, D. (1988, May 24). Med school group seeks reform in curriculum. *Stanford Daily,* p. 1.

Chronological guide to indirect costs at Stanford. (1992, May 28). *Stanford Daily,* p. 1.

Cigarroa, M. (1995, September 13). E-mail, web sites: No more pencils, no more books? *Campus Report.*

Citizens Commission on Graduate Medical Education. (1966). *The Millis Commission Report.* Chicago: American Medical Association.

Clark, B. (1987). *The academic life.* Princeton, NJ: Carnegie Foundation for the Advancement of Teaching.

Clark, B. (1995). *Places of inquiry: Research and advanced education in modern universities.* Berkeley: University of California Press.

Clark, B. (Ed.). (1983). *The higher education system: Academic organization in cross-national perspective.* Berkeley: University of California Press.

Clark, B. (Ed.). (1984). *The academic profession.* Berkeley: University of California Press.

Coggeshall, L. T. (1965). *Planning for progress through medical education.* Evanston, IL: Association of American Medical Colleges.

Cohen, D. (1987). Educational technology, policy, and practice. *Educational Evaluation and Policy Analysis, 9*(2), 153–170.

Cohen, M. & March J. G. (1974). *Leadership ambiguity.* New York: McGraw-Hill.

Colbeck, C. (1996). *Weaving seamless lives: Organizational and disciplinary influences on integration and congruence of faculty work.* Unpublished doctoral dissertation, Stanford University.

Cole, J. R. (1994). Balancing acts: Dilemmas of choice facing research universities. In J. R. Cole, E. Barber, & S. Graubard (Eds.), *The research university in a time of discontent* (pp. 1–36). Baltimore, MD: Johns Hopkins University Press.

Commission on Medical Education. (1992). *The sciences of medical practice, Medical education in transition.* Princeton, NJ: Robert Wood Foundation.

Committee of Five. (1990, October). *Curriculum committee review report.* Available at Stanford University, School of Medicine, Lane Medical Library Archives (Box S1BB, folder 3.17).

Conference of instructors in citizenship. (1923, October 10). Available at Stanford University Special Collections (SC29, box 6, folder 184), Stanford, CA.

Crimmel, H. (1984). The myth of the teacher-scholar. *Liberal Education, 70*(3), 183–198.

Cristakis, N. (1995). The similarity and frequency of proposals to reform U.S. medical education. *Journal of American Medical Association, 274*(9), 706–711.

Cuban, L. (1988). A fundamental puzzle of school reform. *Phi Delta Kappan, 69*(5), 340–344.

Cuban, L. (1990). Reforming again, again, and again. *Educational Researcher, 19*(1), 3–13.

Cuban, L. (1992). Managing dilemmas while building professional communities. *Educational Researcher, 21*(1), 4–11.

Cuban, L. (1993). *How teachers taught: Constancy and change in American classrooms, 1880–1980.* New York: Teachers College Press.

Damrosch, D. (1995). *We scholars.* Cambridge: Harvard University Press.

Danforth, C. H. (1959). *Anatomy: The first hundred years.* Stanford, CA: Stanford University School of Medicine.

Denby, D. (1996). *Great books.* New York: Simon & Schuster.

The Department of History. (1953). [Report]. Available at Stanford University, Special Collections (SC29a, Box 3, folder 80B and SC54, Box 4, folder 31), Stanford, CA.

De Roos, R. (1992, September 9). Edgar Robinson held sway as teacher, author, administrator. *Campus Report,* 10.

Dey, E., Ramirez, C. E., Korn, W., & Astin, A. (1993). *The American college teacher: National norms for the 1992–1993 HERI Faculty Survey.* Los Angeles: Higher Education Research Institute, University of California.

Dictionary of American biography (Vol. 1). (1928). New York: Charles Scribner's Sons.

Dictionary of American biography (Vol. 11, Suppl. 1). (1944). New York: Charles Scribner's Sons.

Dimaggio, P. (1988). Interest and agency in institutional theory. In L. Zucker (Ed.), *Institutional patterns and organizations* (pp. 3–22). Cambridge, MA: Ballinger.

DiMaggio, P., & Powell, W. (1991). The iron cage revisited: Institutional isomorphism and collective rationality. In W. Powell & P. DiMaggio (Eds.), *The new institutionalism in organizational analysis* (pp. 63–82). Chicago: University of Chicago Press.

Dubie, A. (1989). *Frank A. Golder: An adventure of a historian in quest of Russian history.* Boulder, CO: East European Monographs.

Dubin, R., & Taveggia, T. (1968). *Teaching-learning paradox: A comparative analysis of college teaching methods.* Eugene, OR: Center for the Advanced Study of Educational Administration.

Duryea, E. D. (1948). *Background and development of Stanford curricular organization.* Unpublished doctoral dissertation, Stanford University.

Dzuback, M. (1991). *Robert M. Hutchins: Portrait of an educator.* Chicago: University of Chicago.

Ebert, R., & Ginzberg, E. (1988). The reform of medical education. *Health Affairs 7*(Suppl. 2), 5–120.

Educational Testing Service. (1979). *Student instructional report: Comparative data guide for four-year colleges and universities*. Princeton, NJ: Author.

Elliott, O. (1937). *Stanford University: The first twenty-five years*. Stanford, CA: Stanford University Press.

Elmore, R. & McLaughlin, M. (1988). *Steady work*. Santa Monica: Rand.

Enarson, C., & Burg, F. (1992, September 2). An overview of reform initiatives in medical education, 1906–1992. *Journal of American Medical Association, 268*(9), 1141–1143.

Eurich, A. C. (Ed.). (1968). *Campus 1980: The shape of the future in American higher education*. New York: Delacorte Press.

Evangelauf, J. (1994, April 6). A new "Carnegie Classification." *Chronicle of Higher Education,* pp. A17–A26.

Faculty Senate report. (1995, November 15). *Stanford Report*. Stanford, CA: Stanford University.

Fairweather, J. S. (1996). *Faculty work and public trust*. Boston: Allyn & Bacon.

Fairweather, J. S., & Rhoads, R. (1995). Teaching and the faculty role: Enhancing the commitment to instruction in American colleges and universities. *Educational Evaluation and Policy Analysis, 17*(2), 179–194.

Feldman, K. (1987). Research productivity and scholarly accomplishment of college teachers as related to their instructional effectiveness: A review and exploration. *Research in Higher Education, 26*(3), 227–291.

Finkelstein, M. (1984). *The American academic profession*. Columbus: Ohio State University Press.

Fisher, M. (Ed.). (1985). *Teaching at Stanford: An introductory handbook* (Rev. ed.). Stanford, CA: Stanford University, Center for Teaching and Learning.

Flexner, A. (1910). *Medical education in the United States and Canada* (Bulletin No. 4). New York: Carnegie Foundation for the Advancement of Teaching.

Flexner, A. (1925). *Medical education: A comparative study*. New York: Macmillan.

Flexner, A. (1994). *Universities: American, English, German*. New Brunswick, NJ: Rutgers University Press. (Original work published 1930.)

Fox, R. (1990). Training in caring competence. In H. Hendrie & C. Lloyd (Eds.), *Educating competent and humane physicians* (pp. 199–216). Bloomington: Indiana University Press.

Frank, D. J., Schofer, E., & Torres, J. (1994). Rethinking history: Change in the university curriculum, 1910–1990. *Sociology of Education, 67*(4), 231–242.

Freedman, M. (1979). *Academic culture and faculty development*. Berkeley, CA: Montaigne.

Freeland, R. (1992). *Academia's golden age: Universities in Massachusetts, 1945–1990*. New York: Oxford University Press.

Geiger, R. (1986). *To advance knowledge: The growth of American research universities*. New York: Oxford University Press.

Geiger, R. (1990). Organized research units—their role in the development of university research. *Journal of Higher Education, 61*, 1–19.

Giamatti, B. (1988). *A free and ordered space: The real world of the university*. New York: W. W. Norton.

Goldstein, A. (1961). The basic medical sciences in the Stanford plan. *Journal of Medical Education, 36*(6), 686–689.

Gottlieb, J. (1991, January 22). U.S. probe of Stanford may cost other schools. *San Jose Mercury News*.

Graff, G. (1987). *Professing literature*. Chicago: University of Chicago Press.

Graff, G. (1992). *Beyond the culture wars: How teaching the conflicts can revitalize American education*. New York: W. W. Norton.

Graham, H. D., & Diamond, N. (1997). *The rise of American research universities.* Baltimore: Johns Hopkins University Press.

Grant, G., & Riesman, D. (1978). *The perpetual dream: Reform and experiment in the American college.* Chicago: University of Chicago Press.

Gruber, C. (1975). *Mars and Minerva: World War I and the uses of the higher learning in America.* Baton Rouge: Louisiana State University Press.

Gumport, P. (1993). Graduate education and research imperatives: Views from American campuses. In B. Clark (Ed.), *The research foundations of graduate education: Germany, Britain, France, United States, Japan* (pp. 261–293). Berkeley: University of California Press.

Haines, D. (1977). Scientific history as a teaching method: The formative years. *Journal Of American History, 63*(4), 893–912.

Hamilton, J. (1994). A cue from the past. *Stanford, 22*(3), 48–53.

Hangartner, C. A. (1955). *Movements to change American college teaching, 1700–1830.* Unpublished doctoral dissertation, Yale University.

Harvard University. (1946). *General education in a free society.* Cambridge, MA: Harvard University Press.

Hativa, N. (1993, April). *The department-wide approach to improving faculty instruction in higher education: A qualitative evaluation.* Paper presented at the annual meeting of the American Educational Research Association, Atlanta, GA.

Hativa, N. (1995, July). *What are the 'cultures' of teaching of university professors?* [results of a survey for Stanford professors]. Stanford University, Department of Physics, Stanford CA.

Hattie, J., & Marsh, H. W. (1996). The relationship between research and teaching: A meta-analysis. *Review of Educational Research, 66,* 507–542.

Hawkins, H. (1960). *Pioneer: A history of the Johns Hopkins University, 1874–1889.* Ithaca, NY: Cornell University Press.

Hawkins, H. (1972). *Between Harvard and America: The educational leadership of Charles Eliot.* New York: Oxford University Press.

Hawkins, H. (1979). University identity: The teaching and research functions. In A. Oleson & J. Voss (Eds.), *The organization of knowledge in modern America, 1860–1920* (pp. 285–312). Baltimore, MD: Johns Hopkins University Press.

Hefferlin, J. B. (1969). *Dynamics of academic reform.* San Francisco: Jossey-Bass.

Hellerstein, D. (1979). Of horses and zebras: The crisis at Stanford Medical School. *Organ, 7*(22), 1, 3–4.

Hertzberg, H. (1980). The teaching of history. In M. Kammen (Ed.), *The past before us: Contemporary historical writing in the United States* (pp. 474–504). Ithaca, NY: Cornell University Press.

Higham, J. (1965). *History.* Englewood Cliffs, NJ: Prentice-Hall.

Higham, J. (1979). The matrix of specialization. In A. Oleson & J. Voss (Eds.), *The organization of knowledge in modern America, 1860–1920* (pp. 11–13). Baltimore, MD: Johns Hopkins University Press.

Hind, R. (1968). *Evaluation and authority in a university faculty.* Unpublished doctoral dissertation, Stanford University.

History from a Witness. (1893, January 27). *Daily Palo Alto,* 1.

Hofstader, R., & Metzger, W. (1955). *The development of academic freedom in the United States.* New York: Columbia University Press.

Hoopes, R., & Marshall, H. (1957). *The undergraduate in the university: A report to the faculty by the Executive Committee of the Stanford Study of Undergraduate Education, 1954–1956.* Stanford, CA: Stanford University, Board of Trustees.

Horowitz, L. (1978). Stanford School of Medicine: A question of identity. *Stanford M.D., 17*(1), 4–6.

House, E. (1979). Technology versus craft: A ten-year perspective on innovation. *Journal of Curriculum Studies, 11*(1), 1–15.

Howe, I. (1966). *Steady work.* New York: Harcourt, Brace, World.

Hudson, R. (1972). Abraham Flexner in perspective: American medical education, 1865–1910. *Bulletin of the History of Medicine, 46*(6), 545–561.

Jackson, P. (1986). *The practice of teaching.* New York: Teachers College Press.

James, W. (1934). *Memories and studies.* New York: Longman, Green & Co.

Jason, H., & Westberg, J. (1982). *Teachers and teaching in U.S. medical schools.* Norwalk, CT: Appleton-Century-Crofts.

Jauch, L. R. (1976). Relationship of research and teaching: Implications for faculty evaluation. *Research in Higher Education, 5,* 1–13

Jencks, C., & Riesman, D. (1977). *The academic revolution.* Chicago: University of Chicago Press.

Jin He. (1989, May). *Positive, negative, or unrelated: Perspectives on the relationship between teaching and research.* Unpublished manuscript, Stanford University.

Jonas, H., Etzel, S., & Barzansky, B. (1994, September 7). Educational programs in U.S. medical schools, 1993–1994. *Journal of American Medical Association, 272*(9), 697.

Jordan, D. S. (1906). To what extent should the university investigator be relieved from teaching? *Journal of the Association of American Universities 1*(1), 20–26.

Jordan, D. S. (1922). *The days of a man: Being memories of a naturalist, teacher, and minor prophet of democracy.* Yonkers-on-Hudson, NY: World Book Co.

Jordan, D. S. (1929). *The trend in the American university.* Palo Alto, CA: Stanford University.

Joyce, L. (1991). Medical education's brave new world. *Stanford Medicine, 8*(3), 4–9.

Katchadourian, H., & Boli, J. (1985). *Careerism and intellectualism among college students.* San Francisco: Jossey-Bass.

Kaufman, M. (1976). *American medical education: The formative years, 1765–1910.* Westport, CT: Greenwood Press.

Kazak, D. (1995, April 5). Creating the right curriculum. *Palo Alto Weekly,* 3.

Kedes, L. (1978). Another view of the Horowitz survey. *Stanford M.D., 17*(2), 15–16.

Kendall, P., & Reader, G. (1988). Innovations in medical education of the 1950s contrasted with those of the 1970s and 1980s. *Journal of Health and Social Behavior, 29*(4), 279–293.

Kennedy, D. (1984, August 17). *Thomas A. Bailey as textbook author.* Paper presented at the meeting of the Pacific Coast Branch of the American Historical Association, Seattle, WA.

Kennedy, D. (1991, January 8). Statement on indirect costs. *Campus Report,* 8.

Kennedy, D. (1991, March 6). Remarks of President Kennedy to the Stanford community. *Campus Report,* p. 17.

Kennedy, D. (1991, March 11). The improvement of teaching: An essay to the Stanford community. *Campus Report,* p. 16.

Kennedy, D. (1994). Making choices in the research university. In J. R. Cole, E. Barber, & S. Graubard (Eds.), *The research university in a time of discontent* (pp. 85–114). Baltimore, MD: Johns Hopkins University Press.

Kennedy, D. (1996). University and government, university and industry: Examining a changed environment. In K. Arrow, R. Cottle, B. Eaves, & I. Olkin (Eds.), *Education in a research university,* (pp. 101–112), Stanford, CA: Stanford University Press.

Kennedy, D. (1997). *Academic duty.* Cambridge, MA: Harvard University Press.

Keohane, R. (1948). Mary Sheldon Barnes and the origin of the source method of teaching history in the American secondary school, 1885–1896. *American Heritage, 2*(3), 68–69.

Kerr, C. (1982). *The uses of the university* (3rd ed.). Cambridge: Harvard University Press.

Kerr, C. (1994). *Troubled times for American higher education: The 1990s and beyond.* Albany: State University of New York.

Kiester, E., Jr. (1992). *Tresidder.* Stanford, CA: Stanford Historical Society.

Kimball, B. (1986). *Orators and philosophers: A history of the idea of liberal education.* New York: Teachers College Press.

Kriehbiel, E. (1910, October). History courses at Leland Stanford. *The History Teacher's Magazine, 2*(2), 29–30. (Reprinted in Stanford University, *Register, 1894–1895.*)

Kuhn, N., & Calakos, N. (1990, October). *Student Report of Data Collected by the Curriculum Review Committee.* Available at Stanford University, School of Medicine, Lane Medical Library Archives (Box S1BB, folder 3.17).

Ladd, E. C., Jr.; & Lipset, S. M. (1975). *The divided academy: Professors and politics.* New York: McGraw-Hill.

Lampert, M. (1985). How do teachers manage to teach? Perspectives on problems in practice. *Harvard Educational Review, 55*(2), 178–194.

Lathem, E. C. (Ed.). (1994). *Bernard Bailyn: On the teaching and writing of history.* Hanover, NH: Montgomery Endowment of Dartmouth College.

Lee, P. (1962). *Medical schools and the changing times: Nine case reports on experimentation in medical education, 1950–1960.* Evanston, IL: American Association of Medical Colleges.

Levine, A. (1980). *Why innovation fails.* Albany: State University of New York Press.

Levine, A. (Ed.), (1993). *Higher learning in America, 1980–2000.* Baltimore: Johns Hopkins University Press.

Levine, A., & Weingart, J. (1973). *Reform of undergraduate education.* San Francisco: Jossey-Bass.

Levine, L. (1996). *The opening of the American mind.* Boston: Beacon Press.

Liaison Committee on Medical Education. (1965, January). *Report of the Survey of Stanford University School of Medicine.* Liaison Committee on Medical Education of the American Medical Association and Association American Medical Colleges.

Liaison Committee on Medical Education. (1972, April). *Report of the Survey of Stanford University School of Medicine.* Liaison Committee on Medical Education of the American Medical Association and Association American Medical Colleges.

Liaison Committee on Medical Education. (1974). *Report of the Survey of Stanford University School of Medicine.* Liaison Committe on Medical Education of the American Medical Association and Association American Medical Colleges.

Liaison Committee on Medical Education. (1977, February). *Report of the Survey of Stanford University School of Medicine.* Liaison Committee on Medical Education of the American Medical Association and Association American Medical Colleges.

Liebert, L. (1995). "Years of hope, days of rage: Twenty-five years later." *Stanford, 23*(3), 51–58.

Linn, M., & Muilenburg, L. (1996). Creating lifelong science learners: What models form a firm foundation? *Educational Researcher, 25*(5), 18–25.

Lowen, R. (1997). *Creating the Cold War university.* Berkeley: University of California Press.

Ludmerer, K. (1985). *Learning to heal.* New York: Basic Books.

Lyman, R. (1996). Student revolt and campus reform in the 1960s: The case of Stanford's judicial charter. In K. Arrow, R Cottle, B. C. Eaves, & I. Olkin (Eds.), *Education in a Research University* (pp. 113–121). Stanford, CA: Stanford University Press.

Magner, D. (1995, September 22). Doctoral judgments. *The Chronicle of Higher Education,* p. A29.

Manuel, D., & Cigarroa, M. (1996, July/August). A tangible commitment. *Stanford Today,* pp. 28–29.

March, J. G. (1981). Footnotes to organizational change. *Administrative Science Quarterly, 26*(4), 563–577.

March, J. G. (1994). Three lectures on efficiency and adaptiveness in organizations. [Swedish School of Economics and Business Administration Research Reports, 32, Helsinki, Finland].

March, J. G., & Olsen, J. P. (1989). *Rediscovering institutions: The organizational basis of politics.* New York: Free Press.

Matkin, G. (1990). *Technology transfer and the university.* New York: Macmillan.

Mayhew, L. B. (1977). *Legacy of the seventies.* San Francisco: Jossey-Bass.

McCaughey, R. (1993). But can they teach? In praise of college professors who publish. *Teachers College Record, 95*(2), 242–257.

McDonald, F. (1969). Charles Beard. In M. Cunliffe & R. Winks (Eds.), *Pastmasters: Some essays on American historians* (pp. 130–132). New York: Harper & Row.

McKeachie, W. J. (1990). Research on college teaching: The historical background. *Journal of Educational Psychology, 82*(2), 189–200.

McLeish, J. (1976). The lecture method. In N. Gage (Ed.), *The psychology of teaching methods* (pp. 252–301). Chicago: National Society for Study of Education.

Medeiros, F. (1979). *The Sterling years at Stanford: A study in the dynamics of institutional change.* Unpublished doctoral dissertation, Stanford University.

Memo from 23 professors in humanities and social sciences to the Faculty Senate. (1988, January 11). [Faculty Senate Document 3237]. Available at Stanford University, Stanford, CA.

Menand, L. (1996, September 22). How to make a Ph.D. matter. *New York Times Magazine,* pp. 78–81.

Metz, M. (1990). Real school: A universal drama amid disparate experience. In D. Mitchell & M. Goertz (Eds.), *Educational Politics for the New Century* (pp. 75–91). New York: Falmer Press.

Metzger, W. P. (1987). The academic profession in the United States. In B. R. Clark (Ed.), *The academic profession: National, disciplinary, and institutional settings* (pp. 123–208). Berkeley: University of California Press.

Meyer, J. (1992). Innovation and knowledge use in American public education. In J. Meyer & R. Scott (Eds.), *Organizational Environments: Ritual and Rationality* (pp. 233–260). Newbury Park, CA: Sage.

Meyer, J., & Rowan, B. (1977). Institutionalized organizations: Formal structure as myth and ceremony. *American Journal of Sociology, 83*(2), 340–363.

Meyer, J., & Rowan, B. (1978). The structure of educational organizations. In M. W. Meyer (Ed.), *Environments and organizations* (pp. 78–109). San Francisco: Jossey-Bass.

Michitarian, B. (1986, May 21). Kennedy: Change "Western Culture." *Stanford Daily,* 1.

Mirrieless, E. R. (1959). *Stanford: The story of a university.* New York: G. P. Putnam.

Mitchell, J. P. (1958). *Stanford University, 1916–1941.* Stanford, CA: Stanford University, Board of Trustees.

Mooney, C. (1991, May 8). Professors feel conflict between roles in teaching and research. *Chronicle of Higher Education,* pp. A15–A16.

Morrissey, J., Goldman, H., & Klerman, L. (1980). *The enduring asylum.* New York: Grune & Stratton.

Nagel, G. W. (1970). *A Stanford heritage.* Stanford, CA: Stanford Medical Alumni Association.

Nash, G. (1988). *Herbert Hoover and Stanford University.* Stanford, CA: Hoover Institution.

Nisbet, R. (1980). *History of the idea of progress.* New York: Basic Books.

Northway, W., Jr., (1976, August). The university and the medical school: A view of the relationship at Stanford. Unpublished report. Stanford University School of Medicine.

Novick, P. (1988). *That noble dream*. New York: Cambridge University Press.

Oakley, F. (1996). Historical perspectives and our current educational discontents. In R. Orrill (Ed.), *The condition of American liberal education* (pp. 134–139). New York: The College Board.

Oscherwitz, T. (1987, April 15). Track changes spark protest. *Stanford Daily*, 1.

O'Toole, K. (1995, June 14). Efficiency in higher education poses problems, March Argues. *Campus Report*, pp. 9–10.

Panel on the general professional education of the physician. (1984). *Physicians for the twenty-first century*. Washington, DC: Association of American Medical Colleges.

Pascarella, E. T., & Terenzini, P. T. (1991). *How college affects students*. San Francisco: Jossey-Bass.

Pfeffer, J., & Salancik, G. R. (1978). *The external control of organizations: A resource dependence perspective*. New York: Harper & Row.

Pierson, G. (1955). *Yale: The university college, 1921–1937*. New Haven: Yale University Press.

Pihakis, J. (1996). *Teachers rethinking teaching: A peek inside the black box of instructional consultation Stanford University*. Unpublished doctoral dissertation, Stanford University.

Planning in an Era of Change. (1995, December). [Faculty Senate Document 4512]. Report of the Planning and Policy Board of the Senate of the Academic Council of Stanford University, Stanford, CA.

Powell, A., Farrar, E., & Cohen, D. (1985). *The shopping mall high school*. Boston: Houghton Mifflin.

Powell, W., & Owen–Smith, J. (1998). Universities and the market for intellectual property in the life sciences. *Journal of Policy Analysis and Management, 17*(2), 253–277.

Problems of Citizenship. (1925, April 15). Stanford University, Special Collections (SC29, box 6, folder 182), Stanford, CA.

Quaratiello, F. (1988, April 1). A new era: CIV sweeps in Fac Sen. *Stanford Daily*, 1.

Quinlan, K. (1996). *Collaboration and cultures of teaching in university departments: Faculty beliefs about teaching and learning in history and engineering*. Unpublished doctoral dissertation, Stanford University.

Rappleye, W. C. (1932). *Medical education: Final report of the commission on medical education*. New York: Association of American Medical Colleges' Commission on Medical Education.

Remarks of President Gerhard Casper. (1992, April 1). *Campus Report*, 6.

Report of the Commission on Undergraduate Education, 1994. (1994). Stanford University, Stanford, CA.

Report of the Committee on the B.A. in History. (1959). Available at Stanford University, Special Collections (SC29a, Box3, folder 89), Stanford, CA.

Report of the Committee on the Professoriate at Stanford to Faculty Senate. (1974, February). Available at Stanford University, Faculty Senate, Stanford, CA.

Report of the Committee of the School of Social Sciences upon the course in citizenship. (1935, February 7). Available at Stanford University, Special Collections (SC29, box 6, folder 182), Stanford, CA.

Reuben, J. (1996). *The making of the modern university*. Chicago: University of Chicago Press.

Ringer, F. (1979). The German academic community. In A. Oleson & J. Voss (Eds.), *The organization of knowledge in modern America, 1860–1920* (pp. 409–429). Baltimore, MD: Johns Hopkins University Press.

Roberts, R. (1994). Teaching non–Western history at Stanford. In L. Kramer, D. Reid, & W. L. Barney (Eds.), *Learning history in America: Schools, cultures, and politics* (pp. 53–70). Minneapolis: University of Minnesota Press.

Roberts, R. (1995). History. In Stanford University, *Newsletter on Teaching, 7*(1), 5.

Robinson, C. (1950). *The work of eight major educational associations toward the improvement of college teaching, 1920–1940.* Unpublished doctoral dissertation, Stanford University.

Robinson, E. E. (n.d.). [Unpublished memoirs]. Available at Stanford University, Special Collections (SC29b, Box 85), Stanford, CA.

Robinson, E. E. (1947). *Scholarship and cataclysm: Teaching and researching American history, 1939–1945.* Stanford, CA: Stanford University Press.

Robinson, E. E., & Edwards, P. C. (Eds.). (1960). *The memoirs of Ray Lyman Wilbur, 1875–1949.* Stanford, CA: Stanford University Press.

Rosenberg, C. (1987). *The care of strangers; The rise of America's hospital system.* New York: Basic Books.

Rosenzweig, R. (1998). *The political university: Policy, politics, and presidential leadership in the American research university.* Baltimore, MD: Johns Hopkins Press.

Rosovsky, H. (1990). *The university: An owner's manual.* New York: W. W. Norton.

Rothman, D. (1980). *Conscience and convenience.* Boston: Little, Brown & Co.

Rothstein, W. (1987). *American medical schools and the practice of medicine.* New York: Oxford University Press.

Rudolph, F. (1977). *Curriculum: A history of the American undergraduate course of study since 1636.* San Francisco: Jossey-Bass.

Rudolph, F. (1990). *The American college and university: A history.* Athens: University of Georgia Press. (Original work published 1962.)

Samuelowicz, K., & Bain, J. D. (1992). Conceptions of teaching held by academic teachers. *Higher Education, 24,* 93–111.

Sarason, S. (1971). *The culture of the school and the problem of change.* Boston: Allyn & Bacon.

Sarason, S. (1990). *The predictable failure of educational reform.* San Francisco: Jossey-Bass.

Schmidt-Posner, J. (1989). Electronic ivory towers: Organizational approaches to faculty microcomputing. Unpublished doctoral dissertation, Stanford University.

School of Medicine curriculum evaluation subcommittee teport. (1978, November 1). *Campus Report,* pp. 8–9.

Scott, W. R. (1987). *Organizations.* Englewood Cliffs, NJ: Prentice-Hall, 1987.

Scott, W. R., Meyer, J., & Associates. (1994). *Institutional environments and organizations: Structural complexity and individualism.* Thousand Oaks, CA: Sage.

Seixas, P. (1993). The community of inquiry as a basis for knowledge and learning: The case of history. *American Educational Research Journal, 30*(2), 305–324.

Shils, E. (1979). The order of learning: The ascendancy of the university. In A. Oleson & J. Voss (Eds.), *The organization of knowledge in modern America, 1860–1920* (pp. 19–47). Baltimore, MD: Johns Hopkins University.

Show, A. (1917). Field and method of the elementary college course. *The History Teacher's Magazine 8*(4): 111–128.

Shulman, L. (1987). Those who understand teach: Knowledge growth in teaching, *Educational Researcher, 15,* 4–14.

Shulman, L., & Quinlan, K. (1993, August 2). *S-CEIT Focus Group Report.*

Shurkin, J. (1991, March 14). Congressional committee criticizes Stanford's accounting procedures, suggests some employees may be guilty of fraud in indirect
cost issue. *Campus Report,* 1.

Skeff, K., & Noddings, N. (1985, September). *Teaching improvement in the university:
The views of faculty.* Stanford University, Stanford, CA.

Skilling, H. H. (1969). *Do you teach? Views on college teaching.* New York: Holt, Rine-
hart & Winston.

Slosson, E. E. (1910). *Great American universities.* New York: Macmillan.

Smircich, L. (1983). Concepts of culture and organizational analysis. *Administrative
Science Quarterly, 28,* 339–358.

Smith, E. (1949). *Conceptions of leading nineteenth century educators concerning the
relationship of teaching and research.* Unpublished doctoral dissertation, Stanford University.

Smith, P. (1990). *Killing the spirit: Higher education in America.* New York: Viking.

Smith, R. N. (1986). *The Harvard century: The making of a university to a nation.* New
York: Simon & Schuster.

Spoehr, L. (1975). *Progress' pilgrim: David Starr Jordan and the circle of reform,
1891–1931.* Unpublished doctoral dissertation, Stanford University.

Stanford Alumni Association. (1991). *The Stanford century.* Stanford, CA: Author.

Stanford University. (1891). *Circular of Information, No. 6.* Stanford, CA: Author.

Stanford University. (1892–1949). *Register.* Stanford, CA: Author.

Stanford University. (1900–1997). *Annual report of the president.* Stanford, CA: Author.

Stanford University. (1913–1995). *Bulletin for the School of Medicine.* Stanford, CA:
Author.

Stanford University. (1965–1997). *Courses, degrees, and information.* Stanford, CA: Author.

Stanford University. (1968). *The Study of education at Stanford: Report to the university* (Vols. 1–8). Stanford, CA: Author.

Stanford University. (1987, April 29). *Campus report.* Stanford, CA: Author.

Stanford University. (1988, January 19). *Stanford news.* Stanford, CA: Author.

Stanford University.(1988, April 1, 6). *Campus report.* Stanford, CA: Author.

Stanford University. (1995, Fall). *Stanford observer.* Stanford, CA: Author.

Stanford University. (1997, February 12). Faculty Senate Committee meeting. *Stanford
report.* Stanford, CA: Author.

Stanford University, Department of History. *A history of history at Stanford, 1932–1943.*
Stanford, CA: Author.

Stanford University, Department of History. (1966–1996). *Stanford history newsletter*
[later renamed *Stanford historian*]. Stanford, CA: Author.

Stanford University, Department of History. (1970). *Committee on Priorities and History Undergraduate Student Association: Undergraduate survey, 1969–1970.* Stanford, CA: Author.

Stanford University, Department of History. (1991). *Revisions of the history undergraduate curriculum.* Stanford, CA: Author.

Stanford University, Department of History. (1997). *History department statistics: Graduation year-by-year, 1987–1996.* Stanford, CA: Author.

Stanford University, Faculty Senate. (1976, December 2). Faculty Senate minutes. Stanford, CA: Author.

Stanford University, Faculty Senate. (1987, November). *Materials for area one requirement debate.* Stanford, CA: Author.

Stanford University, Faculty Senate. (1995, April). *Toward greater excellence in teaching at Stanford: Final report of the C-AAA Subcommittee on the evaluation and
improvement of teaching.* Stanford, CA: Author.

Stanford University, Office of the Dean of Undergraduate Studies. (1973). *A Stanford education.* Stanford, CA: Author.

Stanford University, Office of the President. (1988, December). *Stanford statistics* (Vol. 6). Stanford, CA: Author.

Stanford University, Office of the Registrar. (1986, 1988, 1990, 1992). *Statistical summary of senior survey.* Stanford, CA: Author.

Stanford University, Office of Undergraduate Admissions. (1997). Undergraduate students, freshman class, 1965–1996. *Stanford, 24*(4), 66.

Stanford University, Provost Office. (1993). *Faculty handbook.* Stanford, CA: Author.

Stanford University, School of Medicine. (1952). *Stanford Medical School Council report, 1952.* Stanford, CA: Author.

Stanford University, School of Medicine. (1957–1992). [Unpublished papers and documents]. Stanford University, Lane Medical Library Archives in School of Medicine (S1BA & S1BB).

Stanford University, School of Medicine. (1959). *The first hundred years.* Stanford, CA: Author.

Stanford University, School of Medicine. (1965). *Report from the committee on lectures and curriculum.* Stanford, CA: Author.

Stanford University, School of Medicine. (1972). *Joint report and recommendations of the subcommittee.* Stanford, CA: Author.

Stanford University, School of Medicine. (1972). Editorial. *The Organ, 2*(1).

Stanford University, School of Medicine. (1979, April). Their petition. *The Organ, 7*(15), 4.

Stanford University, School of Medicine. (1979, November). *The Organ, 7*(2), 4.

Stanford University, School of Medicine. (1982, December 3). Interview with Charlotte Jacobs. *The Organ, 11*(2), 2.

Stanford University, School of Medicine. (1982) *Report of the committee on courses and curriculum concerning the required curriculum in basic sciences.* Stanford, CA: Author.

Stanford University, School of Medicine (1986). *Annual report of the division of human anatomy, department of surgery.* Stanford, CA: Author.

Stanford University, School of Medicine. (1990). *Liaison committee on medical education: Self-survey.* Stanford, CA: Author.

Stanford University, School of Medicine. (1994). Student orientation packet, PCM-C [Terry Blaschke, Course Director]. Stanford, CA: Author.

Stanford University, School of Medicine. (1997). *School Overview* [On-line]. Available: http://www.med.stanford.edu.

Starr, P. (1982). *The social transformation of American medicine.* New York: Basic Books.

Stern, F. (Ed.). (1956). *Varieties of history.* Cleveland, OH: Meridian Books.

Steward, J., & Rich, C. (1976). Is the elective curriculum working? *Stanford M.D., 15*(2), 2–8.

Stowe, L. (1959). The Stanford plan *Journal of Medical Education, 34*(11), 1059–1069.

Survey on relative importance of research: Teaching finds faculty perceive peers favor former—slightly. (1994, June 1). *Campus Report.*

Susman, W. (1984). *Culture as history: The transformation of American society in the twentieth century.* New York: Pantheon Books.

Sykes, C. (1988). *Profscam: Professors and the demise of higher education.* Washington, DC: Regnery Gateway.

Thielens, W., Jr. (1987, April). *The disciplines and undergraduate lecturing.* Paper presented at annual meeting of the American Educational Research Association, Washington, DC.

Tosteson, D. (1990). New pathways in general medical education. *New England Journal of Medicine, 322,* 234–238.

Traub, J. (1994). *The school upon the hill.* New York: Addison-Wesley.

Trice, H. M., & Beyer, J. (1993). *The cultures of work organizations.* Englewood Cliffs, NJ: Prentice-Hall.

Tyack, D. (1967). *George Ticknor and the Boston Brahmins.* Cambridge, MA: Harvard University Press.

Tyack, D., & Cuban, L. (1995). *Tinkering toward utopia.* Cambridge, MA: Harvard University Press.

Tyack, D., & Hansot, E. (1982). *Managers of virtue.* New York: Basic Books.

University of California, Berkeley Academic Senate's Select Committee on Education. (1968). *Education at Berkeley.* Berkeley: University of California Press.

Vader, J. E. (1992). Are teaching and research compatible? *Stanford, 20*(4), 29–37.

Vaughn, D. (1996). *The Challenger launch decision.* Chicago: University of Chicago Press.

Veblen, T. (1957). *The higher learning in America.* New York: Hill & Wang. (Original work published 1918.)

Veysey, L. (1965). *The emergence of the American university.* Chicago: University of Chicago Press.

Veysey, L. (1973). Stability and experiment in the American undergraduate curriculum. In C. Kaysen (Ed.), *Content and context: Essays on college education* (pp. 1–64). New York: McGraw-Hill.

Wagner, J. (1991, March 14). House subcommittee lambasts Stanford. *Stanford Daily,* 1.

Watzlawick, P., Frisch, R., & Weakland, J. (1974). *Change: Principles of problem formation and problem resolution.* New York: Norton.

Weaver, R. L. (1991). Langdell's legacy: Living with the case method. *Villanova Law Review,* pp. 517–594.

Webster, D. (1986). *Academic quality rankings of American colleges and universities.* Springfield, IL.: Charles Thomas Publishers.

Weick, K. (1976). Educational organizations as loosely coupled systems. *Administrative Science Quarterly, 21*(1), 1–19.

Weick, K. (1984). Contradictions in a community of scholars: The cohesion–accuracy tradeoff. In J. Bess (ed.) *College and University Organization* (pp. 155–219). New York: New York University Press.

Weiskotten, H. G., & Ireland, M. W. (1936). *Review of Stanford University medical school for Liaison Committee of American Medical Association and Association of American Medical Colleges.*

Whitfield, R. (1949). *Historical development of the Stanford School of Medicine.* Unpublished doctoral dissertation, Stanford University.

Williams, G. (1980). *Western Reserve's experiment in medical education and its outcome.* New York: Oxford University Press.

Wilshire, B. (1990). *The moral collapse of the university.* Albany: State University of New York Press.

Wilson, L. (1979). *American academics: Then and now.* New York: Oxford University Press.

Wilson, R. C. (1997, February 7). A decade of teaching "reform calculus" has been a disaster, critics charge. *Chronicle of Higher Education,* 1, 16.

Wilson, R. C., & Graff, J. G. (1974). *College professors and their impact on students.* New York: John Wiley & Sons.

Wineburg, S. (1991). Reading historical texts: Notes on the breach between school and academy. *American Educational Research Journal, 28*(3), 495–520.

Wineburg, S., & Wilson, S. (1991). Subject-matter knowledge in the teaching of history. In J. E. Brophy (Ed.), *Advances in research on teaching* (Vol. 2, pp. 305–347). Greenwich, CT: JAI Press.

INDEX

Academic Council, 18, 23, 30, 41, 47, 66
Academic freedom. *See* Faculty autonomy
Academic rank, 57–58, 59, 107, 164, 175, 193, 200, 203
Adams, Charles Kendall, 118
Adams, Ephraim Douglass
  and AHA, 94
  and appointments, 109, 119
  and citizenship, 93
  departmental autonomy and, 172
  influence on Bailey of, 123, 125, 126
  lectures of, 92
  professional career of, 91–94
  and purposes of History Department, 110, 131
  required courses and, 110
  as scholar-teacher, 91–94, 118, 121–22, 125, 131, 181
  and tenure and promotion, 109
Advising
  changes in, 84, 171–72, 189, 194
  complaints about, 20, 33
  as department responsibility, 26
  between 1891–1968, 20, 26–27, 33–34, 38, 44, 47, 54
  evaluation of, 44
  and faculty as advisors, 20, 54, 171–72, 187
  faculty indifference to, 47, 54, 84–85, 187
  and faculty influence, 51
  and Faculty Senate, 38, 39
  and faculty-student relationship, 47–48, 172
  and general education, 47–48
  in History Department, 105–7, 115, 129–30, 171
  inability to improve, 171–72
  and major-subject system, 17–21, 26, 54
  in Medical School, 149–50, 171
  as process, 63
  and research, 89
  reviews of, 30, 33, 38, 47, 84, 105

  and reward system, 47
  special staff for, 54, 171, 187
  student criticism of, 20, 47, 54, 105–7, 171–72
  teaching divorced from, 54, 187
  and tenure and promotion, 38, 44
All-elective system. *See* Elective system
American Historical Association (AHA), 94, 125
American Medical Association, 137
Anatomy teaching, 8, 135, 139–43, 147, 150–53, 157, 158, 174, 188, 195, 205
Appointments
  criteria for, 41, 58–59, 95, 109, 188
  as department function, 172
  and department functions, 58–59
  and evaluation of teaching, 70, 185
  at Harvard University, 191
  in History Department, 95, 109, 128
  and incremental change, 76
  in Medical School, 152, 153, 174
  recommendations about, 205, 206
  and research, 48, 54
  and research and teaching, 9, 48, 188, 205, 206
  of star-quality faculty, 105, 122, 193, 196
  and teaching, 39, 49, 76, 84, 109, 122, 174, 205
Apprenticeship, 56, 135–36
Arrowsmith, William, 200
Association of American Medical Colleges (AAMC), 156–57
Association of American Universities (AAU), 5, 83, 191
Authority, 66–68, 71, 88
Autonomy
  of departments, 25, 33, 34, 51, 59, 89, 161, 167, 172–76, 187–88, 189
  in History Department, 108, 167, 172–76, 181
  and intractable dilemmas, 187–88

Autonomy *(continued)*
  and level of change, 67
  in Medical School, 161, 167, 172–76
  in teaching, 6, 37, 38, 53, 108, 173, 181
  See also Faculty autonomy
Awards for teaching
  and change, 198–99
  and History Department, 114–15, 130
  Kennedy's [Donald] views about, 4, 84
  in Medical School, 152, 153, 174, 181
  and political processes, 198–99
  recommendations concerning, 31, 40
  and research and teaching, 13, 49, 50, 189
  and status, 176
  and tenure and promotion, 6, 176
  at University of Chicago, 81

Bailey, Thomas A., 101, 107–8, 109, 122–28, 131, 181
Barnes, Mary Sheldon, 95, 96, 118–19, 121–22, 127, 131, 181
Barzun, Jacques, 1–2, 61, 74
Basic medical sciences, 146, 149, 152, 156, 175. *See also* Anatomy teaching
"Basic Medical Sciences" (course), 146
Becker, Carl, 93
Bell, Daniel, 79, 81
Bennett, William, 86
Berg, Paul, 180
Biological Sciences, School of, 141
Bisection plan, 21, 51–52, 80, 179, 188–89
Bok, Derek, 1, 28, 79, 86
Branner, John, 22
Brinkley, Alan, 48
British universities, 14
Bureaucracy, 89, 206

Cannon, Henry, 108, 109
Canon. *See* Required reading list
Career choices, in medical education, 162–63
Carnegie Council for Policy Studies, 191
Carnegie Foundation, 2, 83, 136–37
Case-Western Reserve University, 137, 161
Casper, Gerhard, 3, 43–44, 47, 48, 179
CCC. *See* Curriculum Committee on Courses
"Cell Structure and Function" (course), 146, 147, 148–49
Center for Teaching and Learning (CTL), 40, 50, 76, 84, 85, 176
Change
  adaptation to, 164, 200
  adopted, 62, 66–68
  breadth of, 62, 65–66
  context of, 62
  and cultures, 88, 89, 193, 194, 199
  deliberative, 62–74
  depth of, 62–65
  dimensions of, 62–74

elapsed time of, 62, 68–69
  and expectations, 81–83
  fundamental, 63, 64–65, 69–74, 84, 89, 128, 131, 197, 199, 201, 203, 206
  how much, 191–206
  implementation of, 62, 66, 68, 77
  level of, 66–68
  mechanics of, 195–99
  and political processes, 195–99, 206
  and processes, 3, 88, 89
  proposed, 62, 66–68
  reform and, 59, 61, 62, 64, 75–86, 164, 195–99
  and stability, 194–95
  and structures, 3, 88, 89, 193, 194, 195, 198, 199, 201
  summary of, 177
  symbolic, 76, 85, 87, 197, 199, 205
  top-ranked programs and, 197
  types of, 61
  typology of, 62–74
  unintentional, 72–74
  See also Incremental change; *specific topic*
Character building, 9, 13–14, 17, 51, 78, 178, 192, 202
Chase, Robert, 152–53, 174, 188
Citizenship, 9, 23–24, 51, 79, 86, 93–94, 111, 126, 192, 198. *See also* Problems of Citizenship
City University of New York (CUNY), 66
Clark, Burton, 66
Clark University, 2, 14, 178, 197
Classes, size of, 18, 47
Classical curriculum, 55, 78
Classrooms, fundamental change applied to, 65
Clerkships, 154, 158, 175
Clinical practices, 65, 141, 143, 154, 158, 169
Colbeck, Carol, 185–86
Collaboration
  among departments, 4, 26, 146, 173
  among faculty, 25–26, 51, 53, 80–81, 148–49, 166–67, 205
College of Old Westbury (SUNY), 65
Colloquia, 37, 46–47, 56, 73, 101, 102, 130, 171, 173
Columbia University, 2, 22–23, 78, 79, 83, 86, 137, 178–79
Commission on Undergraduate Education (CUE) (1993–1994), 3, 43–44, 46, 84, 171, 179, 182–83
Committee on Advising and Counseling (1968), 39
Committee on the Evaluation and Improvement of Teaching (1995), 49–50, 84
Committee of Five (1919–1920), 23
Committee of Five (Medical School), 155
Committee on General Studies (1955), 33
Committee on the Lower Division (1920), 26

Committee on the Professoriate (1974),
    40–41
Commonwealth Fund, 121
Computer-based instruction, 38, 153, 157
Computers, 46, 64
Conant, James Bryce, 28, 29, 79
"Contemporary Civilization" (Columbia
    course), 78, 79
Content
    comparison of History Department and
        Medical School, 167–69
    instructional practices and, 53–54, 88, 89,
        116, 117–18, 128, 170–71, 202
    role of teaching as disseminator of, 170
Cooper Lane, Levi, 138
Cooper Medical College, 21–22, 138, 139–40
Core curriculum
    and comparison of History Department
        and Medical School, 168
    in medical education, 144, 148, 155, 156,
        158
    See also Distribution requirements;
        Required courses
Cornell University, 14, 16, 137
Corner of the College program (Kresge, UC-
    Santa Cruz), 72
Corporations, 28, 203–4
Council on Medical Education (AMA), 137
Course Review (Stanford), 70
Courses. *See* Curriculum; *specific course*
Craig, Gordon, 105, 182
CUE. *See* Commission on Undergraduate
    Education
Cultures
    and change, 88, 89, 193, 194, 199
    definition of, 63
    and elective system, 193
    research, 3, 188
    and research and teaching, 76, 176
    and resilience of universities, 84
    teaching, 44–45, 54, 114, 115, 130, 172, 173,
        174, 185, 188
"Cultures, Ideas, and Values" (course), 43,
    44, 205
Curriculum
    and breadth and depth of knowledge, 6, 9,
        41, 43, 52, 80, 179, 187, 193
    change in, 22–24, 51–52, 76–77, 86–89, 186
    classical, 55, 78
    comparison of History Department and
        Medical School, 167–69
    content and structure of, 86–89, 167–69
    continuous review of, 86–89
    four-year, 20–21, 24, 80, 179
    and job market, 168
    See also Bisection plan; Elective system;
        Major-subject system; Preclinical cur-
        riculum; Undergraduate curriculum;
        specific committee, course, or program

Curriculum Committee on Courses (CCC)
    (Medical School), 149, 150, 151–52, 156
Curriculum Coordinating Committee (CCC),
    174–75
Curriculum Review Committee (Medical
    School), 156–57, 159
Curriculum Study Committee (Medical
    School), 145

Danforth Foundation, 40
Dartmouth College, 23
De Voto, Bernard, 179
Demonstrations, 142, 146, 150, 157
Departments
    advising responsibility of, 26
    annual reports of, 19
    authority of, 88
    autonomy of, 25, 33, 34, 51, 59, 89, 161,
        167, 172–76, 187–88, 189
    and change, 66, 88, 194
    and characteristics of high-status institu-
        tions, 6
    collaboration among, 4, 26, 146, 173
    compromises by, 85, 168–69
    conflicts among, 6
    cultures of, 63, 176
    and curriculum reform, 33
    dominance of, 198
    and elective system, 89, 193
    functions of, 58–59, 138, 172
    and future of research and teaching
        relationship, 203
    institutionalization of, 59
    intractable dilemmas facing, 187–88
    lack of viable alternatives to, 198
    and major-subject system, 17, 21, 52
    in Medical School, 138, 161, 167, 168, 172–76
    mission of, 9
    organization of, 5, 6
    power of, 89, 205
    as quasi-independent units, 7
    recommendations about, 204–5
    and research, 89
    and research and teaching, 172, 176, 189,
        204–5
    and specialization, 45
    as structure, 63
    super, 22
    and tradition of reform, 195
    and university-college, 9, 198
    variation and commonalities among, 8
    See also specific department
Dilemmas, managing of, 199–206. *See also
    specific dilemma*
Disciplines
    hard and soft, 166–67
    pure and applied, 167
Discussion sections, 19, 25, 30, 31, 37, 46,
    52–53, 79, 80, 111, 169

Dissection, teaching of, 143, 147, 150, 151, 158
Distribution requirements
  and breadth and depth of knowledge, 36
  at Columbia, 78
  debates about, 24
  and elective system, 36–37, 56
  and general education, 43
  at Harvard, 29
  in History Department, 166
  incremental change in, 64, 66, 77
  introduction of, 23, 52
  and research and teaching, 56, 186
  reviews of, 36–37
  at University of Chicago, 81
Doctoral students/degrees
  and elective system, 56
  foreign recognition of, 83
  German origins of concept of, 57
  in History Department, 101, 104, 107, 111, 113–16, 121, 129, 168, 169, 181
  oral examinations for, 101
  and organizational field, 83
  preparation for teaching of, 113–16, 181
  and research, 56, 58–59
  as structure, 57–58, 59
  See also Graduate programs/students
Doctors, vision of first-rate, 134, 158
Duke University, 137

Elective system
  advising and, 149–50
  anatomy teaching and, 150–53
  and breadth and depth of knowledge, 52, 56
  and Casper presidency, 43
  and change, 77, 88, 193, 195
  as characteristic of high-status institutions, 6
  and comparison of History Department and Medical School, 168
  and departments, 89, 193
  and distribution requirements, 36–37, 56
  and faculty autonomy, 37, 38, 55, 89, 175
  and Faculty Senate, 3, 39
  and general education, 9, 41, 56
  and graduate program, 52, 56
  of Harvard/Eliot, 55, 78, 179
  in History Department, 102, 104–5, 107, 121, 128
  institutionalization of, 51, 59
  and instructional practices, 56
  and introductory courses, 56
  Jordan's views about, 16, 51, 55
  and laboratory teaching, 37, 56
  major-subject system and, 16–17, 51–52
  in Medical School, 134, 139, 141, 144, 146, 148–53, 154, 156, 158
  between 1920–1956, 24

  between 1968–1980, 34–41
  pioneering efforts with, 16
  principle of, 16–17, 55–57
  and research and teaching, 52, 55–57, 89, 104, 141, 186, 188, 193
  reviews of, 3, 30, 36, 37, 41
  and specialization, 23, 51, 52, 55, 56, 104, 193
  stability/durability of, 3, 5
  student criticism of, 149, 150–53, 155–56
  at University of Chicago, 81
  and university-college, 9, 14, 34–41, 55, 179, 195
Eliot, Charles, 20–21, 37, 55, 78, 179, 191–92, 201–2
Enclaving, 70–72, 84, 89, 195, 198
Engineering School (Stanford University), 27
Engle, E. T., 141
English composition (course), 17, 23, 51
English Department (Stanford), 44
"Entrepreneurial consumerism," 52
Entrepreneurs, 6, 89, 164, 203, 204
Environmental determinism, 194–95
Evaluation
  of advising, 44
  of faculty, 32–33
  of Five-Year Plan, 149
  of students, 30, 80, 146, 154
Evaluation of teaching
  and appointments, 70, 185
  and change, 69–70, 76, 195
  and elective system, 56
  and faculty autonomy, 57
  and Faculty Senate, 4, 70, 84, 176
  forms for, 40, 50, 70, 85
  and History Department, 92, 124–25, 130
  and incremental change, 69–70
  in Medical School, 147, 152, 153–54, 157
  peer, 4, 44, 49, 50, 53, 70, 84, 108, 204
  recommendations about, 204–5
  and research and teaching, 76, 185, 204–5
  reviews of, 31–33, 38, 39, 40, 184
  and tenure and promotion, 70, 185
Examinations
  comprehensive, 80
  in History Department, 117
  NBME, 150, 153, 160
  oral, 101, 135

Faculty
  accessibility of, 105–6, 114, 157, 171
  as advisors, 20, 54, 171–72, 187
  career stages of, 131, 189
  collaboration among, 25–26, 51, 53, 80–81, 148–49, 166–67, 205
  evaluation of, 32–33
  indifference to advising of, 47, 54, 84–85, 187
  influence of, 51
  job offers of, 107–8

and major-subject system, 17–18, 20
power of, 86
as star-quality, 105, 122, 193, 196
See also Academic Council; Appointments;
    Faculty autonomy; Faculty Senate; Fac-
    ulty-student relationship; Tenure and
    promotion; *specific person*
Faculty autonomy
    and change, 67, 88, 194, 195
    as characteristic of high-status institu-
        tions, 6
    effects of, 172–76
    and elective system, 37, 38, 55, 89, 175
    and evaluation of teaching, 57
    in History Department, 94–95, 108, 115,
        128, 167, 172–76
    institutionalization of, 59
    and instructional practices, 173
    intractable dilemmas of, 187–88
    in Medical School, 134, 161, 163, 167,
        172–76, 195
    origins of ideal of, 13
    recommendations about, 204
    and research, 89, 108, 115, 173, 174
    and research and teaching, 4, 51, 172, 175,
        176, 187, 189, 203, 204
    and specialization, 52, 173
    and teaching, 38, 45, 84–86, 108, 173–74
Faculty Senate
    and advising, 38, 39
    and elective system, 3, 39
    and evaluation of teaching, 4, 70, 84, 176
    formation of, 41
    and general education, 42–43
    Goldstein as chair of, 155
    and level of change, 66
    and medical education, 156
    and research and teaching, 40
    and teaching, 39, 40, 84, 174, 176
    and tenure and promotion, 39, 40
Faculty-student relationship
    and advising, 47–48, 172
    and instructional practices, 46–47
    at Kresge College, 71–72
    and major-subject system, 17, 20
Farrand, Max, 108, 109
Ferrulo, Stephen, 48
Five-Year Plan (Medical School), 143–48,
    149, 154, 156, 158, 161, 168–69, 170, 171,
    174, 195
Flexner, Abraham, 136–37, 158, 164
Flexner Report, 136–37, 138
Four-year curriculum, 20–21, 24, 80, 179
Franklin, H. Bruce, 35
Fuhrman, Frederick, 148–49
Fund for the Advancement of Education, 29
Funding
    and comparison of History Department
        and Medical School, 168

course enrollments and, 174–75
curriculum adaptation and, 168
federal, 43, 81, 166, 181, 197, 203
federal investigation of, 6
for History Department, 113, 121, 166,
    168
and instructional practices, 175
for Medical School, 137, 159, 163, 164, 166,
    168, 174–75
between 1940–1970s, 35
for research, 6, 14, 27, 28, 43, 81, 159, 164,
    166, 168, 181, 197, 203, 205
and research and teaching tensions, 14
for research universities, 203
as structure, 63
for teaching, 14, 45, 113, 174, 175, 185,
    204–5

General education
    and advising, 47–48
    at Columbia, 78, 79, 86
    decline of, 193
    and distribution requirements, 43
    and elective system, 9, 41, 56
    and faculty autonomy, 175
    at Harvard, 78
    in History Department, 166
    and incremental change, 64, 74, 77
    introduction of, 52, 168, 193
    and introductory courses, 44, 193
    between 1980–1995, 42–51
    and required courses, 9, 193
    and research, 44–47, 56
    and research and teaching, 42, 48–51
    reviews of, 30, 33, 36
    and specialization, 9–10, 83, 179, 193
    and teaching, 44–47
    at University of Chicago, 79–81
    in university-college framework, 9, 42–51
General Education in a Free Society (Har-
    vard), 29, 79
General Studies Program, 30, 33, 36–37
German university model, 13–14, 38, 56, 57,
    117, 178, 182
G.I. Bill, 27, 81
Gilman, Daniel C., 80
Goals. *See* Mission/goals
Goldstein, Avram, 145, 149, 154–55
Gores [Walter J.] Award, 40, 176, 185
Governance, 51, 63, 68, 71, 84, 204
Graduate programs/students
    and change, 72–74
    as characteristic of research universities, 3
    and departmental autonomy, 172
    and elective system, 52
    growth of, 179, 188
    at Harvard, 179
    in History Department, 92, 102, 104, 107,
        111, 113–16, 117, 121, 128, 129, 130, 131

preparation for teaching of, 45, 113–16
reputation of, 34
and research, 9, 72–74, 102, 104, 203
support for, 107
Graduate programs/students *(continued)*
  teaching by, 19, 25, 26, 31, 57–58, 111, 113,
    114, 121, 129, 175, 189
  in undergraduate curriculum, 72–74, 115,
    128, 129, 131, 169, 192
  in university-college framework, 14
  See also Doctoral students/degrees
Graduate School of Business (Stanford), 44,
  185, 205
Grant, Gerald, 64–65
Grants. *See* Funding
"Great courses" (Columbia), 78, 79
"Great ideas" model (University of Chicago),
  79–81
"Great men" courses (Harvard), 79
Greulich, William, 142–43

Harkness, Edward, 73, 79
Harper, William Rainey, 20, 80, 81, 197
Harvard University
  appointments at, 191
  as basis for Stanford comparison, 95
  change without reform at, 78–79, 86
  citizenship at, 79
  curriculum at, 29, 79, 168
  elective system at, 55, 78, 179
  graduate education at, 179
  House system at, 73–74, 79
  as hybrid of British and German ideals, 14
  incremental change at, 78–79
  length of college studies and, 20–21
  medical education at, 136, 161
  mission of, 191–92
  as model for reform, 2
  problem-based learning at, 161
  as "real" university, 83
  reputation of, 34, 95, 196
  required courses at, 179
  research and teaching at, 79, 191–92
  as research-driven institution, 192
  specialization at, 78, 79
  as success, 196
  teaching at, 179
  university-college at, 22, 178–79
  See also Eliot, Charles
Hativa, Nira, 46
Hiring of faculty. *See* Appointments
"Historical Method" (course), 117
"Historical Training" (course), 110, 117
"Historical Writing" (course), 113
History, as science, 116–17, 119, 126
History Department (Stanford University)
  appointments in, 95, 109, 128
  autonomy in, 108, 167, 172–76, 181
  change in, 127–29, 131, 132, 167, 169, 186–90

culture of, 114, 115, 130, 172
curriculum of, 94–110, 128–29, 166, 167–69
demographics of, 96, 99, 165–66
dilemmas in, 186–90
doctoral students in, 101, 104, 107, 111,
  113–16, 121, 129, 168, 169, 181
elective system in, 102, 104–5, 107, 121,
  128
faculty autonomy in, 94–95, 108, 115, 128,
  167, 172–76
funding for, 113, 121, 166, 168
graduate students/program in, 102, 104,
  107, 111, 113–16, 117, 121, 128, 129, 130,
  131
growth of, 94, 95, 96, 99
and history as science, 116–17, 119, 126
instructional practices in, 101–2, 116,
  117–18, 129–30, 167, 173, 186–87
job bargaining in, 107–8
and job market, 129, 168
Medical School compared with, 164,
  165–69, 186–90
mini-graduate program in undergraduate,
  74, 115, 128, 129, 131, 169
mission/goals of, 110–16, 130–32, 166
preparing generalists and specialists in,
  110–11
publishing in, 102, 104, 109–10, 111, 115,
  120, 125–27, 129, 166
reputation of, 94, 102, 104
required courses in, 95, 101, 110, 113, 129,
  168, 169
research and teaching in, 111–13, 115–28,
  130, 181, 186–90
research/scholarship in, 102, 104, 107–10,
  111, 115, 117–18, 127–28, 130, 131,
  166–67, 172
scholars and teachers in, 91–94, 116–28,
  129, 131, 181
selection as case study of, 8, 89
small-group instruction in, 108, 113, 114,
  123, 129–30
specialization in, 95, 96, 99, 102, 104–5,
  107, 113, 115, 128, 167
student criticism in, 26, 42–43
teaching in, 94–110, 111–16, 129–30, 172,
  173, 181
tenure and promotion in, 95, 109–10, 115,
  120, 128, 130
See also specific person or topic
History Undergraduate Student Association,
  106
Honors Program, 73, 101, 120
Hoover, Herbert, 22, 27, 28, 92
Hoover Institute and Library, 27–28
Horowitz, Lawrence, 162–63
Howard, George, 17, 95
Hughes, H. Stuart, 58
Hulme, E. M., 109

Humanities, 46, 166, 184, 205
Hutchins, Robert, 64, 79–80, 81, 83, 86,
    197–98

The Idea of a University (Newman), 182–83
Ideals. *See* Cultures; Mission/goals
Incremental change
    accumulating into fundamental change,
        72–74, 230
    at Columbia, 78
    and complexity of universities, 199
    depth of, 63–64
    distinguishing between fundamental and,
        199
    environmental expectations and, 81–83
    examples of, 64, 65, 69–70, 80, 186, 203–4
    explanations for, 81–86
    fundamental change into, 69–72, 201
    in History Department, 127–28, 131, 167,
        169
    and managing dilemmas, 204–6
    in medical education, 134, 143, 161, 167,
        169
    organizational field and, 83
    at other universities, 77–81
    and political processes, 198
    recommendations about, 204–6
    and research and teaching, 186, 190, 204–6
    and stability, 194–95
    strategic, 204–6
    and tradition of reform, 88, 89, 195
    unintentional, 72–74
    and universities as successes, 197
    without reform, 75–81
    See also specific topic
Independent study, 25, 30, 37, 56, 120, 144,
        157, 169, 171, 175, 187, 189
Indiana University, 15, 16, 19
Institution, and level of change, 66–67
Institutional purpose. *See* Mission/goals
Instructional practices
    and change, 52–53, 65, 87–88, 194
    and comparison of History Department
        and Medical School, 169–72
    content divorced from, 53–54, 88, 89, 116,
        117–18, 128, 170–71, 202
    continuity in, 52–53
    and elective system, 56
    and faculty autonomy, 173
    and faculty-student relationship, 46–47
    and funding, 175
    in History Department, 101–2, 116, 117–18,
        129–30, 167, 173, 186–87
    in medical education, 136–37, 146–48, 153,
        157, 158, 167, 186–87
    nontraditional, 4, 169, 194
    range in, 38
    and research, 56
    reviews of, 30, 38

survey about, 37
technological, 38, 44, 46–47, 53, 87–88,
    101–2, 129, 153, 158
and tenure and promotion, 87
See also specific practice
Intellectual property, ownership of, 203
Interdisciplinary courses. *See* Multidiscipli-
    nary courses
"Introduction to Clinical Medicine"
    (course), 146
Introductory courses
    and academic rank, 58, 80
    and departmental autonomy, 172
    durability of, 187
    and elective system, 56
    and faculty autonomy, 173
    and general education, 44, 193
    graduate students teaching in, 175
    in History Department, 99, 111–13, 117,
        123, 125, 129
    in medical education, 162
    and research, 56
    and research and teaching, 175
    in university-college framework, 179
    See also Survey courses

Jackson, Jesse, 43
Jacobs, Charlotte, 181
James, William, 51, 57
Job market, and History Department, 129,
    168
Job offers, of faculty, 107–8
Johns Hopkins University
    Albert Shaw Lectures at, 91–92
    as basis for Stanford comparison, 95
    Gilman and, 80
    medical education at, 136, 137, 141
    as model for reform, 2
    as multiversity, 82
    as research-driven institution, 14, 178,
        192, 197
    university-college model at, 22, 197
Jordan, David Starr
    appointment as president of, 15
    appointments by, 91, 119, 140–41
    and bisection plan, 21, 51–52, 80, 179, 197
    curricular organization of, 16–17, 37, 43
    and departments, 172
    and elective system, 16, 51, 55
    firing of professors by, 15, 38, 95
    and medical education, 138, 140
    professional career of, 15, 16
    and research, 18, 19, 54, 55, 178, 182
    and research and teaching, 48, 75, 182
    on social betterment, 201–2
    as teacher, 18
    and teaching, 38, 39, 109, 178, 182, 201–2
    and tenure and promotion, 94, 109
    university-college model and, 179, 197

Junior colleges, 14, 21, 179

Kennedy, David, 102, 112, 115, 124, 126, 127, 131, 171, 181
Kennedy, Donald, 3–4, 43, 48, 50, 52, 75, 84, 86, 188, 193
Kerr, Clark, 70–71, 80, 82, 196
Knoles, George, 120
Knowledge
  breadth and depth of, 6, 9, 36, 41, 43, 52, 56, 80, 179, 187, 193
  expansion of historical, 168
  expansion of medical, 135, 137, 139, 144, 168
  See also Mission/goals
Kresge College (University of California, Santa Cruz), 70–72
Kristol, Irving, 1, 61, 74

Laboratory sciences, 133. See also Anatomy teaching; Laboratory teaching
Laboratory teaching
  and change in instructional practices, 52–53
  and comparison of History Department and Medical School, 169
  durability of, 187
  and elective system, 37, 56
  and fundamental change, 65
  growth in use of, 37, 171
  as instructional practice, 25
  introduction of, 18
  in medical education, 133, 136, 139, 141, 143, 145, 146–47, 148, 151, 158, 174, 175
  and research, 56
  and research and teaching, 189
  and Study of Undergraduate Education, 30, 31
Law School (Stanford University), 44, 70, 185
Leadership, 204, 205, 206. See also Presidents
Lectures
  as active-learning experience, 142
  alternatives to, 147–48
  anatomy, 139–40, 142
  and comparison of History Department and Medical School, 169–70
  and demonstrations, 142
  as dominant teaching practice, 4, 25, 31, 37, 46–47, 52–53, 169–70, 171
  durability of, 169, 187
  elective system and, 56, 150–51
  and funding, 175
  "great men," 79
  in History Department, 25–26, 92, 99, 102, 103, 108–9, 111, 112, 116, 117, 120, 123, 124–25, 129–30, 169
  and House system, 79

increase in, 175
  and incremental change, 64
  as instructional practice, 56
  Kennedy's views about, 112
  in medical education, 135, 136, 137, 139–40, 142, 143, 147–48, 150–52, 157, 158, 169, 174, 175
  peers visitation to, 44
  reduction in use of, 171
  and Study of Undergraduate Education (1967–68), 30, 31
  televised, 38
Levi, Edward, 81
Liaison Committee on Medical Education, 154
Liberal education, 14, 23, 24, 52, 56, 87, 110, 167, 193. See also General education
Licensing requirements, medical, 166, 168
Lowell, A. Lawrence, 78–79, 179
Lyman, Richard, 35, 75, 101

McDonald, Forrest, 112
Maclean, Norman, 31
McMaster University Medical School (Canada), 161
Major-subject system, 16–21, 22, 23, 26, 51–52, 54, 76–77
Mall, Franklin, 141
Managing dilemmas, 199–206
Mechanical engineering, 44
Medical education
  basic medical sciences in, 146, 149, 152, 156, 175
  central issues for nineteenth century, 134–37
  change in, 65, 136–37, 143, 161, 162, 164, 167, 169, 186–90, 195
  clinical practices in, 65, 141, 143, 154, 158
  demonstrations in, 142, 146
  durability of curriculum model in, 157–64
  elective system in, 134, 139, 141, 144, 146, 148–53, 154, 156, 158
  entrance requirements for, 136
  examinations in, 135, 150, 153, 160
  expansion of knowledge in, 135, 137, 139, 144, 167, 168
  and hard and soft disciplines, 166
  instructional practices in, 136–37, 146–48, 153, 157, 158, 167, 169, 186–87
  introductory courses in, 162
  in late nineteenth century, 134–37
  length of, 136, 145, 146, 153
  and licensing requirements, 166, 168
  mission/goals of, 133–34, 137, 138–39, 144, 149, 154, 155–56, 166, 179–80, 181
  multidisciplinary courses in, 146, 147, 161, 173–74
  problem-based learning in, 65, 161
  in proprietary schools, 135–37

publishing in, 142–43, 162, 166, 181
and pure and applied disciplines, 167
before reform movement, 135–36
reform movement in, 136–37
required courses in, 134, 138, 139, 146, 147, 149, 150, 153–57, 158, 159
research in, 136, 137, 138, 139, 141–43, 145, 146, 149, 153, 154, 155, 158, 162, 163, 164, 166
research and teaching in, 136, 139, 143, 181, 186–90
and science, 136
specialization in, 134, 138, 139, 143, 146, 168
teaching in, 144, 148, 150–53, 156, 158, 161, 172, 173–74, 181, 185
2×2 curriculum in, 136, 137, 138, 144, 145, 149, 150, 158, 159, 160–61, 162, 164, 169
university-based, 136, 158
in university-college framework, 179–80
and vision of first-rate doctors, 134, 158
See also Anatomy teaching; Medical School; Preclinical curriculum
Medical School (Stanford)
accrediting of, 137, 153–54, 175
appointments in, 152, 153, 174
autonomy in, 161, 167, 172–76
awards for teaching in, 152, 153, 174, 181
career choices of graduates from, 162–63
compromises in, 158, 161–62, 168–69
consolidation of campuses for, 28, 144
as consortium member, 137–38
culture of, 172, 174
curriculum of, 138–39, 144–46, 148, 155, 156, 157–64, 167–69
demographics of, 165–66
departments in, 138, 161, 167, 168, 172–76
dilemmas in, 186–90
evaluation of teaching in, 147, 152, 153–54, 157
faculty autonomy in, 134, 161, 163, 167, 172–76, 195
Five-Year Plan of, 143–48, 149, 154, 156, 158, 161, 168–69, 170, 171, 174, 195
funding for, 137, 159, 163, 164, 166, 168, 174–75
growth of, 167
History Department compared with, 164, 165–69, 186–90
political compromises in, 161–62, 164
reputation of, 159–60
reviews in, 156–57
selection as case study of, 8, 89
student criticisms of, 143, 147–48, 149, 150–52, 155–56, 161, 174
student evaluation in, 146, 154
teaching assistants in, 139
tensions within, 143, 145, 147–48, 150, 163
tenure and promotion in, 181

turmoil of 1960s in, 147–48, 149
workloads in, 175
See also Anatomy teaching; Medical education; Preclinical curriculum
Medical Science Training Program, 154
Meier, Gerald, 38
Meiklejohn, Alexander, 197–98
"Methods of Teaching History" (course), 113
Meyer, Arthur W., 140–42
Michigan State University, 137, 161
Minorities, 34, 35, 42, 96, 99
Mission/goals
and change, 82–83, 86–87, 198, 199
and commercialization of research, 203
and cultures, 63
debates about, 86–87
Eliot's views about, 191–92
of History Department, 110–16, 130–32, 166
institutionalization of, 51
intractable dilemmas concerning, 177, 178–80, 187
of medical education, 133–34, 137, 138–39, 144, 149, 154, 155–56, 166, 179–80, 181
and political processes, 192, 198, 199
and research and teaching, 70, 180–82, 202
of research universities, 8–9, 192
and resiliency of universities, 191
of Stanford University, 20, 177, 178, 192
as structure, 63
of university-college, 14, 88, 178–80, 187, 198, 200, 202
See also specific mission
Moral mission, 9, 13–14, 17, 20, 24, 34, 192, 202. *See also* Character building
Multidisciplinary courses, 146, 147, 161, 173–74, 198, 204, 205
"Multiversities," 65, 82

National Board of Medical Examiners (NBME), 150, 153
National university, 179
Newman, John Henry, 182–83
Nontraditional teaching forms, 4, 169–70, 194
Norms. *See specific norm*

Objectivity, 93–94, 126
Ophuls, William, 139
Organization of American Historians (OAH), 125
"Organizational field," 83
Organizational forgetfulness, 88, 89

"The Pacific Slope" (course), 95, 119
Packer, Herbert, 35, 38
Pedagogy. *See* Instructional practices; *specific method*

Peer evaluations
  of research, 196
  of teaching, 4, 44, 49, 50, 53, 70, 84, 108, 204
Ph.D.s. *See* Doctoral students/degrees
Pitzer, Kenneth, 35
Plummer, R. H., 140
Political processes, 192, 195–99, 206
Potter, David, 105, 171, 173
Preclinical curriculum
  and autonomy, 174, 175
  durability of, 158–60, 161
Preclinical curriculum *(continued)*
  and elective system, 148–53
  and Five-Year Plan, 144, 146, 147
  instructional practices in, 170, 171
  and required courses, 153–57
  and specialization, 168–69
  and 2×2 curriculum, 138, 169
  See also Anatomy teaching; "Basic med-
    ical sciences"; *specific course*
"Preparation for Clinical Medicine"
    (course), 161, 170
Presidents
  early-nineteenth century, 9
  governance by, 7
  recommendations about, 204, 205, 206
  and research, 54
  tenure of, 205
  See also specific person
Problem-based learning, 65, 161
"Problems of Citizenship" (course), 23–24,
    25–26, 95, 120, 121
"Problems of Civilization" (course), 173, 205
Processes
  and change, 3, 88, 89, 199, 201
  and change without reform, 84
  and characteristics of high-status institu-
    tions, 6
  definition of, 63
  political, 192, 195–99
  and research and teaching, 76
  and resilience of universities, 84
Promotions. *See* Tenure and promotions
Publishing
  as advancing mission of research
    universities, 2–3
  and annual reports of departments, 19
  discipline-specific formats for, 166–67
  and doctoral degrees, 58
  dominance of, 5, 30, 38
  and hard and soft disciplines, 166
  in History Department, 102, 104, 109–10,
    111, 115, 120, 125–27, 129, 166
  and major-subject system, 18
  in medical education, 142–43, 159, 162,
    166, 181
  and research and teaching tensions, 6
  and review of 1967, 38
  rewards for, 54, 143

  and Stanford's reputation, 164
  and teaching, 53
  and tenure and promotion, 10, 19, 49, 109,
    115, 120, 176, 181
  and university-college framework, 10
  Wilbur's views about, 25
  See also Research; Scholar-teachers;
    Teacher-scholars

Quarter system, 20, 21, 22, 30, 44, 52

Reading courses, 56
"Real" universities, 83
Recitations, 18, 19, 25, 52–53, 116
Redbook (Harvard), 29, 79, 86
Reform
  change and, 59, 61, 62, 64, 75–86, 164,
    195–99
  as continuous, 1, 5
  examples of, 64
  failure of, 199–206
  mechanics of, 195–99
  models for, 2
  in public schools, 4
  and research and teaching, 5, 10
  rhetoric of, 77, 84, 85, 89, 162
  as solution for managing dilemmas, 200
  and stability, 5, 192–95
  symbolic, 10
  taming of, 84, 195, 198
  telic, 64–65
  tradition of, 86–89, 128, 162, 195
  See also Change; *specific program*
Required courses
  and breadth and depth of knowledge, 56
  and Casper presidency, 43
  and change without reform, 77
  and elective system, 41
  and general education, 9, 193
  at Harvard, 29, 179
  in History Department, 95, 101, 110, 113,
    129, 168, 169
  in medical education, 134, 138, 139, 146,
    147, 149, 150, 153–57, 158, 159
  between 1920–1956, 24
  in 1970s, 41
  reviews of, 23, 30, 41, 44
  at University of Chicago, 81
  and university-college framework, 3, 14, 179
  See also Distribution requirements
Required reading list, 42, 43, 80
Research
  and academic rank, 58–59
  and advising, 89
  and appointments, 48, 54
  and change, 54–55, 72–74, 206
  commercialization of, 203–4, 205
  and comparison of History Department
    and Medical School, 168, 169

as core mission of universities, 1–2
cultures, 3, 188
definitions of, 50
and departments, 89
and distribution requirements, 56
and doctoral students/degrees, 56, 58–59
dominance of, 1, 5, 30, 38, 48, 51, 55–59, 107, 120, 125–26, 138, 186–90, 192
between 1891–1920, 17–21
and faculty autonomy, 89, 108, 115, 173, 174
funding for, 6, 14, 27, 28, 43, 81, 159, 164, 166, 168, 181, 197, 203, 205
and general education, 44–47, 56
and graduate programs/students, 9, 72–74, 102, 104, 203
hard versus soft, 166, 167
in higher education literature, 5
in History Department, 102, 104, 108, 109, 111, 115, 117, 127–28, 130, 131, 166–67, 172
institutional bias toward, 39
institutional framework for, 55–59
institutionalization of, 59, 107, 115, 128, 130, 131
and instructional practices, 56
and introductory courses, 56
and major-subject system, 17–21
in medical education, 136, 137, 138, 139, 141, 142–43, 145, 146, 149, 153, 154, 155, 158, 159–60, 162, 163, 164, 166
between 1920–1954, 24–27
between 1954–1968, 30–34
between 1968–1980, 37–41
between 1980–1995, 44–48
peer evaluations of, 196
pure versus applied, 167
redefinitions of, 53
and reputation, 189
reviews of, 38
rewards for, 143, 184, 193, 199, 203
seminars, 56, 117–18
and specialization, 74
and structures, 164
and tenure and promotion, 4–5, 10, 40, 41, 44, 164
undergraduate, 32, 37
and workload, 59
See also Research and teaching; Research universities; specific person
Research and teaching
and appointments, 9, 48, 188, 205, 206
and awards for teaching, 13, 49, 50, 189
and change/reform, 5, 51, 75–76, 88, 186, 190, 199, 204
compatibility between, 4, 48, 49, 76, 88, 181, 182–83, 188, 193
compromises between, 9, 34, 53, 54–55, 84–85
conflict between, 13, 40–41, 48, 50, 183–86, 188

continuous review of, 59
and cultures, 76, 176
and departments, 172, 176, 189, 205, 206
and distribution requirements, 56, 186
and dominance of research, 1–2, 40, 51, 53, 76, 84, 85, 87, 130, 176, 182, 186–90, 201
and elective system, 52, 55–57, 89, 104, 141, 186, 188, 193
and evaluation of teaching, 76, 185, 204–5
and faculty autonomy, 4, 51, 172, 175, 176, 187, 189, 203, 204
future of relationship between, 199–206
and general education, 42, 48–51
at Harvard, 79, 191–92
in History Department, 111–13, 115–28, 130, 181, 186–90
institutionalization of, 75
intractable dilemmas concerning, 178–86
and introductory courses, 175
level of relationship between, 188–89
linkages between, 48–51
in medical education, 136, 139, 143, 181, 186–90
and mission/goals, 70, 181, 202
as mutually reinforcing, 38, 45, 50, 53, 130, 181, 182
in professional schools, 84
realignment of imbalance between, 201–6
reasons for correcting imbalance between, 202–3
recommendations concerning, 204–6
and redefinition of research, 53
reviews of, 30–34, 38–39, 183–84
and rewards, 193
and structures, 76, 84, 176
teaching imperative and, 8–9, 40–41, 48–52, 175–76, 185–86
tensions between, 6, 10, 25, 33, 40, 41, 48, 139, 176, 180–82, 193, 199
and tenure and promotion, 41, 48, 76, 188, 189, 193, 203, 205
in university-college, 9, 10, 50, 53, 54–55, 75, 84, 88, 178–80, 187, 189, 192–94, 200–201, 205
and workloads, 33, 188
See also Anatomy teaching; Research; Teaching
Research universities
adaptive powers of, 194
characteristics of, 2–3
classification/ranking of, 83, 196
emergence of, 1–2
funding for, 203
governance at, 7
laboratory sciences in, 133
mission/goals of, 8–9, 192
and publishing, 2–3
reputation of, 2–3, 189, 206
resiliency of, 191

similarities among, 194
as successes, 196
See also specific institution
Rewards
and advising, 47
for publishing, 54, 143
recommendations about, 204–5
for research, 143, 184, 193, 199, 203, 204–5
for teaching, 30, 48, 49, 85, 156, 184, 185, 193, 204–5
See also Awards for teaching; Tenure and promotions
Riesman, David, 64–65
Roberts, Richard, 114
Robinson, Edgar E.
and Bailey, 107–8, 123, 125, 126
departmental autonomy and, 172
graduate assistants and, 26, 121
and preparing doctoral students for teaching, 113
and purposes of History Department, 112, 113, 131
as teacher-scholar, 118, 119–22, 127, 131, 181
as Wilbur's adviser, 120
Rogers, Carl, 71
Rosovsky, Henry, 79
Ross, Edward A., 15–16
Rosse, James, 43

Sabbatical leaves, 3, 59, 115, 130, 188
Salary bargaining, 107–8
Scholar-teachers
Adams as, 91–94, 118, 121–22, 131, 181
Bailey as, 122–28, 131, 181
and compatibility of research and teaching, 188
in History Department, 116–28, 129, 131
institutionalization of, 59
reaffirmation of ideal of, 41
teacher-scholars versus, 55, 116–28, 131
Scholars, admiration for, 41
Scholarship, teaching as, 4, 49, 50, 84, 188.
See also Research; Scholar-teachers; Teacher-scholars
Schwab, Joseph, 31
Science
history as, 116–17, 119, 126
and medical education, 136
See also Basic medical sciences
"Scientific historians," 116–17, 121. *See also* Adams, Ephraim Douglass
Scientific inquiry, 8
Semester system, 20, 21, 22, 44, 52
Seminars
for both undergraduates and graduates, 74
and change, 52–53, 65
and comparison of History Department and Medical School, 169

durability of, 187
and elective system, 56
freshmen, 36
and funding, 175
growth in use of, 46–47, 171
in History Department, 99, 101, 102, 103, 107, 108, 113, 116, 117–18, 123–24
institutionalization of, 99, 101
in medical education, 175
at other schools, 103, 104, 105
peer visitation of, 44
research, 56, 73, 117–18
and research and teaching, 189
reviews of, 25, 30, 31, 36, 47
with senior faculty, 47
for undergraduates, 19, 36, 37, 74
Senior faculty, 36, 58, 79
Servicemen's Readjustment Act (G. I. Bill), 27, 81
Sheehan, James, 43
Sheldon, Edward A., 118
Show, Arley, 117
Skillings, Hugh, 38
Slosson, Edward E., 19, 109–10
Small-group instruction
and comparison of History Department and Medical School, 169, 170
durability of, 187
and elective system, 56
and faculty autonomy, 173
and funding, 175
and general education, 46–47, 78
growth in use of, 169, 171, 173
in History Department, 99, 101, 102, 105, 108, 113, 114, 123, 129–30
at Kresge College, 71
in medical education, 136, 139, 155, 157, 158, 161, 175
and research, 56
Social betterment, teaching for, 201–2
Specialization
and breadth and depth of knowledge, 56
and change, 77, 193
departments as basis for, 45
dominance of, 52
and elective system, 23, 51, 52, 55, 56, 104, 193
and faculty autonomy, 52, 173
and general education, 9–10, 83, 179, 193
at Harvard University, 78, 79
in History Department, 95, 96, 99, 102, 107, 113, 115, 128, 167
and major-subject system, 23
in medical education, 133, 134, 138, 139, 143, 146, 168
and research, 74
at University of Chicago, 81
in university-college framework, 9–10
See also Research

Stanford, Jane, 15–16, 95
Stanford, Leland, 15, 18, 95
Stanford Research Institute, 27
Stanford Research Park, 28
Stanford Study of Education. *See* Study of
    Undergraduate Education (1954)
Stanford University
    adaptation at, 206
    bureaucracy at, 20
    demographics of, 42, 168
    endowment of, 35
    federal investigation of federal funding of, 6
    founding of, 15–16
    governance at, 6, 7–8
    growth of, 19–20, 21, 22, 28, 35, 42, 57
    as hybrid of British and German univer-
        sity ideals, 14
    incremental becoming fundamental
        change at, 74
    mission/goals of, 20, 177, 178, 192
    organization of, 6
    organization field of, 95
    reputation of, 6, 22, 28–29, 34, 122, 164,
        196–97
    as research-driven university, 178, 189
    schools in, 22
    selection as case study of, 5–8
    stability at, 22
    Sterling's vision for, 28–29, 196
    structural and cultural features of, 6
    as success, 196
    turmoil in 1960s at, 34–35, 52, 147–48, 149
    as typical institution, 6
    university-college model at, 10, 15–16,
        178–79, 197–98
    See also specific person or topic
State University of New York, 65, 66
Stegner, Wallace, 27
Sterling, J. E. Wallace, 26–30, 48, 75, 104,
    122, 143–44, 196
Strategic incremental change, 204–6
Structures
    and change/reform, 3, 88, 89, 193, 194,
        195, 198, 199, 201
    and characteristics of high-status institu-
        tions, 6
    comparison of History Department and
        Medical School, 167–69
    definition of, 63
    in History Department, 128
    and medical education, 143
    and research, 164
    and research and teaching, 76, 84, 175,
        176, 203
    and resilience of universities, 84
    See also specific structure
Students
    evaluation of, 30, 80, 146, 154
    selectivity in admitting, 83

university-college framework, 9, 14
    See also Evaluation of teaching; *specific
        course*
Students for an Improved Curriculum, 156
Study cards, 20, 21, 26, 54
Study of Education at Stanford (1967–1968),
    34, 35–41, 50, 69, 84, 102, 173
The Study of Education at Stanford (Stanford
    faculty), 38, 184–85
Study of Undergraduate Education
    (1954–56), 29–34, 50, 69, 102, 105, 168,
    183–84
Success, of universities, 195, 196–97
Survey courses, 23–24, 25–26, 175. *See also*
    Introductory courses

Teacher-scholars
    Barnes as, 118–19, 127, 131, 181
    and elective system, 38
    emergence of concept of, 38
    in History Department, 116–28, 131
    recommendations about, 206
    Robinson as, 118, 119–21, 127, 131, 181
    scholar-teachers versus, 55, 116–28
Teaching
    and advising, 54, 187
    and appointments, 39, 49, 76, 84, 109, 122,
        174, 205
    autonomy/freedom in, 6, 37, 38, 53, 108,
        173, 181
    and change, 52–54, 84–86, 169–72, 206
    and class size, 18
    cultures, 44–45, 54, 114, 115, 130, 172, 173,
        174, 185, 188
    as department mission, 9
    and doctoral students/degrees, 57–58,
        113–16, 181
    "effective" and "good," 31–32
    between 1891–1920, 17–21
    and elective system, 56–57
    and faculty autonomy, 38, 45, 84–86, 108,
        173–74
    and Faculty Senate, 39, 40, 84, 174, 176
    funding for, 14, 45, 113, 174, 175, 185, 204–5
    and general education, 44–47
    genetic basis of, 25, 124
    goals/task of, 9, 31–32, 108, 170
    by graduate students, 19, 25, 26, 31, 111,
        113–16, 121, 129, 175, 189
    "hack," 24
    at Harvard University, 179
    importance at Stanford of, 3–4
    institutionalization of, 59
    integration/fragmentation of, 185–86
    intractable dilemmas about, 184
    and major-subject system, 17–21
    marginalization of, 107
    in medical education, 144, 146–48, 150–53,
        156, 158, 161, 172, 173–74, 181, 185

motivation of faculty for, 201–2
negative connotations of, 109
between 1920–1954, 24–27
between 1954–1968, 30–34
between 1968–1980, 37–41
between 1980–1995, 44–48
origin of ideal of, 13–14
as process, 63
publishing and, 10, 53
recommendations about, 204–5
and reputation of institutions, 189
rewards for, 30, 48, 49, 85, 156, 184, 185, 193
rhetoric of, 41, 130, 176
Teaching *(continued)*
satisfaction from, 202
as scholarship, 4, 49, 50, 84, 188
for social betterment, 201–2
student criticisms of, 174
symbolic value of, 198
as technical moves, 202
and tenure and promotion, 4, 6, 13, 25, 39, 40, 41, 44, 45, 49, 115, 122, 181, 193, 199, 205
at University of Chicago, 31, 80–81
See also Anatomy teaching; Awards for teaching; History Department: teaching in; Preclinical curriculum; Workload, teaching; *specific teacher, president, method, type of courses or individual course*
Teaching assistants
in Medical School, 139, 152
See also Graduate programs/students
Team teaching, 53, 114, 146, 148–49, 161, 173
Technology. *See* Instructional practices: technological
Telic reforms, 64–65
Tenure and promotions
and advising, 38, 44
and awards for teaching, 6, 176
change in, 189
criteria for, 4, 10, 13, 25, 94, 109, 115, 120, 176, 188, 189, 193, 203
as department function, 58–59, 172
and evaluation of teaching, 70, 185
and Faculty Senate, 39, 40
in History Department, 95, 109–10, 115, 120, 128, 130
and instructional practices, 87
in Medical School, 181
and publishing, 10, 19, 49, 109, 115, 120, 176, 181
recommendations about, 205
and research, 4–5, 10, 40, 41, 44, 164
and research and teaching, 41, 48, 76, 188, 189, 193, 203, 205
student criticisms of, 176
and teaching, 4, 6, 13, 25, 39, 40, 41, 44, 45, 49, 115, 122, 181, 193, 199, 205

Terman, Frederick, 27, 28, 29, 104, 197
Thielens, Wagner Jr., 46
Time, change and elapse of, 68–69
Tresidder, Donald, 27, 28
Turner, Frederick Jackson, 119–20
Tutorial system, 79, 102
2×2 curriculum (medical education), 136, 137, 138, 144, 145, 149, 150, 158, 159, 160–61, 162, 164, 169

Undergraduate curriculum
adaptation in, 167–69
changing, 3, 21–27, 29–30, 36–37, 42–44, 51–52, 86–89
faculty-student relationship and, 17
graduate school practices in, 72–74, 115, 128, 129, 131, 169, 192
and House system, 73–74
mission and, 86–87
Sterling's reviews of, 29, 196
Wilbur's reorganization of, 21–27
See also Advising; Bisection plan; Curriculum; Elective system; Instructional practices; Introductory courses; Major-subject system; Multidisciplinary courses; Required courses; Teaching
Universities
bottom-heavy, 66–68, 89, 194
and change, 1, 61, 192–99, 201
classification/ranking of, 83, 196
complexity of, 199
demands from constituencies on, 82
emergence of American, 64
expectations of, 81–83, 84, 88
imitation among, 83
managing dilemmas of, 199–206
missions of, 82–83
"organizational field" of, 83
"real," 83
as reflection of society, 206
resilience of, 82, 84, 88, 89, 191, 200, 202, 204
satisfaction with, 196–98
stability in, 192–95
as successes, 195, 196–97
survival of, 82
top-heavy, 7, 67
See also Research universities; *specific university*
University of Buffalo, 66
University of California at Berkeley, 22, 34, 82, 105, 107–8, 192, 196, 198
University of California at Santa Cruz, 70–72, 198
University of Chicago
advising at, 47
change/reform at, 64, 79–81, 86
distribution requirements at, 81
elective system at, 81

expansion of curriculum at, 168
general education at, 79–81
"great ideas" model at, 79–81
as hybrid of British and German ideals, 14
length of studies at, 20
medical education at, 137
as model for reform, 2
as multiversity, 82
as "real" university, 83
as research-driven institution, 81
specialization at, 81
survey courses at, 23
teaching at, 31, 80–81
university-college at, 22, 178–79, 197–98
See also Hutchins, Robert
University of Indiana, 119
University of Michigan, 22, 104, 192, 198
University of New Mexico Medical School,
161
University of Pennsylvania, 137
University of Pittsburgh, 137
University of Rochester, 137
University Student Evaluation Rating Form
(Stanford), 40, 50, 70
University of Virginia, 103
University of Washington, 137
University of Wisconsin, 197–98
University-college
abandonment of, 21
and breadth and depth of knowledge, 193
and change/reform, 36, 192–95, 197–99
as characteristic of high-status institutions, 6
characteristics of, 200–201
and compromises, 55, 130, 179, 187, 192,
200
conclusions about, 51–55
curriculum tinkering in, 21–34
and departments, 198
dilemmas/conflicts within, 9–10, 14, 22, 34,
36, 77, 87, 107, 130, 133, 167, 178–80,
187, 194, 202
and elective system, 34–41, 55, 179, 195
and general education, 42–51
invention of, 9, 13–15
lack of viable alternative to, 195, 197–99
major-subject system in, 16–21
and medical education, 179–80
mission/goals of, 14, 88, 178–80, 187, 198,
200, 202
and models of historians, 131
recommendations about, 205
reputation of, 206
and research, 55–59
research and teaching in, 9, 10, 50, 53,
54–55, 75, 84, 88, 178–80, 187, 189,
192–94, 200–201, 203, 205
and specialization, 9–10
stability in, 195

Veblen, Thorstein, 182
Veysey, Laurence, 178

Wessells, Norman K., 182
"Western Civilization" (course), 26, 31, 36,
58, 95, 111, 120, 121, 173, 205
"Western Culture" (course), 3, 13, 41, 42–43,
64, 86, 205
"Westward Movement" (course), 95, 120
White, Andrew, 16, 37, 55
Wilbur, Ray Lyman
curriculum reorganization of, 22, 23, 179
departmental autonomy and, 172
and medical education, 22, 133–34, 139,
143, 163
professional career of, 21–22
and research, 25, 133
and research and teaching, 48, 75
retirement of, 27
Robinson as adviser to, 120
and specialization, 133–34, 143
and teaching, 24–25, 109
university-college tension and, 179
Williams College, 23
Workload, teaching
average, 37, 44
and change, 64, 65
and elective system, 37
in History Department, 99, 100, 102, 107–8,
115, 129, 130, 175
and major-subject system, 20
in Medical School, 175
and outside job offers, 108
reduction in, 3, 4, 37, 59, 65, 94, 107, 129,
130, 175, 188
and research and teaching, 33, 59, 188
Wright, Gordon, 101
"Writing and Teaching of History" (course),
121

Yale University, 14, 22, 47, 73–74, 95, 137,
178–79, 192

ABOUT THE AUTHOR

Larry Cuban is Professor of Education at Stanford University, Stanford, California, where he teaches courses in the history of school reform, leadership, and policy analysis. He has been faculty sponsor of the Stanford Schools Collaborative and The Stanford Teacher Education Program.

Professor Cuban's background in the field of education prior to becoming a professor includes 14 years of teaching high school social studies in inner city schools, administering teacher-training programs at school sites, and serving 7 years as a district superintendent.

Trained as an historian, Professor Cuban received a B.A. degree from the University of Pittsburgh in 1955 and an M.A. from Cleveland's Case Western Reserve University three years later. On completing his Ph.D. work at Stanford University in 1974, he assumed the superintendency of the Arlington, Virginia Public Schools, a position he held until returning to Stanford in 1981.

His major research interests focus on the history of curriculum and instruction, educational leadership, school reform, and the effectiveness of schools. As a practitioner, he continues to work with teachers and administrators in Stanford's Professional Development Center; from August 1988 to January 1989, Professor Cuban taught an 11th grade class in United States History at Los Altos (California) High School.

The author of many articles, Dr. Cuban's books include *Teachers and Machines: The Use of Classroom Technology Since 1920* (1986); *How Teachers Taught: Constancy and Change in American Classrooms, 1890–1980* (1984); *Urban School Chiefs Under Fire* (1976); and *To Make a Difference: Teaching in the Inner City* (1970). His most recent book, published by State University of New York (SUNY) Press is *The Managerial Imperative: The Practice of Leadership in Schools* (1988).

Dr. Cuban is married to Barbara Cuban who is a clinical social worker. They are the parents of two daughters. They make their home in Palo Alto.